BARRON'S

SAT*

CRITICAL READING
WORKBOOK

14TH EDITION

Sharon Weiner Green
Former Instructor in English
Merritt College, Oakland, California

Mitchel Weiner
Former Member, Department of English
James Madison High School, Brooklyn, New York

BARRON'S

*SAT is a registered trademark of the College Board, which was not involved in the production of, and does not endorse, this book.

ACKNOWLEDGMENTS

The authors gratefully acknowledge the following copyright holders for permission to reprint material used in reading passages:

PAGE 4: From *A Handbook to Literature, 6/E* by Holman. © 1992. Reprinted by permission of Prentice-Hall, Inc.

PAGES 22–23: From "Symbolic Language of Dreams" by Erich Fromm in *Language: An Enquiry into Its Meaning and Function* by Ruth Nanda Anshen, ed. Copyright 1957. HarperCollins Publishers, Inc.

PAGE 29: From "The Spider and the Wasp" by Alexander Petrunkevitch. Copyright © 1952 by *Scientific American, Inc.* All rights reserved.

PAGE 33: From *Small Town America* by Richard Lingerman. Copyright © 1980 with permission of Putnam Publishing Group.

PAGE 34: From *A Pocket History of the United States* by Alan Nevins and Henry Steele Commager. Copyright 1991. Alfred A. Knopf, New York.

PAGES 109–110: From *The Most Beautiful House in the World* by Witold Rybczynski. Copyright 1989. With permission of Viking Penguin.

PAGE 112: From *La Vida* by Oscar Lewis. Reprinted by permission of Harold Ober Associates Incorporated. Copyright © 1965 by Oscar Lewis.

PAGES 112–113: From "What is Poverty?" by Jo Goodwin Parker. Originally published in *America's Other Children: Public Schools Outside Suburbia* by George Henderson, ed. Copyright 1971. University of Oklahoma Press.

PAGE 115: From "Living in Two Cultures" by Jeanne Wakatsuki Houston in *Outlooks and Insights*. Copyright 1983. St. Martin's Press.

PAGE 117: Reprinted by permission from "Introduction" by Antonio Castro Leal to *Twenty Centuries of Mexican Art*. © 1940 The Museum of Modern Art, New York.

PAGES 118–120: From *The Press and the Presidency* by John Tebbel and Sarah Miles Watts. Copyright 1985. Oxford University Press, New York.

PAGES 122–123: From "The Desert Smells Like Rain: A Naturalist in Papago Indian Country" by Gary Nabhan. With permission of North Point Press; div. of Farrar, Straus & Giroux, Inc.

PAGES 125–126: "Native Earth," from *Indian Country* by Peter Matthiessen, copyright © 1979, 1980, 1981, 1984 by Peter Matthiessen. Used by permission of Viking Penguin, a division of Penguin Group (USA) Inc.

PAGES 127–128: From "Social Characteristics and Socialization of Wild Chimpanzees" by Yukimaru Sugiyama in *Primate Socialization* by Frank E. Poirer, ed. Copyright 1972. Random House, New York.

PAGES 129–130: From *War, Peace and International Politics* by David W. Zeigler, Copyright 1977. Reprinted by permission of Addison-Wesley Educational Publishers, Inc.

PAGES 132–133: From *Picasso on Art: A Selection of Views* by Dore Ashton. Copyright 1972. The Viking Press, New York.

PAGE 133: From *Picasso: The Early Years* by Jiri Padrta. Undated. Tudor Publishing Co., New York.

PAGES 137–138: From "The Dynamic Abyss" by Charles D. Hollister, Arthur R. M. Nowell, and Peter A. Jumars. Copyright © 1984 by *Scientific American, Inc.* All rights reserved.

PAGES 139–140: From *Organizing the World's Money* by Benjamin J. Cohen. Copyright 1977. Basic Books, a div. of HarperCollins Publishers, Inc.

PAGE 142: From *F. Scott Fitzgerald* by Kenneth Eble. Copyright 1963. Twayne Publishers, an imprint of Simon & Schuster Macmillan.

PAGES 142–143: From "F. Scott Fitzgerald" by Edmund Wilson in *Shores of Light.* © 1985 with permission from Farrar, Straus & Giroux, Inc.

PAGES 234–235: Reprinted by permission from *Picasso: Fifty Years of His Art* by Alfred H. Barr. © 1946 The Museum of Modern Art, New York.

PAGE 240: From *The Magic Years* by Selma H. Fraiberg. Copyright 1959. By permission of Scribner, a division of Simon & Schuster.

PAGES 240–241: From *Essentials of Psychology and Life* by Philip G. Zimbardo. Reprinted with permission of Addison-Wesley Educational Publishers, Inc. Copyright 1980. Scott, Foresman and Co., Glenview, Illinois.

PAGES 256–257: From *The Joy of Music* by Leonard Bernstein. Copyright 1959. Used by permission of Doubleday, a div. of BDD Publishing Group.

PAGES 262–263: From "The Canopy of the Tropical Rain Forest" by Donald R. Perry. Copyright © 1984 by *Scientific American, Inc.* All rights reserved.

PAGE 268: From *The Politics of Prejudice* by Roger Daniels. Copyright 1962. University of California Press, Berkeley.

PAGES 268–269: From "American Antisemitism Historically Reconsidered" by John Higham, in *Jews in the Mind of America* by Herbert Stember, et al., eds. Copyright 1966. American Jewish Committee, Basic Books, New York. Reprinted in *Antisemitism in the United States* by Leonard Dinnerstein, ed. Copyright 1971. Holt, Rinehart, and Winston, Inc., New York.

PAGES 284–285: From "The Man Who Hitched the Reindeer To Santa Claus's Sleigh" by X. J. Kennedy in *The New York Times Book Review*, December 5, 1993. © 1993 The New York Times Co.

PAGE 290: From *The Way to Rainy Mountain* by N. Scott Momaday. Copyright 1969. University of New Mexico Press.

PAGES 291–292: From "Huge Conservation Effort Aims to Save Vanishing Architect of the Savanna" by William K. Stevens, © 1989 by The New York Times Co. Reprinted with permission.

PAGE 296: From *Montana 1948* by Larry Watson. Copyright © 1993 by Larry Watson (Milkweed Editions, 1993).

All inquiries should be addressed to:
Barron's Educational Series, Inc.
250 Wireless Boulevard
Hauppauge, New York 11788
www.barronseduc.com

ISSN: 2166-8191

ISBN: 978-1-4380-0027-5

PRINTED IN THE UNITED STATES OF AMERICA

9 8 7 6 5

10% POST-CONSUMER WASTE
Paper contains a minimum of 10% post-consumer waste (PCW). Paper used in this book was derived from certified, sustainable forestlands.

Contents

Preface

Welcome to the world of the SAT, where *air* and *lumber* can be verbs, and *apathy* and *phenomena* are common everyday words. It's a tricky world, but nothing you can't master: if you can navigate Facebook, you can navigate the SAT.

Welcome also to the fourteenth edition of Barron's *SAT Critical Reading Workbook*. If you are looking for a trusty guide as you make your way through the critical reading sections of the SAT, this is the guide for you.

Here's how this book can help:

- It introduces you to today's SAT, providing you with four complete critical reading tests, each three sections long. Here are four crucial "dress rehearsals" for the day you walk into the examination room.
- It briefs you on the vocabulary-in-context and passage-based reading questions, giving you key tips on how to tackle these important types of questions.
- It teaches you how to create your own quirky, memorable flash cards—personal study aids that will help you master SAT vocabulary.
- It takes you through the double reading passages, showing you how to work your way through a pair of passages without wasting effort or time.
- It offers you enough material for a year-long study program so that you don't have to settle for last-minute cram sessions. If you've got the time, pace yourself. Remember, you're training for a marathon, not a 50-yard dash.
- It gives you the SAT High-Frequency Word List, incorporating vocabulary from actual SAT tests through 2011. These words are *vital*—computer analysis shows that they occur test after test on actual SATs. Master them, and you'll be well on your way to building a college-level vocabulary.

As you work your way through the book, take note of the following icons, which will alert you to helpful tips:

 shows you a time-saving tip.

 indicates something you should give special attention.

points out words you might want to look up.

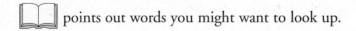 shows you when to apply a "plus or minus" test—when it helps you to know if a word is positive or negative.

Let Barron's *SAT Critical Reading Workbook* give you the inside scoop on the sometimes scary world of the SAT. Don't let the SAT get you down. With the Barron's team behind you, go for your personal best: take time today to build your skills for the SAT.

This edition of Barron's *SAT Critical Reading Workbook* is a sign of Barron's ongoing commitment to make this publication America's outstanding guide to the critical reading sections of the SAT. It has benefited from the dedicated labors of the editorial staff of Barron's, in particular Linda Turner, and from the research and writing skills of John Seal and Lexy Green. We are greatly indebted to them.

PART 1

INTRODUCING THE SAT: CRITICAL READING SKILLS

Nature of the Test

Overview and Content

The Critical Reading Sections

Before the Test

During the Test

Nature of the Test

What is the SAT? Educational Testing Service (ETS) says it's a standardized test designed to help predict how well high school students are likely to do in their academic work as college freshmen. From your viewpoint, it probably looks more like one extra set of hurdles you have to jump before you get to the next level of the college admissions game.

This particular set of hurdles, however, doesn't demand any specialized knowledge on your part, just general test-taking savvy. You're not required to recall great chunks of history or literature or science. You're not even required to recall most math formulas—they're printed right in the test booklet.

Assessment tests are basically multiple-choice tests. Your score depends upon how many correct answers you get within a definite period of time. Speed is important, but so is accuracy. You have to pace yourself so that you don't sacrifice speed to gain accuracy (or sacrifice accuracy to gain speed).

Overview and Content

This is the actual format of the SAT. The total testing time allowed is 3¾ hours. There are ten sections on the test. You are given 25 minutes apiece to complete seven of them. They are:

- 1 essay-writing section
- 2 critical reading sections
- 2 mathematics sections
- 1 writing skills section
- 1 "experimental" section (critical reading, writing skills, or mathematics)

The eighth and ninth sections take 20 minutes apiece. They are:

- 1 critical reading section
- 1 mathematics section

Finally, there is an additional 10-minute section. It is:

- 1 writing skills section

These sections will all appear on the SAT. However, the order in which they appear is likely to vary from test to test.

Not counting the experimental section, the three critical reading sections should contain a total of 19 sentence completion questions and 48 passage-based reading questions. *More than half* of the critical reading questions on the SAT directly test how well you understand what you read.

Pay particular attention to how these critical reading sections are organized. All three sections contain groups of sentence completion questions followed by groups of passage-based reading questions. The sentence completion questions are arranged in order of difficulty: they start out with easy "warm-up" questions and get more and more difficult as they go along. (The passage-based reading questions do not necessarily get more difficult as they go along. In general, questions about material found early in the passage come before questions about material occurring later.

The Critical Reading Sections

Here are examples of the two types of critical reading questions you can expect:

Sentence Completion Questions

Sentence completion questions ask you to fill in the blanks. Your job is to find the word or phrase that best completes the sentence's meaning.

> **Directions:** Choose the word or set of words that, when inserted in the sentence, *best* fits the meaning of the sentence as a whole.

Brown, this biography suggests, was an _____ employer, giving generous bonuses one day, ordering pay cuts the next.

  (A) indifferent
  (B) objective
  (C) unpredictable
  (D) ineffectual
  (E) unobtrusive

If you insert the different answer choices in the sentence, (C) *by definition* makes the most sense. Someone who gives bonuses one day and orders pay cuts the next clearly is *unpredictable*—no one can tell what he's going to do next.

To learn how to handle sentence completion questions, turn to Part III.

Passage-Based Reading Questions

Passage-based reading questions ask about a passage's main idea or specific details, the author's attitude to the subject, the author's logic and techniques, the implications of the discussion, or the meaning of specific words.

> **Directions:** The passage below is followed by questions based on its content. Answer the questions on the basis of what is *stated* or *implied* in that passage.

    Certain qualities common to the sonnet should be noted. Its definite restrictions make it a challenge to the artistry of the poet and
Line call for all the technical skill at the poet's
(5) command. The more or less set rhyme patterns occurring regularly within the short space of fourteen lines afford a pleasant effect on the ear of the reader, and can create truly musical effects. The rigidity of the form precludes a
(10) too great economy or too great prodigality of words. Emphasis is placed on exactness and perfection of expression. The brevity of the form favors concentrated expression of ideas or passion.

1. The author's primary purpose is to

    (A) contrast different types of sonnets
    (B) criticize the limitations of the sonnet
    (C) describe the characteristics of the sonnet
    (D) explain why the sonnet has lost popularity as a literary form
    (E) encourage readers to compose formal sonnets

2. In line 7, "afford" most nearly means

    (A) initiate
    (B) exaggerate
    (C) are able to pay for
    (D) change into
    (E) provide

3. The author's attitude toward the sonnet form can best be described as

    (A) amused toleration
    (B) grudging admiration
    (C) strong disapprobation
    (D) effusive enthusiasm
    (E) scholarly appreciation

The first question asks you to find the author's main idea. In the opening sentence, the author says certain qualities of the sonnet should be noted or observed. He then goes on to tell you which of these qualities deserve your attention, characterizing them in some detail. Thus, he *describes certain of the sonnet's* qualities or *characteristics*. The correct answer is (C). You can eliminate the other answers with ease. The author is upbeat about the sonnet: he doesn't say that the sonnet has limitations or that it has become less popular. Similarly, he doesn't discuss different types of sonnets. And while he talks about the challenge of composing formal sonnets, he never invites his readers to try writing them.

The second question asks you to figure out a word's meaning from its context. The rhyme patterns have a pleasant effect on the ear of the listener; indeed they *provide* or afford this effect. The correct answer is (E).

The third question asks you to determine how the author feels about his subject. All the author's comments about the sonnet form are positive, but he doesn't go so far as to gush (he's not *effusive*). The only answer that reflects this attitude is (E), *scholarly appreciation.*

See Part IV for tactics that will help you handle the entire range of passage-based reading questions.

Before the Test

What you do on your actual test day clearly matters greatly. However, what you do *before the test*, as you organize yourself and learn how to handle tests such as the SAT, may in the long run matter even more.

Six Months Before

EXPAND YOUR VERBAL HORIZONS

If you haven't started studying for the test by this time, you'd better get started now. There's no point killing yourself with last-minute cramming sessions and overnight flash-card marathons. Now's the time to pick up some good habits that will expand your verbal horizons and increase your verbal skills.

Make a habit of reading a high-quality newspaper every day. Try *The Wall Street Journal, The New York Times*, or *The Washington Post*, not something written in short sound bites like *USA Today*. Good newspapers, written for **discriminating** readers, **exemplify** what is best in journalism today. Note how their editorials address the day's issues **dispassionately**, **delineating** schemes to **rectify** society's ills.

Note also the number of boldface words in the preceding two sentences. We have highlighted them because they are key SAT words: you can find them all on our SAT High-Frequency Word List (Part V). Were any of them unfamiliar to you? Then turn to the high-frequency list. You can jumpstart your SAT preparations if you follow the directions given there for building your vocabulary. You have the time— get to it!

Two Months Before

REGISTER

First, get the paperwork out of the way. Unless you like paying late registration fees, be sure to pick up a test registration form at your high school guidance office and send it in to the College Board at least 6 or 7 weeks before the date on which you want to take the test. Plan ahead: if you want to take the test in October, you have to mail your form in early September, when you are bound to be busy getting off to a good start with your new classes at school.

To get a registration form, or to order a copy of *The SAT Preparation Booklet*, a guide to the test including a sample SAT, go online, call, e-mail, or write the College Board:

(866) 756-7346
(8:00 A.M.–9:00 P.M. Eastern Time, weekdays)
http://sat.www.collegeboard.org/contact

College Board SAT Program
P.O. Box 025505
Miami, FL 33102

REHEARSE

The best way to practice for a race is to run the course in advance. Likewise, the best way to practice for a test is to take a simulated test, going over all the different question types in advance.

First, memorize the directions in this book for each type of question. These are only slightly different from the exact words you'll find on the SAT. The test time you would normally spend reading directions can be better spent answering questions.

Then take your practice test. In this workbook, you have four model tests—one self-assessment test in the next chapter, plus three more at the end of the book. To get the most out of these tests, try taking them under test conditions—no breaks in midsection, no talking, no help from friends.

You'll find this kind of run-through will help build your test-taking stamina and strengthen you for those four vital hours after you walk through the test-center door.

LEARN TO PACE YOURSELF

In taking the SAT, your job is to answer as many questions as you can, rapidly, economically, *correctly*, without getting hung up on any one question and wasting time you could have used to answer two or three additional ones.

As you go through this book, if you find you do get bogged down on an individual question, think things through. First, ask yourself whether it's a question you might be able to answer if you had a bit more time or whether it's one you have *no* idea how to tackle. If you think it's one you can answer if you give it a second try, mark it with a check or an arrow, and plan to come back to it after you've worked through the easy questions in the section. If, however, you think it's a lost cause, mark it with an X and come back to it only after you've answered all the other questions in the section and double-checked your answers. With practice, you should be able to distinguish a "second chancer" from a lost cause. In any case, if you're taking too long, your best bet is to move on.

LEARN WHEN (AND WHEN NOT) TO GUESS

Students always worry about whether they should or shouldn't guess on standardized tests. Because wrong answers do count fractionally against you on the SAT, you may think that you should never guess if you aren't sure of the right answer to a question. But even if you guessed wrong four times for every time you guessed right, you would still come out even. A wrong answer costs you only ¼ of a point. *On the multiple-choice questions,* the best advice for top students is to guess if you can eliminate one or two of the answer choices. You have a better chance of hitting the right answer when you make this sort of "educated" guess.

As you go through this book, try this experiment to find out what kind of guesser you are. Take part of any test that you have not taken before. You don't have to take an entire test section, but you should tackle at least 25 questions. First, answer only the questions you are sure about. Then, with a different color pen, answer the remaining questions for which you can make educated guesses. Finally, with yet another color pen, guess blindly on all the other questions.

Score each of the three tests separately. Compare your scores from the three different approaches to the test. For many people, the second score (the one with the educated guesses) will be the best one. But you may be different. Maybe you are such a poor guesser that you should never guess at all. That's okay. Or maybe you are such a good guesser that you should try every question. That's okay, too. The important thing is to know yourself.

LEARN TO CONCENTRATE

Another important technique for you to work on is building your powers of concentration. As you go through the practice exercises and model tests, notice when you start to lose your focus. Does your mind drift off in the middle of long reading passages? Do you catch yourself staring off into space, or watching the seconds ticking away on the clock? The sooner you spot these momentary lapses of concentration, the sooner you'll be back working toward your goal.

By the way, there's nothing wrong with losing focus for a moment. Everybody does it. When you notice you're drifting, smile. You're normal. Breathe in slowly and let the air ease out. Then take a fresh look at that paragraph or question you were working on. You've had your minibreak. Now you're ready to pick up a few points.

LEARN THERE'S NO NEED TO PANIC

Despite all rumors to the contrary, *your whole college career is not riding on the results of this one test.* The SAT is only one of the factors that colleges take into account when they are deciding about admissions. Admissions officers like the test because the scores give them a quick way to compare applicants from different high schools without worrying whether a B+ from the district high school is the equivalent of a B+ from the elite preparatory school. But colleges never rely on SAT scores alone. Admissions officers are perfectly well aware that there are brilliant students who fall apart on major tests, that students who are not feeling well can do much worse than normal on a test, and that all sorts of things can affect SAT scores on any given day. What's more, every college accepts students with a *wide* range of SAT scores.

You do not need to answer every question on the SAT correctly to be accepted by the college of your choice. In fact, if you answer only 50–60 percent of the questions correctly, you'll get a better than average score, and that, plus a decent GPA, will get you into most colleges.

As you can see, *there's no need to panic about taking the SAT.* However, not everybody taking the SAT realizes this simple truth.

It's hard to stay calm when those around you are tense, and you're bound to run into some pretty tense people when you take the SAT. (Not everyone works through this book, unfortunately.) If you do experience a slight case of "exam nerves" just before the big day, don't worry about it.

- Being keyed up for an examination isn't always bad; you may outdo yourself because you are so worked up.
- Total panic is unlikely to set in; by the time you face the exam, you'll know too much.

Keep these facts in mind, and those tensions should just fade away.

The Night Before

REST

The best thing you can do for yourself before any test is to get a good night's sleep. If you find you're so keyed up that you don't think you'll be able to sleep, try listening to relaxing music, or exercising and then taking a warm bath. If you're lying in bed wakefully, try concentrating on your breathing: breathe in for 4 to 6 counts, hold your breath for another 4 to 6 counts, exhale for 4 to 6 counts. Concentrating on breathing or on visualizing an image of a person or place often helps people to block out distractions and enables them to relax.

ORGANIZE YOUR GEAR

The night before the test, set out everything you're going to need the next day. You will need your admission ticket, a photo ID (a driver's license or a nondriver picture ID, a passport, or a school ID), four or five sharp No. 2 pencils (with erasers), plus a map or directions showing how to get to the test center. Set out an accurate watch (one that doesn't beep) plus a calculator with charged batteries to use on the math sections.

Lay out comfortable clothes for the next day, including a sweater in case the room is cold. Consider bringing along a snack, a treat you can munch on during the break.

PLAN YOUR ROUTE

Allow plenty of time for getting to the test site. If you haven't been there before, locate the test center on a map and figure out the best route. To be sure you know the way, take a trip to the site *before* the day of the test. The test starts at 8:00 AM—you've no time to get lost. If you're using public transportation, check your bus or subway schedule, and be sure you've got a token or ticket or the correct change. If you're driving, check that there's gas in the car. Your job is taking the test. You don't need the extra tension that comes from worrying about whether you will get to the test on time, or the extra distraction that comes from kicking yourself for losing test time by being late.

During the Test

Use Time Wisely

In the course of working through the model tests and practice exercises in this book, you should develop your own personal testing rhythm. You know approximately how many questions you need to get right to meet your academic goals.

Don't get bogged down on any one question. By the time you get to the SAT, you should have a fair idea of how much time to spend on each question (about 30–40 seconds for a sentence completion question, 75 seconds for a passage-based reading question if you average in your passage reading time). If a question is taking too long, leave it and move on to the next ones. Keep moving on to maximize your score.

NOTE DOWN QUESTIONS YOU SKIP

Before you move on, put a mark in your test booklet next to the question you're skipping. You're probably going to want to find that question easily later on.

What sort of mark? First, ask yourself whether it's a question you might be able to answer if you had a bit more time or whether it's one you have *no* idea how to tackle. If you think it's one you can answer if you give it a second try, mark it with a check or an arrow and plan to come straight back to it after you've worked through the easy questions in the section. If you think it's a lost cause, mark it with an X and come back to it only after you've answered all the other questions in the section and double-checked your answers. Either way, mark the test booklet and move on.

Whenever you skip a question, check frequently to make sure you are answering later questions in the right spots. No machine is going to notice that you made a mistake early in the test, by answering question 9 in the space for question 8, so that all your following answers are in the wrong places. Line up your answer sheet with your test booklet. That way you'll have an easier time checking that you're getting your answers in the right spots.

Never just skip for skipping's sake. Always try to answer each question before you decide to move on. Keep up that "can do" spirit—the more confident you are that you can answer the SAT questions, the more likely you are to give each question your best shot.

ANSWER EASY QUESTIONS FIRST

First answer all the easy questions; *then* tackle the hard ones if you have time. You know that the questions in each segment of the test get harder as you go along (except for the passage-based reading questions). But there's no rule that says you have to answer the questions in order. You're allowed to skip; so, if the last three sentence completion questions are driving you crazy, move on to the reading passages right away. Take advantage of the easy questions to boost your score.

TACKLE SHORTER QUESTIONS BEFORE LONGER ONES

If you're running out of time on a critical reading section and you're smack in the middle of a reading passage, look for the shortest questions on that passage and try answering them. Aim for questions with answer choices that are only two or three words long. You don't need much time to answer a vocabulary-in-context question or a straightforward question about the author's attitude or tone, and one or two extra correct answers can boost your score an additional 10 to 20 points.

ELIMINATE WRONG ANSWERS AS YOU GO

Eliminate as many wrong answers as you can. Sometimes you'll be able to eliminate all the choices until you have just one answer left. Even if you wind up with two choices that look good, deciding between two choices is easier than deciding among five. What's more, the reasoning that helped you decide which answer choices to eliminate may also give you new insights into the question and help you figure out which of the remaining answer choices is correct.

Draw a line through any answer you decide to eliminate. Then, if you decide to move on to another question and come back to this one later, you won't forget which answer choices you thought were wrong. (However, when you cross out an answer choice, do so *lightly*. Don't obliterate it totally. You may want to look it over again later if you decide your first impulse to eliminate it was wrong.)

Even if you can't settle on a correct answer and decide to guess, every answer you eliminate as definitely wrong improves your chances of guessing right.

Center on the Test

Focus on the question in front of you. At this moment, it's all that matters. Answer it and fill in your answer choice, *being careful you're filling in the right space*. Then move on to the next question, and the next. Find your steady, even testing rhythm and keep it going.

BLOCK OUT DISTRACTIONS

When Tiger Woods plays golf, he has his mind on one thing: the game, not the movements of the enthusiastic crowd, not the occasional plane flying overhead, not the applause of the spectators, not even the photographers in the gallery. He blocks them out.

The SAT is your game. To play it well, block out the distractions. Don't start looking around at the other students taking the test. You don't get any points for watching other people answer questions. You get points only for answering questions yourself. Keep your eye on the test booklet and your mind on the game.

WHEN THINGS GET TIGHT, STAY LOOSE

Sooner or later, as you go through the test, you're going to hit a tough spot. You may run into a paragraph that seems totally unintelligible, or a couple of hard questions that throw you, so that you stop thinking about the question you're working on and sit there panicking instead.

If you come to a group of questions that stump you, relax. There are bound to be a few brain-benders on a test of this nature. *Remember: You don't have to answer every question correctly to do just fine on the test.*

There will be a break about halfway through the test. Use this period to clear your thoughts. Take a few deep breaths. Stretch. Close your eyes and imagine yourself floating. In addition to being under mental pressure, you're under physical pressure from sitting so long in a hard seat with a No. 2 pencil clutched in your hand. Anything you can do to loosen up and get the kinks out will ease your body and help the oxygen get to your brain.

KEEP A POSITIVE OUTLOOK

The best thing you can do for yourself during the test is to keep a positive frame of mind. Too many people walk into tests and interviews defeated before they start. Instead of feeling good about what they have going for them, they worry about what can go wrong instead. They let negative thoughts distract them and drag them down.

You are a motivated, hard-working student. That's why you've chosen to work through this book. You're exactly the sort of person for whom colleges are looking. For you, the SAT isn't an unknown terror. It's something you can handle, something for which you are prepared. It's okay for you not to answer every question. It's okay to get some questions wrong. You'll do better figuring out the answers to the questions you tackle if you know you're doing okay. Have confidence in yourself.

NOTE WHAT'S GOING RIGHT

Whenever you cross out an answer you *know* is incorrect, whenever you skip a question so that you can come back to it later, notice that you're doing the right thing. Whenever you catch yourself drifting off and quickly get back to work, whenever you stretch to get out the kinks, recognize how much you're in control. In applying these tactics you've mastered, you're showing you know how to do the job and do it right.

PAT YOURSELF ON THE BACK

As you go through the test, each time you get a correct answer, pat yourself on the back. "Yes! Ten more points!" Enjoy your successes, and keep an eye out for more successes, more correct answer choices ahead. Feel good about the progress you're making and the rewarding college years to come.

PART 2

SELF-ASSESSMENT

Introduction

Self-Assessment Test

Answer Key

Analysis of Test Results

Answer Explanations

Introduction

How do you get a high score on the SAT? Practice, practice, practice.

Call this chapter "Seventy Minutes to a Better Score on the SAT." Just a little over an hour from now you will have a much better idea of how well prepared you are to face the critical reading sections of the SAT.

This chapter contains a full test's worth of critical reading test sections, just like the ones on the official practice test for the SAT. There are three critical reading sections. You are allowed 25 minutes each for Sections 1 and 2, and 20 minutes for Section 3. Make every minute count. Take each test section under exam conditions, or as close to exam conditions as possible—no talking, no consulting dictionaries, no taking soda breaks. Limit yourself to the time allowed; that way you'll develop a sense of how to pace yourself on the SAT.

As soon as you've completed all three sections, see how many questions you've answered correctly. (The correct answers are given on page 37.) Then read the answer explanations and go back over any questions you got wrong. Note unfamiliar words you came across so that you can look them up in your dictionary. Check to see whether any particular question types are giving you special trouble. Do this follow-up thoroughly to get the most out of the time you've spent.

Answer Sheet 1

ANSWER SHEET FOR SELF-ASSESSMENT

Section 1

1. Ⓐ Ⓑ Ⓒ Ⓓ Ⓔ
2. Ⓐ Ⓑ Ⓒ Ⓓ Ⓔ
3. Ⓐ Ⓑ Ⓒ Ⓓ Ⓔ
4. Ⓐ Ⓑ Ⓒ Ⓓ Ⓔ
5. Ⓐ Ⓑ Ⓒ Ⓓ Ⓔ
6. Ⓐ Ⓑ Ⓒ Ⓓ Ⓔ
7. Ⓐ Ⓑ Ⓒ Ⓓ Ⓔ

8. Ⓐ Ⓑ Ⓒ Ⓓ Ⓔ
9. Ⓐ Ⓑ Ⓒ Ⓓ Ⓔ
10. Ⓐ Ⓑ Ⓒ Ⓓ Ⓔ
11. Ⓐ Ⓑ Ⓒ Ⓓ Ⓔ
12. Ⓐ Ⓑ Ⓒ Ⓓ Ⓔ
13. Ⓐ Ⓑ Ⓒ Ⓓ Ⓔ

14. Ⓐ Ⓑ Ⓒ Ⓓ Ⓔ
15. Ⓐ Ⓑ Ⓒ Ⓓ Ⓔ
16. Ⓐ Ⓑ Ⓒ Ⓓ Ⓔ
17. Ⓐ Ⓑ Ⓒ Ⓓ Ⓔ
18. Ⓐ Ⓑ Ⓒ Ⓓ Ⓔ
19. Ⓐ Ⓑ Ⓒ Ⓓ Ⓔ

20. Ⓐ Ⓑ Ⓒ Ⓓ Ⓔ
21. Ⓐ Ⓑ Ⓒ Ⓓ Ⓔ
22. Ⓐ Ⓑ Ⓒ Ⓓ Ⓔ
23. Ⓐ Ⓑ Ⓒ Ⓓ Ⓔ
24. Ⓐ Ⓑ Ⓒ Ⓓ Ⓔ
25. Ⓐ Ⓑ Ⓒ Ⓓ Ⓔ

Section 2

1. Ⓐ Ⓑ Ⓒ Ⓓ Ⓔ
2. Ⓐ Ⓑ Ⓒ Ⓓ Ⓔ
3. Ⓐ Ⓑ Ⓒ Ⓓ Ⓔ
4. Ⓐ Ⓑ Ⓒ Ⓓ Ⓔ
5. Ⓐ Ⓑ Ⓒ Ⓓ Ⓔ
6. Ⓐ Ⓑ Ⓒ Ⓓ Ⓔ
7. Ⓐ Ⓑ Ⓒ Ⓓ Ⓔ

8. Ⓐ Ⓑ Ⓒ Ⓓ Ⓔ
9. Ⓐ Ⓑ Ⓒ Ⓓ Ⓔ
10. Ⓐ Ⓑ Ⓒ Ⓓ Ⓔ
11. Ⓐ Ⓑ Ⓒ Ⓓ Ⓔ
12. Ⓐ Ⓑ Ⓒ Ⓓ Ⓔ
13. Ⓐ Ⓑ Ⓒ Ⓓ Ⓔ

14. Ⓐ Ⓑ Ⓒ Ⓓ Ⓔ
15. Ⓐ Ⓑ Ⓒ Ⓓ Ⓔ
16. Ⓐ Ⓑ Ⓒ Ⓓ Ⓔ
17. Ⓐ Ⓑ Ⓒ Ⓓ Ⓔ
18. Ⓐ Ⓑ Ⓒ Ⓓ Ⓔ
19. Ⓐ Ⓑ Ⓒ Ⓓ Ⓔ

20. Ⓐ Ⓑ Ⓒ Ⓓ Ⓔ
21. Ⓐ Ⓑ Ⓒ Ⓓ Ⓔ
22. Ⓐ Ⓑ Ⓒ Ⓓ Ⓔ
23. Ⓐ Ⓑ Ⓒ Ⓓ Ⓔ
24. Ⓐ Ⓑ Ⓒ Ⓓ Ⓔ
25. Ⓐ Ⓑ Ⓒ Ⓓ Ⓔ

Section 3

1. Ⓐ Ⓑ Ⓒ Ⓓ Ⓔ
2. Ⓐ Ⓑ Ⓒ Ⓓ Ⓔ
3. Ⓐ Ⓑ Ⓒ Ⓓ Ⓔ
4. Ⓐ Ⓑ Ⓒ Ⓓ Ⓔ
5. Ⓐ Ⓑ Ⓒ Ⓓ Ⓔ
6. Ⓐ Ⓑ Ⓒ Ⓓ Ⓔ
7. Ⓐ Ⓑ Ⓒ Ⓓ Ⓔ

8. Ⓐ Ⓑ Ⓒ Ⓓ Ⓔ
9. Ⓐ Ⓑ Ⓒ Ⓓ Ⓔ
10. Ⓐ Ⓑ Ⓒ Ⓓ Ⓔ
11. Ⓐ Ⓑ Ⓒ Ⓓ Ⓔ
12. Ⓐ Ⓑ Ⓒ Ⓓ Ⓔ
13. Ⓐ Ⓑ Ⓒ Ⓓ Ⓔ

14. Ⓐ Ⓑ Ⓒ Ⓓ Ⓔ
15. Ⓐ Ⓑ Ⓒ Ⓓ Ⓔ
16. Ⓐ Ⓑ Ⓒ Ⓓ Ⓔ
17. Ⓐ Ⓑ Ⓒ Ⓓ Ⓔ
18. Ⓐ Ⓑ Ⓒ Ⓓ Ⓔ
19. Ⓐ Ⓑ Ⓒ Ⓓ Ⓔ

20. Ⓐ Ⓑ Ⓒ Ⓓ Ⓔ
21. Ⓐ Ⓑ Ⓒ Ⓓ Ⓔ
22. Ⓐ Ⓑ Ⓒ Ⓓ Ⓔ
23. Ⓐ Ⓑ Ⓒ Ⓓ Ⓔ
24. Ⓐ Ⓑ Ⓒ Ⓓ Ⓔ
25. Ⓐ Ⓑ Ⓒ Ⓓ Ⓔ

1 1 1 1 1 1 1 1 1 1 1 1

SELF-ASSESSMENT TEST

Section 1

TIME—25 MINUTES
24 QUESTIONS

For each of the following questions, select the best answer from the choices provided and fill in the appropriate circle on the answer sheet.

Each of the following sentences contains one or two blanks; each blank indicates that a word or set of words has been left out. Below the sentence are five words or phrases, lettered A through E. Select the word or set of words that best completes the sentence.

Example:

Fame is ----; today's rising star is all too soon tomorrow's washed-up has-been.

(A) rewarding   (B) gradual
(C) essential   (D) spontaneous
(E) transitory

1. While there were some tasks the candidate could _____, others she had to attend to herself.

   (A) perform
   (B) endorse
   (C) delegate
   (D) misconstrue
   (E) rehearse

2. His dislike of _____ made him regard people who flaunted their wealth or accomplishments as _____.

   (A) flattery...charlatans
   (B) poverty...misers
   (C) boasting...braggarts
   (D) failure...opportunists
   (E) procrastination...spendthrifts

3. Although caterpillars and spiders belong to distinctly different classes of arthropods and come to produce silk quite independently, the silks they produce have remarkably _____ compositions.

   (A) delicate
   (B) diaphanous
   (C) mutable
   (D) similar
   (E) durable

4. Concrete actually is _____, like a sponge—it can absorb up to 10 percent of its weight in water.

   (A) delicate
   (B) elastic
   (C) porous
   (D) ubiquitous
   (E) washable

5. Some of Kandinsky's artistic innovations are now so much a part of our visual world that they appear on everything from wallpaper to women's scarves without causing the slightest _____.

   (A) profit
   (B) remorse
   (C) boredom
   (D) effort
   (E) stir

GO ON TO THE NEXT PAGE

6. Short stories, in Hemingway's phrase, have plots that show only "the tip of the iceberg"; such stories _____ a _____ shape below but do not describe that shape in detail.

   (A) cover up...distinctive
   (B) hint at...bulkier
   (C) depart from...nebulous
   (D) thaw out...colder
   (E) revolve around...grimmer

7. The title *Rage of a Privileged Class* seems _____, for such a privileged group would seem on the surface to have no _____ sustained anger with anyone.

   (A) incongruous...time for
   (B) paradoxical...reason for
   (C) ambiguous...familiarity with
   (D) ironic...indifference to
   (E) witty...capacity for

8. Darwin's ideas, which viewed nature as the result of cumulative, _____ change, triumphed over the older, catastrophist theories, which _____ that mountains and species were created by a few sudden and dramatic events.

   (A) gradual...maintained
   (B) drastic...anticipated
   (C) regular...denied
   (D) frequent...disproved
   (E) abrupt...insinuated

1 1 1 1 1 1 1 1 1 1 1 1

Read each of the passages below, and then answer the questions that follow the passage. The correct response may be stated outright or merely suggested in the passage.

Questions 9 and 10 are based on the following passage.

How did the term "spam" come to mean unsolicited commercial e-mail? Flash back to 1937, when Hormel Foods creates a new
Line canned spiced ham, SPAM. Then, in World
(5) War II, SPAM luncheon meat becomes a staple of soldiers' diets (often GIs ate SPAM two or three times a day). Next, SPAM's wartime omnipresence perhaps inspired the 1987 Monty Python skit in which a breakfast-
(10) seeking couple unsuccessfully tries to order a SPAM-free meal while a chorus of Vikings drowns them out, singing "Spam, spam, spam, spam . . . ." To computer users drowning in junk e-mail, the analogy was obvious.
(15) "Spam," they said, "it's spam."

9. The tone of the passage can best be characterized as

   (A) nostalgic
   (B) sardonic
   (C) detached
   (D) chatty
   (E) didactic

10. The parenthetic remark in lines 6 and 7 ("often . . . day") serves primarily to

   (A) establish the soldiers' fondness for SPAM
   (B) provide evidence of SPAM's abundance
   (C) refute criticisms of wartime food shortages
   (D) illustrate the need for dietary supplements
   (E) point out the difference between military and civilian diets

Questions 11 and 12 are based on the following passage.

How does an artist train his eye? "First," said Leonardo da Vinci, "learn perspective; then draw from nature." The self-taught eigh-
Line teenth century painter George Stubbs followed
(5) Leonardo's advice. Like Leonardo, he studied anatomy, but, unlike Leonardo, instead of studying human anatomy, he studied the anatomy of the horse. He dissected carcass after carcass, peeling away the five separate
(10) layers of muscles, removing the organs, baring the veins and arteries and nerves. For 18 long months he recorded his observations, and when he was done he could paint horses muscle by muscle, as they had never been painted
(15) before. Pretty decent work, for someone self-taught.

11. The primary purpose of the passage is to

   (A) explain a phenomenon
   (B) describe a process
   (C) refute an argument
   (D) urge a course of action
   (E) argue against a practice

12. The use of the phrase "pretty decent" (line 15) conveys

   (A) grudging enthusiasm
   (B) tentative approval
   (C) ironic understatement
   (D) bitter envy
   (E) fundamental indifference

GO ON TO THE NEXT PAGE

1 1 1 1 1 1 1 1 1 1 1 1 1

Questions 13–24 are based on the following passage.

In this excerpt from an essay on the symbolic language of dreams, the writer Erich Fromm explores the nature of symbols.

One of the current definitions of a symbol is that it is "something that stands for something else." We can differentiate between three
Line kinds of symbols: the *conventional*, the *acci-*
(5) *dental*, and the *universal* symbol.

The *conventional* symbol is the best known of the three, since we employ it in everyday language. If we see the word "table" or hear the sound "table," the letters *t-a-b-l-e* stand for
(10) something else. They stand for the thing "table" that we see, touch, and use. What is the connection between the *word* "table" and the *thing* "table"? Is there any inherent relationship between them? Obviously not. The
(15) *thing* table has nothing to do with the *sound* table, and the only reason the word symbolizes the thing is the convention of calling this particular thing by a name. We learn this connection as children by the repeated experience
(20) of hearing the word in reference to the thing until a lasting association is formed so that we don't have to think to find the right word.

There are some words, however, in which the association is not only conventional. When
(25) we say "phooey," for instance, we make with our lips a movement of dispelling the air quickly. It is an expression of disgust in which our mouths participate. By this quick expulsion of air we imitate and thus express our
(30) intention to expel something, to get it out of our system. In this case, as in some others, the symbol has an inherent connection with the feeling it symbolizes. But even if we assume that originally many or even all words had
(35) their origins in some such inherent connection between symbol and the symbolized, most words no longer have this meaning for us when we learn a language.

Words are not the only illustration for con-
(40) ventional symbols, although they are the most frequent and best known ones. Pictures also can be conventional symbols. A flag, for instance, may stand for a specific country, and yet there is no intrinsic connection between
(45) the specific colors and the country for which they stand. They have been accepted as denoting that particular country, and we translate the visual impression of the flag into the concept of that country, again on conventional
(50) grounds.

The opposite to the conventional symbol is the *accidental* symbol, although they have one thing in common: there is no intrinsic relationship between the symbol and that which it
(55) symbolizes. Let us assume that someone has had a saddening experience in a certain city; when he hears the name of that city, he will easily connect the name with a mood of sadness, just as he would connect it with a mood
of joy had his experience been a happy one.
(60) Quite obviously, there is nothing in the nature of the city that is either sad or joyful. It is the individual experience connected with the city that makes it a symbol of a mood.

(65) The same reaction could occur in connection with a house, a street, a certain dress, certain scenery, or anything once connected with a specific mood. We might find ourselves dreaming that we are in a certain city. We ask
(70) ourselves why we happened to think of that city in our sleep and may discover that we had fallen asleep in a mood similar to the one symbolized by the city. The picture in the dream represents this mood, the city "stands for" the
(75) mood once experienced in it. The connection between the symbol and the experience symbolized is entirely accidental.

GO ON TO THE NEXT PAGE →

1 1 1 1 1 1 1 1 1 1 1

The *universal* symbol is one in which there is an intrinsic relationship between the symbol
(80) and that which it represents. Take, for instance, the symbol of fire. We are fascinated by certain qualities of fire in a fireplace. First of all, by its aliveness. It changes continuously, it moves all the time, and yet there is constancy
(85) in it. It remains the same without being the same. It gives the impression of power, of energy, of grace and lightness. It is as if it were dancing, and had an inexhaustible source of energy. When we use fire as a symbol, we
(90) describe the *inner experience* characterized by the same elements which we notice in the sensory experience of fire—the mood of energy, lightness, movement, grace, gaiety, sometimes one, sometimes another of these elements
(95) being predominant in the feeling.

The universal symbol is the only one in which the relationship between the symbol and that which is symbolized is not coincidental, but intrinsic. It is rooted in the experience
(100) of the affinity between an emotion or thought, on the one hand, and a sensory experience, on the other. It can be called universal because it is shared by all men, in contrast not only to the accidental symbol, which is by its very nature
(105) entirely personal, but also to the conventional symbol, which is restricted to a group of people sharing the same convention. The universal symbol is rooted in the properties of our body, our senses, and our mind, which
(110) are common to all men and, therefore, not restricted to individuals or to specific groups. Indeed, *the language of the universal symbol is the one common tongue developed by the human race, a language which it forgot before*
(115) *it succeeded in developing a universal conventional language.*

13. The passage is primarily concerned with

(A) refuting an argument
(B) illustrating an axiom
(C) describing a process
(D) proving a thesis
(E) refining a definition

14. In line 9, "stand for" most nearly means

(A) tolerate
(B) represent
(C) withstand
(D) endorse
(E) rise

15. According to lines 8–33, "table" and "phooey" differ in that

(A) only one is a conventional symbol
(B) "table" is a better known symbol than "phooey"
(C) "phooey" has an intrinsic natural link with its meaning
(D) children learn "phooey" more readily than they learn "table"
(E) only one is used exclusively by children

16. It can be inferred from the passage that another example of a word with both inherent and conventional associations to its meaning is

(A) hiss
(B) hike
(C) hold
(D) candle
(E) telephone

GO ON TO THE NEXT PAGE

1 1 1 1 1 1 1 1 1 1 1 1

17. The author contends that conventional symbols

    (A) are less meaningful than accidental ones
    (B) necessarily have an innate connection with an emotion
    (C) can be pictorial as well as linguistic
    (D) are less familiar than universal symbols
    (E) appeal chiefly to conventionally minded people

18. Which of the following would the author be most likely to categorize as a conventional symbol?

    (A) a country road
    (B) a patchwork quilt
    (C) a bonfire
    (D) the city of London
    (E) the Statue of Liberty

19. According to the author's argument, a relationship between the city of Paris and the mood of joy can best be described as

    (A) innate
    (B) dreamlike
    (C) elemental
    (D) coincidental
    (E) immutable

20. A major factor distinguishing a universal symbol from conventional and accidental symbols is

    (A) its origins in sensory experience
    (B) its dependence on a specific occasion
    (C) the intensity of the mood experienced
    (D) its unmemorable nature
    (E) its appeal to the individual

21. By saying "Take . . . the symbol of fire" (lines 80 and 81), the author is asking the reader to

    (A) grasp it as an element
    (B) consider it as an example
    (C) accept it as a possibility
    (D) prefer it as a category
    (E) assume it as a standard

22. Which of the following would the author most likely categorize as a universal symbol?

    (A) the letters f-i-r-e
    (B) the letters p-h-o-o-e-y
    (C) a red dress
    (D) an American flag
    (E) water in a stream

23. In line 108, "properties" most nearly means

    (A) possessions
    (B) attributes
    (C) investments
    (D) titles
    (E) grounds

24. The author contends in lines 112–116 that the language of the universal symbol

    (A) antedates the development of everyday conventional language
    (B) restricts itself to those capable of comprehending symbolism
    (C) should be adopted as the common tongue for the human race
    (D) grew out of human efforts to create a universal conventional language
    (E) developed accidentally from the human desire to communicate

STOP

2 2 2 2 2 2 2 2 2 2 2 **2**

Section 2

TIME—25 MINUTES
24 QUESTIONS

For each of the following questions, select the best answer from the choices provided and fill in the appropriate circle on the answer sheet.

Each of the following sentences contains one or two blanks; each blank indicates that a word or set of words has been left out. Below the sentence are five words or phrases, lettered A through E. Select the word or set of words that best completes the sentence.

Example:

Fame is ----; today's rising star is all too soon tomorrow's washed-up has-been.

(A) rewarding   (B) gradual
(C) essential   (D) spontaneous
(E) transitory

---

1. Though their lack of external ears might suggest otherwise, mole rats are able to use _____ to communicate.

   (A) gestures
   (B) touch
   (C) smells
   (D) sounds
   (E) symbols

2. The word *tephra*, from the Greek word meaning ash, has come into use among geologists to describe the assortment of fragments, ranging from blocks of material to dust, that is _____ into the air during a volcanic eruption.

   (A) amassed
   (B) ejected
   (C) repressed
   (D) wafted
   (E) absorbed

3. While most commentators' reaction to the candidate's acceptance speech was _____, a highly positive reaction came from columnist William Safire, who called it a rhetorical triumph.

   (A) enthusiastic
   (B) unrehearsed
   (C) tepid
   (D) groundless
   (E) immediate

4. Scientists are hard-line _____; only after failing to _____ a controversial theory do they accept the evidence.

   (A) militarists...exploit
   (B) optimists...believe
   (C) martinets...punish
   (D) innovators...refute
   (E) cynics...debunk

5. The founder of the Children's Defense Fund, Marian Wright Edelman, strongly _____ the lack of financial and moral support for children in America today.

   (A) advocates
   (B) condones
   (C) feigns
   (D) abets
   (E) decries

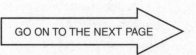
GO ON TO THE NEXT PAGE

2 2 2 2 2 2 2 2 2 2 **2**

Read the passages below, and then answer the questions that follow. The correct response may be stated outright or merely suggested in the passages.

Questions 6–9 are based on the following passages.

Passage 1 is an excerpt from a lecture by American humorist Mark Twain; Passage 2, an excerpt from an essay by English author and critic G. K. Chesterton.

Passage 1

There are several kinds of stories, but only one difficult kind—the humorous. The humorous story is American; the comic story,
Line English; the witty story, French. The humor-
(5) ous story depends for its effect upon the manner of the telling; the comic story and the witty story upon the matter. The humorous story may be spun out to great length, and may wander around as much as it pleases, and
(10) arrive nowhere in particular; but the comic and witty stories must be brief and end with a point. The humorous story bubbles gently along; the others burst.

Passage 2

Line American humor, neither transfiguringly
(15) lucid and appropriate like the French, nor sharp and sensible like the Scotch, is simply the humor of imagination. It consists in piling towers on towers and mountains on mountains; of heaping a joke up to the stars and extending
(20) it to the end of the world. With this distinctively American humor Bret Harte had little or nothing in common. The wild, sky-breaking humor of America has its fine qualities, but it must in the nature of things be deficient in two
(25) qualities, not only supremely important to life and letters, but also supremely important to humor—reverence and sympathy. And these two qualities were knit into the closest texture of Bret Harte's humor.

6. Which of the following most resembles the humorous story as described in Passage 1?

   (A) A paradox
   (B) A fairy tale
   (C) An allegory
   (D) A shaggy-dog story
   (E) An amusing limerick

7. In stating that "The humorous story bubbles gently along; the others burst," the author of Passage 1 is speaking

   (A) melodramatically
   (B) hypothetically
   (C) metaphorically
   (D) nostalgically
   (E) analytically

8. Which generalization about American humor is supported by both passages?

   (A) It is witty and to the point.
   (B) It demonstrates greater sophistication than French humor.
   (C) It depends on a lengthy buildup.
   (D) It is by definition self-contradictory.
   (E) It depends on the subject matter for its effect.

GO ON TO THE NEXT PAGE

2 2 2 2 2 2 2 2 2 2 2 2

9. The author of Passage 1 would most likely respond to the next-to-last sentence of Passage 2 (lines 22–27) by

(A) denying that American humor is deficient in any significant way
(B) apologizing for the lack of reverence in the American humorous story
(C) noting that Bret Harte was not a particularly sympathetic writer
(D) arguing that little is actually known about the nature of humor
(E) agreeing with the author's assessment of the situation

Questions 10–15 are based on the following passage.

In the following excerpt from Jane Austen's Pride and Prejudice, *the members of the Bennet family react to news of the marriage of Lydia, the youngest Bennet daughter, to Mr. Wickham. Elizabeth, oldest of the Bennet daughters and the novel's heroine, is in love with Mr. Darcy and worries how this unexpected marriage may affect her relationship with him.*

A long dispute followed this declaration; but Mr. Bennet was firm: it soon led to another; and Mrs. Bennet found, with amaze-
Line ment and horror, that her husband would not
(5) advance a guinea[1] to buy clothes for his daughter. He protested that she should receive from him no mark of affection whatever, on the occasion of her marriage. Mrs. Bennet could hardly comprehend it. That his anger
(10) could be carried to such a point of inconceivable resentment, as to refuse his daughter a privilege, without which her marriage would scarcely seem valid, exceeded all that she could believe possible. She was more alive to
(15) the disgrace, which the want of new clothes must reflect on her daughter's nuptials, than to any sense of shame at her eloping and living with Wickham, a fortnight before they took place.

(20) Elizabeth was now most heartily sorry that she had, from the distress of the moment, been led to make Mr. Darcy acquainted with their fears for her sister; for since her marriage would so shortly give the proper termination
(25) to the elopement, they might hope to conceal its unfavorable beginning, from all those who were not immediately on the spot.

She had no fear of its spreading farther, through his means. There were few people on
(30) whose secrecy she would have more confidently depended; but at the same time, there was no one, whose knowledge of a sister's frailty would have mortified her so much. Not, however, from any fear of disadvantage from
(35) it, individually to herself; for at any rate, there seemed a gulf impassable between them. Had Lydia's marriage been concluded on the most honorable terms, it was not to be supposed that Mr. Darcy would connect himself with a
(40) family, where to every other objection would now be added, an alliance and relationship of the nearest kind with the man whom he so justly scorned.

From such a connection she could not
(45) wonder that he should shrink. The wish of procuring her regard, which she had assured herself of his feeling in Derbyshire, could not in rational expectation survive such a blow as this. She was humbled, she was grieved; she
(50) repented, though she hardly knew of what. She became jealous of his esteem, when she could no longer hope to be benefitted by it. She wanted to hear of him, when there seemed the least chance of gaining intelligence. She
(55) was convinced that she could have been happy with him, when it was no longer likely they should meet.

---

[1]A British coin.

GO ON TO THE NEXT PAGE

2 2 2 2 2 2 2 2 2 2 2

10. All of the following statements about Mrs. Bennet may be inferred from the passage EXCEPT

(A) She finds a lack of proper attire more shameful than a lack of proper conduct.
(B) She is ready to welcome home her newly married daughter.
(C) She is sensitive to the nature of her husband's scruples about the elopement.
(D) She is unable to grasp the degree of emotion her daughter's conduct has aroused.
(E) She is primarily concerned with external appearances.

11. The "privilege" that Mr. Bennet refuses to grant his daughter (line 12) is the privilege of

(A) marrying Mr. Wickham
(B) buying a new wardrobe
(C) running away from home
(D) seeing her mother and sisters
(E) having a valid wedding ceremony

12. According to the passage, Elizabeth Bennet presently

(A) has ceased to crave Darcy's affection
(B) regrets having told Darcy of her sister's elopement
(C) no longer desires to conceal Lydia's escapade
(D) fears Darcy will spread the word about the sudden elopement
(E) cares more for public opinion than for her family's welfare

13. The expression "a sister's frailty" (lines 32 and 33) refers to Elizabeth's sister's

(A) delicate health since birth
(B) embarrassing lack of proper wedding garments
(C) reluctant marriage to a man whom she disdained
(D) fear of being considered an old maid
(E) moral weakness in running away with a man

14. According to lines 38–43, Mr. Darcy feels contempt for

(A) Lydia's hasty marriage
(B) secrets that are entrusted to him
(C) Elizabeth's confession to him
(D) Lydia's new husband
(E) Mr. Bennet's harshness

15. The passage can best be described as

(A) a description of the origins of a foolish and intemperate marriage
(B) an account of one woman's reflections on the effects of her sister's runaway marriage
(C) an analysis of the reasons underlying the separation of a young woman from her lover
(D) a description of a conflict between a young woman and her temperamental parents
(E) a discussion of the nature of sacred and profane love

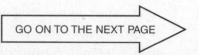

GO ON TO THE NEXT PAGE

2 2 2 2 2 2 2 2 2 2 2 **2**

Questions 16–24 are based on the following passage.

The following passage is taken from a classic study of tarantulas published in Scientific American *in 1952.*

A fertilized female tarantula lays from 200 to 400 eggs at a time; thus it is possible for a single tarantula to produce several thousand
Line young. She takes no care of them beyond
(5) weaving a cocoon of silk to enclose the eggs. After they hatch, the young walk away, find convenient places in which to dig their bur-rows and spend the rest of their lives in soli-tude. Tarantulas feed mostly on insects and
(10) millipedes. Once their appetite is appeased, they digest the food for several days before eating again. Their sight is poor, being limited to sensing a change in the intensity of light and to the perception of moving objects. They
(15) apparently have little or no sense of hearing, for a hungry tarantula will pay no attention to a loudly chirping cricket placed in its cage unless the insect happens to touch one of its legs.
(20) But all spiders, and especially hairy ones, have an extremely delicate sense of touch. Laboratory experiments prove that tarantulas can distinguish three types of touch: pressure against the body wall, stroking of the body
(25) hair and riffling of certain very fine hairs on the legs called trichobothria. Pressure against the body, by a finger or the end of a pencil, causes the tarantula to move off slowly for a short distance. The touch excites no defensive
(30) response unless the approach is from above, where the spider can see the motion, in which case it rises on its hind legs, lifts its front legs, opens its fangs and holds this threatening pos-ture as long as the object continues to move.
(35) When the motion stops, the spider drops back to the ground, remains quiet for a few sec-onds, and then moves slowly away.

The entire body of a tarantula, especially its legs, is thickly clothed with hair. Some of it
(40) is short and woolly, some long and stiff. Touching this body hair produces one of two distinct reactions. When the spider is hungry, it responds with an immediate and swift attack. At the touch of a cricket's antennae the
(45) tarantula seizes the insect so swiftly that a motion picture taken at the rate of 64 frames per second shows only the result and not the process of capture. But when the spider is not hungry, the stimulation of its hairs merely
(50) causes it to shake the touched limb. An insect can walk under its hairy belly unharmed.

The trichobothria, very fine hairs growing from disklike membranes on the legs, were once thought to be the spider's hearing organs,
(55) but we now know that they have nothing to do with sound. They are sensitive only to air movement. A light breeze makes them vibrate slowly without disturbing the common hair. When one blows gently on the trichobothria,
(60) the tarantula reacts with a quick jerk of its four front legs. If the front and hind legs are stimu-lated at the same time, the spider makes a sud-den jump. This reaction is quite independent of the state of its appetite.
(65) These three tactile responses—to pressure on the body wall, to moving of the common hair, and to flexing of the trichobothria—are so different from one another that there is no possibility of confusing them. They serve the
(70) tarantula adequately for most of its needs and enable it to avoid most annoyances and dan-gers. But they fail the spider completely when it meets its deadly enemy, the digger wasp *Pepsis.*

GO ON TO THE NEXT PAGE ⟹

2 2 2 2 2 2 2 2 2 2 2

16. According to the author, which of the following attributes is (are) characteristic of female tarantulas?

   I. Maternal instincts
  II. Visual acuity
 III. Fertility

   (A) I only
   (B) II only
   (C) III only
   (D) I and III only
   (E) II and III only

17. Lines 6–9 primarily suggest that the female tarantula

   (A) becomes apprehensive at sudden noises
   (B) is better able to discern pressure than stroking
   (C) must consume insects or millipedes daily
   (D) constructs a cocoon for her young
   (E) is reclusive by nature

18. In line 29, "excites" most nearly means

   (A) irritates
   (B) delights
   (C) stimulates
   (D) exhilarates
   (E) infuriates

19. The author's attitude toward tarantulas would best be described as
   (A) fearful
   (B) sentimental
   (C) approving
   (D) objective
   (E) incredulous

20. The main purpose of the passage is to

   (A) report on controversial new discoveries about spider behavior
   (B) summarize what is known about the physical and social responses of tarantulas
   (C) challenge the findings of recent laboratory experiments involving tarantulas
   (D) explain the lack of social organization in the spider family
   (E) discuss the physical adaptations that make tarantulas unique

21. The description of what happens when one films a tarantula's reaction to the touch of a cricket (lines 44–48) chiefly is intended to convey a sense of the tarantula's

   (A) omnivorous appetite
   (B) photogenic appearance
   (C) graceful movement
   (D) quickness in attacking
   (E) lack of stimulation

22. In line 63, "independent" most nearly means

   (A) individualistic
   (B) self-governing
   (C) affluent
   (D) regardless
   (E) detached

GO ON TO THE NEXT PAGE ⇒

2 2 2 2 2 2 2 2 2 2 **2**

23. In the passage, the author does all of the following EXCEPT

(A) deny a possibility
(B) describe a reaction
(C) correct a misapprehension
(D) define a term
(E) pose a question

24. In the paragraphs immediately following this passage, the author most likely will

(A) explain why scientists previously confused the tarantula's three tactile responses
(B) demonstrate how the tarantula's three tactile responses enable it to meet its needs
(C) point out the weaknesses of the digger wasp that enable the tarantula to subdue it
(D) report on plans for experiments to explore the digger wasp's tactile sense
(E) describe how the digger wasp goes about attacking tarantulas

STOP

If you finish before time is called, you may check your work on this section only. Do not work on any other section in the test.

Self-Assessment Test

3 3 3 3 3 3 3 3 3 3 3

Section 3

TIME—20 MINUTES
19 QUESTIONS

For each of the following questions, select the best answer from the choices provided and fill in the appropriate circle on the answer sheet.

Each of the following sentences contains one or two blanks; each blank indicates that a word or set of words has been left out. Below the sentence are five words or phrases, lettered A through E. Select the word or set of words that best completes the sentence.

Example:

Fame is ----; today's rising star is all too soon tomorrow's washed-up has-been.

(A) rewarding   (B) gradual
(C) essential   (D) spontaneous
(E) transitory

1. Excavation is, in essence, an act of _____: to clear a site down to the lowest level means that all the upper levels are completely obliterated.

   (A) exploration
   (B) destruction
   (C) validation
   (D) malice
   (E) spontaneity

2. Hummingbirds use spider silk to strengthen nest walls to better _____ the weight and pressure of wriggling hatchlings.

   (A) withstand
   (B) discern
   (C) expose
   (D) transmute
   (E) induce

3. A map purporting to show that Vikings charted North America long before Columbus, _____ as a fraud in 1974, could turn out to be _____ after all, according to California scientists.

   (A) honored...questionable
   (B) condemned...superficial
   (C) branded...genuine
   (D) labeled...fragmentary
   (E) dismissed...extant

4. Although the poet Stevie Smith had a childhood that was far from _____, she always envied children, believing they alone had the ideal life.

   (A) idyllic
   (B) envious
   (C) indifferent
   (D) dubious
   (E) neutral

5. In Christopher's _____ family, _____ begun over dinner frequently carried over for days.

   (A) contentious...arguments
   (B) abstemious...accusations
   (C) garrulous...doubts
   (D) assiduous...conversations
   (E) irreverent...rituals

6. A prudent, thrifty New Englander, DeWitt was naturally _____ of investing money in junk bonds, which he looked on as _____ ventures.

   (A) enamored...worthless
   (B) terrified...sound
   (C) chary...risky
   (D) tired...profitable
   (E) cognizant...provincial

GO ON TO THE NEXT PAGE

3 3 3 3 3 3 3 3 3 3 3 3

The questions that follow the next two passages relate to the content of both, and to their relationship. The correct response may be stated outright in the passage or merely suggested.

Questions 7–19 are based on the following passages.

The following passages describe the settling of the American West during the nineteenth century. The first was written by a social historian and scholar. The second comes from a widely used textbook in American history.

Passage 1

The populating of nearly one billion acres of empty land west of the Mississippi occurred in a series of peristaltic waves, beginning in
Line the 1840s and continuing for the rest of the
(5) century. First to arrive was the advance guard, the trailblazers—explorers, trappers, and mountain men, hide and tallow traders, freelance adventurers, the military. Then the settlers in their wagon trains lumbering over the
(10) Oregon Trail to the lush meadows of the Oregon Territory and the inland valleys of California. Next, the gold-seekers, bowling across the plains and deserts pell-mell in 1848, working up and down the California mountain
(15) ranges, then backtracking to the gold and silver country in the Rockies and the Southwest. And finally, a last great wave, first by wagons, then by railroads, to mop up the leapfrogged Great Plains. By 1890 the great movement
(20) west was over, ending in a final hurrahing stampede of boomers into Oklahoma Territory, a rush of humanity that created entire towns in an afternoon.

The vast, empty land demanded new tools,
(25) new social organizations, new men and women. And it produced a new canon of myths and heroes—the stuff of countless dime novels, Wild West shows, movies, and television series for later generations. The heroes
(30) are familiar enough—the cowboys, the lawmen, the gamblers, the gold-hearted dancehall girls, the bad men too, for heroes need evil to conquer. The western town played a part, too, mainly as backdrop and chorus,
(35) before which the central figures enacted their *agon* (struggle; contest). The fictional western town was as rigidly formalized as the set for a Japanese No play—the false-front stores on a dusty street lined with hitching rails, the
(40) saloons with bar, gambling tables, and stage for the dancers, the general store, the jail, and the church. The people of the chorus had a stereotypical form—women in crinolines and the men in frock coats and string ties, their
(45) striped pants tucked into boots. Their lives were projected as dim, ordinary, law-abiding shadows, against which were contrasted the bold-hued dramas of the principals. These were the "decent folk," whom the heroic law-
(50) men died for; they were the meek who would inherit the set after the leading actors left and the last wild cowboy was interred in Boot Hill. Colorless, sober, conservative, salt-of-the-earth, they represented the future—and a dull one it
(55) was. Occasionally, as in the film *High Noon*, their passive virtues were transmogrified into hypocrisy and timidity, mocking the lonely courage of the marshal they had hired to risk his life for them. The implication was: Are
(60) these dull, cautious folk really the worthy heirs of the noble cowboys? In Steven Crane's short story *The Bride Comes to Yellow Sky*, the last cowboy is a drunken anachronism, wearing his nobility in tatters, yet not to be
(65) scorned.

GO ON TO THE NEXT PAGE →

3 3 3 3 3 3 3 3 3 3

Passage 2

It was the miners who established the first outpost of the Far West. The discovery of gold in California had transformed that com-
Line monwealth from a pastoral outpost of New
(70) Spain to a thriving American state and had opened up new and varied economic activities—farming, shipping, railroading, and manufacturing. That experience was to be repeated again and again in the history of the mining
(75) kingdom; in the rush to Pike's Peak country in 1859, to Alder Gulch and Last Chance in Montana and the banks of the Sweetwater in Wyoming in the middle sixties, to the Black Hills of the Dakota country in the seventies.
(80) Everywhere the miners opened up the country, established political communities, and laid the foundations for more permanent settlements. As the gold and silver played out or fell into the hands of eastern corporations and mining
(85) fever abated, the settlers would perceive the farming and stock-raising possibilities around them or find work on the railroads that were pushing in from the East and West. Some communities remained almost exclusively
(90) mining, but the real wealth of Montana and Colorado, Wyoming and Idaho, as of California, was in their grass and their soil. Even in mineral wealth the value of the precious metals which had first lured adventurers
(95) was shortly exceeded by that of the copper and coal and oil which were so abundant. . . .
Even while the miners were grubbing in the hills of Nevada and Montana, a new and more important chapter was being written in
(100) the history of the West. This was the rise of the cattle kingdom. The physical basis of the kingdom was the grasslands of the West, stretching unbroken from the Rio Grande to the northern frontier, from Kansas and
(105) Nebraska into the Rocky Mountain valleys. Here millions of buffaloes had roamed at will, but within two decades the buffalo was to

become almost extinct and its place taken by even more millions of Texas longhorns and
(110) Wyoming and Montana steers. . . .
The cattle kingdom, like the mining, had its romantic side, and the remembrance of this has persisted in the American consciousness after the cattle kingdom itself has vanished.
(115) The lonely life on the plain, the roundup, the hieroglyphic brands, the long drive, the stampede, the war with cattle rustlers, the splendid horsemanship, the picturesque costume designed for usefulness, not effect—the wild
(120) life of the cow towns like Abilene and Cheyenne, all have found their way into American folklore and song. Children array themselves now in imitation cowboy suits, moving-picture ranchmen shoot down rustlers
(125) with unerring aim, and the whole country sings what was reputed to be President Franklin Roosevelt's favorite song:
Home, home on the range,
Where the deer and the antelope play
(130) Where seldom is heard, a discouraging word,
And the skies are not cloudy all day.

7. According to Passage 1, the settling of the West took place

(A) during a steady migration that lasted for 60 years
(B) intermittently as people went farther and farther west
(C) in two waves, the first during the 1840s, the last in the 1890s
(D) in no discernible order
(E) sometimes slowly and sometimes rapidly during a 50-year period

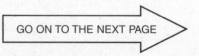
GO ON TO THE NEXT PAGE

3 3 3 3 3 3 3 3 3 3 3

8. Passage 1 implies that the settlers went to the West largely for

   (A) economic advancement
   (B adventure
   (C a desire for more space
   (D free land
   (E) more individual liberty

9. The comparison between western towns and the set of a Japanese No play (line 38) is intended to make the point that

   (A) in the Old West, people mattered more than towns
   (B) all towns in the Old West looked alike
   (C) the towns looked good on the surface but not underneath
   (D) in books and films, western towns are all the same
   (E) towns were all show and no substance

10. The author of Passage 1 believes that after the westward migration the settlers were portrayed as people who

    (A) settled into routine lives
    (B) yearned for a return to the romantic days of the past
    (C) turned into hypocrites
    (D) failed to do what was expected of them
    (E) were worthy heirs of their noble cowboy predecessors

11. The allusion to the cowboy in *The Bride Comes to Yellow Sky* (lines 62–65) is meant to show that

    (A) the people rejected the heroes of the Old West
    (B) many of the myths of the Old West were false
    (C) the legendary heroes of the Old West became obsolete
    (D) drunkenness and reckless behavior tarnished the image of the heroic cowboys of the Old West
    (E) all glamorous and romantic eras eventually die out

12. The center of the so-called "mining kingdom" (lines 67–82), as described in Passage 2,

    (A) was located in California
    (B) stretched from the Mississippi River to the western mountains
    (C) shifted from place to place
    (D) began in the Far West and then jumped to the East
    (E) drifted west throughout the second half of the nineteenth century

13. According to Passage 2, when the gold and silver ran out, the miners switched to

    (A) working on the land
    (B) searching for oil and other fuels
    (C) cattle rustling
    (D) their previous occupations
    (E) digging for other minerals

GO ON TO THE NEXT PAGE

3 3 3 3 3 3 3 3 3 3 **3**

14. The author of Passage 2 believes that the defining event in the history of the West was

   (A) the founding of new cities and towns
   (B) the discovery of precious metals
   (C) the growth of the cattle industry
   (D) the development of the mining kingdom
   (E) the coming of the railroad

15. Passage 2 implies that the buffalo became almost extinct in the Great Plains because

   (A) they roamed westward
   (B) their land was fenced off for agriculture
   (C) the land could no longer support huge buffalo herds
   (D) they were killed to make room for cattlegrazing
   (E) they were driven north to Canada and south to Mexico

16. According to Passage 2, the cowboy of the Old West is remembered today for all of the following EXCEPT his

   (A) distinctive clothing
   (B) ability to ride horses
   (C) law-abiding nature
   (D) fights with cattle thieves
   (E) rugged individualism

17. Both passages suggest that settlers were attracted to California because of its

   (A) gold
   (B) mountains
   (C) seacoast
   (D) scenic splendor
   (E) fertile valleys

18. The authors of Passage 1 and Passage 2 seem to have a common interest in

   (A) defining the American dream
   (B) political history
   (C) mining
   (D) American folklore and legend
   (E) the social class structure in America

19. Compared to the account of the westward movement in Passage 1, Passage 2 pays more attention to the role of

   (A) pioneer families
   (B) miners
   (C) politicians
   (D) entrepreneurs
   (E) outlaws discussion of the *miner*.

STOP

Answer Key

Section 1

1. **C**	7. **B**	13. **E**	19. **D**
2. **C**	8. **A**	14. **B**	20. **A**
3. **D**	9. **D**	15. **C**	21. **B**
4. **C**	10. **B**	16. **A**	22. **E**
5. **E**	11. **B**	17. **C**	23. **B**
6. **B**	12. **C**	18. **E**	24. **A**

Section 2

1. **D**	7. **C**	13. **E**	19. **D**
2. **B**	8. **C**	14. **D**	20. **B**
3. **C**	9. **A**	15. **B**	21. **D**
4. **E**	10. **C**	16. **C**	22. **D**
5. **E**	11. **B**	17. **E**	23. **E**
6. **D**	12. **B**	18. **C**	24. **E**

Section 3

1. **B**	6. **C**	11. **C**	16. **C**
2. **A**	7. **E**	12. **C**	17. **A**
3. **C**	8. **A**	13. **A**	18. **D**
4. **A**	9. **D**	14. **C**	19. **B**
5. **A**	10. **A**	15. **D**	

Self-Assessment Test

Analysis of Test Results

I. Check your answers against the answer key.

II. Fill in the following chart.

Sentence Completion Number Correct	Section 1 (Questions 1–8) _____		Section 2 (Questions 1–5) _____	Section 3 (Questions 1–6) _____		Total _____
Passage-Based Reading Number Correct	Section 1 (Questions 9–24) _____		Section 2 (Questions 6–24) _____	Section 3 (Questions 7–19) _____		Total _____

III. Interpret your results.

Sentence Completion   Number Correct _____

Passage-Based Reading   Number Correct _____

Subtotal _____

Guessing Penalty: Subtract 1/4 point for each incorrect answer.   _____
(Do not take off points for questions you left blank.)

TOTAL SCORE _____

	Sentence Completion Score	Passage-Based Reading Score	Total
Excellent	18–19 Correct	43–48 Correct	60–67
Very Good	14–17 Correct	33–42 Correct	46–59
Good	11–13 Correct	25–32 Correct	35–45
Fair	9–10 Correct	20–24 Correct	28–34
Poor	6–8 Correct	12–19 Correct	17–27
Very Poor	0–5 Correct	0–11 Correct	0–16

You can get a rough idea of which areas you most need to work on by comparing your sentence completion and passage-based reading scores.

The College Board uses a guessing formula to compensate for the effect of wild guesses on people's scores. The formula is

$$\text{Raw score} = \underset{\text{no. correct}}{\underline{\hspace{2cm}}} - (\underset{\text{no. incorrect}}{\underline{\hspace{2cm}}} \text{ divided by 4})$$

In calculating your raw score,* do not count any questions you left blank as incorrect.

Raw scores of 60 to 67 (Critical Reading) are excellent.
Raw scores of 46 to 59 (Critical Reading) are very good.
Raw scores of 35 to 45 (Critical Reading) are above average.
Raw scores of 23 to 34 (Critical Reading) are below average to average.

If your raw score differs from your total number of correct answers by more than 3 points, you should be very cautious about guessing on this test. Guess intelligently. Guess only when you can eliminate one or more of the five answer choices to the question.

IV. List any unfamiliar words you came across. Then look the words up in a dictionary and write down their definitions.

Word	Definition
_____	_____
_____	_____
_____	_____
_____	_____
_____	_____

V. Read the answer explanations and think about your performance.

Go over the questions you omitted as well as the ones you got wrong. Did you mark any answers in the wrong spot? Did you run out of time and have to leave out questions you could have answered correctly? Did you misread any questions, overlooking key words such as "except" and "best"? Were you too cautious about guessing, omitting questions that you had a chance of getting right if you had guessed? If necessary, reread the relevant sections in Part I. Then get to work on mastering the different question types.

---

*A very precise formula is used to convert raw scores to scaled scores for the SAT, and the results may vary slightly from test to test. This book uses a broad-range approximation to give you a ballpark estimate of how you will perform on an actual SAT.

Answer Explanations

Section 1

1. **(C)** If you *delegate* or assign a task to someone else, you do not have to attend to it yourself.

2. **(C)** Someone who flaunts or shows off his or her achievements or possessions is by definition a *braggart*, one who *boasts*.

3. **(D)** If you realize how very different caterpillars and spiders are, you will find it remarkable that they produce silks that are *similar*.

4. **(C)** Like a sponge, concrete can soak up water because it is *porous*, or permeable to fluids.

5. **(E)** We are now so used to Kandinsky's innovative designs that they can turn up anywhere without causing any widespread notice, or *stir*.

6. **(B)** Just as the tip of the iceberg suggests or hints at the greater mass of the iceberg under the water, to Hemingway short stories *hint at* a *bulkier*, heavier tale underlying the small part of the story the reader gets to see.

7. **(B)** To have so many advantages that one would have no reason for anger and yet to be angry all the same is clearly *paradoxical* (puzzling; contradictory).

8. **(A)** The catastrophist theories hypothesized or *maintained* that mountains and species were created by sudden dramatic events or catastrophes. Darwin, however, theorized that nature was the result of cumulative, *gradual* change.

9. **(D)** From its casual direction, "Flash back to 1937," to its quotes from computer users, the passage has a *chatty*, informal tone.

10. **(B)** Given that SPAM was available for the soldier to eat three times a day, clearly it was *abundant* (plentiful).

11. **(B)** The author's primary purpose is to *describe a process*—the process by which Stubbs taught himself to draw horses.

12. **(C)** It is clear that the author admires Stubbs's achievement. To teach oneself to paint horses as they had never been painted before is a major accomplishment. To term that accomplishment only "pretty decent" is an example of *ironic understatement.*

13. **(E)** The author begins by giving a definition of the term *symbol* and proceeds to analyze three separate types of symbols. Thus, he is *refining* or further defining his somewhat rudimentary original definition.

14. **(B)** For a group of letters to stand for an object, the letters must in some way *represent* that object to the people who accept the letters as a conventional symbol for the object.

15. **(C)** In describing the associations of the word "phooey," the author states that "the symbol has an inherent connection with the feeling it symbolizes." In other words, there is an *intrinsic natural link* between the symbol and its meaning.

16. **(A)** When we say "hiss," we expel air in a sibilant manner, making a sharp "s" sound as we thrust our tongue toward the tooth ridge and dispel the air quickly. Thus we express our disapproval of something, our desire to push it away from us, so that the meaning of "hiss" has both inherent and conventional associations.

17. **(C)** The author gives the example of the flag as a conventional symbol that is *pictorial* rather than linguistic.
18. **(E)** To the author, the *Statue of Liberty* would be a conventional symbol, one agreed upon by a group of people to stand for the abstract idea of freedom.
19. **(D)** If by some accident you were to have a memorably joyful time in Paris, the city of Paris might come to have some symbolic value for you, bringing a mood of joy to your mind. However, the relationship between the city and the mood is not an inherent, built-in one; it is purely *coincidental.*
20. **(A)** The author describes how one's inner experience of a universal symbol is rooted in or grows out of one's *sensory experience.*
21. **(B)** The author offers fire as an *example* of a universal symbol and asks the reader to consider it.
22. **(E)** Like fire, *water* is a universal symbol that we experience through our senses, feeling its fluidity, its movement, its power. The words "*fire*" and "*phooey*" are conventional symbols, as is the flag. A red dress, if it has any symbolic value at all, is an accidental symbol at best.
23. **(B)** The "*properties*" mentioned here are our body's *attributes* or characteristics. To answer vocabulary-in-context questions, substitute each of the answer choices in the sentence in place of the word in quotes.
24. **(A)** The closing sentence states that the human race forgot the language of universal symbols before it developed conventional language. Thus, the language of the universal symbol *antedates* or comes before the development of our everyday conventional tongues.

Section 2

1. **(D)** Our experience suggests to us that a creature without visible ears would be unable to hear *sounds.*
2. **(B)** In a volcanic eruption, ash and other matter is *ejected* or forced out of the volcano.
3. **(C)** The opposite of a highly positive response is a *tepid* or lukewarm one. Note that *while* signals a contrast.
4. **(E)** *Cynics* distrust human nature and motives. Such persons would suspect the motives of anyone advancing a controversial theory and would accept evidence in favor of that theory only after having tried hard to *debunk* that evidence (expose it as a sham or false).
5. **(E)** As the founder of a fund for children, Edelman would be likely to *decry* (condemn) a lack of support for young people.
6. **(D)** Twain states that the "humorous story may be spun out to great length, and may wander around as much as it pleases, and arrive nowhere in particular." In this way it resembles the *shaggy-dog story*, by definition a long, rambling joke whose humor derives from its pointlessness.
7. **(C)** Twain is using figurative language to contrast a humorous story and a witty or comic story. He is speaking *metaphorically.*
8. **(C)** In Passage 1, Twain states that the American "humorous story may be spun out to great length"; in Passage 2, Chesterton states that American humor "consists in piling towers on towers and mountains on mountains; of heaping a joke up to the stars and extending it to the end of the world." Both passages thus support the generalization that American humor *depends on a lengthy buildup.*

9. **(A)** Twain considers the American humorous story difficult to bring off properly; to him, that is its challenge and its charm. He speaks positively about the humorous story's "bubbling gently along." He finds the manner of its telling pleasing rather than irreverent or unsympathetic Thus he would most likely respond to Chesterton's criticism by *denying* that this distinctively *American humor is deficient in any significant way.*

10. **(C)** Far from being *sensitive to the nature of her husband's scruples* or ethical considerations about his daughter's elopement, Mrs. Bennet can hardly comprehend them.

11. **(B)** The "privilege" Mr. Bennet refuses his daughter is *buying a new wardrobe*. In the opening sentence, we learn that Mr. Bennet would not come up with any money ("would not advance a guinea") to buy his daughter new clothes. To Mrs. Bennet, the purchase of new clothes on the occasion of a wedding was a privilege automatically granted the bride.

12. **(B)** The opening sentence of the second paragraph indicates Elizabeth's *regret*: she "was most heartily sorry."

13. **(E)** Frailty here is the *moral weakness* of giving way to temptation and running off to "live in sin" with a man.

14. **(D)** The concluding sentence of the third paragraph indicates that Darcy scorned or felt contempt for *Lydia's new husband.*

15. **(B)** Three of the four paragraphs trace Elizabeth's *reflections* or thoughts in detail.

16. **(C)** Neither maternal instincts nor visual acuity is characteristic of female tarantulas. Only *fertility* (the quality of being prolific) is.

17. **(E)** Since it is stated that young tarantulas go off to spend their lives in solitude, it follows that female tarantulas are *reclusive* or solitary by nature.

18. **(C)** To excite a defensive response is to *stimulate* that kind of reaction.

19. **(D)** The author's presentation of factual information about tarantulas is evidence of a scientifically *objective* (impartial) attitude toward them.

20. **(B)** Rather than covering new ground or challenging current theories, the passage *summarizes* general knowledge.

21. **(D)** The key words here are "seizes the insect so swiftly," which describe the spider's quickness in attacking.

22. **(D)** Under these conditions, the spider will jump whether or not it is hungry. Thus its reaction occurs quite *regardless* of the state of its appetite.

23. **(E)** Use the process of elimination to answer this question.

- In lines 65–69 the author *denies the possibility* that the viewer could confuse the spider's three tactile responses. You can eliminate (A).

- In the second, third, and fourth paragraphs the author *describes* the spider's three tactile responses or *reactions*. You can eliminate (B).

- In lines 52–56 the author *corrects the misapprehension* that the trichobothria might be hearing organs. You can eliminate (C).

- In lines 52 and 53, the author *defines* trichobothria as very fine hairs growing from disklike membranes on the spider's legs. You can eliminate (D).

- Only (E) is left. At no time does the author *pose* or ask *a question*. By elimination, (E) is the correct answer.

24. (**E**) The concluding sentence of the passage states that the tarantula's tactile responses do not help it when it meets (that is, is attacked by) its deadly enemy, the digger wasp. It follows that subsequent paragraphs will discuss *digger wasp attacks* in more detail.

Section 3

1. (**B**) If, during an archeological excavation, a site's upper levels are obliterated or destroyed, then excavation is an act of *destruction*.
2. (**A**) If the silk makes the nest walls stronger, they will be more able to *withstand* or resist the weight and pressure of the small birds.
3. (**C**) Although once *branded* (stigmatized or discredited) as a fake, the map may turn out to be authentic or *genuine* after all.
4. (**A**) Despite Stevie Smith's belief in an ideal childhood, her childhood was not *idyllic* or charmingly simple.
5. (**A**) A *contentious* (quarrelsome, disputatious) family by definition is given to *arguments*.
6. (**C**) Someone prudent or cautious would look on junk bonds as *risky*, uncertain investments. Such a person would be *chary* of (cautiously hesitant about) investing in such poor risks.
7. (**E**) As described in the first paragraph of Passage 1, the settling of the West occurred in "peristaltic waves." In other words, it did not occur at a steady rate. Rather, it took place *sometimes slowly and sometimes rapidly during a 50-year period* from the 1840s to the 1890s. Nor did the settlers go farther and farther west. California was settled before the Rockies and the Great Plains.
8. (**A**) Those who went west were, among others, trappers and traders, gold- and oil-seekers, all hoping for *economic advancement* by cashing in on the rich resources of the area.
9. (**D**) The "fictional western town was as rigidly formalized (lines 36 and 37) as the set for a Japanese No play." It follows, therefore, *that in books and films, western towns are all the same*. In reality, of course, towns vary considerably.
10. (**A**) The passage describes a stereotype of townspeople frequently used in books, movies, and plays set in the period. The people seem always to be portrayed as "decent folk" (line 49) who had *settled into routine lives*.
11. (**C**) The cowboy in Crane's story is called a "drunken anachronism" (line 63), a label implying that he is a sad relic of a bygone era. In other words, he's a *hero of the Old West who became obsolete*.
12. (**C**) The original center of the mining kingdom was California. Then, the center shifted to Colorado (Pike's Peak), to Montana, Wyoming, and the Black Hills of South Dakota. As new sources of precious metals were discovered throughout the nineteenth century, the center *shifted from place to place*.
13. (**A**) Many ex-miners turned to farming and to raising cattle, occupations that required them to *work on the land*.
14. (**C**) Passage 2 says that, although mining had been a major influence in shaping the history of the American West, the *growth of the cattle industry* was an even "more important chapter" (line 99).

15. **(D)** The passage indicates that, before becoming "almost extinct" (line 108), millions of buffalo had "roamed at will" (line 106) throughout the Great Plains. Because ranchers needed the land to graze their "Texas longhorns and Wyoming and Montana steers," the buffalo *were killed to make room for cattle.*

16. **(C)** The qualities of the cowboy mentioned in the passage are his "picturesque costume," his "splendid horsemanship," his "war with cattle rustlers," and his "lonely life on the plain." Only the cowboy's *law-abiding nature* is not mentioned.

17. **(A)** Passage 1 tells of *gold*-seekers "working up and down the California mountain ranges" (lines 14 and 15). Passage 2 says that "the discovery of *gold* in California" (lines 67 and 68) triggered a rush of settlers to the area.

18. **(D)** Both authors discuss the impact of the westward movement on American culture, *folklore and legend.* In particular, the cowboy epitomizes the romanticism of the westward movement.

19. **(B)** In Passage 1 the *miner* is mentioned as one of several figures who participated in the settling of the West. On the other hand, almost half of Passage 2 is devoted to a discussion of the *miner.*

PART 3

SENTENCE COMPLETION QUESTIONS

Overview

Tips on Handling Sentence Completion Questions

Sentence Completion Exercises

Answers to Sentence Completion Exercises

Answer Explanations

Overview

Sentence completion questions are the first critical reading questions you encounter as you take the SAT. These questions test your ability to use your vocabulary and to recognize how the different parts of a sentence fit together to make sense.

The sentence completion questions ask you to choose the best way to complete a sentence from which one or two words have been omitted. You must be able to recognize the logic, style, and tone of the sentence, so that you will be able to choose the answer that makes sense in this context. You must also be able to recognize the different ways in which words are normally defined. At some time or another, you have probably had a vocabulary assignment in which you were asked to define a word and use it in a sentence. In questions of this type, you have to *fit* words into sentences. Once you understand the implications of a sentence, you should be able to choose the answer that will make the sentence clear, logical, and consistent in style and tone.

The subject matter of these sentences comes from a wide variety of fields—music, art, science, literature, history. However, you are not being tested on your general knowledge. Though at times your knowledge of a particular fact may guide you in choosing the correct answer, you should be able to handle any of the sentences using your understanding of the English language.

Tips on Handling Sentence Completion Questions

Before You Look at the Answer Choices, Think of a Word That Makes Sense

Your first step in answering a sentence completion question is, *without looking at the answer choices,* to try to come up with a word that fits in the blank. The word you think of may not be the exact word that appears in any of the answer choices, but it will probably be similar in meaning to the right answer. Then, when you turn to the answer choices, you'll have an idea of what you're looking for.

Try going through the sentence substituting the word *blank* for each missing word. Doing this will give you a feel for what the sentence means.

Example:

Unlike her gabby brother Bruce, Bea seldom __blanks__ .

Just from looking at the sentence, you know the answer must be *chatters, talks,* or a synonym.

At this point, look at the answer choices. If the word you thought of is one of the five choices, select it as your answer. If the word you thought of is *not* a choice, look for a synonym of that word.

See how the process works in dealing with a more complex sentence.

The psychologist set up the experiment to test the rat's ____; he wished to see how well the rat adjusted to the changing conditions it had to face.

> **Did You Notice?**
>
> The sentence above is actually two statements linked by a semicolon (;). The punctuation mark is your clue that the two statements support each other.
>
> A semicolon signals you that the second statement develops the idea expressed in the first statement.
>
> Statement 1:   The psychologist set up the experiment to test the rat's adaptability. Why?
>
> Statement 2:   He wished to see how well the rat adjusted to the changing conditions it had to face.

Even before you look at the answer choices, you can figure out what the answer *should* be.

Look at the sentence. A psychologist is trying to test some particular quality or characteristic of a rat. What quality? How do you get the answer?

Note how the part of the sentence following the semicolon (the second clause, in technical terms) is being used to define or clarify what the psychologist is trying to test. He is trying to see how well the rat *adjusts*. What words does this suggest to you? Either *flexibility* or *adaptability* could complete the sentence's thought.

Here are the five answer choices given:

> (A) reflexes
> (B) communicability
> (C) stamina
> (D) sociability
> (E) adaptability

The answer clearly is *adaptability*, (E).

Be sure to check out all five answer choices before you make your final choice. Don't leap at the first word that seems to fit. You are looking for the word that *best* fits the meaning of the sentence as a whole. In order to be sure you have not been hasty in making your decision, substitute each of the answer choices for the missing word. That way you can satisfy yourself that you have come up with the answer that best fits.

TIP

2   Spot Clues in the Sentence: Signal Words

Writers use transitions to link their ideas logically. These transitions or signal words are clues that can help you figure out what the sentence actually means.

Support Signals

Look for words or phrases that indicate that the omitted portion of the sentence continues a thought developed elsewhere in the sentence. Examples are *and, moreover, in addition*, and *furthermore*. In such cases, a synonym or near-synonym should provide the correct answer.

Here is an example of a sentence completion question in which a support signal provides a helpful clue.

> He was habitually so docile and ____ that his friends could not understand his sudden outburst against his employers.
>
> (A) submissive
> (B) incorrigible
> (C) contemptuous
> (D) erratic
> (E) hasty

The signal word *and* is your clue that the writer is trying to reinforce the notion of docility introduced in the sentence. Not only is this person docile, he is also *blank*. Look through the answer choices for a synonym or near-synonym of *docile* or obedient. You find one immediately: (A), *submissive*. Check through the other answer choices. Nothing else makes sense. The correct answer is (A).

Contrast Signals

Look for words or phrases that indicate a contrast between one idea and another. Examples are *but, although, nevertheless, despite, however, even though,* and *on the other hand.* In such cases, an antonym or near-antonym for another word in the sentence should provide the correct answer.

Here is an example of a sentence completion question in which a contrast signal pinpoints the correct answer for you.

> We expected her to be jubilant over her victory, but she was ____ instead.
>
> (A) triumphant
> (B) adult
> (C) morose
> (D) loquacious
> (E) culpable

The signal word *but* suggests that the winner's expected reaction contrasts with her actual one. Instead of being "jubilant" (extremely joyful), she is sad. Look through the answer choices to find a word that is the *opposite* of jubilant. The correct answer is (C), *morose* or gloomy.

Cause and Effect Signals

Look for words or phrases that indicate that one thing causes another. Examples are *because, since, therefore, consequently, accordingly, hence, thus,* and *as a result.*

Here is an example of a sentence completion question in which a cause and effect signal should prove helpful to you.

> Because his delivery was ____, the effect of his speech on the voters was nonexistent.
>
> (A) plausible
> (B) moving
> (C) audible
> (D) halting
> (E) respectable

What sort of delivery would cause a speech to have no effect? A *plausible* (superficially pleasing and persuasive) delivery would probably have some effect on the voters. A *moving* or eloquent delivery certainly would. An *audible* delivery, one the audience could hear, would be more likely to have an effect than an inaudible one would. A *respectable*, appropriate delivery probably would have some impact as well. Only a *halting* or stumbling delivery would mar the voters' appreciation of the speech and cause it to have little or no effect on them. Thus, the correct answer is (D).

How's Your Word Power?

Did you know all the words in the answer choices? Look up any unfamiliar words in our Word List, in a dictionary, or online at sites like *www.onelook.com* or *www.dictionary.com*.

TIP

3   Notice Negatives

Watch out for negative words and words with negative prefixes: *no, not, none; non-, un-, in-*. These negative words and word parts are killers, especially in combination.

> The damage to the car was insignificant.
>   ("Don't worry about it—it's just a scratch.")
> The damage to the car was not insignificant.
>   ("Oh, no, Bart! We totaled Mom's car!")

In particular, watch out for *not*: it's easy to overlook, but it's a key word, as the following sentence clearly illustrates.

> Madison was not _____ person and thus made few public addresses; but those he made were memorable, filled with noble phrases.
>
>   (A) a reticent
>   (B) a stately
>   (C) an inspiring
>   (D) an introspective
>   (E) a communicative

What would happen if you overlooked *not* in this question? Probably you'd wind up choosing (A): Madison was a *reticent* (quiet; reserved) man. *For this reason* he made few public addresses.

Unfortunately, you'd have gotten things backward. The sentence isn't telling you what Madison was like. It's telling you what he was *not* like. And he was not a *communicative* person; he didn't express himself freely. However, when he did get around to speaking, he had some good things to say.

Try the Plus or Minus Test

Work out whether the missing word is positive (+) or negative (−). Then test the answer choices for their positive or negative sense. Eliminate those that don't work.

TIP

4

Words Have Many Meanings: Stay Alert

Watch out for words that have more than one meaning. Before you rule out an answer choice, consider whether the word has any secondary meanings. *Lie*, for example, can mean recline. It can also mean fib. Similarly, the adjective *partial* means incomplete, as in "a partial list of contributors." It can also mean biased, as in "too partial to be fair to both sides," or having a liking for, as in "I am highly partial to chocolate."

Be on the lookout for familiar-looking words defined in unfamiliar ways. Try this example:

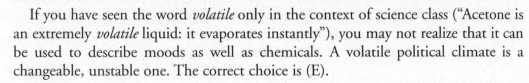

The political climate today is extremely _____: no one can predict what the electorate will do next.
   (A) malevolent
   (B) pertinent
   (C) claustrophobic
   (D) lethargic
   (E) volatile

Before you can answer this question, you need to think of a word that makes sense in the context. If no one can *predict* what the voters will do, then the political climate must be *unpredictable*. The correct answer is a synonym for *unpredictable* or *changeable*.

Now consider the answer choices. *Malevolent* (wicked; malicious) is not a synonym for *unpredictable*. *Pertinent* (relevant; applicable) is not a synonym for *unpredictable*. *Claustrophobic* (afraid of closed-in places) is not a synonym for *unpredictable*. *Lethargic* (sluggish; drowsily dull) is not a synonym for *unpredictable*. Only *volatile* is left.

Did You Notice?

The sentence above is actually two statements linked by a colon (:). The punctuation mark is your clue that the two statements support each other.

A colon signals you that the second statement serves to explain or clarify the first. It gives examples, or it defines terms.

Statement 1: The political climate today is extremely volatile.
What does volatile mean?
Statement 2: *No one can predict* what the electorate will do next.
Volatile means unpredictable. To be volatile is to do things no one can predict.

If you have seen the word *volatile* only in the context of science class ("Acetone is an extremely *volatile* liquid: it evaporates instantly"), you may not realize that it can be used to describe moods as well as chemicals. A volatile political climate is a changeable, unstable one. The correct choice is (E).

TIP

5

Break Down Unfamiliar Words, Looking for Familiar Word Parts

To determine the meaning of an unfamiliar word, either in a sentence or among the answer choices, use what you know about word parts, the building blocks of our language: prefixes, suffixes, and most important of all, roots.

(A list of word parts appears on pages 203–219.)

Consider the following sentence:

> Interviewing the flood victims on her show, Oprah Winfrey was wholly _____:
> she appeared to feel their loss as if it had been her own.

Note how the part of the sentence following the colon (the second clause) is being used to clarify Winfrey's attitude or behavior. She *appeared to feel* the victims' loss. The correct answer must have something to do with *feeling*.

Here are the five answer choices:

> (A) self-possessed
> (B) empathetic
> (C) obsessive
> (D) perceptive
> (E) theoretical

From your study of word parts, you know that the root *path* means feeling or disease. *Antipathy* is a hostile feeling; *sympathy*, a kindly one. *Empathy* is an understanding of and identification with the feelings of another person. In identifying with the feelings of the flood victims, Winfrey was *empathetic*.

More Signals to Spot!

Look for signals that indicate a word is being defined—phrases such as *in other words, that is,* or *which means,* and special punctuation clues. Commas, hyphens, and parentheses all are used to set off definitions.

TIP

6

Take One Blank at a Time

Dealing with double-blank sentences can be tricky. Testing the first word of each answer pair helps you narrow things down.

Here's how to do it. Read through the entire sentence. Then insert the first word of each answer pair in the sentence's first blank. Ask yourself whether this particular word makes sense in this blank. If the initial word of an answer pair makes no sense in the sentence, you can eliminate the entire pair.

Next, check out the second word of each of the answer pairs that you haven't ruled out. Be careful. Remember: just as each word of the correct answer pair must make sense in its individual context, both words must make sense when used together.

Try this question to practice working with double-blank sentences.

> The opossum is _____ the venom of snakes in the rattlesnake subfamily and thus views the reptiles not as _____ enemies but as a food source.
>
> (A) vulnerable to...natural
> (B) indicative of...mortal
> (C) impervious to...lethal
> (D) injurious to...deadly
> (E) defenseless against...potential

Your first job is to eliminate any answer choices you can on the basis of their first word.

- Opossums might be *vulnerable* to snake poison. Keep (A).
- Opossums are unlikely to be *indicative* or suggestive *of* snake poison. Cross out (B).
- Opossums could be *impervious to* (unaffected by; immune to) snake poison. Keep (C).
- Opossums couldn't be *injurious* or harmful *to* snake poison. Cross out (D).
- Opossums could be *defenseless against* snake poison. Keep (E).

Now examine the second half of the sentence. Opossums look on rattlesnakes as a food source. They can eat rattlers for a reason. Why? Is it because opossums are *vulnerable to* or *defenseless against* the poison? No. It's because they're *impervious* to the poison (that is, unharmed by it). That's the reason they can treat the rattlesnake as a potential source of food and not as a *lethal,* or deadly, enemy. The correct answer is (C).

Note the cause-and-effect signal *thus.* The nature of the opossum's response to the venom explains *why* it can look on a dangerous snake as a possible prey.

Sentence Completion Exercises

To develop your ability to handle sentence completion questions, work your way through the following three series of exercises. Warning: These series of exercises are graded in difficulty. The further you go, the harder the going gets, just as on a video game. Go all the way. Even if you do less well on Level C than you did on Level A, look on every error as an opportunity to learn. Study all the sentences that you found difficult. Review all the vocabulary words that you didn't know. Remember: these are all college-level sentences, set up to test your knowledge of college-level words.

After completing each exercise, see how many questions you answered correctly. (The correct answers are given on pages 85–86.) Then *read the answer explanations* for questions you answered incorrectly, questions you omitted, and questions you answered correctly but found difficult.

Level A

You should feel reasonably comfortable answering most of the sentence completion questions on this level of difficulty. Consider the four practice exercises that follow to be a warm-up for the harder questions to come.

Note: Whether you are working on Level A, Level B, or Level C, each section of the following practice exercises will begin with one or two relatively easy questions; each will also include some challenging vocabulary words. Do not expect to answer every question correctly.

Each of the following sentences contains one or two blanks; each blank indicates that a word or set of words has been left out. Below the sentence are five words or phrases, lettered A through E. Select the word or set of words that best completes the sentence.

Example:

Fame is ----; today's rising star is all too soon tomorrow's washed-up has-been.

(A) rewarding   (B) gradual
(C) essential   (D) spontaneous
(E) transitory

EXERCISE 1

1. The Cabinet member's resignation was not a total _____: rumors of his imminent departure had been making the rounds in Washington for a week.

   (A) withdrawal
   (B) success
   (C) shock
   (D eclipse
   (E) pretense

2. The wagon train leaders chose to _____ their route when they realized that the heavy rains had made fording the river too _____ a task.

   (A) question...uncomplicated
   (B) disregard...common
   (C) abandon...legitimate
   (D) alter...impracticable
   (E) follow...elusive

3. It is possible to analyze a literary work to death, _____ what should be a living experience as if it were a laboratory specimen.

   (A) questioning
   (B) dissecting
   (C) amending
   (D) nurturing
   (E) reviving

4. Anthropologists traditionally argue that the male-female division of labor in hunter-gatherer societies arose because it _____ the nuclear family's joint interests and thereby represented a sound, _____ strategy.

   (A) impaired...collaborative
   (B) respected...divisive
   (C) ignored...disinterested
   (D) restricted...provisional
   (E) promoted...cooperative

5. Because of its strength, adhesiveness, and invaluable qualities as a nest-building material, many species of birds _____ silk into their nests.

   (A) smuggle
   (B) jettison
   (C) incorporate
   (D) entice
   (E) dissolve

6. The recruit was _____ by the sergeant's scathing rebuke; nobody had ever _____ him like that before.

   (A) flattered...honored
   (B) touched...noticed
   (C) stung...reprimanded
   (D) astonished...questioned
   (E) discouraged...intrigued

7. Her memoirs are quite unlike those of her predecessors, for she is bold and aggressive where they are _____ and conventional.

   (A) audacious
   (B) exuberant
   (C) reticent
   (D) brazen
   (E) contentious

8. The report was relentlessly _____ to the scientist, interpreting one complex event after another to his _____.

   (A) generous...dismay
   (B) disparaging...initiative
   (C) complex...indifference
   (D) hostile...discredit
   (E) polite...detriment

9. People who don't outgrow their colleges often don't grow in other ways; there remained in Forster's life and imagination a _____ of the undergraduate, clever but _____.

   (A) dislike...talented
   (B) touch...judicious
   (C) trace...immature
   (D) fear...dormant
   (E) vestige...sincere

10. She _____ recognition and fame, yet she felt a deep suspicion and ___ for the world in which recognition and fame are granted, the world of money and opinion and power.

    (A) mistrusted...antagonism
    (B) worked for...respect
    (C) endured...veneration
    (D) shunned...enmity
    (E) yearned for...contempt

11. Unfortunately, excessive care in choosing one's words often results in a loss of _____.

    (A) precision
    (B) atmosphere
    (C) selectivity
    (D) spontaneity
    (E) credibility

12. Just as the earliest stone tools left by humans may seem nothing more than rock fragments to a layperson, so a lot of fossils require a trained eye to _____ them.

    (A) excavate
    (B) appreciate
    (C) disseminate
    (D) antedate
    (E) educate

13. According to a noted art critic, one would have to be completely immune to the sensuous pleasures of painting to be _____ Lucien Freud's mesmerizing art.

    (A) drawn to
    (B) overcome by
    (C) enamored of
    (D) unaffected by
    (E) consistent about

14. Skulls are the Rosetta stones of anthropology because they bear unique features that let scientists _____ whether two fossil samples come from the same type of creature.

    (A) determine
    (B) prophesy
    (C) disregard
    (D) initiate
    (E) recollect

15. For years no one could make this particular therapy work in animals larger than rodents, but now two research groups have demonstrated its _____ in dogs.

    (A) efficacy
    (B) defects
    (C) variability
    (D) origin
    (E) virulence

16. Thanks to the emerging technology of active noise control, automakers may soon be able to _____ noise inside a car and create the long-promised "quiet ride."

    (A) mute
    (B) endure
    (C) undertake
    (D) concentrate
    (E) augment

17. Despite her father's _____ that "a woman's place is in the home" and a _____ reception from her professors and fellow graduate students, Marian Cleeves went on to become the first woman to receive a doctorate in anatomy from the University of California at Berkeley.

    (A) warning...gratifying
    (B) reprimand...lavish
    (C) encouragement...respectful
    (D) admonition...cool
    (E) maxim...hospitable

18. John Keats, Dylan Thomas, Arthur Rimbaud—all these were poets who *had* to be poets, whom no one or nothing short of death could have _____ their courses.

    (A) confirmed in
    (B) derailed from
    (C) lauded for
    (D) interested in
    (E) convinced of

19. By arguing that much of what scientists think they know about the focusing mechanism of the eye is untrue, this radical scholar has gained a reputation as _____ in the field.

    (A) a fugitive
    (B) a convert
    (C) an artisan
    (D) a maverick
    (E) a peacemaker

20. The philosopher Auguste Comte _____ the term *altruism* to _____ unselfish regard for the welfare of others.

    (A) avoided...rationalize
    (B) coined...denote
    (C) applied...lessen
    (D) explained...refute
    (E) understood...terminate

EXERCISE 2

1. Given the ability of modern technology to _____ the environment, it is clear that, if we are not careful, the human race may soon be as extinct as the dinosaur.

    (A) enhance
    (B) destroy
    (C) analyze
    (D) repair
    (E) nurture

2. As founder and president of the Children's Defense Fund, Marian Wright Edelman has ensured that, even though the young cannot vote or make campaign contributions, they are nevertheless not _____ in Washington.

    (A) represented
    (B) distrusted
    (C) ignored
    (D) committed
    (E) welcome

3. Using novel concepts and techniques previously unknown in commercial advertising, the _____ advertising campaign broke new ground in the field of marketing.

    (A) questionable
    (B) interminable
    (C) imitative
    (D) inadequate
    (E) innovative

4. The attorney's vibrant voice and _____ sense of timing were as useful to him as his prodigious preparation, attention to detail, and _____ of the law.

    (A) deficient...conception
    (B) excellent...ignorance
    (C) shaky...command
    (D) outstanding...mastery
    (E) impeccable...deprecation

5. By putting the entire Woolf archive on microfilm, the project directors hope to make the contents of the manuscripts more _____ to scholars.

    (A) accessible
    (B) objective
    (C) appealing
    (D) implicit
    (E) relevant

6. Some spiderwebs are sheets or tangles of threads that delay the _____ of prey, allowing the spider, _____ by vibrations that travel through the threads, time to make its way over to the entangled victim.

   (A) escape...alerted
   (B) consumption...frightened
   (C) capture...thwarted
   (D) pursuit...soothed
   (E) sighting...irritated

7. Janet Malcolm depicts the biographer as a nosy, intrusive figure, _____ his subject's private papers.

   (A) protecting
   (B) restoring
   (C) invading
   (D) acknowledging
   (E) compiling

8. Because fruit juice fills babies' small stomachs and ruins their appetite for foods that contain nutrients they _____, consuming large quantities can actually prove _____ to babies less than 24 months old.

   (A) prefer...beneficial
   (B) choose...counterproductive
   (C) require...helpful
   (D) need...detrimental
   (E) ingest...advantageous

9. Telling gripping tales about a central character engaged in a mighty struggle with events, modern biographies satisfy the American appetite for _____ narratives.

   (A) brief
   (B) colloquial
   (C) digressive
   (D) undemanding
   (E) epic

10. According to poet John Berryman, there were so many ways to _____ a poem that it was quite amazing good ones ever got written.

    (A) dedicate
    (B) begin
    (C) ruin
    (D) recite
    (E) categorize

11. Musk oxen survived in isolated arctic habitats, but in the nineteenth century they declined rapidly even there, their numbers _____ by the armed enthusiasm of explorers, whalers, fur traders, and Eskimo.

    (A) swelled
    (B) augmented
    (C) devastated
    (D) underestimated
    (E) calculated

12. The aorta is like a tree trunk from which other major arteries _____.

    (A) escape
    (B) subtract
    (C) clamber down
    (D) branch off
    (E) strip away

13. He loved his friends, but he held people in general in _____ and maintained that human virtues were unworthy of comparison with a dog's devotion.

    (A) reverence
    (B) abeyance
    (C) contempt
    (D) affection
    (E) honor

14. Rejecting Professor Marian Diamond's work showing that rat-brain structure can increase by 5 to 7 percent, one _____ neuroanatomist stated flatly, "Young lady, that brain cannot _____!"

    (A) astounded...function
    (B) aghast...deteriorate
    (C) dumbfounded...think
    (D) skeptical...grow
    (E) finicky...die

15. For all his protestations of _____, Judge Learned Hand had been deeply _____ at being passed over for the United States Supreme Court, where Oliver Wendell Holmes, Jr., Benjamin Cardozo, and countless others said he belonged.

    (A) innocence...embarrassed
    (B) disbelief...enervated
    (C) indifference...disappointed
    (D) despondency...frustrated
    (E) affection...commiserated

16. Always trying to look on the bright side of every situation, she is a born _____.

    (A) opportunist
    (B) antagonist
    (C) optimist
    (D) maverick
    (E) zealot

17. The most crucial issue for wildlife in this arid land is unimpeded _____ water.

    (A) passage through
    (B) freedom from
    (C) access to
    (D) saturation in
    (E) overflow of

18. According to Lionel Trilling, the paradox of liberalism is that in its quest for freedom it must move toward greater organization, stricter legislation, and increasing _____.

    (A) anarchy
    (B) self-realization
    (C) stagnation
    (D) control
    (E) levity

19. Our mood swings about the economy grow more extreme: when things go well, we become _____; when things go poorly, _____ descends.

    (A) restive...anxiety
    (B) euphoric...gloom
    (C) prudent...benevolence
    (D) ascetic...misery
    (E) ambivalence...optimism

20. Abandoning the moral principles of his youth, the aging emperor Tiberius led a _____, wanton life.

    (A) celibate
    (B) rudimentary
    (C) dissipated
    (D) circumspect
    (E) peripatetic

EXERCISE 3

1. Although a few of her contemporaries _____ her book, most either ignored it or mocked it.

    (A) dismissed
    (B) disregarded
    (C) deprecated
    (D) misconstrued
    (E) appreciated

2. All critics have agreed that the opera's score is _____, but, curiously, no two critics have agreed which passages to praise and which to damn.

   (A) intolerable
   (B) melodious
   (C) unsurpassed
   (D) conventional
   (E) uneven

3. A man incapable of _____ action, he never had an opinion about something that he had not worked up beforehand, fashioning it with lengthy care.

   (A) premeditated
   (B) coherent
   (C) spontaneous
   (D) calculated
   (E) self-conscious

4. Even as the local climate changed from humid to arid and back—a change that caused other animals to become extinct—our almost-human ancestors _____ by learning how to use the new flora.

   (A) anticipated
   (B) survived
   (C) diverged
   (D) deteriorated
   (E) migrated

5. Marketing specialists have begun _____ what had once been a _____ audience into innumerable segments based on age, sex, income, and a host of pop sociological categories.

   (A) carving up...mass
   (B) bringing together...fragmented
   (C) tearing apart...sophisticated
   (D) unifying...distinct
   (E) transforming...responsive

6. Like a balloon that is _____, aneurysms (swellings in the walls of arteries) sometimes enlarge so much that they _____.

   (A) expanding...contract
   (B) punctured...dilate
   (C) elastic...stratify
   (D) weightless...stretch
   (E) overinflated...burst

7. Critics _____ the _____ in developing the new weather satellite to unexpected problems in manufacturing and testing its components.

   (A) credit...timeliness
   (B) impute...success
   (C) attribute...delay
   (D) assign...importance
   (E) deny...threat

8. As former Supreme Court Justice Warren Burger was fond of pointing out, many lawyers are not legal hotshots; they often come to court _____ and _____ professional skills.

   (A) ill prepared...lacking
   (B) hot-tempered...criticizing
   (C) reluctant...demonstrating
   (D) argumentative...manifesting
   (E) conservative...excelling

9. A hypothesis must not only account for what we already know, but must also be _____ by continued observation.

   (A) refuted
   (B) interrupted
   (C) verified
   (D) discredited
   (E) outmoded

10. *Elizabeth Gaskell: A Habit of Stories* is a considerable _____, superseding Winifred Gerin's learned biography of the English novelist.

    (A) failure
    (B) rationalization
    (C) accomplishment
    (D) recollection
    (E) muddle

11. Boccherini was a good and interesting composer whose reputation has not sufficiently _____ the decline into which it fell after his death.

    (A) contributed to
    (B) benefited from
    (C) recovered from
    (D) conflicted with
    (E) derived from

12. Having billed himself as "Mr. Clean," Hosokawa could not _____ the _____ of a major financial scandal.

    (A) survive...acclaim
    (B) withstand...notoriety
    (C) identify...exposure
    (D) resist...charms
    (E) censure...temptation

13. A curious _____ of Florence's history is that this great center of Italian _____ should time and again have been home to acts of appalling savagery and inhumanity.

    (A) example...conflict
    (B) paradox...civilization
    (C) result...brutality
    (D) convention...culture
    (E) distinction...quality

14. Illness can be _____ as how disease *feels*, the experience of being sick: at once a physical or natural condition and a social and cultural one.

    (A) cured
    (B) survived
    (C) acclaimed
    (D) defined
    (E) deprecated

15. Lamenting that something horrid had recently befallen the craft of biography, biographer Arthur Schlesinger _____ the glut of gossipy new lives on the market.

    (A) deplored
    (B) forgot
    (C) acclaimed
    (D) composed
    (E) abridged

16. Instead of taking exaggerated precautions against touching or tipping or jarring the bottle of wine, the waitress handled it quite _____, being careful only to use a napkin to keep her hands from the cool bottle itself.

    (A) fastidiously
    (B) reverently
    (C) nonchalantly
    (D) tentatively
    (E) ambivalently

17. The eighteenth century was a kind of golden age in deaf history because, with the establishment of schools for the deaf, these people emerged from _____ and began to appear in positions of eminence and _____—as writers, engineers, philosophers, and intellectuals.

    (A) retirement...ambiguity
    (B) seclusion...compromise
    (C) obscurity...responsibility
    (D) hiding...ignominy
    (E) solicitude...disrepute

18. The crisis is not ____; it will not affect us for years to come.

    (A) specious
    (B) fleeting
    (C) meaningless
    (D) minute
    (E) imminent

19. When Dorothy and her friends realized that, despite his claims, the Wizard of Oz didn't know how to get them back to Kansas, they were sure they'd been ____ by a ____.

    (A) befriended...philanthropist
    (B) succored...magician
    (C) captured...genius
    (D) duped...charlatan
    (E) delayed...miser

20. Now better known for its racetrack, Saratoga Springs first gained attention for the ____ qualities of its famous "healing waters."

    (A) diagnostic
    (B) commercial
    (C) therapeutic
    (D) overlooked
    (E) experimental

EXERCISE 4

1. Repeat offenders who continue to drive under the influence of alcohol face having their drivers' licenses permanently ____.

    (A) issued
    (B) recorded
    (C) authorized
    (D) revoked
    (E) disregarded

2. Excited and unafraid, the ____ child examined the stranger with bright-eyed curiosity.

    (A) apathetic
    (B) drowsy
    (C) timorous
    (D) inquisitive
    (E) hesitant

3. Though masterminded by the Metropolitan Museum's Guy Bauman, this survey of Flemish paintings in America was clearly a ____ operation, aided by scholars throughout North America.

    (A) marginal
    (B) derivative
    (C) worthwhile
    (D) circuitous
    (E) collective

4. I am seeking an ____ solution to this dispute, one that will be fair and acceptable to both sides.

    (A) equivocal
    (B) infamous
    (C) equitable
    (D) idiosyncratic
    (E) overrated

5. A New World lizard, the basilisk, occasionally does something that seems to ____ physics: it runs across the surface of water for distances of up to 30 feet.

    (A) defy
    (B) quantify
    (C) assess
    (D) exemplify
    (E) corroborate

6. The most consistent qualities of Forster's novels are the human isolation and passivity in them; his principal characters stand slightly apart and _____, but rarely _____.

(A) sneer...collapse
(B) interact...adapt
(C) mourn...recollect
(D) observe...act
(E) domineer...participate

7. Far from being distracted or immobilized by his inner conflicts, Keynes was _____ by them into becoming one of the most productive, effective, and buoyant personalities of the twentieth century.

(A) neutralized
(B) energized
(C) incapacitated
(D) enervated
(E) inhibited

8. A born teller of tales, Olsen used her impressive _____ skills to advantage in her story "I Stand Here Ironing."

(A) domestic
(B) metaphysical
(C) narrative
(D) diagnostic
(E) argumentative

9. Waving broadly at the still-applauding crowd, the speaker was highly _____ by the _____ response to her talk.

(A) exasperated...vehement
(B) gratified...enthusiastic
(C) bewildered...profound
(D) intimidated...sincere
(E) delighted....skeptical

10. As a scientific document, the book should stand for several years until further _____ again make revision _____.

(A) developments...impossible
(B) obstacles...optional
(C) attempts...undesirable
(D) failures...detrimental
(E) advances...necessary

11. The jazz musician cannot play well if he is completely _____, as if lying half asleep in a Jacuzzi.

(A) untruthful
(B) autonomous
(C) sincere
(D) relaxed
(E) talented

12. Why do some plant stems develop a protective bark that enables them to survive the winter, while others _____ at the first frost?

(A) blossom
(B) adapt
(C) shrivel
(D) mature
(E) wake

13. Salvador Dali's tendency to fabricate events makes it difficult for the biographer to tell the story of his life with any degree of _____.

(A) vividness
(B) accuracy
(C) solemnity
(D) spontaneity
(E) artistry

14. If Amelia Earhart's acceptance was by no means _____, her fame was unusually widespread and her popularity long-lived.

    (A) universal
    (B) ambiguous
    (C) expedient
    (D) partial
    (E) genuine

15. Throughout his career he demonstrated strong belief in individual faith but powerful _____ about the organized church.

    (A) modesty
    (B) skepticism
    (C) devotion
    (D) discernment
    (E) ambition

16. The text abounds with details, but there are no overarching theses to _____ them.

    (A) specify
    (B) exaggerate
    (C) confound
    (D) unify
    (E) modify

17. The senator contended that, rather than being a _____ concern, global warming is a critical problem that imperils not just Americans but all life on Earth.

    (A) significant
    (B) hazardous
    (C) strategic
    (D) planetary
    (E) peripheral

18. It would be beneficial if someone so radical could be brought to believe that old customs need not necessarily be _____ and that change may possibly be _____.

    (A) defensible...premature
    (B) outdated...required
    (C) evil...salutary
    (D) invaluable...temporary
    (E) worthless...inadvisable

19. T. S. Eliot, famous for his _____, nevertheless accepted posterity's interest in his life, _____ that his correspondence with his lady friends eventually would be read.

    (A) reticence...assuming
    (B) modesty...prohibiting
    (C) boastfulness...remembering
    (D) vanity...intimating
    (E) curiosity...regretting

20. Waiting impatiently in line to see Santa Claus, even the best-behaved children grow _____ and start to fret.

    (A) fidgety
    (B) noisome
    (C) sonorous
    (D) pungent
    (E) ambivalent

Level B

Most high school students have some difficulty answering sentence completion questions on this level. Consider the four practice exercises that follow to be a good sample of the mid-range sentence completion questions you will face on the SAT.

Each of the following sentences contains one or two blanks; each blank indicates that a word or set of words has been left out. Below the sentence are five words or phrases, lettered A through E. Select the word or set of words that best completes the sentence.

Example:

Fame is ----; today's rising star is all too soon tomorrow's washed-up has-been.

(A) rewarding   (B) gradual
(C) essential   (D) spontaneous
(E) transitory

Ⓐ Ⓑ Ⓒ Ⓓ ●

EXERCISE 1

1. In the 1920s Hollywood became a magnet for men and women on the cutting edge—_____ artists genuinely excited by the possibilities of the up-and-coming film medium.

    (A) impecunious
    (B) innovative
    (C) unprepossessing
    (D) impenitent
    (E) apathetic

2. A leading philosopher of our time, Ludwig Wittgenstein, laid down a _____ to which good historians _____: "Of that of which nothing is known nothing can be said."

    (A) burden...protest
    (B) law...amend
    (C) rule...adhere
    (D) maxim...succumb
    (E) weapon...surrender

3. One by one, she _____ almost all of her supporters until, at the end, only a handful of her closest allies really wanted her to stay in office.

    (A) promoted
    (B) alienated
    (C) represented
    (D) exaggerated
    (E) liberated

4. The banquet had _____ effect on the overfed guests: they began to nod off in their seats.

    (A) a soporific
    (B) a cumulative
    (C) an immoderate
    (D) an invigorating
    (E) a negligible

5. Thomas Jefferson called *The Federalist* papers "the best commentaries on the principles of government ever written," and two centuries later they still _____ as the most _____ statements of American political philosophy.

   (A) stand...derivative
   (B) rate...abstruse
   (C) rank...impressive
   (D) fascinate...ambiguous
   (E) compete...underrated

6. Left to endure a penniless old age, the _____ man lived to regret his _____ youth.

   (A) miserly...friendless
   (B) reclusive...affable
   (C) eccentric...fleeting
   (D) egotistical...frugal
   (E) improvident...prodigal

7. Peter has a bad habit of making _____ remarks that wander so far off topic that we forget the gist of what he is saying.

   (A) awkward
   (B) pertinent
   (C) digressive
   (D) telling
   (E) tentative

8. Though set in a mythical South American country, Isabel Allende's novel is _____ the tragic history of Chile.

   (A) irrelevant to
   (B) rooted in
   (C) inconsistent with
   (D) exceeded by
   (E) indifferent to

9. The marketers' _____ in donating the new basketball backboards to the school system are not solely _____; they plan to sell advertising space on the backboards, turning them into miniature billboards.

   (A) losses...obvious
   (B) expectations...peculiar
   (C) aims...mercenary
   (D) reasons...sensitive
   (E) motivations...philanthropic

10. Justice Harry Blackmun's retirement, while unlikely to bring about a drastic change in the Supreme Court, will remove a distinctly _____ voice from the Court's often featureless mix.

    (A) bland
    (B) personal
    (C) moderate
    (D) neutral
    (E) derivative

11. Having just published his fourth novel in an almost 40-year career, Gaddis describes himself, with some _____, as a writer who has never been in a _____ to get into print.

    (A) expectation...mood
    (B) impatience...technique
    (C) understatement...rush
    (D) indecision...position
    (E) exaggeration...school

12. Actors fade out of view with depressing frequency; the theater is a _____ profession at best.

    (A) romantic
    (B) demanding
    (C) precarious
    (D) disinterested
    (E) degenerate

13. Though Phil had expected to feel overawed when he met Joe Montana, he found the world-famous quarterback friendly and ____.

    (A) querulous
    (B) acerbic
    (C) domineering
    (D) unintimidating
    (E) taciturn

14. Flying in the face of ____, the writer George Sand shocked her contemporaries by taking lovers and by wearing men's clothes.

    (A) immodesty
    (B) reconciliation
    (C) emancipation
    (D) convention
    (E) modernism

15. In the poem "Annabel Lee," the speaker reveals that he is not ____ to the death of his beloved; on the contrary, he is ____.

    (A) indifferent...apathetic
    (B) reconciled...acquiescent
    (C) resigned...inconsolable
    (D) accustomed...inured
    (E) relevant...responsive

16. The artists of the Chinese avant-garde have used Western styles ____ and meaningfully to accomplish artistic ends of their own.

    (A) obsequiously
    (B) shamefully
    (C) cannily
    (D) indifferently
    (E) problematically

17. Despite the poem's archaic and tortuous language, the thrust of the poet's argument is surprisingly ____.

    (A) vapid
    (B) dated
    (C) blunted
    (D) intelligible
    (E) idiosyncratic

18. Splitting the country into conflicting factions, pitting brother against brother, the Civil War was ____ experience for the American people.

    (A) an ephemeral
    (B) a divisive
    (C) a peripheral
    (D) an illuminating
    (E) a salutary

19. Because of the trauma they have experienced, survivors of a major catastrophe are likely to exhibit ____ of behavior and may require the aid of competent therapists.

    (A) concessions
    (B) diminutions
    (C) aberrations
    (D) restrictions
    (E) altercations

20. The reader has the happy impression of watching an extraordinarily inventive and intellectually ____ novelist working at the ____ of her powers.

    (A) dishonest...apex
    (B) creative...eclipse
    (C) fecund...height
    (D) effete...limits
    (E) amenable...diminution

EXERCISE 2

1. While some Southern writers see the past as a heavy burden, others see it as a subject for _____ reflection.

   (A) gloomy
   (B) wearisome
   (C) interminable
   (D) nostalgic
   (E) bleak

2. One of Detroit's great success stories was Lee Iacocca's revitalization of the moribund Chrysler Corporation, turning it into a _____ competitor.

   (A) vigorous
   (B) tentative
   (C) marginal
   (D) negligent
   (E) superficial

3. A journalist rather than a scholar, Mr. Cose seems nevertheless to be _____ most of the serious studies relevant to his topic.

   (A) overawed by
   (B) ignorant of
   (C) associated with
   (D) wearied by
   (E) familiar with

4. Egocentric, at times vindictive when he believed his authority was being questioned, White could also be kind, gracious, and even _____ when the circumstances seemed to require it.

   (A) self-deprecating
   (B) authoritarian
   (C) provocative
   (D) taciturn
   (E) disdainful

5. Far from being in the _____ condition promised by the realtor, the condo was shabby and dilapidated.

   (A) vacant
   (B) indifferent
   (C) pristine
   (D) marginal
   (E) euphoric

6. Polls indicate that many prospective voters in the next presidential election are _____ about the outcome; they do not seem to care who wins.

   (A) enthusiastic
   (B) inadequate
   (C) antagonistic
   (D) apathetic
   (E) suspicious

7. If you need car parts that the dealers no longer stock, try _____ for odd bits and pieces at the auto wreckers' yards.

   (A) waiting
   (B) bantering
   (C) scavenging
   (D) riveting
   (E) insuring

8. Grateful as we are for these splendid books, they remain isolated examples of excellence in a literature of _____.

   (A) competition
   (B) distinction
   (C) grandeur
   (D) mediocrity
   (E) affirmation

9. Despite the _____ discussions of recent months, observers say that the administration and the developer have made progress in their negotiations and are close to _____ on a purchase price.

   (A) amicable...haggling
   (B) acrimonious...defaulting
   (C) heated...agreeing
   (D) fruitful...settling
   (E) constructive...compromising

10. People expected Winston Churchill to take his painting lightly, but Churchill, no ____, regarded his artistic efforts most seriously indeed.

    (A) virtuoso
    (B) zealot
    (C) dilettante
    (D) altruist
    (E) renegade

11. Aimed at curbing European attempts to seize territory in the Americas, the Monroe Doctrine was a warning to ____ foreign powers.

    (A) magnanimous
    (B) credulous
    (C) reticent
    (D) predatory
    (E) allied

12. It is a spotty sort of book, with many pages that, if not exactly ____, are less than ____.

    (A) bland...tedious
    (B) pretentious...conventional
    (C) dull...exciting
    (D) eventful...newsworthy
    (E) murky...obscure

13. Although Miss Watson never joined the temperance movement, she was a strict teetotaler and would not ____ drinking alcohol.

    (A) recall
    (B) rebuke
    (C) condone
    (D) evade
    (E) relinquish

14. In discussing Rothko's art, Breslin is ____ in keeping to the facts and resisting the ____ of fanciful interpretation.

    (A) scrupulous...temptation
    (B) meticulous...integrity
    (C) ungainly...reward
    (D) uninterested...echo
    (E) inept...bias

15. Burdened by debt, Lydgate abandons his dreams of reforming medicine to take a conventional but ____ practice in London.

    (A) lucrative
    (B) ordinary
    (C) innovative
    (D) intangible
    (E) exotic

16. Numerous studies have found that people who choose to represent themselves in court on the whole exercise pretty good judgment—they seem to have a ____ sense of when they need a lawyer and when they don't.

    (A) faulty
    (B) capricious
    (C) reliable
    (D) transient
    (E) drastic

17. When I listened to her cogent arguments, all my ____ were ____ and I was forced to agree with her point of view.

    (A) senses...stimulated
    (B) opinions...confirmed
    (C) preconceptions...substantiated
    (D) questions...interpolated
    (E) doubts...dispelled

18. What made Ann such a fine counselor was her ____, her ability to put herself in her client's place and feel his emotions as if they were her own.

    (A) integrity
    (B) empathy
    (C) tenacity
    (D) impartiality
    (E) aloofness

19. Samuel Johnson gave more than ____ cooperation to his biographer, James Boswell; he made himself available to Boswell night after night, furnished Boswell with correspondence, even read his biographer's notes.

    (A) innocuous
    (B) collusive
    (C) tacit
    (D) edifying
    (E) diplomatic

20. Where lesser scholars would have been ____ by the vast collection of unpublished letters, rough drafts, and journals left by Henry James, Leon Edel was emboldened by its discovery and began to plan an ambitious series of studies on the life and works of the novelist.

    (A) intrigued
    (B) encouraged
    (C) incensed
    (D) taxed
    (E) daunted

EXERCISE 3

1. In their determination to discover ways to ____ human life, doctors fail to take into account that longer lives are not always happier ones.

    (A) ease
    (B) prolong
    (C) eradicate
    (D) recuperate
    (E) dissect

2. In this survey of Revolutionary America, the author finds a remarkable homogeneity of opinion from Massachusetts to Georgia; the differences between the sections are ____, almost always explainable by differences in climate or topography.

    (A) sharp
    (B) nonexistent
    (C) irreconcilable
    (D) superficial
    (E) enormous

3. Halls and audiences for *lieder* recitals tend to be smaller than those for opera and thus more ____ the intimacy and sense of close involvement, which is the recital's particular charm.

    (A) inauspicious for
    (B) destructive of
    (C) conducive to
    (D) compromised by
    (E) indifferent to

4. Despite their reputations as soothing love songs sung by mothers to lull fretful infants to sleep, many lullabies are of a dark, even ____ nature.

    (A) soporific
    (B) manipulative
    (C) threatening
    (D) auspicious
    (E) innocuous

5. The mayor and school superintendent let their dispute over budget cuts ____ to ugly and destructive proportions.

    (A) escalate
    (B) automate
    (C) stagnate
    (D) condense
    (E) dwindle

6. Wherever Lao Li travels, he makes slides of contemporary works of art; his archives ____ every meaningful artistic effort in modern China.

    (A) deride
    (B) ignore
    (C) perpetrate
    (D) document
    (E) abridge

7. Contrary to her customary ____ behavior, Susan began leaving parties early to seek the solitude of her room.

    (A) reclusive
    (B) circumspect
    (C) decorous
    (D) gregarious
    (E) altruistic

8. Science is always ____, expecting that modifications of its present theories will sooner or later be found necessary.

    (A) conclusive
    (B) irrefutable
    (C) original
    (D) tentative
    (E) inflexible

9. One of the great killers until barely 50 years ago, tuberculosis ("consumption" as it was then named) seemed a scourge or ____ rather than the long-term ____ illness it was.

    (A) plague...chronic
    (B) detriment...ominous
    (C) antiseptic...prevalent
    (D) vestige...contemporary
    (E) epidemic...salutary

10. Gaddis is a formidably talented writer whose work has been, unhappily, more likely to intimidate or ____ his readers than to lure them into his fictional world.

    (A) entice
    (B) strengthen
    (C) invigorate
    (D) transform
    (E) repel

11. Compared with the ostentatious glamour of opera, classical song (increasingly called *lieder* everywhere) is a more ____ tradition.

    (A) articulate
    (B) unrepresentative
    (C) subdued
    (D) broad-minded
    (E) worldly

12. This well-documented book is ____ researched, fluently written, and unfailingly intelligent in tracing the ____ course of its subject's tormented career.

    (A) indifferently...triumphant
    (B) inadequately...unfortunate
    (C) painstakingly...tragic
    (D) carefully...auspicious
    (E) thoroughly...promising

13. Lexy's joy at finding the perfect Christmas gift for John was ____, for she still had to find presents for the cousins and Uncle Bob.

    (A) transitory
    (B) antithetical
    (C) exuberant
    (D) exhaustive
    (E) incontrovertible

14. Life is a ____ of the sacred and the profane, of good and evil; to try to ____ them is futile.

    (A) rejection...embrace
    (B) commingling...separate
    (C) misalliance...endure
    (D) defamation...reform
    (E) confusion...promulgate

15. Under the rule of the foreign invaders, the land seemed asleep, save for a small group of rebels who sought to kindle the ____ nationalism of the people.

    (A) valid
    (B) blatant
    (C) dormant
    (D) pretentious
    (E) contemplated

16. Many of the early Hollywood moguls sought to ____ themselves and enhance their celluloid empires by snaring ____ writers and intellectuals as screenwriters.

    (A) advance...presumptuous
    (B) aggrandize...prestigious
    (C) intimidate...unsuspecting
    (D) glorify...superannuated
    (E) sabotage...distinguished

17. The Turner Network's production is an absorbing *Heart of Darkness*, watchful, surreptitious, almost ____ as it waits to ____ our emotions.

    (A) lighthearted...cater to
    (B) melancholy...cheer up
    (C) mercenary...pay for
    (D) predatory...pounce on
    (E) furtive...figure out

18. Helen valued people who behaved as if they respected themselves; nothing irritated her more than an excessively ____ waiter or a fawning salesclerk.

    (A) austere
    (B) domineering
    (C) grave
    (D) obsequious
    (E) contentious

19. Whereas most scholars have tended to regard Monteverdi's opera *L'Orfeo* as the beginning of a tradition, Mr. Pickett sensibly considers it the ____ of one.

    (A) origin
    (B) example
    (C) presence
    (D) culmination
    (E) birthright

20. Though ostensibly teaching posture, Feher brings into play techniques of ballet, yoga, and vocal projection to come up with lessons that can best be described as ____.

    (A) problematic
    (B) eclectic
    (C) homogeneous
    (D) unpretentious
    (E) doctrinaire

EXERCISE 4

1. During the troubles of 1750, the extent of ____ in Scotland was terrible; many Scots could afford nothing to eat but oatmeal porridge.

    (A) anarchy
    (B) detriment
    (C) punishment
    (D) apathy
    (E) destitution

2. The biographer of Tennyson is confronted with the problem, rarely solved, of how to make a basically _____ life interesting.

   (A) dramatic
   (B) bewildering
   (C) intriguing
   (D) controversial
   (E) uneventful

3. If, like the mole rat, you could run backward as easily as forward but had weak eyes that could see only dim shadows of light and dark, you too might want touch-sensitive whiskers to help _____ you through the tunnels of your underground home.

   (A) carry
   (B) illuminate
   (C) excavate
   (D) distract
   (E) guide

4. Getting into street brawls is no minor matter for professional boxers, who are required by law to restrict their _____ impulses to the ring.

   (A) humorous
   (B) aggressive
   (C) obligatory
   (D) amateurish
   (E) legitimate

5. For all of his turn-of-the-century trappings, the novel's hero is basically a _____ voice; his values and cultural _____ are of the present more than the 1890s.

   (A) derivative...antecedents
   (B) modern...antiquity
   (C) contemporary...sensibility
   (D) familiar...descendants
   (E) hollow...premises

6. She wondered whether triangles, which had only three sides, _____ as polygons, which she thought of as many-sided.

   (A) theorized
   (B) estimated
   (C) qualified
   (D) subsisted
   (E) multiplied

7. Kepler's observations of the supernova would have been more _____ and valuable had they been made with a telescope; unfortunately, Kepler's supernova lighted the night skies five full years before Galileo made the first _____ telescopic scan of the heavens.

   (A) remote...skeptical
   (B) solemn...unseemly
   (C) infamous...extraneous
   (D) detailed...documented
   (E) fortuitous...recorded

8. As a product of the Soviet literary establishment, the author was brave enough to _____ the hand that fed him, but not heroic enough to bite it.

   (A) give up
   (B) nibble at
   (C) cringe from
   (D) worship
   (E) devour

9. It is a relief to see people who can be interested in the arts without being "arty"—collectors who collect for their own _____ rather than for _____.

   (A) enjoyment...satisfaction
   (B) interest...pleasure
   (C) reputation...amusement
   (D) pleasure...show
   (E) education...fulfillment

10. The periodic nature of her complaints began to concern us: alarmed by these _____ attacks, we decided to consult a doctor in spite of her opposition.

    (A) trivial
    (B) recurrent
    (C) superficial
    (D) spontaneous
    (E) tentative

11. Though critic John Simon seldom had a good word to say about most contemporary plays, his review of *All in the Timing* was a total _____.

    (A) mistake
    (B) dismissal
    (C) fraud
    (D) rave
    (E) farce

12. Traditional Chinese painters trained by copying their teachers; _____ was reserved for old age, when you might make changes so _____ that they were almost invisible.

    (A) imitation...ubiquitous
    (B) emulation...dramatic
    (C) novelty...marked
    (D) originality...slight
    (E) honor...petty

13. Satisfied that her name had been _____, she dropped her libel suit after the newspaper finally published a _____ of its original defamatory statement.

    (A) praised...summary
    (B) maligned...glossary
    (C) vindicated... repetition
    (D) enhanced...reaffirmation
    (E) cleared...retraction

14. Like Machiavelli before him, Henry Kissinger has a keen appreciation for the hard-headed, even _____, use of power, to the point of admiring some traits in leaders who were otherwise _____.

    (A) cynical...benevolent
    (B) gentle...insignificant
    (C) ruthless...detestable
    (D) resentful...charismatic
    (E) forceful...exemplary

15. Some thought Dali was a brilliant painter; others _____ him as a conceited poseur.

    (A) respected
    (B) venerated
    (C) dismissed
    (D) vindicated
    (E) exasperated

16. The late James Beard was _____ with his time and knowledge—a _____ trait in the narrow world of food writing, a milieu notorious for its pettiness and infighting.

    (A) unselfish...common
    (B) unconcerned...standard
    (C) stingy...remarkable
    (D) occupied...negative
    (E) generous...rare

17. *New Yorker* short stories often include _____ allusions to _____ people and events: the implication is, if you are in the in-crowd, you'll get the reference; if you come from Cleveland, you won't.

    (A) esoteric...obscure
    (B) redundant...celebrated
    (C) tedious...notorious
    (D) provincial...major
    (E) passing...common

18. Her growing bitterness was _____ by her professional rivalry with her sister, whose fortunes rose while her own _____.

    (A) represented...ascended
    (B) mitigated...dwindled
    (C) exemplified...soared
    (D) nurtured...multiplied
    (E) exacerbated...declined

19. Mr. Levi is _____ learned; he has read everything bearing on his subject and on poetry in general (in several languages), and he has forgotten little if anything.

    (A) moderately
    (B) spottily
    (C) inadvertently
    (D) formidably
    (E) inadequately

20. Because vast organizations are an inevitable element in modern life, it is _____ to aim at their abolition.

    (A) necessary
    (B) important
    (C) customary
    (D) realistic
    (E) futile

Level C

Most high school students have trouble answering many sentence completion questions on this level of difficulty. Consider the four practice exercises that follow to be a chance for you to acquaint yourself with the toughest sorts of sentence completion questions that occur on the SAT.

Each of the following sentences contains one or two blanks; each blank indicates that a word or set of words has been left out. Below the sentence are five words or phrases, lettered A through E. Select the word or set of words that best completes the sentence.

Example:

Fame is ----; today's rising star is all too soon tomorrow's washed-up has-been.

(A) rewarding   (B) gradual
(C) essential   (D) spontaneous
(E) transitory

Ⓐ Ⓑ Ⓒ Ⓓ ●

EXERCISE 1

1. The moon was hidden and the night had grown very dark; she had to _____ to see.

   (A) blink
   (B) strain
   (C) mask
   (D) remember
   (E) reflect

2. The Battle of Lexington was not, as most of us have been taught, a _____ rising of individual farmers, but was instead a tightly organized, well-planned event.

   (A) premeditated
   (B) cautionary
   (C) spontaneous
   (D) coordinated
   (E) theoretical

3. The book will arouse antagonism, disagreement, and animosity among theologians because it will _____ many _____ rituals and beliefs.

   (A) undermine...iconoclastic
   (B) tolerate...accepted
   (C) undermine...established
   (D) disregard...forgotten
   (E) observe...pious

4. The , by definition, possesses wisdom; the virtuoso, by definition, possesses _____.

   (A) scholar...morality
   (B) sage...expertise
   (C) zealot...sincerity
   (D) visionary...idealism
   (E) pedant...proficiency

5. For a young person, Winston seems remarkably _____; you'd expect someone his age to show a little more life.

   (A) sophomoric
   (B) vigorous
   (C) stodgy
   (D) tidy
   (E) sensitive

6. The true historian finds the facts about Marlowe and Shakespeare far more interesting than people's unfounded _____.

   (A) complaints
   (B) evidence
   (C) conjectures
   (D) qualms
   (E) certainty

7. Even Cormac McCarthy, Don DeLillo, and William Gaddis—eminent novelists who are notoriously _____ when it comes to _____—have surrendered to the exigencies of modern publishing and agreed to be the subjects of magazine articles.

   (A) prolific...writing
   (B) egotistical...fame
   (C) overrated...style
   (D) irate...delays
   (E) shy...publicity

8. Tom prided himself on knowing the latest news, the secrets of the rich and the poor; it _____ him that there was something he did not know about his friend.

   (A) delighted
   (B) flattered
   (C) reminded
   (D) galled
   (E) reassured

9. Uncertain which suitor she ought to marry, the princess _____, saying now one, now the other.

   (A) improvised
   (B) vacillated
   (C) threatened
   (D) compromised
   (E) divulged

10. Factory trawlers, large fishing vessels that drag heavy nets over the seafloor, "vacuum" the North Pacific seas, trapping fish _____.

    (A) unintentionally
    (B) indiscriminately
    (C) paradoxically
    (D) collaboratively
    (E) temporarily

11. Elizabeth Barrett, whose _____ father would brook no interference or disagreement with his plans for his daughter, eloped in order to _____ his autocratic rule.

    (A) attentive...underscore
    (B) vindictive...preserve
    (C) domineering...escape
    (D) idiosyncratic...accommodate
    (E) authoritarian...extend

12. Duke Ellington's jazz symphonies were attacked by classical critics who felt that the entire attempt to fuse jazz as a form with classical music should be _____.

    (A) promoted
    (B) documented
    (C) discouraged
    (D) acclaimed
    (E) repeated

13. During the last four decades of Tennyson's long life, his creative powers never _____, some of his most remarkable work coming after the age of 70.

    (A) recovered
    (B) manifested
    (C) flagged
    (D) blossomed
    (E) broadened

14. The villagers fortified the town hall, hoping this improvised _____ could _____ them from the guerrilla raids.

    (A) citadel...alienate
    (B) refuge...distinguish
    (C) stronghold...protect
    (D) venture...intimidate
    (E) disguise...safeguard

15. Lovejoy, the hero of Jonathan Gash's mystery novels, is an antiques dealer who gives the reader advice on how to tell _____ antique plate from the real thing.

    (A) a priceless
    (B) a spurious
    (C) a classical
    (D) an authentic
    (E) an antiquated

16. The omniscient narrator stands above the story he is telling, _____ his knowledge of what will occur.

    (A) disheartened by
    (B) unlimited in
    (C) ostracized for
    (D) vindicated by
    (E) uncertain of

17. Today employers no longer speak of firing or discharging employees; instead, according to the latest _____, they simply "effect a separation."

    (A) digression
    (B) overstatement
    (C) euphemism
    (D) paradox
    (E) proverb

18. The TV news magazine sits precisely at the _____ of information and entertainment, for while it is not a silly sitcom, it is not a documentary either.

    (A) foundation
    (B) juncture
    (C) cessation
    (D) institution
    (E) eclipse

19. Even though nonbreeding female mole rats are _____, when the queen mole rat dies, several females suddenly _____ their sexual and reproductive powers and battle one another to replace her.

    (A) prolific...accept
    (B) sterile...regain
    (C) barren...relinquish
    (D) fecund...recover
    (E) fragile...lose

20. _____ by life's _____, the last emperor of China worked as a lowly gardener in the palace over which he had once ruled.

    (A) Fortified...generosity
    (B) Deluded...coincidences
    (C) Humbled...vicissitudes
    (D) Venerated...survivors
    (E) Recognized...impostors

EXERCISE 2

1. The observers hope to find out how important _____ foraging is to these endangered shorebirds in order to _____ the importance of restricting nighttime human use of beaches to specific places or times.

    (A) nocturnal...ascertain
    (B) aerial...convey
    (C) underwater...rectify
    (D) sporadic...mitigate
    (E) desultory...mandate

2. Most people who are color-blind actually can distinguish several colors; some, however, have a truly _____ view of a world all in shades of gray.

    (A) monochromatic
    (B) opalescent
    (C) translucent
    (D) astigmatic
    (E) roseate

3. Even when being _____ in method, people can come up with incorrect answers by basing their arguments on false premises.

   (A) original
   (B) logical
   (C) slipshod
   (D) realistic
   (E) careless

4. Was he so thin-skinned, then, to _____ any small _____ at his expense?

   (A) support...purchase
   (B) repeat...compliment
   (C) comprehend...mystery
   (D) resent...jest
   (E) disregard...insult

5. We look with pride at our new bridges and dams, for they are works of art as well as of _____.

   (A) leisure
   (B) aesthetics
   (C) drudgery
   (D) utility
   (E) anachronism

6. When clay dries out, it loses its plasticity and becomes less _____.

   (A) synthetic
   (B) expensive
   (C) malleable
   (D) tangible
   (E) brittle

7. For many years an unheralded researcher, Barbara McClintock gained international _____ when she won the Nobel Prize in Physiology and Medicine.

   (A) condemnation
   (B) notoriety
   (C) renown
   (D) affluence
   (E) camaraderie

8. In judging the degree of his guilt, the question remains whether he acted out of purely _____ motives or whether he acted with thoughts of his own _____ in mind.

   (A) benevolent...fame
   (B) disinterested...advantage
   (C) selfish...benefit
   (D) mercenary...profit
   (E) malicious...cleverness

9. Rosa was such a last-minute worker that she could never start writing a paper till the deadline was _____.

   (A) known
   (B) problematic
   (C) imminent
   (D) superseded
   (E) recent

10. Rather than feeling toward Miss Havisham the _____ due a benefactor, Estella became resentful and even _____ to her patron.

    (A) esteem...effusive
    (B) obligation...dutiful
    (C) altruism...quarrelsome
    (D) gratitude...hostile
    (E) condescension...benign

11. Trying to prove Hill a liar, Senator Specter repeatedly questioned her _____.

    (A) intelligence
    (B) veracity
    (C) optimism
    (D) autonomy
    (E) brevity

12. It was only the first day of summer vacation, but his nerves were already _____ by the constant clamor of the children.

    (A) eliminated
    (B) alleviated
    (C) replete
    (D) vacillated
    (E) frayed

13. Donald Trump's former casino in Atlantic City once was the most _____ gambling palace in the East, easily outglittering its competitors.

    (A) professional
    (B) speculative
    (C) ostentatious
    (D) lucrative
    (E) restrained

14. Mrs. Thatcher had a better eye for the weaknesses and _____ of her contemporaries than for their virtues.

    (A) responsibilities
    (B) foibles
    (C) merits
    (D) talents
    (E) attractions

15. American culture now stigmatizes, and sometimes even heavily _____, behavior that was once taken for granted: overt racism, cigarette smoking, the use of sexual stereotypes.

    (A) advocates
    (B) penalizes
    (C) ignores
    (D) indoctrinates
    (E) advertises

16. Because we have completed our analysis of the major components of the proposed project, we are free to devote the remainder of this session to a study of the project's _____ details.

    (A) lurid
    (B) scrupulous
    (C) unquestionable
    (D) incidental
    (E) involuntary

17. When we encounter a tentative thought of our own in someone else's writings, any _____ we may have had of its validity is _____, and what we were hesitant to believe is confirmed as truth.

    (A) assurance...unfounded
    (B) intimation...imprudent
    (C) doubt...dispelled
    (D) proof...unjustified
    (E) suspicion...reinforced

18. Determined to hire employees on the basis of their merits rather than on the basis of their family connections, Johnson refused to _____ nepotism and other forms of favoritism in the engagement of new workers.

    (A) obscure
    (B) proscribe
    (C) countenance
    (D) misrepresent
    (E) discern

19. Just as sloth is the mark of the idler, _____ is the mark of the _____.

    (A) grief...miser
    (B) obsequiousness...toady
    (C) wanderlust...trespasser
    (D) suspicion...tyrant
    (E) brevity...wit

20. Unlike Sartre, who was born into a cultivated environment, receiving culture in his feeding bottle, so to speak, the child Camus had to fight to _____ a culture that was not _____.

    (A) acquire...innate
    (B) encourage...barbarous
    (C) develop...frivolous
    (D) restrain...inferior
    (E) justify...conventional

EXERCISE 3

1. Because the damage to his car had been _____, Michael decided he wouldn't bother to report the matter to his insurance company.

   (A) intermittent
   (B) gratuitous
   (C) negligible
   (D) spontaneous
   (E) significant

2. Such was Brandon's _____ that he was frequently described as being honest as the day was long.

   (A) vigilance
   (B) munificence
   (C) probity
   (D) gravity
   (E) eminence

3. While the movie *Spellbound* is in many ways a glowing testimonial to the powers of psychoanalysis to overcome the evils of unreason, its portrait of the analytic profession is not entirely _____.

   (A) malignant
   (B) obscure
   (C) adulatory
   (D) vehement
   (E) derivative

4. Hoping for a rave review of his new show, the playwright was _____ when the critics _____ it unanimously.

   (A) gloomy...condoned
   (B) incredulous...appraised
   (C) vexed...selected
   (D) miserable...panned
   (E) impressed...divulged

5. Because it had not been blasted into a stable orbit, the satellite moved _____ through space.

   (A) innocuously
   (B) terminally
   (C) erratically
   (D) effortlessly
   (E) routinely

6. When railroads first began to supplant rivers and canals as highways of commerce, they were regarded as blessings and their promoters were looked upon as _____.

   (A) hucksters
   (B) upstarts
   (C) atheists
   (D) benefactors
   (E) diehards

7. Though she tried to be happy living with Clara in the city, Heidi _____ for the mountains and for her gruff but loving grandfather.

   (A) pined
   (B) searched
   (C) cheered
   (D) labored
   (E) trembled

8. The discovery by George Poinar and Roberta Hess that amber can preserve intact tissue from million-year-old insects _____ the possibility, since proved correct, that it also can preserve intact DNA.

   (A) eliminated
   (B) distorted
   (C) raised
   (D) precluded
   (E) predestined

9. The new dance troupe's gravest problem, one that mars the current production, is a desire for correctness and technical accuracy that ____ both energy and musical response.

   (A) enhances
   (B) stifles
   (C) transforms
   (D) reflects
   (E) supplies

10. New judges often fear that the influence of their own backgrounds will ____ their verdicts, no matter how sincere they are in wanting to be ____.

    (A) contradict...revered
    (B) corroborate...silent
    (C) condition...impartial
    (D) disclose...secretive
    (E) falsify...humane

11. Because he had abandoned his post and joined forces with the Indians, his fellow officers considered the hero of *Dances with Wolves* a ____.

    (A) martinet
    (B) braggart
    (C) renegade
    (D) skinflint
    (E) laggard

12. To take a ____ attitude, looking down on others as one's inferiors, often is to ____ any chance of favorable relations with them.

    (A) promising...negate
    (B) patronizing...eliminate
    (C) modest...reduce
    (D) pertinent...violate
    (E) benign...deny

13. Contemporary critics often ____ the poet Longfellow as a simple sentimentalist who relied too much on poetic meters only suitable for light verse.

    (A) heed
    (B) endorse
    (C) dismiss
    (D) embellish
    (E) acclaim

14. On some occasions Monteverdi clearly specifies the instruments he wishes to make up his orchestra, but more often he is ____ or silent on the issue.

    (A) enigmatic
    (B) precise
    (C) eloquent
    (D) resolute
    (E) vehement

15. Just as an ____ dish lacks flavor, an inane remark lacks ____.

    (A) intriguing...spice
    (B) insipid...sense
    (C) inedible...listeners
    (D) occasional...implications
    (E) offensive...taste

16. Deeply ____ by the insult to his dignity, he maintained that no true gentleman would accept such an ____ calmly.

    (A) mortified...opportunity
    (B) incensed...affront
    (C) puzzled...honor
    (D) shamed...iconoclasm
    (E) gratified...admonition

17. Isozaki's love for detail is apparent everywhere in the new museum, but happily the details are _____ to the building's larger formal composition, which is _____ by the unfortunate busyness of much recent architecture.

    (A) important...harmed
    (B) irrelevant...fragmented
    (C) subordinated...unencumbered
    (D) appropriate...echoed
    (E) incidental...nullified

18. Although most worthwhile criticism concentrates on the positive, one should not _____ praise everything.

    (A) argumentatively
    (B) constructively
    (C) derogatorily
    (D) analytically
    (E) indiscriminately

19. The biographer may not have _____ the depths of her subject's self-contradictory character, but she has traced its intriguingly complex _____.

    (A) plumbed...tedium
    (B) sounded...surface
    (C) thwarted...background
    (D) reached...insipidity
    (E) disregarded...psyche

20. Learned though she was, her _____ never degenerated into _____.

    (A) erudition...pedantry
    (B) knowledge...ignorance
    (C) scholarship...research
    (D) speculation...thought
    (E) education...inquiry

EXERCISE 4

1. Biologists categorize many of the world's environments as deserts: regions where the _____ availability of some key factor, such as water, sunlight, or an essential nutrient, places sharp constraints on the existence of living things.

    (A) ready
    (B) gradual
    (C) limited
    (D) nearby
    (E) unprecedented

2. The sea was so rough that the safest thing to do was to seize the railing of the ship and hang on; walking was too _____ a pastime.

    (A) leisurely
    (B) pleasant
    (C) tempting
    (D) precarious
    (E) prosaic

3. Though the ad writers had come up with a highly creative campaign to publicize the company's newest product, the head office rejected it for a more _____, down-to-earth approach.

    (A) innovative
    (B) drastic
    (C) prosaic
    (D) noteworthy
    (E) philosophic

4. The Americans and the British seem to have a dog-in-the-manger attitude toward the island of Malta, no longer needing it themselves but nevertheless wishing to _____ it to others.

    (A) interpret
    (B) offer
    (C) deny
    (D) praise
    (E) reveal

5. Increasingly silent and withdrawn, he changed from a fluent, articulate speaker to someone who gave only _____ answers to any questions asked of him.

   (A) bookish
   (B) effusive
   (C) idiomatic
   (D) pretentious
   (E) monosyllabic

6. When you learn archaeology solely from lectures, you get only _____ sense of the concepts presented, but when you hold a 5,000-year-old artifact in your hands, you have a chance to involve your senses, not just your intellect.

   (A) an invalid
   (B) an anachronistic
   (C) an abstract
   (D) a specious
   (E) a tangential

7. Paradoxically, while it is relatively easy to prove a fraudulent work of art is a fraud, it is often virtually impossible to prove that an authentic one is _____.

   (A) unpretentious
   (B) objective
   (C) impartial
   (D) dubious
   (E) genuine

8. The humorist Mark Twain had a great _____ for history and historians, observing that each year the antiquarians shed new darkness on the past.

   (A) reverence
   (B) affinity
   (C) tolerance
   (D) contempt
   (E) empathy

9. Since novelty of presentation is apt to add to a performer's popularity, the most successful troubadours were those who were also the most _____ in their delivery.

   (A) spontaneous
   (B) lyrical
   (C) academic
   (D) practiced
   (E) repetitious

10. Unfortunately, in developing countries rapid economic growth often _____ the overexploitation of natural resources and _____ distribution of wealth.

    (A) halts...indiscriminate
    (B) holds off...inadequate
    (C) leads to...inequitable
    (D) continues...evenhanded
    (E) goes beyond...ungrateful

11. Untempered by any _____, she spread an ever more militant message to her followers.

    (A) conviction
    (B) enthusiasm
    (C) radicalism
    (D) hardship
    (E) discretion

12. The idea that people are basically economic creatures, intent only upon their own material advantage, induces disbelief in the _____ of any seemingly _____ motive.

    (A) purpose...natural
    (B) desirability...ulterior
    (C) stupidity...altruistic
    (D) seemliness...egoistic
    (E) integrity...unselfish

13. Leavening his decisions with humorous, down-to-earth anecdotes, Judge Wapner was not at all the _____ legal scholar.

    (A) considerate
    (B) pedantic
    (C) indecisive
    (D) competent
    (E) pragmatic

14. The Apache are a _____ society, where husbands typically move into wives' dwellings and women take the leadership role in family affairs.

    (A) sedentary
    (B) defunct
    (C) fragmented
    (D) matrilineal
    (E) xenophobic

15. _____ James Baldwin, who wrote of black Americans as being in a perpetual state of rage, Mr. Cose asserts that few human beings could _____ the psychic toll of uninterrupted anger.

    (A) Corroborating...endure
    (B) Refuting...enhance
    (C) Dismissing...refine
    (D) Challenging...survive
    (E) Upholding...weather

16. Rather than allowing these dramatic exchanges between her characters to develop fully, Ms. Norman unfortunately tends to _____ the discussions involving the two women.

    (A) exacerbate
    (B) protract
    (C) truncate
    (D) augment
    (E) elaborate

17. "The show must go on" is the oldest _____ of show business; every true performer lives by that creed.

    (A) euphemism
    (B) allegory
    (C) precursor
    (D) tenet
    (E) corroboration

18. The _____ with which musicians and lovers of fine instruments _____ Paul Irvin's professional services attests to his great expertise and craftsmanship as a harpsichord maker.

    (A) hesitation...acquire
    (B) avidness...solicit
    (C) persistence...supersede
    (D) harmony...conjure
    (E) vehemence...reject

19. From the critic's perspective, M. F. K. Fisher is a writer who _____ classification, for her food writing reads like love stories, her fiction like memoirs.

    (A) remembered
    (B) relished
    (C) skirted
    (D) complied with
    (E) matured with

20. Because the apelike members of *Australopithecus afarensis* were capable both of walking and of swinging through trees, the anthropologist described them as a mosaic, bipedal from the waist down and _____ from the waist up.

    (A) ethereal
    (B) arboreal
    (C) dysfunctional
    (D) articulated
    (E) pedestrian

Answers to Sentence Completion Exercises

Level A

Sentence Completion Exercise 1

1. C	3. B	5. C	7. C	9. C	11. D	13. D	15. A	17. D	19. D
2. D	4. E	6. C	8. D	10. E	12. B	14. A	16. A	18. B	20. B

Sentence Completion Exercise 2

1. B	3. E	5. A	7. C	9. E	11. C	13. C	15. C	17. D	19. B
2. C	4. D	6. A	8. D	10. C	12. D	14. D	16. C	18. D	20. C

Sentence Completion Exercise 3

1. E	3. C	5. A	7. C	9. C	11. C	13. B	15. A	17. C	19. D
2. E	4. B	6. E	8. A	10. C	12. B	14. D	16. C	18. E	20. C

Sentence Completion Exercise 4

1. D	3. E	5. A	7. B	9. B	11. D	13. B	15. B	17. E	19. A
2. D	4. C	6. D	8. C	10. E	12. C	14. A	16. D	18. E	20. A

Level B

Sentence Completion Exercise 1

1. B	3. B	5. C	7. C	9. E	11. C	13. D	15. C	17. D	19. C
2. C	4. A	6. E	8. B	10. B	12. C	14. D	16. C	18. B	20. C

Sentence Completion Exercise 2

1. D	3. E	5. C	7. C	9. C	11. D	13. C	15. A	17. E	19. C
2. A	4. A	6. D	8. D	10. C	12. C	14. A	16. C	18. B	20. E

Sentence Completion Exercise 3

1. B	3. C	5. A	7. D	9. A	11. C	13. A	15. C	17. D	19. D
2. C	4. C	6. D	8. D	10. E	12. C	14. B	16. B	18. D	20. B

Sentence Completion Exercise 4

1. E	3. E	5. C	7. D	9. D	11. D	13. E	15. C	17. A	19. D
2. E	4. B	6. C	8. B	10. B	12. D	14. C	16. E	18. E	20. E

Level C

Sentence Completion Exercise 1

1. B	3. C	5. C	7. E	9. B	11. C	13. C	15. B	17. C	19. B
2. C	4. B	6. C	8. D	10. B	12. C	14. C	16. B	18. B	20. C

Sentence Completion Exercise 2

1. A	3. B	5. D	7. C	9. C	11. B	13. C	15. B	17. C	19. B
2. A	4. D	6. C	8. B	10. D	12. E	14. B	16. D	18. C	20. A

Sentence Completion Exercise 3

1. C	3. C	5. C	7. A	9. B	11. C	13. C	15. B	17. C	19. B
2. C	4. D	6. D	8. C	10. C	12. B	14. A	16. B	18. E	20. A

Sentence Completion Exercise 4

1. C	3. C	5. E	7. E	9. A	11. E	13. B	15. D	17. D	19. C
2. D	4. C	6. C	8. D	10. C	12. E	14. D	16. C	18. B	20. B

Answer Explanations

Level A

Sentence Completion Exercise 1

1. **(C)** If Washington political circles had been aware for a week that the Cabinet member was on the way out, his resignation did not come as a *shock* or surprise to them.

2. **(D)** Because the heavy rains had made their original route *impracticable* or impassable, the leaders decided to *alter* their route.

3. **(B)** The key phrase "as if it were a laboratory specimen" signals you that excessive literary analysis is analogous to the *dissecting* or cutting apart of animals and plants done in a biology lab.

4. **(E)** Customs generally arise because they serve a function. In this case, the division of labor by gender probably came about because it *promoted* or furthered the interests of the family and in this way was a sensible *cooperative* strategy.

5. **(C)** Silk possesses qualities invaluable in nest building. Therefore birds *incorporate* or introduce silk into their nests, including it as a component.

6. **(C)** Because no one had ever rebuked or *reprimanded* the recruit so harshly, the sergeant's words particularly *stung* or smarted.

7. **(C)** The earlier writers differ from this writer in being *reticent* (reserved) and conventional.

8. **(D)** A report that constantly interpreted things to reflect badly on or *discredit* someone would clearly be unfriendly or *hostile* to that person.

9. **(C)** There remained in Foster, who had not grown up fully, a *trace* (small bit; hint) of the undergraduate; he was clever but in some ways *immature*.

10. **(E)** Although she felt *contempt* (scorn) for the world of money and opinion and power, she nevertheless desired or *yearned for* the fame that only that world could give.

11. **(D)** If you are excessively careful about what you say, you are not likely to be *spontaneous* or free in your choice of words.

12. **(B)** A layperson or nonexpert by definition lacks the training to *appreciate* or recognize the importance of fossils and ancient artifacts.

13. **(D)** It would be extremely hard to be *unaffected* or unmoved by truly mesmerizing, enchanting art.

14. **(A)** Anthropologists attempt to *determine* (discover; learn) the origins of the fossils they find.

15. **(A)** If the therapy has been shown to work in dogs (animals larger than rodents), then its *efficacy* or effectiveness in larger animals has been proven.

16. **(A)** To *mute* or muffle the noise inside a car should make a trip in the car quieter.

17. **(D)** Neither her father's *admonition* (warning or counsel) nor her classmates' *cool* (unsociable; distant) reception stopped Cleeves from following her chosen path.

18. **(B)** To *derail* someone *from* his course is to throw him off track.

19. (**D**) By definition, a *maverick* (dissenter; nonconformist) is someone who takes a stand that differs from that of his or her associates.

20. (**B**) Comte *coined* (invented; created) a term to *denote* (stand for; mean) the concept of unselfishness.

Sentence Completion Exercise 2

1. (**B**) If we manage to *destroy* the environment, we will be well on the way to extinction as a species.

2. (**C**) "Even though" children cannot influence affairs in the usual ways, thanks to Edelman's work they are nevertheless not *ignored.*

3. (**E**) A campaign that breaks new ground is by definition *innovative.*

4. (**D**) Both an *outstanding* sense of timing and a *mastery* of the law would be helpful to an attorney.

5. (**A**) The goal of the project is to make Woolf's work more *accessible* or available to scholars.

6. (**A**) The entangling threads that slow down the victim's *escape* vibrate from the prey's struggles. These vibrations *alert* (warn; inform) the spider that something is trapped in its web.

7. (**C**) In poking through the subject's private papers, the biographer *invades* the subject's privacy.

8. (**D**) If the babies drink so much fruit juice that they do not get the varied nourishment they *need,* then drinking large amounts of juice could be *detrimental* (harmful) to them.

9. (**E**) An *epic* or account of heroic exploits by definition narrates the mighty struggles of a central character or protagonist.

10. (**C**) If it is so amazing that good poems ever get written, there must be many ways to *ruin* poems.

11. (**C**) The musk oxen declined or grew fewer in number because the herds were *devastated* (destroyed; ravaged) by hunters.

12. (**D**) Just as the limbs of a tree *branch off* from the trunk, the major arteries branch off from the aorta.

13. (**C**) Someone who looks on human virtues as less worthy than canine virtues clearly views people in general with *contempt* (scorn).

14. (**D**) The dumbfounded neuroanatomist disbelieved Diamond's work. *Skeptical* of the results of her experiments, he maintained that a rat's brain could not increase or *grow.*

15. (**C**) Though he maintained that he did not care (protested his *indifference*), Judge Hand was *disappointed* that he had not been nominated to the Supreme Court.

16. (**C**) Someone consistently hopeful is by definition an *optimist.*

17. (**C**) In an arid, extremely dry land, wildlife needs *access to* water.

18. (**D**) One would expect that a liberal political movement advocating freedom would favor less authority, not more. However, Trilling asserts that, paradoxically, contrary to expectations, liberalism must move in the direction of increasing *control.*

19. (**B**) The contrast here is between the extremes of *euphoria* (elation) and *gloom* (melancholy; depression).

20. **(C)** By definition, to lead a lewd or wanton life is to be *dissipated* (corrupted by sensuality; self-indulgent).

Sentence Completion Exercise 3

1. **(E)** Though most people disregarded or made fun of her book, some *appreciated* it (admired it; grasped its worth).

2. **(E)** If the critics all say the opera's score has both praiseworthy and wretched sections, then they agree that the score varies in quality. In other words, it is *uneven*.

3. **(C)** Someone who plans everything in advance is not *spontaneous*.

4. **(B)** Our almost-human ancestors did not become extinct. Instead, they *survived*.

5. **(A)** The marketing experts have divided or *carved up* the *mass* (whole) audience into segments.

6. **(E)** Like an *overinflated* balloon, aneurysms *burst*.

7. **(C)** Critics *attribute* the *delay* to unexpected problems, a common cause of slowdowns.

8. **(A)** A hotshot is someone conspicuously talented and successful. Many lawyers are *not* legal hotshots. They are *ill prepared* and they *lack* professional skills.

9. **(C)** Scientists continue to test hypotheses against experience, *verifying* them or establishing their accuracy by keeping on making observations.

10. **(C)** To supersede or replace a learned, scholarly biography, this new life of Gaskell must be a very good book. In other words, it must be a considerable *accomplishment* or achievement for the author.

11. **(C)** After Boccherini's death, the composer's reputation fell into a decline, or weakened. It has not yet *recovered* or improved enough to satisfy the writer of this sentence.

12. **(B)** Because he had emphasized his scandal-free, virtuous reputation, Hosokawa could not *withstand* or successfully resist the *notoriety* (ill fame) of being connected with a scandal.

13. **(B)** It is *paradoxical* (incongruous; puzzlingly contradictory) that a *civilized* center should have been the site of horribly uncivilized, inhumane acts.

14. **(D)** The sentence serves to *define* the term *illness*.

15. **(A)** If Schlesinger laments or mourns the state of biography, then he is unhappy about the gossipy new biographies currently on sale. Thus, he *deplores* (disapproves of) them.

16. **(D)** The waitress handled the bottle *nonchalantly* or casually, without undue concern.

17. **(C)** To begin to appear in prominent, *responsible* positions is to emerge from *obscurity* or anonymity into the public view.

18. **(E)** If the crisis will not affect us for years, then by definition it is not *imminent* (immediately looming; near).

19. **(D)** A *charlatan* falsely pretends to know more than he actually does. When Dorothy finds out that the Wizard does not know how to get her home, she thinks he has *duped* or made a fool of her.

20. **(C)** Healing waters are by definition *therapeutic* (curative).

Sentence Completion Exercise 4

1. (**D**) To *revoke* a license is to cancel it, to make it void.
2. (**D**) A curious child is by definition *inquisitive*.
3. (**E**) Since many scholars helped to put together the survey, it was a *collective* (combined; cooperative) effort, not an individual one.
4. (**C**) A fair solution is by definition *equitable* or just.
5. (**C**) It is physically impossible for most living creatures to walk on water. Thus, by running across the surface of water, the basilisk seems to *defy* or challenge the laws of physics.
6. (**D**) Passive, inactive people tend to *observe* rather than to *act*.
7. (**B**) Keynes was not immobilized. Instead, he was *energized* or invigorated.
8. (**C**) The telling of tales is by definition *narrative*.
9. (**B**) An *enthusiastic*, spirited response would be likely to please or *gratify* a speaker.
10. (**E**) *Advances* or new developments in science would make it *necessary* to revise the book.
11. (**D**) Someone lying half asleep in a hot tub is clearly *relaxed*.
12. (**C**) Plants that do not survive *shrivel* (wither) and die.
13. (**B**) To fabricate events is to make them up, to invent them. Dali's tendency to make things up makes it hard for biographers to portray his life with *accuracy*.
14. (**A**) Many people accepted and liked Earhart ("her fame was unusually widespread and her popularity long-lived"). However, not everyone did: her acceptance was not *universal*.
15. (**B**) His belief in individual faith contrasts with his doubts (*skepticism*) about the organized church.
16. (**D**) *Theses* is the plural form of *thesis*, which here means theory or contention. The details are disconnected; no overarching or encompassing theories bring them together or *unify* them.
17. (**E**) If global warming poses a threat to all life on Earth, then by definition it is not a *peripheral* (marginal; minor) issue.
18. (**E**) Radicals tend to believe that old customs are nonsense and that change is always a good idea. This author thinks it would be good for radicals to rethink their beliefs. They need to realize that old customs are not always *worthless* and that change can sometimes be a bad idea (be *inadvisable*).
19. (**A**) Though Eliot was personally *reticent* (reserved; uncommunicative about himself), he was realistic enough to *assume* that his private papers someday would be read.
20. (**A**) To be *fidgety* by definition is to exhibit or be marked by impatience.

Level B

Sentence Completion Exercise 1

1. (**B**) People on the cutting edge—at the forefront of a new movement—are likely to be *innovative*.
2. (**C**) Wittgenstein's comment is a *rule* to which good historians should *adhere* or stick. It says, "If you don't know anything about a subject, you can't say anything about it." In other words, write about what you know.

3. (**B**) If only a few of her allies stood by her, she must have *alienated* or estranged all the others.

4. (**A**) A *soporific* effect by definition puts people to sleep, causing them to nod off.

5. (**C**) The papers *rank* as (have the status or position of) the most *impressive* statements of American political philosophy.

6. (**E**) Someone who has *improvidently* squandered his money without thinking about the future would regret his *prodigal,* wasteful ways.

7. (**C**) *Digressive* remarks that wander from the topic may make us forget the gist or main point of what's being said.

8. (**B**) Allende's book is based on or *rooted* in actual Chilean history.

9. (**E**) If they plan on selling ad space, their *motivations* in making the donation are at least partially financial and not solely charitable or *philanthropic.*

10. (**B**) Blackmun's voice stood out from the featureless mix of the other Justices' voices: it was an individual, *personal* voice.

11. (**C**) It is somewhat of an *understatement* for Gaddis to describe himself as never having been in a *rush* to get into print. At a rate of one book every 10 years, he's been markedly slow to publish.

12. (**C**) *Precarious* means uncertain in prospects; risky. Acting as a career certainly is that.

13. (**D**) Montana was *unintimidating*: he did not frighten or overawe those who met him.

14. (**D**) In Sand's time, for a woman to take lovers or wear men's clothes was a shocking departure from *convention* (usual social custom).

15. (**C**) The speaker is not *resigned* or reconciled to her death. Instead, he is *inconsolable* (heartbroken; unable to be comforted or consoled).

16. (**C**) The Chinese artists have been clever. They have made *canny* (shrewd) use of Western styles.

17. (**D**) One would expect the use of outmoded, archaic vocabulary and twisted, tortuous phrasing to make a poem unintelligible. However, contrary to expectations, the poet's argument is *intelligible.*

18. (**B**) By definition, an experience that splits a nation into factions or conflicting groups is *divisive* (dissension creating).

19. (**C**) Traumas or major shocks can lead to *aberrations* or abnormalities of behavior in survivors.

20. (**C**) Someone intellectually *fecund* (fertile; prolific) is bursting with ideas. Clearly, this productive novelist is at the *height* of her powers.

Sentence Completion Exercise 2

1. (**D**) The writers who are not negative about the past look on it positively, even *nostalgically* (sentimentally, with a sense of wistful longing).

2. (**A**) By revitalizing Chrysler, Iacocca made it a *vigorous,* energetic company.

3. (**E**) One expects a scholar to know the serious works on his subject. Though Cose is not a scholar, he nevertheless is *familiar with* the appropriate serious works.

4. (**A**) Despite his self-centeredness, White could be kind to others and even belittle or be modest about himself (be *self-deprecating*).

5. **(C)** The contrast here is between the apartment's actual state ("shabby and dilapidated") and its promised condition: *pristine* (spotlessly clean).

6. **(D)** By definition, someone *apathetic* does not care.

7. **(C)** To *scavenge* is to hunt through discarded items to find useful bits.

8. **(D)** Most of the books are not excellent, but are *mediocre* (of moderate or low quality) instead.

9. **(C)** Angry, *heated* discussions suggest no settlement is near. However, the two sides actually are close to *agreeing*.

10. **(C)** Churchill was not a *dilettante* or dabbler; he was a serious artist.

11. **(D)** Foreign powers that look on territory in the Americas as prey to be seized are by definition *predatory*.

12. **(C)** A spotty book is uneven in quality. This particular book suffers from sections that are relatively uninteresting, less than *exciting* though not precisely *dull*.

13. **(C)** A strict teetotaler (person who abstains from drinking alcohol) would not *condone* (overlook or disregard) anyone's drinking intoxicants.

14. **(A)** To interpret art fancifully, inventing things, is a *temptation* to the critic. This critic resists the temptation; he is *scrupulous* (carefully painstaking) in sticking to the facts.

15. **(A)** Because he owes money, Lydgate must take a *lucrative* (well-paying) position.

16. **(C)** The writer is relatively positive about people's decisions in choosing to represent themselves in court. He or she concludes that people have a *reliable* or dependable sense of when lawyers are and are not necessary.

17. **(E)** For the listener to come to agree with the speaker, any *doubts* he might have had must have been *dispelled* (made to vanish).

18. **(B)** *Empathy* by definition is sensitivity to the feelings and thoughts of others.

19. **(C)** *Tacit* cooperation is implied but not expressed actively. Johnson's cooperation with Boswell went far beyond this.

20. **(E)** Lesser scholars would have been intimidated or *daunted* by the amount of material to be explored.

Sentence Completion Exercise 3

1. **(B)** The key phrase here is "longer lives." The doctors are trying to lengthen or *prolong* human life.

2. **(D)** If the colonies appeared remarkably homogeneous or uniform in opinion, then clearly there were only *superficial* or very minor differences among them.

3. **(C)** A small hall would tend to promote a sense of closeness appropriate to recitals. In other words, such a hall would be particularly *conducive* to the intimacy that is the recital's special charm.

4. **(C)** "Even" intensifies what is being said. Lullabies not only have a dark side; many also have a *threatening*, menacing quality.

5. **(A)** For a dispute to become ugly and destructive, the level of disagreement must *escalate* (intensify; increase).

6. **(D)** Lao Li's archives *document* or record contemporary Chinese art.

7. **(D)** Someone who leaves parties in order to go off alone clearly can no longer be described as *gregarious* (sociable).

8. **(D)** If science is always ready to change or modify its theories, it clearly is *tentative* (provisional) rather than absolute in making its statements.

9. (**A**) Because we today are able to cure tuberculosis, we think of it as simply another long-term *chronic* illness. In the past, however, people regarded it as a pestilence or *plague*.

10. (**E**) Rather than lure or attract readers, Gaddis's work tends to *repel* or drive them away.

11. (**C**) Instead of being showily glamorous like opera, classical song is more restrained or *subdued*.

12. (**C**) The writer is uniformly positive about the book being reviewed, calling it *painstakingly* or carefully researched. The life the book describes, however, is not positive: the subject's tormented career was *tragic*.

13. (**A**) Lexy's pleasure did not last long; it was *transitory*, or fleeting.

14. (**B**) *Commingling* is a thorough combining of parts. It would be futile or pointless to try to *separate* elements that have been thoroughly mixed.

15. (**C**) By describing the land as asleep, the writer means that the nation had yet to rouse itself to confront the foreign invaders. Clearly the people's sense of nationalism was *dormant* or sleeping.

16. (**B**) In order to enhance or improve their empires, the moguls (cinema magnates) needed the services of *prestigious* writers whose eminence would rub off on them. In this way the moguls would *aggrandize* themselves, making themselves appear greater through their association with great intellectuals.

17. (**D**) The production is described metaphorically as if it were a jungle creature, alert, stealthy, almost *predatory* (ready to seize its victim) as it waits to *pounce*.

18. (**D**) *Obsequious* means servile or fawningly attentive.

19. (**D**) "Whereas" signals a contrast. *L'Orfeo* is not the beginning of a tradition. Instead, it is the *culmination* or highest achievement of one.

20. (**B**) In combining so many different approaches, Feher's lessons are clearly *eclectic* (composed of elements drawn from different sources).

Sentence Completion Exercise 4

1. (**E**) If you could afford only such meager nourishment, clearly you would be very poor—in other words, suffering from *destitution*, or utter poverty.

2. (**E**) An *uneventful* life, one in which nothing much important or notable happened, would be difficult to make interesting.

3. (**E**) Unable to rely on its poor vision to help it move in the darkness, the mole rat depends on the sensitivity of its whiskers to what they touch to give it a feel for its surroundings. Thus, the whiskers help *guide* the mole rat.

4. (**B**) *Aggressive*, belligerent impulses push people to get into street brawls. However, professional boxers are allowed to fight only in professional competitions—that is, in the ring.

5. (**C**) The phrase "for all" as used here means "in spite of." It signals a contrast. The novel's hero does not really belong in the 1890s. He is a *contemporary* voice and has a contemporary cultural *sensibility* or capacity for appreciation.

6. (**C**) She wondered whether triangles *qualified* (demonstrated the required characteristics) to be called polygons.

7. (**D**) Telescopic observations are more *detailed* (complete) than ones made with the naked eye. However, the first *documented* or recorded use of the telescope came after Kepler saw the supernova.

8. **(B)** The author was not brave enough to attack the people who had the power to prevent his books from being published; he did not bite the hand that fed him. However, he was brave enough to make an occasional negative remark about these people; thus, he *nibbled at* the hand that fed him.

9. **(D)** People who are "arty" are showily or pretentiously artistic: they collect art in order to show off their belongings. True art lovers, however, collect for their own *pleasure,* not for *show.*

10. **(B)** *Recurrent* (periodically reappearing) attacks or bouts of illness could well alarm someone's friends and family.

11. **(D)** "Though" signals a contrast. In this case, Simon's review of a contemporary play is a *rave* (extravagant praise).

12. **(D)** In their old age, Chinese painters no longer copied their teachers. However, their *originality* did not involve major changes; they made *slight,* barely visible ones.

13. **(E)** If you had your reputation damaged by a libelous statement, you would want your name *cleared* or freed of blame. Thus, you would welcome a *retraction* (disavowal; withdrawal) of the libel.

14. **(C)** Kissinger appreciates the hard-headed, realistic use of power. He even appreciates power when it is used *ruthlessly,* without compassion or remorse. For this reason, he is able to admire the ability to use power effectively even when he sees it in people who are otherwise *detestable* (odious).

15. **(C)** Poseurs by definition pretend to be something they are not. Some people thought Dali was a great artist. Others *dismissed* (slighted; made little of) him as a painter who pretended to be great.

16. **(E)** If the world of food writing is known for its pettiness (small-mindedness) and infighting (internal quarrels), then an author who was *generous* would be *rare* in this milieu.

17. **(A)** *Esoteric* allusions are by definition references that are understood by only a small, restricted group. References to *obscure,* little-known people and events clearly would not be understood by people in general.

18. **(E)** To see her sister's fortunes rise while her own *declined* or fell would be likely to *exacerbate* or intensify the subject's bitterness.

19. **(D)** To have retained so much information is to be *formidably* or awe inspiringly learned.

20. **(E)** It is *futile* or useless to try to abolish something whose existence is inevitable (unavoidable).

Level C

Sentence Completion Exercise 1

1. **(B)** In the dark, one's eyes have to work hard or *strain* to be able to see.

2. **(C)** The uprising was organized and planned. Thus, it was not *spontaneous* or unpremeditated.

3. **(C)** Theologians (specialists in the study of religious faith and practices) would be upset by a book that *undermined* or weakened *established* rituals and beliefs.

4. **(B)** By definition, a *sage* is a wise person. Likewise, a virtuoso is a skilled person, one who has *expertise*.

5. **(C)** Someone old for his years, slow and conservative, could well be called *stodgy*.

6. **(C)** Preferring facts, the historian is uninterested in speculations or *conjectures*.

7. **(E)** By agreeing to be the subjects of magazine articles, these famously *shy* novelists have given in to their publishers' insistence on *publicity*.

8. **(D)** Caring so much about being in the know, Tom was vexed or *galled* by his ignorance.

9. **(B)** To waver between choices is by definition to *vacillate*.

10. **(B)** With their huge nets, the trawlers scoop up everything in their path. Thus, they trap fish *indiscriminately*, hauling them in without distinguishing among them.

11. **(C)** A father who rules autocratically and will brook or allow no disagreement is by definition *domineering* (overbearing; tyrannical). His daughter eloped to *escape* his control.

12. **(C)** The symphony is a classical music form. In writing jazz symphonies, Ellington was combining or fusing jazz with a classical form. He was attacked by critics who wished to *discourage* such fusions.

13. **(C)** If Tennyson managed to produce particularly impressive work in his last years, clearly his creative powers had not declined or *flagged*.

14. **(C)** A *stronghold* (fortified area) by definition is a place set up to *protect* people from attack.

15. **(B)** Lovejoy advises the reader how to avoid being fooled by fake or *spurious* antiques.

16. **(B)** Someone omniscient (all-knowing) would by definition be *unlimited in* knowledge.

17. **(C)** A *euphemism* is a mild expression used in place of a blunt, unpleasant one.

18. **(B)** By definition, a *juncture* is a point of convergence, here the point where televised information and entertainment are joined in a new format.

19. **(B)** For a nonbreeding female to be able to replace a queen, taking over her breeding functions, the female must *regain* her reproductive abilities. In other words, the nonbreeding female suddenly reverses her *sterility* (barrenness; inability to reproduce).

20. **(C)** *Vicissitudes* are the changes of fortune one experiences in the course of a lifetime. Going from ruling an empire to laboring in a garden, China's last emperor clearly would have been *humbled* or lowered in condition by these changes.

Sentence Completion Exercise 2

1. **(A)** Before they can *ascertain* or figure out how important it is to limit the human use of the beaches at night, the observers must determine just how much the shorebirds depend on their *nocturnal* (nighttime) feeding.

2. **(A)** If you can see only shades of gray, your view is by definition *monochromatic* (made up of one color or hue).

3. **(B)** A faulty premise or underlying assumption can undermine the most *logically* reasoned argument.

4. **(D)** To be thin-skinned by definition is to be quick to *resent* any insult or joking remark (*jest*) that might reflect on one's dignity.

5. **(D)** Bridges and dams are built to serve useful functions: they are works of *utility*. However, this writer asserts that the new bridges and dams are works of art as well.

6. **(C)** By definition, something that loses its plasticity (capacity for being molded or shaped) is less *malleable* (capable of being shaped).

7. **(C)** McClintock went from being unheralded (not celebrated or famous) to being *renowned* (celebrated; acclaimed).

8. **(B)** A *disinterested* (unselfishly motivated) act would not be motivated by selfish thoughts of one's own *advantage*.

9. **(C)** *Imminent* means near at hand, hanging threateningly over one's head. A procrastinator or last-minute worker often delays till the deadline is nearly upon her.

10. **(D)** Conventionally, one owes a benefactor *gratitude*. Rather than feeling thankful, however, Estella felt resentful and even *hostile* (unfriendly; antagonistic).

11. **(B)** *Veracity* means truthfulness. By questioning someone's truthfulness, you hope to prove he or she is a liar.

12. **(E)** Nerves would be *frayed* or strained by constant clamor (noise).

13. **(C)** Something that outglitters its rivals is more showy or *ostentatious* than they are.

14. **(B)** *Foibles* by definition are minor flaws or weaknesses. The support signal *and* suggests that the missing word must be a synonym or near-synonym for "weaknesses."

15. **(B)** To stigmatize behavior is to characterize or mark it as disgraceful or wicked. To *penalize* behavior is to go even further and punish it.

16. **(D)** Now that they have dealt with the major items, they can move on to the minor or *incidental* ones.

17. **(C)** If you now believe what you had been reluctant to believe, your *doubts* or uncertainties have been *dispelled* (dissipated; driven away).

18. **(C)** Johnson would not *countenance* (tolerate; approve) such unfair hiring practices.

19. **(B)** A *toady* (sycophant; flatterer in search of getting favors) is characterized by *obsequiousness* (servile attentiveness).

20. **(A)** Camus had to fight to *acquire* or gain a culture that was not his by birth (in other words, was not *innate* or inborn).

Sentence Completion Exercise 3

1. **(C)** One wouldn't bother to make an insurance claim for *negligible* (small; inconsequential) damage.

2. **(C)** *Probity* is by definition honesty or integrity.

3. **(C)** In calling *Spellbound* a glowing testimonial to (expression of the benefits received from) the powers of psychoanalysis to do good, the writer maintains that the movie presents a favorable picture of psychoanalysis. However, it is not an exclusively admiring, *adulatory* picture.

4. (**D**) To have his work *panned* or harshly criticized would be likely to make a playwright *miserable*.

5. (**C**) The satellite is off course and is moving *erratically* (irregularly or inconsistently) through space.

6. (**D**) A *benefactor* by definition is someone who confers benefits or blessings on others.

7. (**A**) "Though" signals a contrast. In spite of her attempts to be happy, Heidi was unhappy because she *pined* (fruitlessly longed) to be back home.

8. (**C**) The couple's discovery *raised* or suggested a possibility that further investigation showed to be correct.

9. (**B**) An overemphasis on correctness that *stifled* or repressed the performers' liveliness would mar or spoil a production.

10. (**C**) Your background can *condition* or determine your thinking, subtly prejudicing you so that you cannot be truly *impartial* or fair.

11. (**C**) A *renegade* by definition deserts one allegiance in favor of another.

12. (**B**) A *patronizing* or condescending attitude may offend others and *eliminate* or rule out the possibility of good relations.

13. (**C**) To *dismiss* Longfellow in this way is to reject him as unworthy of serious critical consideration.

14. (**A**) By not specifically stating his wishes, Monteverdi leaves them a mystery. Thus, he is *enigmatic* (mysterious).

15. (**B**) By definition, *insipid* means lacking flavor. By definition, inane means lacking *sense*.

16. (**B**) An *affront* (deliberate offense or insult) would clearly *incense* or anger someone.

17. (**C**) Because the details are *subordinated* or made less important than the building's total design, the building is *unencumbered* (unimpeded; unhampered) by a sense of busyness.

18. (**E**) To praise things *indiscriminately*, making no distinctions between treasures and trash, is to fail to exercise proper critical selectivity.

19. (**B**) To *sound* the depths is to ascertain just how deep something is. This biographer has not reached the depths, but she has examined the *surface*.

20. (**A**) *Erudition* means great learning or scholarship. *Pedantry*, however, is a great show of learning, an excessive attention to petty details that lacks the true scholarly spirit.

Sentence Completion Exercise 4

1. (**C**) A *limited* availability of necessities would put constraints or restrictions on the creatures needing them.

2. (**D**) Under such rough conditions, it would be too risky or *precarious* to walk without holding on.

3. (**C**) "Though" signals a contrast. Rather than being creative, the eventual publicity campaign was *prosaic* or unimaginative.

4. (**C**) To *deny* or refuse to others something you yourself do not need or want is to behave like the proverbial dog-in-the-manger, who did not want to eat the hay in the manger but refused to let the hungry cattle get at it.

5. **(E)** No longer fluent and prone to speech, he became *monosyllabic*, answering in words of one syllable.

6. **(C)** Something understood only theoretically or intellectually is known only in the *abstract*.

7. **(E)** It is incongruous that it is easier to prove something a fake than to prove it *genuine* or real.

8. **(D)** When we say historians shed new light on or illuminate the past, we express respect for historians. When Twain observed that the antiquarians (students of ancient things) shed new darkness on the past, he expressed *contempt* or scorn for historians.

9. **(A)** *Spontaneous* performances, performances arising from the impulse of the moment, tend to be fresh or *novel*.

10. **(C)** The key word here is "unfortunately." To have rapid economic growth *lead* to the overexploitation or excessive, unjust use of resources and the unfair or *inequitable* sharing of wealth is truly unfortunate.

11. **(E)** If she became increasingly militant (aggressively active), then she was not tempered (mellowed) by a spirit of *discretion* or caution.

12. **(E)** If you think that people are motivated only by selfish thoughts of their own advantage, you will be unlikely to believe in the *integrity* or trustworthiness of any *unselfish* motive.

13. **(B)** Wapner was not a *pedantic* scholar, fussing about minute points of law.

14. **(D)** By definition, a *matrilineal* society, in which inheritance is determined through the female line, is one in which women have a significant role.

15. **(D)** In remarking that few humans could *survive* living in a state of uninterrupted anger, Cose *challenges* or disputes Baldwin's statement about anger as a constant in black American life.

16. **(C)** Instead of allowing the exchanges to develop fully, the playwright cuts short or *truncates* them.

17. **(D)** By definition, a *tenet* is a belief generally held to be true. Here it is used as a synonym for guiding principle or "creed."

18. **(B)** Musicians *solicit* or seek out Irvin's services with *avidness* (eagerness) because he is a highly skilled artisan.

19. **(C)** Fisher's work evades or *skirts* classification because it does not fall neatly into set categories.

20. **(B)** *Arboreal* means inhabiting or frequenting trees.

PART 4

PASSAGE-BASED READING QUESTIONS

Overview

SAT passage-based reading questions test your ability to understand what you read—both content and technique. Each critical reading section on the SAT will include one or two long reading passages of different length, followed by six to thirteen questions of assorted types. Two of the three critical reading sections will also include a pair of quite short reading passages—about 100 words in length—each followed by a couple of reading questions.

Passages on the tests fall into certain types. Some will be **narrative**: a passage from a novel, a short story, an autobiography, or a personal essay. Some will deal with the **sciences** (including medicine, botany, zoology, chemistry, physics, geology, astronomy); others, with the **humanities** (including art, literature, music, philosophy, folklore); still others, with the **social sciences** (including history, economics, sociology, government). Some of the above passages may be what the College Board calls **argumentative**; these passages present definite points of view on the subjects. One passage most likely will be "**ethnic**" in content: whether it is a history passage, a personal narrative, or a passage on music, art, or literature, it will deal with concerns of a particular minority group.

The questions that follow each passage are not arranged in order of difficulty. Rather, they are arranged to suit the way the passage's content is organized. Thus, a question based on information presented at the beginning of the passage will come before a question based on information at the end. However, questions based on the short reading passages tend to be easier than those based on the longer passages. Tackle the short reading passages *first*.

Tips on Handling
Passage-Based Reading Questions

TIP
1   Try to Anticipate What the Passage Is About

As you read the italicized introductory material preceding the passage and tackle the passage's opening sentences, try to anticipate what the passage will be about. Ask yourself who or what the author is writing about. Recollect what else you may have read about the topic. You'll be in a better position to understand what you read.

On sections with both short and long reading passages, tackle the short passages first. Consider the paired short reading passages a warmup for the paired long reading passages that appear later in the test.

TIP
2   Pick Your Questions to Answer

On sections with two long reading passages, head straight for the passage that appeals to you more. It is hard to concentrate when you read about something wholly unfamiliar to you. Give yourself a break. First tackle the reading passage that interests you or deals with topics in which you are well grounded. Then move on to the other passage. You'll do better that way.

Similarly, when you're ready to answer questions on a long passage, consider taking a quick glance at *all* the questions on that passage and starting off with answering the ones you feel you can handle easily. Check out the questions with answer choices that are only two or three words long. (Usually these are vocabulary-in-context questions, or questions on attitude or tone.) Answer them. Then focus on the longer, more difficult questions.

> **TIP**
>
> Vocabulary-in-context questions take hardly any time to answer. If you're running out of time, answer them first.

If you are stumped by a tough reading question, don't automatically skip the other questions on that passage. As stated on page 101, the reading questions following each passage are not arranged in order of difficulty. Instead, they tend to be arranged sequentially: questions on paragraph 1 come before questions on paragraph 2. Therefore, it pays to look over all the questions on the passage. An essay question may be just one question away from a tough one.

> **TIP**
>
> Logic/application questions take lots of time to think through. If you're running out of time, you may want to skip that logic question and try a detail or vocabulary one.
>
> Why get bogged down answering one time-consuming question when in the same amount of time you can answer two less demanding ones?

Recognize the questions to bear down on as opposed to the questions to skip. Spot the most time-consuming questions; then, decide whether any given time-consumer is one you should skip. Questions containing the word EXCEPT in capital letters tend to be tricky; they may be ones to take a pass on. Questions using Roman numerals (I only, I and II only, and so on) that require you to use the process of elimination to reach your answer may be time-consuming. Similarly, the following sorts of questions may take a lot of time:

- ones that ask about the author's underlying assumptions;
- ones that ask what additional information would help to clarify points in the passage;
- ones that compare or contrast two passages in great detail;
- ones with extremely lengthy answer choices.

You may decide you want to skip one or more of them.

However…*try to answer all the questions* on one passage before you move on to the second. Often, working through one or two questions will provide you with information you can use in answering other questions on that passage.

Whenever you skip from question to question, or from passage to passage, *be sure you're filling in the right spaces on your answer sheet.*

TIP

3

Read Purposefully: Passage, Questions, and Answer Choices

As you work through the passage, try to identify what *kind* of writing it represents, what *techniques* are being used, who the intended *audience* may be, and what *feel-*

ing (if any) the author has toward this subject. Try to retain names, dates, and places for quick reference later. In particular, try to remember where in the passage the author makes *major* points. Underline key words, if you like, or indicate main ideas with a star (*) or arrow. Then, when you start looking for a phrase or sentence to justify your answer, you may be able to save time by going back to that section of the passage immediately without having to reread the whole thing.

Read as rapidly as you can with understanding, but do not force yourself. Do not worry about the time element. If you worry about not finishing the test, you will begin to take short-cuts and miss correct answers in your haste.

Figure out whether it ever helps you to read the questions before you read through the passage. For the long passages, our general advice is, to read the passage first; then read the questions. We find most students do better tackling reading exercises in this way. However, if you habitually read slowly and methodically, you may be better off reading an individual question and then scanning the passage to find its answer. Likewise, in dealing with an extra-long, 800-word reading passage, you may want to try skimming the questions *before* you read the passage to get a sense of what you should be on the lookout for. You have to know your strengths and weaknesses as a reader before you can select the approach that is right for you.

> **The Questions-First Approach**
>
> - As you read each question, be on the lookout for key words, either in the question itself or among the answer choices.
> - Run your eye down the passage, looking for those key words or their synonyms. (That's called *scanning*.)
> - When you spot a key word in a sentence, read that sentence and a couple of sentences around it.
> - Decide whether you can confidently answer the question on the basis of just that part of the passage.
> - Check to see whether your answer is correct.

Use the practice exercises at the end of this chapter to find out whether or not the "questions first" approach works for you. Select an 800-word passage and skim the questions on it. Next, read the passage and answer the questions. Check your answers. Then think over your experience.

- Did you get through the passage and all 12 questions in 15 minutes or less?
- Did you answer a reasonable number of questions correctly?
- Did you feel in control as you started to read the passage, or did you feel as if you had a jumble of question words dancing around in your head?
- Did you feel that skimming the questions in advance slowed you down too much and wasted your time?

Try another 800-word passage, this time reading the passage first, and compare how you did on this passage with your result on the first one. Then decide what's right for you.

In answering questions, don't just settle for the first answer choice that looks good. Read each choice, and compare what it says to the actual words of the passage. When you come to an answer choice that contradicts information in the passage or that doesn't answer the question being asked, cross it out.

Go Back to the Passage to Double-Check Your Answer Choices

When you tackle the questions, *go back to the passage* to verify the answers you chose. Do not rely on your memory alone; above all, do not ignore the passage and just answer questions on the basis of other things you've read. Remember: the questions are asking you about what *this* author has to say about the subject, not about what some other author you once read said about it in another book.

Use the line references in the questions to be sure you've gone back to the correct spot in the passage. Most reading passages on the SAT tend to be long. Fortunately, all the lines are numbered, and the questions often refer you to specific lines in the passage by number. It takes less time to locate a line number than to spot a word or phrase. Use the line numbers to orient yourself in the text.

Tackle Paired Passages One Passage at a Time

If the double-passage section has you worried, relax. It's not that formidable, especially if you deal with it our way. The double reading passage is usually found in a separate section. First you'll see a few lines in italics introducing both passages. Then will come the two passages. Their lines will be numbered as if they were one *enormous* passage: thus, if **Passage 1** ends on line 42, **Passage 2** will begin on line 43. However, they are two separate passages, and you should tackle them one at a time. Remember: the questions are organized sequentially: questions about **Passage 1** will come before questions about **Passage 2**. Therefore, do things in order. *First* read Passage 1; then jump straight to the questions and answer all those based on Passage 1. Most of the time, the Passage 1 questions will immediately follow the excerpts. Once in a great while, one or two questions that refer to both passages will precede the questions about Passage 1. In that case, don't get sidetracked. Skip the questions referring to both passages, and focus on those based on Passage 1. *Next* read Passage 2; then answer all the questions based on Passage 2.

COMMON LITERARY TERMS

allusion	reference to something
analogy	comparison; similarity of functions or properties; likeness
anecdote	short account of an incident (often autobiographical)
antithesis	direct opposite
argumentative	presenting a logical argument
assertion	positive statement; declaration
cite	to refer to; to quote as an authority
euphemism	mild or indirect expression substituted for one felt offensive or harsh (Example: "Downsizing employees" is a euphemism for firing them.)
expository	concerned with explaining ideas, facts, and so on
generalization	simplification; general idea or principle
metaphor	an expression used to suggest a similarity between two things that are not literally equivalent (Example: "He's a tiger!")
narrative (adj.)	relating to telling a story
paradox	statement that contradicts itself (Example: "I always lie.")
rhetorical	relating to the effective use of language
thesis	the central idea in a piece of writing; a point to be defended

Finally, tackle the three or four questions that refer to *both* passages. Go back to both passages as needed.

Passage-Based Reading Exercises

To develop your ability to handle passage-based reading questions, work your way through the following four exercises. Each exercise contains a full test's worth of long reading passages and questions: one 400-word passage followed by 6 questions, one 550-word passage followed by 9 questions, one 800-word passage followed by 12 questions, plus one pair of passages followed by 13 questions. The passages have been taken from published sources—the same sort of sources that are tapped by the makers of the SAT.

Warning: These exercises are graded in difficulty. Although the questions don't necessarily get harder the further you go, the reading passages definitely do. Go all the way. Even if you do less well on Level C than you did on Level A, look on every error as an opportunity to learn. Reread all the passages you found difficult. Review all the vocabulary words that you didn't know. Remember: these passages and questions are *all* comparable to the ones on the SAT.

After completing each exercise, see how many questions you answered correctly. (The correct answers are given on page 146.)

Then *read the answer explanations*.

Level A

You should feel reasonably comfortable interpreting most of the reading passages on this level of difficulty. Consider the reading passages that follow to be a warm-up for the harder excerpts to come.

EXERCISE 1

Read each of the passages below, and then answer the questions that follow the passage. The correct response may be stated outright or merely suggested in the passage.

Questions 1–5 are based on the following passage.

The following passage is taken from a review of a general survey of the natural and physical sciences published in 1964.

"Idle speculation" has no place in science, but "speculation" is its very lifeblood, a well-known physicist believes.

Line　　"The more fundamental and far-reaching a
(5)　scientific theory is, the more speculative it is
likely to be," Dr. Michael W. Ovenden, author
and lecturer at the University of Glasgow,
Scotland, states in his book "Life in the
Universe." Dr. Ovenden says it is erroneous to

(10)　believe that science is only concerned with
"pure facts," for mere accumulation of facts is
a primitive form of science. A mature science
tries to arrange facts in significant patterns to
see relationships between previously unrelated
(15)　aspects of the universe.

　　A theory that does not suggest new ways
of looking at the universe is not likely to make
an important contribution to the development
of science. However, it is also important that
(20)　theories are checked by new experiments and
observations.

Dr. Ovenden discusses recent discoveries in biology, chemistry and physics that give clues to the possibility of life in the solar system (25) and other star systems. He discusses conditions on Mars, Venus, Jupiter and Saturn, and considers whether or not the same conditions may be found on planets of other stars.

Only the planets Venus, Earth, and Mars (30) lie within the temperature zone, about 75,000,000 miles wide, in which life can exist. Venus is covered by a dense layer of clouds which permits no observation of the surface, and the surface temperature of the planet is (35) not known.

Mars is colder than Earth, the average temperature being about minus 40 degrees Fahrenheit, compared with plus 59 degrees Fahrenheit as the average for Earth. However, (40) near the Mars poles during the summer season, temperatures may rise to as much as 70 degrees Fahrenheit, whereas winter temperatures may fall to minus 130 degrees Fahrenheit.

(45) Because of the extreme difference in the Martian seasons, the only life-forms expected to exist, without a built-in temperature control such as warm-blooded animals and humans have, are those which would stay inactive (50) most of the year. These life-forms may be a kind of vegetation that opens its leaves to the sun in the daytime, stores water and closes its leaves in the night for protection against the cold.

(55) Attempts have been made to detect in the spectrum of the dark markings on Mars the absorption lines due to chlorophyll. So far the test has not succeeded. But the infrared spectrum of the Martian markings has been found (60) to be very similar to the spectrum of Earth vegetation when studied at high altitudes.

1. In line 1, "idle" most nearly means

    (A) stationary
    (B) perfect
    (C) empty
    (D) lethargic
    (E) leisurely

2. "Speculation is its [science's] very lifeblood" (line 2) means that scientists must

    (A) fund their research through gambling proceeds
    (B) concern themselves with provable facts
    (C) understand all forms of science
    (D) form opinions about the data they gather
    (E) keep abreast of new developments

3. According to lines 12–15, a mature science

    (A) concerns itself exclusively with gathering and recording facts
    (B) dismisses speculative thinking as overly fanciful
    (C) connects hitherto unlinked phenomena in meaningful ways
    (D) subordinates speculative thought to the accumulation of facts
    (E) differentiates between hypotheses and speculation

4. The similarity from high altitudes between the infrared spectrum of the Martian markings and the Earth spectrum suggests

    (A) the value of speculative thinking
    (B) the absence of chlorophyll on Mars
    (C) a possibility that Mars has vegetation
    (D) that Mars's surface has been cultivated
    (E) the effect of cold on the color of the spectrum

5. The author does all of the following EXCEPT

    (A) make an approximation
    (B) use a metaphor
    (C) state a resemblance
    (D) make a conjecture
    (E) deny a contradiction

Questions 6–15 are based on the following passage.

The following passage is taken from The Souls of Black Folk, *W. E. B. Du Bois's classic study of the African-American's struggle in this country.*

Once upon a time I taught school in the hills of Tennessee, where the broad dark vale of the Mississippi begins to roll and crumple
Line to greet the Alleghanies. I was a Fisk student
(5) then, and all Fisk men thought that Tennessee was theirs alone, and in vacation time they sallied forth in lusty bands to meet the county school-commissioners. Young and happy, I too went, and I shall not soon forget that summer,
(10) seventeen years ago.

First, there was a Teachers' Institute at the county-seat; and there distinguished guests of the superintendent taught the teachers fractions and spelling and other mysteries—white
(15) teachers in the morning, Negroes at night. A picnic now and then, and a supper, and the rough world was softened by laughter and song. I remember how—but I wander.

There came a day when all the teachers
(20) left the Institute and began the hunt for schools. I learn from hearsay (for my mother was mortally afraid of firearms) that the hunting of ducks and bears and men is wonderfully interesting, but I am sure that the man who has
(25) never hunted a country school has something to learn of the pleasures of the chase. I see now the white, hot roads lazily rise and fall and wind before me under the burning July sun; I feel the deep weariness of heart and
(30) limb as ten, eight, six miles stretch relentlessly ahead; I feel my heart sink heavily as I hear again and again, "Got a teacher? Yes." So I walked on and on—horses were too expensive—until I had wandered beyond railways,
(35) beyond stage lines, to a land of "varmints" and rattlesnakes, where the coming of a stranger was an event, and men lived and died in the shadow of one blue hill.

Sprinkled over hill and dale lay cabins and
(40) farmhouses, shut out from the world by the forests and the rolling hills toward the east. There I found at last a little school. Josie told me of it; she was a thin, homely girl of twenty, with a dark-brown face and thick, hard hair. I
(45) had crossed the stream at Watertown, and rested under the great willows; then I had gone to a little cabin where Josie was resting on her way to town. The gaunt farmer made me welcome, and Josie, hearing my errand, told me
(50) anxiously that they wanted a school over the hill; that but once since the war had a teacher been there; that she herself longed to learn—and thus she ran on, talking fast and loud, with much earnestness and energy.

(55) Next morning I crossed the tall, round hill, plunged into the wood, and came out at Josie's home. The father was a quiet, simple soul, calmly ignorant, with no touch of vulgarity. The mother was different—strong, bustling,
(60) and energetic, with a quick, restless tongue, and an ambition to live "like folks." There was a crowd of children. Two growing girls; a shy midget of eight; John, tall, awkward, and eighteen; Jim, younger, quicker, and better-look-
(65) ing; and two babies of indefinite age. Then there was Josie herself. She seemed to be the center of the family: always busy at service, or at home, or berry-picking; a little nervous and inclined to scold, like her mother, yet faithful,
(70) too, like her father. I saw much of this family afterwards, and grew to love them for their honest efforts to be decent and comfortable, and for their knowledge of their own ignorance. There was with them no affectation.
(75) The mother would scold the father for being so "easy"; Josie would roundly berate the boys for carelessness; and all knew that it was a hard thing to dig a living out of a rocky side-hill.

6. The passage as a whole is best characterized as

   (A) an example of the harsh realities of searching for employment
   (B) a description of the achievements of a graduate of a prestigious school
   (C) an analysis of teacher education in a rural setting
   (D) a reminiscence of a memorable time in one man's life
   (E) an illustration of the innocence and gullibility of youth

7. Lines 21–24 suggest that the author had no firsthand knowledge of hunting living creatures because

   (A) he had too much sympathy for the hunter's prey to become a hunter himself
   (B) his studies had left him no time for recreational activities
   (C) small arms weapons had been forbidden in his home
   (D) hunting was an inappropriate activity for teachers
   (E) his mother had once been wounded by a gunshot

8. To the author, his journey through the Tennessee countryside seemed to be all of the following EXCEPT

   (A) gratifying
   (B) interminable
   (C) tiring
   (D) carefree
   (E) discouraging

9. The "stage lines" mentioned by the author in line 35 refer to

   (A) phases of personal growth
   (B) theatrical directions
   (C) horse-drawn transportation
   (D) cultural divisions
   (E) train stations

10. The author sets the word *varmints* in quotation marks (line 35) for which of the following reasons?

    (A) He wishes to indicate he is referring to an authority.
    (B) He is unsure of the correct spelling of the term.
    (C) He recognizes them as hunted creatures.
    (D) He is using the word colloquially.
    (E) He is defining it as a technical term.

11. The author's attitude toward his school-hunting days is predominantly one of

    (A) exasperation
    (B) nostalgia
    (C) bitterness
    (D) self-reproach
    (E) amusement

12. The passage suggests that Josie's interest on meeting the author was

    (A) magnified by her essentially gregarious nature
    (B) sufficiently strong to make her act uncharacteristically
    (C) prompted by her need for distractions on the long road to town
    (D) intensified by her desire to gain an education
    (E) motivated by her longing to escape her impoverished home

13. By saying she wished to live "like folks" (line 61), Josie's mother primarily emphasizes

    (A) apprehension about sinking to the level of mere brutes
    (B) an expanding greed for material possessions
    (C) impatience with people who think themselves too good for their fellows
    (D) a longing for her entire family to better themselves
    (E) an unfortunate inclination toward conformity

14. To the author, Josie appears to

    (A) be far more energetic than her mother
    (B) possess traits of both her parents
    (C) scold her brothers excessively
    (D) look down on her parents for their ignorance
    (E) share her father's calm demeanor

15. The author most likely remembers Josie and her family primarily with feelings of

    (A) measured regret
    (B) grudging condescension
    (C) grateful veneration
    (D) outright curiosity
    (E) distinct affection

Questions 16–27 are based on the following passage.

The book from which the following passage was taken explains architectural methods both past and present.

The ancient Chinese believed that in the features of the natural landscape one could glimpse the mathematically precise order of
Line the universe and all the beneficial and harmful
(5) forces that were harmoniously connected according to the principle of the Tao—the Way. This was not a question of metaphor; the topography did not represent good or evil; it really *was* good or evil. Under these circum-
(10) stances, locating a building in the landscape became a decision of momentous proportions that could affect an individual and his family for generations to come. The result was *feng-shui*, which means "wind and water," and
(15) which was a kind of cosmic surveying tool. Its coherent, scientific practice dates from the Sung dynasty (960–1126), but its roots are much older than that. It was first used to locate grave sites—the Chinese worshiped their
(20) ancestors, who, they believed, influenced the good fortune of their descendants. Eventually it began to be used to locate the homes of the living; and, indeed, the earliest book on *feng-*

shui, published during the Han dynasty (202
(25) B.C.–A.D. 220), was entitled *The Canon of the Dwellings.*

Feng-shui combined an intricate set of related variables that reflected the three great religions of China—Taoism, Buddhism, and
(30) Confucianism. First were the Taoist principles of yang and yin—male and female. The five Buddhist planets corresponded to the five elements, the five directions (north, south, west, east, and center), and the five seasons (the
(35) usual four and midsummer). *Feng-shui* employed the sixty-four epigrams of the *I-Ching*, a classic manual of divination popularized by Confucius, and also made use of the astrological signs: the constellations were
(40) divided into four groups: the Azure Dragon (east), the Black Tortoise (north), the White Tiger (west), and the Red Bird (south).

The first task of the geomancer, who was called *feng-shui hsien sheng*, or "doctor of the
(45) vital force," was to detect the presence of each of these variables in the natural landscape. Hilly ground represented the Dragon; low ground was the Tiger: the ideal was to have the Dragon on the left and the Tiger on the
(50) right (hence, to face south). In a predominantly hilly area, however, a low spot was a good place to build; in flatter terrain, heights were considered lucky. The best site was the junction between the Dragon and the Tiger, which
(55) is why the imperial tombs around Beijing are so beautifully situated, just where the valley floor begins to turn into mountain slopes.

The shape of mountain peaks, the presence of boulders, and the direction of streams
(60) all incorporated meanings that had to be unraveled. Often simple observation did not suffice, and the Chinese had to resort to external aids. The mariner compass was a Chinese invention, but the *feng-shui* compass served a
(65) different purpose. It resembled a large, flat, circular platter. In the center, like the bull's-eye of a dartboard, was a magnetic needle, surrounded by eighteen concentric circles. Each ring represented a different factor and

(70) was inscribed with the constellations, odd and even numbers, the planets and the elements, the seasons, the hexagrams, the signs of the zodiac, the solar orbit, and so on. With the aid of the compass, the geomancer could discover

(75) the existence of these variables even when they were not visible to the naked eye.

It might appear that *feng-shui* made man the victim of fate, but this is not the case. For one thing, there was a moral dimension to the

(80) belief; and to gain the full benefit of an auspiciously placed home, the family itself had to remain honest and upright. Moreover, the geomancer's job was not only to identify bad and good sites but also to advise on how to miti-

(85) gate evil influences or to improve good ones. Trees could be planted to camouflage undesirable views; streams could be rerouted; mounds could be built up or cut down. It is no accident that the greatest Chinese art of all is

(90) gardening.

Many villages in China have a grove of trees or bamboo behind them, and a pond in front. The function of these picturesque features is not as landscaping embellishment, or

(95) at least it is not only that; they are intended to fend off evil influences. The pagodas that can still be seen built on the tops of hills and mounds serve the same purpose. When visiting some recently built farmhouses in the

(100) county of Wuqing, I noticed that the entrances to some of the courtyards were screened by a wall that forced the visitor to wind his way around it, as in a maze or an obstacle course. But the purpose of the *ying-pei*, as the Chinese

(105) walls are called, is not to prevent the passerby from looking in. These are "spirit walls" and are meant to keep out asomatous[1] trespassers. The *ying-pei* is not an isolated superstition, like lucky horseshoes in the West; it too is part

(110) of *feng-shui*.

---

[1]Lacking a body; ghostly; spirit-like.

16. The passage suggests that the ancient Chinese

(A) are not clearly understood by modern-day thinkers
(B) were preoccupied with death
(C) did not understand the basic physical principles that govern the universe
(D) behaved in a peaceful manner
(E) conducted their lives according to a well-defined philosophy

17. As described in the passage, *feng-shui* is a practice that

(A) has spread throughout the world
(B) is used to locate building sites
(C) is widely used near the water's edge
(D) most people consider a foolish superstition
(E) is used to determine the appearance of buildings

18. According to the passage, the Tao apparently

(A) originated about a thousand years ago
(B) is a kind of metaphor
(C) is a way of viewing the world
(D) is a prescription for a happy life
(E) is a moral code that guides human behavior

19. According to the passage, *feng-shui* seems to have developed as a practice mainly because the Chinese believed in

(A) the sayings of Confucius
(B) life after death
(C) astrology
(D) providing for future generations
(E) original sin

20. The best definition of a "geomancer" (line 43) is one who

    (A) knew how to provide spiritual counsel
    (B) understood religion
    (C) could read and interpret the terrain
    (D) guided people in the wilderness
    (E) served as a medium between the living and the dead

21. The principles of *feng-shui* suggest that the best terrain on which to build a house is

    (A) partly flat and partly hilly
    (B) a river valley
    (C) mountainous
    (D) where mountains meet the sea
    (E) rugged with lots of trees

22. The author compares the center of a *feng-shui* compass to the bull's-eye of a dartboard (lines 66 and 67) in order to

    (A) suggest that *feng-shui* is like a game
    (B) clarify the appearance of the compass
    (C) indicate that *feng-shui* requires physical dexterity
    (D) explain that it is extremely difficult to find ideal building sites
    (E) belittle the art of *feng-shui*

23. The author of the passage implies that the city of Beijing was deliberately built

    (A) near mountains
    (B) on a large bay
    (C) at the confluence of two rivers
    (D) to maximize the sun's light and warmth
    (E) close to ancient burial places

24. According to the passage, an ideally situated home

    (A) assures happiness to the family living there
    (B) is no guarantee of good fortune
    (C) empower families to ward off sickness and disease
    (D) helps a family establish financial security
    (E) keeps families together

25. The author calls gardening the "greatest" art in China (line 89) because

    (A) Chinese gardens are usually very beautiful
    (B) the best gardeners in the world come from China
    (C) gardening is a popular pastime in China
    (D) Chinese gardens contain symbolic meanings
    (E) the Chinese know how to grow exotic plants and flowers

26. Which of the following best describes the author's attitude toward *feng-shui*?

    (A) Mild skepticism
    (B) Surprise
    (C) Awe and wonder
    (D) Amused mockery
    (E) Intellectual curiosity

27. To repel evil spirits a family believing in *feng-shui* is likely to pay attention to all of the following EXCEPT

    (A) the distance from their home of large rock formations
    (B) the accessibility of the main entrance
    (C) the placement of trees around the house
    (D) the color of their house
    (E) the appearance of nearby mountains

Questions 28–40 are based on the following pair of passages.

The following passages discuss the problems of being poor in America. The first is an excerpt from a best-selling study of a Puerto Rican family, written by an anthropologist in the 1960s. The second is an excerpt from a speech given at a Florida school in 1965.

Passage 1

Low wages, chronic unemployment and underemployment lead to low income, lack of property ownership, absence of savings,
Line absence of food reserves in the home, and a
(5) chronic shortage of cash. These conditions reduce the possibility of effective participation in the larger economic system. And as a response to these conditions we find in the culture of poverty a high incidence of pawning
(10) personal goods, borrowing from local money-lenders at usurious rates of interest, sponta-neous informal credit devices organized by neighbors, the use of secondhand clothing and furniture, and the pattern of frequent buying of
(15) small quantities of food many times a day as the need arises.

People with a culture of poverty produce very little wealth and receive very little in return. They have a low level of literacy and
(20) education, usually do not belong to labor unions, are not members of political parties, generally do not participate in the national welfare agencies, and make very little use of banks, hospitals, department stores, museums
(25) or art galleries. They have a critical attitude toward some of the basic institutions of the dominant classes, hatred of the police, mis-trust of government and those in high position, and a cynicism which extends even to the
(30) church. This gives the culture of poverty a high potential for protest and for being used in political movements aimed against the exist-ing social order.

People with a culture of poverty are aware
(35) of middle-class values, talk about them and

even claim some of them as their own, but on the whole they do not live by them. Thus it is important to distinguish between what they say and what they do. For example, many will
(40) tell you that marriage by law, by the church, or by both is the ideal form of marriage, but few will marry. To men who have no steady jobs or other sources of income, who do not own property and have no wealth to pass on to their
(45) children, who are present-time oriented and who want to avoid the expense and legal diffi-culties involved in formal marriage and divorce, free unions or consensual marriages make a lot of sense. Women will often turn
(50) down offers of marriage because they feel it ties them down to men who are immature, punishing and generally unreliable. Women feel that consensual union gives them a better break; it gives them some of the freedom and
(55) flexibility that men have. By not giving the fathers of their children legal status as hus-bands, the women have a stronger claim on their children if they decide to leave their men. It [consensual union] also gives women exclu-
(60) sive rights to a house or any other property they may own.

Passage 2

You ask me what is poverty? Listen to me. Here I am, dirty, smelly, and with no "proper" underwear on and with the stench of my rot-
(65) ting teeth near you. I will tell you. Listen to me. Listen without pity. I cannot use your pity. Listen with understanding. Put yourself in my dirty, worn-out ill-fitting shoes, and hear me.

Poverty is getting up every morning from
(70) a dirt- and illness-stained mattress. The sheets have long since been used for diapers. Poverty is living in a smell that never leaves. This is a smell of urine, sour milk, and spoiling food sometimes joined with the strong smell of
(75) long-cooked onions. Onions are cheap. If you have smelled this smell, you did not know how it came. It is the smell of the outdoor privy. It is the smell of young children who cannot walk the long dark way in the night. It
(80) is the smell of the mattresses where years of

"accidents" have happened. It is the smell of
the milk which has gone sour because the
refrigerator long has not worked, and it costs
money to get it fixed. It is the smell of rotting
(85) garbage. I could bury it, but where is the shovel? Shovels cost money.

Poverty is always being tired. I have
always been tired. They told me at the hospital
when the last baby came that I had chronic
(90) anemia caused from poor diet, a bad case of
worms, and that I needed a corrective operation. I listened politely—the poor are always
polite. The poor always listen. They don't say
that there is no money for iron pills, or better
(95) food, or worm medicine. The idea of an operation is frightening and costs so much that, if I
had dared, I would have laughed. . . .

Poverty is looking into a black future.
Your children won't play with my boys. They
(100) will turn to other boys who steal to get what
they want. I can already see them behind the
bars of their prison instead of behind the bars
of my poverty. Or they will turn to the freedom of alcohol or drugs, and find themselves
(105) enslaved. And my daughter? At best, there is
for her a life like mine. . . . Poverty is an acid
that drips on pride until all pride is worn away.
Poverty is a chisel that chips on honor until
honor is worn away. Some of you say that you
(110) would do *something* in my situation, and
maybe you would, for the first week or the
first month, but for year after year after year?

I have come out of my despair to tell you
this. Remember I did not come from another
(115) place or another time. Others like me are all
around you. Look at us with an angry heart,
anger that will help you help me. Anger that
will let you tell of me. The poor are always
silent. Can you be silent too?

28. A defining characteristic of poverty,
according to the author of Passage 1, is
that poor people

(A) lack the imagination to lift themselves
out of poverty
(B) lack the skills to find decent jobs
(C) are constantly in a state of crisis
(D) are somewhat responsible for their
own poverty
(E) are isolated from the mainstream of
society

29. The author of Passage 1 uses the phrase
"culture of poverty" (line 9) to suggest that

(A) causes of poverty have been carefully
studied and analyzed
(B) poor people often take pride in their
poverty
(C) for some people poverty has become a
prevailing way of life
(D) poor people share a common
background
(E) there are several levels and
classifications of poor people

30. By asserting that the culture of poverty
can be used by political movements (lines
30–33), the author is

(A) predicting an uprising by the poor
(B) citing a reason for eliminating poverty
(C) encouraging political movements to
incite rebellions
(D) criticizing the motives of politicians
(E) alluding to a particular historical
event

31. The author's point about the need to
"distinguish between what they [poor
people] say and what they do" (lines
37–39) is meant to suggest that

(A) poor people enjoy being hypocritical
(B) lying is part of the culture of poverty
(C) the poor are often unable to change
the conditions of their lives
(D) the poor are fooling themselves
(E) poverty causes people to have illusions

32. A conclusion to be drawn from the discussion of marriage in Passage 1 is that men and women in the culture of poverty

    (A) avoid legalized marriages for practical and economic reasons
    (B) prefer to be independent
    (C) cannot afford the cost of a marriage license
    (D) do not trust each other to be faithful husbands and wives
    (E) consider themselves unworthy of legal marriage

33. The comparison between the "bars of their prison" and the "bars of my poverty" (lines 102 and 103) is meant to suggest that the speaker believes that

    (A) her sons must choose between a life of crime and a life of poverty
    (B) escaping from poverty is more difficult than escaping from prison
    (C) her sons can escape from poverty but not from prison
    (D) crime results from poverty
    (E) poverty and imprisonment are similar

34. Evidence in Passage 2 suggests that the speaker lives

    (A) on an isolated farm
    (B) in an urban slum
    (C) in a housing project
    (D) in the country
    (E) near a big city

35. The primary emotion conveyed by the speaker in Passage 2 is

    (A) jealousy
    (B) resentment
    (C) discouragement
    (D) hopelessness
    (E) remorse

36. When the speaker says "the poor always listen" (line 93) and "the poor are always silent" (lines 118 and 119) she is implying that poor people

    (A) are more polite than middle-class people are
    (B) cannot express themselves articulately
    (C) prefer to keep to themselves
    (D) suffer from powerlessness
    (E) don't want to antagonize other people

37. The main intent of the speaker in Passage 2 is to

    (A) convey information about poverty to the audience
    (B) enrage the audience
    (C) arouse the audience to action
    (D) define poverty
    (E) describe real differences between the rich and the poor

38. Compared to Passage 1, Passage 2 is more likely to evoke an emotional response from the reader because

    (A) it uses shocking language
    (B) it is written in sentence fragments
    (C) the speaker shows intense emotion
    (D) it repeatedly uses the word *poverty*
    (E) the audience is addressed as "you"

39. In discussing poverty, the authors of both passages seem to agree that poverty

    (A) cannot be clearly defined
    (B) means more than lack of money
    (C) should be viewed with compassion
    (D) cannot be eliminated
    (E) weakens the fabric of society

40. Passage 2 illustrates the contention in Passage 1 that the poor

    (A) suffer from a chronic shortage of cash
    (B) mistrust the government
    (C) have a low level of literacy and education
    (D) rely on neighbors to borrow money
    (E) make little use of banks, hospitals, and department stores

EXERCISE 2

Read each of the passages below, and then answer the questions that follow the passage. The correct response may be stated outright or merely suggested in the passage.

Questions 1–7 are based on the following passage.

The following passage, taken from a memoir by a Japanese-American writer, describes the conflicts she felt as she grew up living in two cultures and trying to meet two very different sets of expectations.

Whenever I succeeded in the *Hakujin* world, my brothers were supportive, whereas Papa would be disdainful, undermined by my
Line obvious capitulation to the ways of the West. I
(5) wanted to be like my Caucasian friends. Not only did I want to look like them, I wanted to act like them. I tried hard to be outgoing and socially aggressive and act confidently, like my girlfriends. At home I was careful not to
(10) show these personality traits to my father. For him it was bad enough that I did not even look Japanese: I was too big, and I walked too assertively. My behavior at home was never calm and serene, but around my father I still
(15) tried to be as Japanese as I could.

As I passed puberty and grew more interested in boys, I soon became aware that an Oriental female evoked a certain kind of interest from males. I was still too young to under-
(20) stand how or why an Oriental female fascinated Caucasian men, and of course, far too young to see then that it was a form of "not seeing." My brothers would warn me, "Don't trust the *Hakujin* boys. They only want one
(25) thing. They'll treat you like a servant and expect you to wait on them hand and foot. They don't even know how to be nice to you." My brothers never dated Caucasian girls. In fact, I never really dated Caucasian boys until
(30) I went to college. In high school, I used to sneak out to dances and parties where I would

meet them. I wouldn't even dare to think what Papa would do if he knew.

What my brothers were saying was that I
(35) should not act toward Caucasian males as I did toward them. I must not "wait on them" or allow them to think I would, because they wouldn't understand. In other words, be a Japanese female around Japanese men and act
(40) as a *Hakujin* around Caucasian men. The double identity within a "double standard" resulted not only in confusion for me of my role, or roles, as a female, but also in who or what I was racially. With the admonitions of my
(45) brothers lurking deep in my consciousness, I would try to be aggressive, assertive and "come on strong" toward Caucasian men. I mustn't let them think I was submissive, passive, and all-giving like Madame Butterfly.
(50) With Asian males I would tone down my natural enthusiasm and settle into patterns instilled in me through the models of my mother and sisters. I was not comfortable in either role.

1. The author's father reacted negatively to her successes in the Caucasian world because

   (A) he wanted her older sisters to be more successful than she was
   (B) his expectations were that she could do even better than he had done
   (C) he realized worldly success alone could not make her happy
   (D) he envied her for having opportunities that he had never known
   (E) he felt her Westernization was costing him his authority over her

2. The author most likely uses the Japanese word *Hakujin* to stand for Caucasians because

   (A) she knows no other word with that meaning
   (B) her brothers insisted that she address white boys in that way
   (C) she enjoys showing off her knowledge of exotic terminology
   (D) that is how her immediate family referred to them
   (E) it is a term that indicates deep respect

3. The father of the author expected her to be

   (A) tranquil and passive
   (B) subservient to Caucasian males
   (C) successful in the *Hakujin* way
   (D) increasingly independent and aggressive
   (E) open about going to school dances

4. By describing the white boys' fascination with Oriental women as "not seeing" (lines 22 and 23), the author primarily wishes to convey that

   (A) the white boys were reluctant to date their Oriental classmates or see them socially
   (B) they had no idea what she was like as an individual human being
   (C) the boys were too shy to look the girls in the eye
   (D) the boys could not see her attractions because she was too large to meet Japanese standards of beauty
   (E) love is nearsighted, if not blind

5. By a "double identity within a 'double standard'" (lines 40 and 41) the author primarily means that

   (A) she had one standard while her brothers had another
   (B) she had one standard while her mother had another
   (C) she was Japanese at home and *Hakujin* outside the home
   (D) she was too assertive at school to be passive at home
   (E) she felt like a double agent, betraying both sides

6. As used in lines 48 and 49, the figure of Madame Butterfly can best be described as

   (A) a model the author sought to emulate
   (B) the pattern the author's brothers wished her to follow
   (C) a particularly generous *Hakujin*
   (D) a role the author eventually found comfortable
   (E) an ethnic stereotype

7. The author's reaction to the roles she was required to adopt was primarily one of

   (A) indifference
   (B) despair
   (C) bemusement
   (D) outrage
   (E) unease

Questions 8–15 are based on the following passage.

The following excerpt is taken from a standard text on the history of Mexican art.

Pre-Spanish history in Mexico is riddled with lacunae or gaps. All that can be stated with certainty is that, quite independent of any
Line European or Oriental influence, peoples
(5) speaking different languages and at various stages of cultural development gradually created a civilization in Mexico which, by the tenth century, already knew the use of certain metals. This civilization has left us temples,
(10) palaces, tombs, ball-courts, images of its gods, ritual masks and funeral urns, mural paintings and codices, jewelry and personal ornaments, pottery for household and religious uses, weapons, and primitive tools. All these do not
(15) belong to the same epoch, style, or culture, but together they form a rich and varied aggregation which is, nevertheless, homogeneous and comparable to Chinese art of the two thousand years from Confucius to the Ming dynasty.
(20) Pre-Spanish art in Mexico served a religious function. It was not content to copy the external world, whose visible forms were for it no more than an outward testimony of great inner forces. It created original compositions,
(25) using real elements with an almost musical freedom. It is not a crude art; they are mistaken who see in its bold simplifications or wayward conceptions an inability to overcome technical difficulties. The ancient Mexican
(30) artist was deliberate and skillful, and, though never led by a merely descriptive aim, he often lingered over his subjects with realistic and minutely observant pleasure. One marvels at his plastic feeling and at his powers of deco-
(35) rative composition.
The Mayas achieved in sculpture a placid and austere beauty of proportion and sensitiveness in modeling which has rarely been surpassed. The works of the Totonacs reveal a
(40) people of keen sensibility and varied means of expression. Their grace and tranquil, formal beauty, their plastic rhythm and interpretation

of psychological values place their makers among the creators of purest art. Aztec works
(45) rival the sober and vigorous solidity of great Egyptian sculpture, which they surpass in human intensity. The colossal statue of Coatlicue shows that equilibrium between a maximum richness of detail and an assertion
(50) of plastic structure which, centuries later, is again to be found in the Mexican baroque.
In its finest works, Mexican sculpture equals the masterpieces of any other period. The plastic feeling of these mysterious people
(55) led them to solutions that are surprising in their modernity. There are Tarascan statuettes that anticipate the essential and drastic simplicity of Brancusi, and Totonac masks that recall the poignant mortality which haunted
(60) Lehmbruck. The reclining figure of Chacmool seems to forecast the lines of "The Mountains" by the English sculptor Henry Moore. The ancient Mexicans tried sculptural caricature also, and even sought to reproduce
(65) color effects plastically . . . These peoples have left us, as Roger Fry affirms, "more masterpieces of pure sculpture than the whole of Mesopotamia, or than the majority of modern European civilizations."

8. In line 1, "riddled" most nearly means

(A) puzzled
(B) questioned
(C) interpreted
(D) sifted
(E) filled

9. The author stresses that our knowledge of pre-Spanish civilization in Mexico is

(A) incomplete
(B) homogeneous
(C) academic
(D) graphic
(E) paradoxical

10. Which of the following statements best expresses the main idea of the passage?

    (A) Religion dominated early Mexican art.
    (B) The artists of ancient Mexico excelled chiefly in decoration.
    (C) Mexican art surpasses European and Asian art.
    (D) Many masterpieces exist among pre-Spanish Mexican art works.
    (E) Modern Mexican art cannot equal pre-Spanish Mexican art.

11. The author implies that distortions in ancient Mexican art were

    (A) reparable
    (B) deliberate
    (C) beautiful
    (D) caused by inferior tools
    (E) inflicted at a later date

12. The statement in lines 33–35 ("One marvels . . . decorative composition") is best interpreted as conveying

    (A) skepticism about the ancient Mexican artist's commitment to decorative art
    (B) distrust of the plastic, synthetic quality of purely decorative art
    (C) perplexity about how the pre-Spanish artist could have achieved his level of technical skill
    (D) admiration for both the artist's technical expertise and artistic sensibility
    (E) a desire to study the origins of Mexican art further

13. In line 38, "modeling" most nearly means

    (A) posing for artists
    (B) imitating the work of others
    (C) displaying fashions
    (D) being good examples
    (E) shaping objects

14. In the last paragraph, the author probably mentions Brancusi, Lehmbruck, and Henry Moore in order to

    (A) prove that he is acquainted with the works of modern artists
    (B) show that their works were influenced by Mexican art
    (C) explain that good art has universal appeal
    (D) add a note of irony to his argument
    (E) relate Mexican art to more familiar works of art

15. It can be inferred from the passage that much of ancient Mexican art depicted

    (A) abstract patterns
    (B) landscapes
    (C) people
    (D) still life
    (E) pure color

Questions 16–27 are based on the following passage.

The following passage is an excerpt from a historical study, done in the 1980s, of the relationship between the press and each American president from George Washington to Ronald Reagan.

In the shifting relationship between the press and the presidency over nearly two centuries, there has remained one primary con-
Line stant—the dissatisfaction of one with the
(5) other. No president has escaped press criticism, and no president has considered himself fairly treated. The record of every administration has been the same, beginning with mutual protestations of goodwill, ending with recrimi-
(10) nations and mistrust.

This is the best proof we could have that the American concept of a free press in a free society is a viable idea, whatever defects the media may have. While the Founding Fathers
(15) and their constituencies did not always agree on the role the press should play, there was a basic

consensus that the newspaper (the only medium of consequence at the time) should be the buffer state between the rulers and the ruled.

(20) The press could be expected to behave like a watchdog, and government at every level, dependent for its existence on the opinions of those it governed, could expect to resent being watched and having its shortcomings, real or

(25) imaginary, exposed to the public view.

Reduced to such simple terms, the relationship of the presidents to the press since George Washington's first term is understandable only as an underlying principle. But this

(30) basic concept has been increasingly complicated by the changing nature of the presidency, by the individual nature of presidents, by the rise of other media, especially television, and by the growing complexity of beliefs

(35) about the function of both press and government.

In surveying nearly two centuries of this relationship, it is wise to keep in mind an axiom of professional historians—that we

(40) should be careful not to view the past in terms of our own times, and make judgments accordingly. Certain parallels often become obvious, to be sure, but to assert what an individual president should or should not have

(45) done, by present standards, is to violate historical context. Historians occasionally castigate each other for this failing, and in the case of press and government, the danger becomes particularly great because the words them-

(50) selves—"press" and "government," even "presidency"—have changed in meaning so much during the past two hundred years.

Recent scholarship, for example, has emphasized that colonial Americans believed

(55) in a free press, but not at all in the sense that we understand it today. Basic to their belief was the understanding, which had prevailed since the invention of the printing press in the fifteenth century, that whoever controlled the

(60) printing press was in the best position to control the minds of men. The press was seen at once as an unprecedented instrument of

power, and the struggle to control it began almost as soon as the Gutenberg (or Mazarin)

(65) Bible appeared at Mainz in 1456, an event which meant that, for the first time, books could be reproduced exactly and, more important, that they could be printed in quantity.

Two primary centers of social and politi-

(70) cal power—the state and the church—stood to benefit most from the invention of the printing press. In the beginning it was mutually advantageous for them to work together; consequently it was no accident that the first

(75) printing press on the North American continent was set up in Mexico City in 1539 by Fray Juan Zumarraga, first Catholic bishop of that country. It gave the church an unprecedented means of advancing conversion, along

(80) with the possibility of consolidating and extending its power, thus providing Catholic Spain with the same territorial advantages that would soon be extended elsewhere in the Americas.

(85) When British colonies were established in North America during the early part of the seventeenth century, it was once again a religious faith, this time Protestant, that brought the first printing press to what is now the

(90) United States. But while colonial printing in Central and South America remained the province of the Catholics for some time and was used primarily for religious purposes, in North America secular publishing became an

(95) adjunct of a church-dominated press almost at once and was soon dominant.

It is part of American mythology that the nation was "cradled in liberty" and that the colonists, seeking religious freedom, immedi-

(100) ately established a free society, but the facts are quite different. The danger of an uncontrolled press to those in power was well expressed by Sir William Berkeley, governor of Virginia, when he wrote home to his superi-

(105) ors in 1671: "I thank God there are no free schools nor printing, and I hope we shall not have these hundred years; for learning has brought disobedience, and heresy, and sects

into the world, and printing has divulged
(110) them, and libels against the best government,
God keep us from both." There are those in
twentieth-century America who would say
"Amen" to Berkeley's view of printing and
"libels against the best government."

16. According to the passage, all American
presidents have experienced

    (A) defects in the quality of their press
    coverage
    (B) goodwill from some reporters in the
    press corps
    (C) alternating periods of antagonism and
    harmony with the press
    (D) hostility between themselves and the
    press
    (E) having untruthful reports published
    about themselves

17. Conflict between the president and the
press indicates that

    (A) the press publishes the truth even
    when it hurts the president
    (B) freedom of the press is alive and well
    in the United States
    (C) presidents have traditionally had little
    respect for the press
    (D) the press is made up mostly of critics
    and cynics
    (E) friendly reporters are rarely assigned
    to cover the president

18. In the early days of the country, the
function of the press was to

    (A) interpret the government's actions for
    the people
    (B) carefully observe and report on the
    work of all elected officials
    (C) serve as a conduit of information
    between the government and the
    people
    (D) preserve, protect, and defend the Bill
    of Rights, especially freedom of the
    press
    (E) mold public opinion

19. Since the early days the relationship
between the president and the press has
been altered by all of the following
EXCEPT

    (A) the president's term of office has
    remained four years
    (B) the position of "Press Secretary" has
    been created
    (C) presidents hold televised news
    conferences
    (D) U.S. presidents are expected to be
    world leaders
    (E) an increasingly large number of news
    people cover the president

20. The author of the passage cautions the
reader about judging presidents of the
distant past because

    (A) press reports of their day cannot be
    trusted
    (B) modern scholars have revised history
    (C) we can't fully grasp the context of the
    past
    (D) second-guessing is unfair to former
    presidents
    (E) history is an imprecise science

21. In colonial America, the phrase "free press" (line 55) meant that

    (A) the same newspapers were published throughout the thirteen colonies
    (B) the press influenced what people thought and did
    (C) aside from the Bible, newspapers were the colonists' favorite reading material
    (D) very few people could afford to own a printing press
    (E) the government was less powerful than the press

22. The assertion that it was "no accident" (line 74) that Juan Zumarraga set up the first printing press in North America means that

    (A) the church refused to allow anyone else to set up a printing press before Zumarraga did
    (B) Zumarraga worked as an agent of the Spanish government
    (C) printing holy bibles raised funds for the church
    (D) the church quickly saw that the printing press could help spread the word of God
    (E) Zumarraga advocated the improvement of the printing press

23. In contrast to printing in South America, printing in North America

    (A) was less politically oriented
    (B) was founded by the Catholic church
    (C) was dominated by religion
    (D) began earlier in the history of the New World
    (E) quickly became less religious in nature

24. In the opening sentence of the final paragraph (lines 97–101), the author seeks primarily to

    (A) define a term
    (B) defend a widely held belief
    (C) correct a misconception
    (D) champion a cause
    (E) pose a question

25. The author refers to Sir William Berkeley as an example of an administrator who

    (A) was concerned for the future of his colony
    (B) was appointed rather than elected to his office
    (C) viewed the press as a tool for spreading heresy
    (D) advocated religious tolerance
    (E) inspired confidence in the press

26. Americans who would say "Amen" to Berkeley's view (lines 112 and 113) are likely to believe

    (A) that limits should be set on freedom of the press
    (B) in the exercise of complete religious freedom for all
    (C) in a *laissez-faire* type of government
    (D) in the separation of church and state
    (E) that extremism in defense of freedom is not justified

27. The passage suggests that issues of a free press

    (A) pertain only to the United States
    (B) have been intertwined with matters concerning the separation of church and state
    (C) still raise controversy in the United States
    (D) are clearly discussed in the Constitution of the United States
    (E) originated during George Washington's administration

Questions 28–40 are based on the following pair of passages.

The following passages are excerpts from the writings of two naturalists with a deep affection for the American wilderness. The first is about the Grand Canyon; the second, about the Sonoran Desert in the state of Arizona.

Passage 1

Those who have long and carefully studied the Grand Canyon of the Colorado do not hesitate for a moment to pronounce it by far the most sublime of all earthly spectacles. If its
(5) sublimity consisted only in its dimensions, it could be sufficiently set forth in a single sentence. It is more than 200 miles long, from 5 to 12 miles wide, and from 5,000 to 6,000 feet deep. There are in the world valleys which
(10) are longer and a few which are deeper. There are valleys flanked by summits loftier than the palisades of the Kaibab. Still the Grand Canyon is the sublimest thing on earth. It is not so alone by virtue of its magnitudes, but
(15) by virtue of the whole—its *ensemble.*

The common notion of a canyon is that of a deep, narrow gash in the earth, with nearly vertical walls, like a great and neatly cut trench. There are hundreds of chasms in the
(20) Plateau Country which answer very well to this notion. Many of them are sunk to frightful depths and are fifty to a hundred miles in length. Some are exceedingly narrow, as the canyons of the forks of the Virgen, where the
(25) overhanging walls shut out the sky. Some are intricately sculptured, and illuminated with brilliant colors; others are picturesque by reason of their bold and striking sculpture. A few of them are most solemn and impressive by
(30) reason of their profundity and the majesty of their walls. But, as a rule, the common canyons are neither grand nor even attractive. Upon first acquaintance they are curious and awaken interest as a new sensation, but they
(35) soon grow tiresome for want of diversity, and become at last mere bores. The impressions they produce are very transient, because of their great simplicity, and the limited range of ideas they present.

(40) It is perhaps in some respects unfortunate that the stupendous pathway of the Colorado River through the Kaibabs was ever called a canyon, for the name identifies it with a baser conception. But the name presents as wide a
(45) range of signification as the word *house.* The log cabin of the rancher, the painted and vine-clad cottage of the mechanic, the home of the millionaire, the places where parliaments assemble, and the grandest temples of
(50) worship are all houses. Yet the contrast between St. Mark's and the rude dwelling of the frontiersman is not greater than that between the chasm of the Colorado and the trenches in the rocks which answer to the ordi-
(55) nary conception of a canyon. So is the chasm an expansion of the simple type of drainage channels peculiar to the Plateau Country. To the conception of its vast proportions must be added some notion of its intricate plan, the
(60) nobility of its architecture, its colossal buttes, its wealth of ornamentation, the splendor of its colors, and its wonderful atmosphere. All of these attributes combine with infinite complexity to produce a whole which at first
(65) bewilders and at length overpowers.

Passage 2

Last Saturday before dusk, the summer's 114 degree heat broke to 79 within an hour. A fury of wind whipped up, pelting houses with dust, debris, and gravel. Then a scatter of rain
(70) came, as a froth of purplish clouds charged across the skies. As the last of the sun's light dissipated, we could see Baboquivari Peak silhouetted on a red horizon, lightning dancing around its head.

(75) The rains came that night—they changed the world.

Crusty dry since April, the desert floor softened under the rain's dance. Near the rain-pocked surface, hundreds of thousands of
(80) bloodroot amaranth are popping off their seedcoats and diving toward light. Barren places will soon be shrouded in a veil of green.

Desert arroyos are running again, muddy water swirling after a head of suds, dung, and
(85) detritus. Where sheetfloods pool, buried animals awake, or new broods hatch. At dawn, dark egg-shaped clouds of flying ants hover over ground, excited in the early morning light.

In newly filled waterholes, spadefoot
(90) toads suddenly congregate. The males bellow. They seek out mates, then latch onto them with their special nuptial pads. The females spew out egg masses into the hot murky water. For two nights, the toad ponds are wild with
(95) chanting while the Western spadefoot's burnt-peanut-like smell looms thick in the air.

A yellow mud turtle crawls out of the drenched bottom of an old adobe borrow pit where he had been buried through the hot dry
(100) spell. He plods a hundred yards over to a floodwater reservoir and dives in. He has no memory of how many days it's been since his last swim, but the pull of the water—*that* is somehow familiar.
(105) This is the time when the Papago Indians of the Sonoran Desert celebrate the coming of the rainy season moons, the *Jujkiabig Mamsad,* and the beginning of a new year.

Fields lying fallow since the harvest of the
(110) winter crop are now ready for another planting. If sown within a month after summer solstice, they can produce a crop quick enough for harvest by the Feast of San Francisco, October 4.

When I went by the Madrugada home in
(115) Little Tucson on Monday, the family was eagerly talking about planting the flashflood field again. At the end of June, Julian wasn't even sure if he would plant this year—no rain yet, too hot to prepare the field, and hardly
(120) any water left in their *charco* catchment basin.

Now, a fortnight later, the pond is nearly filled up to the brim. Runoff has fed into it through four small washes. Sheetfloods have swept across the field surface. Julian imagines
(125) big yellow squash blossoms in his field, just another month or so away. It makes his mouth water.

Once I asked a Papago youngster what the desert smelled like to him. He answered with
(130) little hesitation:

"The desert smells like rain."

His reply is a contradiction in the minds of most people. How could the desert smell like rain, when deserts are, by definition, places
(135) which lack substantial rainfall?

The boy's response was a sort of Papago shorthand. Hearing Papago can be like tasting a delicious fruit, while sensing that the taste comes from a tree with roots too deep to fathom.
(140) The question had triggered a scent—creosote bushes after a storm—their aromatic oils released by the rains. His nose remembered being out in the desert, overtaken: *the desert smells like rain.*

28. Passage 1 indicates that the Grand Canyon is "the sublimest thing on earth" (line 13) because of its

   (A) size
   (B) geologic formations
   (C) mysterious beauty
   (D) overall appearance
   (E) stature among the world's natural wonders

29. Passage 1 implies that visitors to the Grand Canyon are most likely to be

   (A) enthusiastic at first but quick to seek fresh wonders
   (B) astonished by the Grand Canyon's incomparable size
   (C) overwhelmed by the canyon's variety of features
   (D) awestruck by the agelessness of the place
   (E) impressed by the mixture of colors and rock formations

30. The author thinks that the Grand Canyon should not have been called a "canyon" because

    (A) it is far too big for a canyon
    (B) most canyons have vertical walls
    (C) it is made up of several unconnected parts
    (D) the Grand Canyon transcends the common notion of the word
    (E) it was not formed the way most other canyons were

31. One can infer from the passage that St. Mark's (line 51) is

    (A) a large church
    (B) an ornate structure
    (C) an archaeological ruin
    (D) a holy shrine
    (E) a tourist attraction

32. Relating the Grand Canyon to "drainage channels" (lines 56 and 57) helps the author make the point that

    (A) large canyons at one time were very small
    (B) flowing water is necessary in canyon formation
    (C) the Grand Canyon is in a class by itself
    (D) canyons change perpetually in Plateau Country
    (E) the canyons of Plateau Country are unique

33. According to Passage 2, rain showers in the desert

    (A) soak instantly into the earth
    (B) are usually preceded by thunder
    (C) promote the growth of vegetation
    (D) force birds from their nests
    (E) keep the land cool enough for comfortable human habitation

34. In line 72, "dissipated" most nearly means

    (A) squandered
    (B) distributed
    (C) separated
    (D) vanished
    (E) indulged

35. The author's attitude toward the coming of the rains is best described as

    (A) respect for the rains' destructive powers
    (B) awe of their revitalizing effects
    (C) appreciation of the rains' practical utility
    (D) puzzlement at the rains' delayed arrival
    (E) skepticism of their ultimate influence

36. The author of Passage 2 identifies the spadefoot toad by all of the following characteristics EXCEPT

    (A) its relative size
    (B) the time of day it is particularly active
    (C) its manner of propagating offspring
    (D) the sound it makes as its mating call
    (E) its characteristic odor

37. According to the author, the Papago youngster's description of the desert's smell (line 131) would strike most readers as

    (A) incontrovertible
    (B) literal
    (C) tentative
    (D) paradoxical
    (E) hypothetical

38. In contrast to the author of Passage 2, the author of Passage 1 relies almost exclusively on his sense(s) of

    (A) sight and sound
    (B) sight and smell
    (C) sight only
    (D) smell only
    (E) sound only

39. The author of Passage 2 most obviously differs from the author of Passage 1 in that he

   (A) views nature more like a poet than a scientist
   (B) includes information about his personal experiences
   (C) uses figurative language
   (D) is more respectful of nature's wonders
   (E) includes more geological information

40. The two passages differ in that Passage 1 is

   (A) abstract, whereas Passage 2 is concrete
   (B) practical, whereas Passage 2 is speculative
   (C) analytical, whereas Passage 2 is didactic
   (D) cynical, whereas Passage 2 is earnest
   (E) resigned, whereas Passage 2 is argumentative

Level B

Most high school students have some difficulty comprehending reading passages on this level. Consider the reading passages that follow to be a good sample of the mid-range prose excerpts you will face on the SAT.

EXERCISE 1

Read each of the passages below, and then answer the questions that follow the passage. The correct response may be stated outright or merely suggested in the passage.

Questions 1–6 are based on the following passage.

In the following passage, author Peter Matthiessen considers Native American spirituality.

We can no longer pretend—as we did for so long—that Indians are a primitive people: no, they are a traditional people, that is, a
Line "first" or "original" people, a primal people,
(5) the inheritors of a profound and exquisite wisdom distilled by long ages on this earth. The Indian concept of earth and spirit has been patronizingly dismissed as simple hearted "naturalism" or "animism," when in fact it
(10) derives from a holistic vision known to all mystics and great teachers of the most venerated religions of the world.

This universal and profound intuitive knowledge may have come to North America
(15) with the first peoples to arrive from Asia, although Indians say it was the other way around, that the assumption of white historians that a nomadic people made a one-way journey across the Bering Strait from Asia and
(20) down into America, and never attempted to travel the other way, makes little sense. Today most Indians believe that they originated on this continent: at the very least, there was travel in both directions. (In recent years, this the-
(25) ory has been given support by a young anthropologist who, on the basis of stone tools and skull measurements as well as pictographs and cave drawings, goes so far as to suggest that the Cro-Magnon—the first truly modern
(30) men—who came out of nowhere to displace the Neanderthals in Eurasia perhaps 40,000 years ago were a pre-Indian people from North America.) According to the Hopi, runners were sent west across the Bering Strait as
(35) messengers and couriers, and information was exchanged between North America and

Eurasia in very early times, long before European history had begun.

(40) The Old Way—what the Lakota call *wouncage*, "our way of doing"—is very consistent throughout the Indian nations, despite the great variety of cultures. The Indian cannot love the Creator and desecrate the earth, for Indian existence is not separable from Indian (45) religion, which is not separable from the natural world. It is not a matter of "worshiping nature," as anthropologists suggest: to worship nature, one must stand apart from it and call it "nature" or the "human habitat" or "the envi- (50) ronment." For the Indian, there is no separation. Man is an aspect of nature, and nature itself is a manifestation of primordial religion. Even the word "religion" makes an unnecessary separation, and there is no word for it in the (55) Indian tongues. Nature is the "Great Mysterious," the "religion before religion," the profound intuitive apprehension of the true nature of existence attained by sages of all epochs, everywhere on earth: the whole universe is sacred, man is the (60) whole universe, and the religious ceremony is life itself, the miraculous common acts of every day.

1. To the author, the distinction between the words *primitive* and *primal* (lines 2–4) is that

   (A) whereas the former is excessively positive, the latter is neutral in significance
   (B) while the latter is often used metaphorically, the former is not
   (C) the latter reinforces the notion of Indian barbarism that is implicit in the former
   (D) while the former has some negative connotations, the latter has neutral or positive ones
   (E) the former came into common use earlier than the latter did

2. The author most likely used quotation marks around certain words in the last sentence of the first paragraph (lines 6–12) because

   (A) they are quotations from another work
   (B) they are slang
   (C) they come from another language
   (D) he disagrees with their application here
   (E) he wishes to emphasize their appropriateness

3. Which of the following is the most accurate statement about the second paragraph of the passage?

   (A) It develops the idea of the first paragraph.
   (B) It is a digression from the author's argument.
   (C) It provides examples to illustrate the points made in the first paragraph.
   (D) It provides a logical introduction to the third paragraph.
   (E) It is full of totally unsupported assumptions.

4. The author's attitude toward Indian religion is one of

   (A) respect
   (B) idolatry
   (C) condemnation
   (D) pity
   (E) indifference

5. In line 57, "apprehension" most nearly means

   (A) capture
   (B) foreboding
   (C) understanding
   (D) achievement
   (E) approval

6. By calling the common acts of every day miraculous (line 61), Matthiessen is being

    (A) paradoxical
    (B) allusive
    (C) sarcastic
    (D) analytical
    (E) apologetic

Questions 7–15 are based on the following passage.

The following passage, written by a zoological anthropologist, is an excerpt from a field-research study into the organization and behavior of chimpanzee society.

Many primates live in an organized troop in which all ages and both sexes are included, and in which members always move compactly
Line together as a stable social unit. There is a
(5) ranking hierarchy among troop males, although the strictness with which the hierarchy is enforced varies. The ranking relationship is recognized among them and the hierarchy functions to ameliorate conflict. The high-
(10) est-ranking male or males defend, control, and lead the troop; the strong social bond among members and their safety is maintained.

On the other hand, chimpanzees lack a stable social troop. Even members of a region-
(15) al population, who are acquainted with each other, rarely move en masse but move in temporarily formed parties that usually consist of less than ten animals. Such parties maintain associative and friendly contact through their
(20) rich vocal and behavioral communication. Chimpanzee society ensures the free and independent movement of each individual based on highly developed individuality without the restriction of either territoriality or hierarchy.
(25) On the other hand, a chimpanzee enjoys the benefits of group life in that it can avoid the enemy and find fruits with less effort.

Although there is a loose dominant and subordinate relationship among individuals,
(30) chimpanzees are rarely placed under the

restraint of the ranking hierarchy. The rigidly organized troop characteristic of most primates must be an adaptation for avoiding enemies like man and carnivores and for defense
(35) against these enemies. In this context, a group of monkeys is more likely to survive than a single individual. The group provides a social mechanism for survival. Females and young monkeys, especially a female with a baby,
(40) must be protected by others. As their food, fruits, nuts, leaves, and some kinds of insects, is scattered in a wide area in the natural habitat, a dominant animal does not control the entire food source, nor does a subordinate ani-
(45) mal starve when the former is satiated. An important problem in the rigid hierarchical social organization is that each animal must adjust its movements and behaviors to those of the troop. A rigidly organized troop cannot be
(50) maintained when individuals do not subordinate their personal desires for the good of troop unity or solidarity. The flexible social organization of the chimpanzee may be one resolution of this problem. This kind of social
(55) organization may be one of the original factors raising individuality to the level of personality. Chimpanzees have not rejected group life, but they have rejected individual uniformity and the pressure of a dominance hierarchy.
(60) That a number of experienced big males can serve as leader, appropriately coping with critical situations, and that followers can appropriately react to a leader's behavior, prove that chimpanzee society is not a simple
(65) chaotic gathering but a developed society based on highly developed psychological processes and individuality. The identity of fellow chimpanzees is formed in the mind of those chimpanzees who utilize the same range.
(70) The size of the regional population must be restricted by the upper limit of members that an animal can identify and have friendly relations with. Another factor restricting population size must be environmental conditions,
(75) that is, the volume and the distribution of food and shelter and the geophysical condition of the habitat. The latter may influence the mov-

ing pattern, moving range, and the grouping pattern of each individual and group of indi-
(80) viduals. Chimpanzees form regional populations even in continuous habitats such as those found in the Budongo Forest.

7. In many primate troops, the social hierarchy consists of

   (A) females only
   (B) males only
   (C) males of all ages
   (D) females of all ages
   (E) both males and females of all ages

8. According to the passage, primate societies are

   (A) generally unstable
   (B) flexible
   (C) extremely competitive
   (D) dominated by adult males
   (E) frequently in conflict with each other

9. The author believes that primates establish strong bonds within a troop in order to

   (A) protect the members of the troop
   (B) facilitate food-gathering
   (C) establish loyalty to the group
   (D) keep other troops from encroaching on their territory
   (E) teach the youngest members how to survive

10. Unlike other primates, chimpanzees

    (A) are not bound to troops
    (B) lack a strict hierarchy within their troops
    (C) share the raising of their young
    (D) are hostile to chimpanzees from alien populations
    (E) form troops that consist of fewer than ten members

11. The author compares chimpanzees to other primates mainly to emphasize the point that

    (A) chimpanzees are more easily trained than other kinds of monkeys
    (B) great variations in behavior exist among primates of different species
    (C) chimpanzees are different
    (D) all primates have man as their common enemy
    (E) primate behavior is well understood

12. The passage implies that chimpanzees are more human-like than other primates because

    (A) the basic unit of chimpanzee society is the family
    (B) chimpanzees know how to express their emotions
    (C) each chimpanzee has a distinct personality
    (D) chimpanzees learn from their mistakes
    (E) loyalty to the group takes precedence over individuality

13. As described in the passage, the major difference between a rigid and a flexible social structure among primates is

    (A) the ability of each to withstand predators
    (B) the frequency of communication among members
    (C) the distances a member may travel from the main group
    (D) the amount of individual freedom afforded to members
    (E) the relative size of the main group

14. According to the passage, the chimpanzee population in a given area is partly determined by

    (A) dominant chimpanzee males
    (B) the proximity of humans
    (C) predators
    (D) the size of the food supply
    (E) the degree of compatibility between troops of chimpanzees

15. The author cites the Budongo Forest (line 82) as an example of a place where

    (A) chimpanzee troops have distinctive personalities
    (B) troops of chimpanzees have formed a melting pot
    (C) several species of primates coexist
    (D) chimpanzee troops are severely restricted in size
    (E) regional populations of chimpanzees have developed

Questions 16–27 are based on the following passage.

The following passage, taken from a historical study of war, discusses a research project undertaken to determine the real causes of war.

There has been no lack of theories on the cause of war. But we do lack theories that hold up when tested against the facts of history.
Line This deficiency of all existing theories has led
(5) a group of scholars to try to reverse the typical way of arriving at an explanation for war. Instead of coming up with a theory and then looking for the evidence, they have decided to look first at the evidence. Their first undertak-
(10) ing was to collect the most precise information possible about wars, their length, destructiveness, and participants. But before they could do even this they needed careful definitions of terms, so it would be clear which events
(15) belonged in the category of "war," when a state could be considered "participating in a war," what in fact a "state" was, and so on. Like all definitions, theirs were somewhat

arbitrary, but they carefully justified their
(20) choices and, more important, they drew up their definitions first, before arriving at their conclusions so that they could not be accused of defining events in a way that would prove their presuppositions.
(25) After agreeing on definitions, they set out to collect data. Even though they confined themselves to wars fought in the last 150 years, they encountered difficulties in getting precise information on items such as the number of
(30) casualties. Nevertheless, they argue, their results are better than any that preceded them. These basic facts about wars they published in a handbook, *The Wages of War 1865–1965*, edited by two leaders of the project, J. David
(35) Singer and Melvin Small. Even though this is only the beginning of the project, it already provides some answers to questions about wars. You might hear a street corner preacher tell you that the end of the world is at hand,
(40) because the number of wars is increasing just as the Bible prophesies. If you want to check the validity of such an assertion, you could turn to *The Wages of War* and answer the question using the best available data.
(45) The next step in the project is to identify conditions or events that seem to be associated with wars. They are not looking for explanations, but just for correlations, that is, items that usually accompany each other. It is for
(50) this reason that they have named their project "The Correlates of War." Starting with their collection of data on wars, they could examine the hypothesis of Woodrow Wilson that autocracies are the cause of wars. If this were true,
(55) then autocracies would fight other autocracies and democracies might fight autocracies in defense but democracies would never fight democracies. After defining "democracy" in a way that could be measured (for example, the
(60) frequency with which officeholders change office), they would see if any of the wars they had identified in the last 150 years had been fought between two countries clearly identifiable as democracies. If they could find no
(65) such wars, they could say there was a *correla-*

tion between democracy and peace. It would not yet be a *proof* that autocracies cause war. There could be other explanations—the world might contain only one or two democracies.
(70) But a correlation would be an important first step.

The Correlates of War project is just entering this second stage. It will be some time before a full theory appears. Even when the
(75) project does produce a theory of war (if it finds evidence to warrant such a theory), it may not provide the final word on the subject. Any such project must make decisions early in the research, such as what counts as a war and
(80) what does not. These decisions can crucially affect the outcome, even though it might not be evident for a long time that they will. Here is an example of this problem. The Correlates of War project counts the wars fought by
(85) Prussia under Bismarck as three separate wars because each stopped before the next one started. On the other hand, Hitler's belligerent moves against neighboring countries in 1939 and 1940 (Poland, Denmark, Belgium, France,
(90) Norway) are counted as only one war because they took place in rapid succession. If these data are used in specific ways, they could "demonstrate" that Bismarck was more war-like than Hitler. For some purposes this might
(95) be satisfactory but not for others.

Another problem is revealed by this example. Because the Danes capitulated to the Germans in 1940, that encounter is not listed as a war at all. Because the Belgians did resist,
(100) that is counted as part of World War II. But the difference between these two situations was not the willingness of Germany to fight but the willingness of Germany's victim to resist. What is measured, then, is not so much the
(105) willingness of states to go to war (which may be the most important phenomenon to explain) but the willingness of other states to resist aggression. In spite of such objections, however, the Correlates of War project is an
(110) important effort, in many ways superior to earlier studies on the causes of war.

16. The goal of the research project described in the passage is to

    (A) put an end to war once and for all
    (B) develop a superior theory to explain the causes of war
    (C) correct errors in history books about the causes of war
    (D) reverse the method customarily used to study wars
    (E) compare and contrast several important wars

17. Historians participating in the study have devised new research methods because

    (A) evidence becomes harder to find as time goes on
    (B) past assumptions are being challenged by a new, younger generation of historians
    (C) professional historians are divided into two groups—theoreticians and practitioners
    (D) historians continually revise history as new evidence comes to light
    (E) existing theories fail to coincide with facts

18. By calling the scholars' definitions of terms "somewhat arbitrary" (lines 18 and 19), the author of the passage is suggesting that

    (A) the procedures used in the study were sloppy
    (B) the scholars should have used dictionary definitions
    (C) too much effort was wasted on defining terms
    (D) the scholars had no better alternatives
    (E) writing precise definitions was not important to the study

19. In the opening paragraph, the author of the passage commends the researchers for

    (A) not being discouraged by the vast amount of factual information on war
    (B) condemning inadequate theories about the causes of war
    (C) thoroughly surveying all the previous theories about the subject
    (D) defining their terms as objectively as possible
    (E) devising a theory and then supporting it with evidence

20. The author uses the example of the street corner preacher (line 38) in order to make the point that

    (A) many Americans are ignorant about history
    (B) you should not trust the word of people who speak on street corners
    (C) facts speak louder than opinions
    (D) ancient wars described in the Bible were not included in the study
    (E) the Bible is not a reliable source of historical information

21. After collecting factual data about wars, the scholars devoted themselves to studying

    (A) the political and social conditions that have often led to war
    (B) democracies and autocracies
    (C) the effectiveness of wartime propaganda
    (D) the important figures (e.g., Wilson, Hitler) associated with various wars
    (E) what caused the actual outbreak of hostilities

22. The study described in the passage has derived its name, "The Correlates of War," from

    (A) the name of the theory on which the study is based
    (B) a common explanation of the causes of war
    (C) the title of an important book on the subject
    (D) the researchers' expectation that their project involves the collection of data
    (E) the research method used by the participants

23. According to the author, a potential weakness of the study is that

    (A) the limits of the study are not clearly defined
    (B) the correlations may be misinterpreted
    (C) other historians will not accept the findings of the study
    (D) the present study ignores previous studies of the same subject
    (E) most correlations are unreliable

24. The author of the passage implies that research studies like "The Correlates of War"

    (A) are an essential function of the academic world
    (B) add immeasurably to the world's fund of knowledge
    (C) may fail to produce definitive results
    (D) lack the precision of earlier studies of war
    (E) serve as a valuable resource for policy makers

25. The author compares the warlike qualities of Bismarck and of Hitler in order to illustrate that
    (A) researchers generally prove whatever they want
    (B) research design and procedure may invalidate the findings
    (C) "The Correlates of War" project is notorious for its faulty research techniques
    (D) the preliminary findings of "The Correlates of War" project are invalid
    (E) Bismarck was more belligerent than Hitler

26. According to the final paragraph, the author seems to think that "The Correlates of War" project
    (A) is being carried out by hard-working researchers
    (B) is a formidable challenge for the researchers
    (C) has the potential to prevent future wars
    (D) is too flawed to be useful
    (E) is the best of its kind

27. Which pair of adjectives best describes the author's overall feelings about "The Correlates of War" project?
    (A) amazed and astonished
    (B) scornful and cynical
    (C) optimistic and hopeful
    (D) resentful and bitter
    (E) casual and indifferent

Questions 28–40 are based on the following pair of passages.

Pablo Picasso was probably the most influential painter of the twentieth century. In the first passage, written by Picasso himself, the artist explains his views on art. The second passage discusses Cubism, the type of modern art originated by Picasso.

Passage 1

I can hardly understand the importance given to the word *research* in connection with modern painting. In my opinion to search
Line means nothing in painting. To find, is the
(5) thing. Nobody is interested in following a man who, with his eyes fixed on the ground, spends his life looking for the pocketbook that fortune should put in his path. The one who finds something no matter what it might be, even if
(10) his intention were not to search for it, at least arouses our curiosity, if not our admiration.

Among the several sins that I have been accused of committing, none is more false than the one that I have, as the principal objec-
(15) tive in my work, the spirit of research. When I paint, my object is to show what I have found and not what I am looking for. In art intentions are not sufficient and, as we say in Spanish: love must be proved by facts and not by rea-
(20) sons. What one does is what counts and not what one had the intention of doing.

We all know that Art is not truth. Art is a lie that makes us realize truth, at least the truth that is given us to understand. The artist must
(25) know the manner whereby to convince others of the truthfulness of his lies. If he only shows in his work that he has searched, and researched, for the way to put over lies, he would never accomplish anything.
(30) The idea of research has often made painting go astray, and made the artist lose himself in mental lucubrations.[1] Perhaps this has been the principal fault of modern art. The spirit of research had poisoned those who have not
(35) fully understood all the positive and conclusive elements in modern art and has made them

attempt to paint the invisible and, therefore, the unpaintable.

(40) They speak of naturalism in opposition to modern painting. I would like to know if anyone has ever seen a natural work of art. Nature and art, being two different things, cannot be the same thing. Through art we express our conception of what nature is not.

_____

[1]Meditation; study.

Passage 2

(45) Cubism, with Picasso and Braque at its head, rejected the conventional notions of beauty. Discarding the world of perspectives and naturalism, they put in their place a new world obeying only the laws of the artist's
(50) inner vision. Picasso succeeded in freeing the technique of painting from its slavish adherence to the description of nature, and he gave it new laws of harmony and balance. This break with the past had far-reaching conse-
(55) quences. From then on the painter became a free creator, a poet.

Through the break in the wall, poetry crept into painting, with all that is unusual, miraculous, and disturbing. Things around us
(60) which do not seem worthy of the artist's glance, things often considered ugly, were revealed in Picasso's pictures in their most ordinary essence but also in a new, extraordinary significance.

(65) "I put into my pictures all the things I enjoy," said Picasso, and so he does, with his pipe, glass, packet of tobacco, and guitar. He is tireless in seeking to define the forms of these objects and their essential volume, trans-
(70) forming them into poetic images, and treating them freely and naturally as in daily life. In this connection André Breton wrote of Picasso: "It rested with a failure of the will of this man, and what we are concerned about
(75) would have been at least postponed, if not utterly lost." To which Paul Eluard added: "Yes, for this man held in his hands the fragile key to the problem of reality. He sought to see

what he sees, to set vision free, to attain sight.
(80) He achieved this."

Picasso considers art a process that is never completed; he studies the problem that interests him over and over again, from different angles. Thus he does not create pictures in
(85) the conventional, picture-gallery sense of the word; he does not seek, but finds, in the words of the aphorism attributed to him. The elemental side of his talent never allows him to rest content with what he has achieved. He is
(90) always interested exclusively in the present, in the picture on which he is working. "Everything must be done anew, and not just patched up," he says, and these words sum up his programme.

(95) The constant creativity which has no regard for the nature of anything he has painted before gives Picasso the freedom to move at will in the boundless spaces of free expression. It gives him the freedom to draw on all
(100) sources of inspiration for the most varied motifs, opening up all spheres of culture, contemporary, distant, or historic.

Thus this restless, disturbing spirit, one of the most truthful witnesses to the conflict-torn
(105) century we live in, goes again and again into the attack on the gates of the unknown. Each new development in his art does more than merely increase the number of pictures he has painted: it turns against his very work itself,
(110) testing the foundations on which it rests. Picasso confounds his followers and turns inside out the aesthetic principles he himself has just established.

28. To Picasso, the author of Passage 1, the man who spends his life "with his eyes fixed on the ground" (lines 5 and 6) represents artists who

   (A) don't appreciate modern art
   (B) try hard but have no artistic talent
   (C) contemplate their subjects too much before painting
   (D) paint only to make money
   (E) study the works of the great masters

29. The sentence "When I paint, my object is to show what I have found and not what I am looking for" (lines 15–17) is

    (A) a digression from the main point of the passage
    (B) a denial of an accusation
    (C) an explanation of one of "several sins" (line 12)
    (D) a paraphrase of what art critics have said about Picasso
    (E) a false statement that the author intends to disprove

30. The statement "Art is not truth" (line 22) implies that

    (A) artists are liars and are basically untrustworthy
    (B) we should not take art too seriously
    (C) art gives us more than truth; it gives us understanding
    (D) we should be prepared to suspend our disbelief when we view art
    (E) we must accept the idea that truth comes in many forms

31. To Picasso, the most successful art is that which

    (A) shows what the artist has seen
    (B) reveals what the artist has found
    (C) arouses our curiosity but not our admiration
    (D) accurately portrays the subject
    (E) conceals the artist's techniques

32. As used in Passage 1, "naturalism" in art (line 39) refers to

    (A) realism
    (B) a school of contemporary art
    (C) pre-twentieth-century painting
    (D) outdoor paintings
    (E) paintings using colors found only in nature

33. The aspect of Picasso's art that is emphasized in Passage 2 is his

    (A) profundity
    (B) enormous output of work
    (C) innovations
    (D) technical achievement
    (E) appeal to art lovers

34. Passage 2 implies that, before Picasso, artists

    (A) were held back by the social customs of the day
    (B) lacked the technique to portray nature realistically
    (C) were dependent on patrons for success
    (D) adhered to strict rules of art
    (E) restricted their paintings to one acceptable style

35. According to Passage 2, Picasso broke painting tradition in all of the following ways EXCEPT by

    (A) ignoring the need for harmony and balance
    (B) expanding the subject matter of paintings
    (C) throwing out the rules of perspective
    (D) expressing himself more freely
    (E) discarding the need for realistic painting

36. The statement "Everything must be done anew, and not just patched up" (lines 91 and 92) suggests that Picasso believes that

    (A) artists should practice leaving well enough alone
    (B) artists can benefit from their mistakes
    (C) bad pictures need more than just patching up
    (D) spontaneity is lost when artists start tinkering with their pictures
    (E) patching up a picture restricts artists' freedom of expression

37. The author of Passage 2 seems to believe that Picasso is not only an energetic artist but also

    (A) an observer of the politics of his time
    (B) a social revolutionary
    (C) a bold experimenter
    (D) an inspiration to other artists
    (E) an intellectual

38. Eluard's view that Picasso sought to "attain sight" (line 79) coincides with Picasso's statement in Passage 1 that

    (A) "to search means nothing" (lines 3 and 4)
    (B) "my object is to show what I have found" (line 16)
    (C) "what one does is what counts" (line 20)
    (D) "art is a lie" (lines 22 and 23)
    (E) "Nature and art . . . cannot be the same thing" (lines 41–43)

39. Both Passage 1 and Passage 2 describe Picasso as an artist who

    (A) transforms objects into "poetic images" (line 70)
    (B) "does not seek, but finds" (line 86)
    (C) is never "content with what he has achieved" (line 89)
    (D) attacks the "gates of the unknown" (line 106)
    (E) "confounds his followers" (line 111)

40. Compared to Passage 2, Passage 1 is

    (A) less controversial
    (B) more up-to-date
    (C) more argumentative
    (D) more historical
    (E) less rhetorical

Level C

Most high school students have trouble following reading passages at this level of difficulty. Consider the excerpts that follow as a chance for you to acquaint yourself with the toughest prose that occurs on the SAT.

EXERCISE 1

Read each of the passages below, and then answer the questions that follow the passage. The correct response may be stated outright or merely suggested in the passage.

Questions 1–7 are based on the following passage.

The following passage is taken from Cranford, *Elizabeth Gaskell's nineteenth-century novel set in a small English town.*

In the first place, in Cranford all the holders of houses, at least those above a certain rent, are women. If a married couple come to
Line settle in the town, somehow the gentleman
(5) disappears; he is either fairly frightened to

death by being the only man in the Cranford evening parties, or is accounted for by being with his regiment, his ship, or closely engaged in business all the week in the great neighbor-

(10) ing commercial town of Drumble, distant only twenty miles on a railroad. In short, whatever does become of the gentlemen, they are not at Cranford. What could they do if they were there? The surgeon has his round of thirty

(15) miles, and sleeps at Cranford; but every man cannot be a surgeon. For keeping the trim gardens full of choice flowers without a weed to speck them; for frightening away little boys who look wistfully at the said flowers through

(20) the railings; for rushing out at the geese that occasionally venture into the gardens if the gates are left open; for deciding all questions of literature and politics without troubling themselves with unnecessary reasons or argu-

(25) ments; for obtaining clear and correct knowledge of everybody's affairs in the parish; for keeping their neat maid-servants in admirable order; for kindness (somewhat dictatorial) to the poor, and real tender good offices to each

(30) other whenever they are in distress—the ladies of Cranford are quite sufficient. "A man," as one of them observed to me once, "is *so* in the way in the house!" Although the ladies of Cranford know all each other's proceedings,

(35) they are exceedingly indifferent to each other's opinions. Indeed, as each has her own individuality, not to say eccentricity, pretty strongly developed, nothing is so easy as verbal retaliation; but, somehow, goodwill reigns

(40) among them to a considerable degree.

The Cranford ladies have only an occasional little quarrel, spurted out in a few peppery words and angry jerks of the heads; just enough to prevent the even tenor of their lives

(45) from becoming too flat. Their dress is very independent of fashion; as they observe, "What does it signify how we dress here at Cranford, where everybody knows us?" And if they go from home, their reasoning is equally

(50) cogent, "What does it signify how we dress here, where nobody knows us?" The materials of their clothes are, in general, good and plain,

and most of them are nearly as scrupulous as Miss Tyler, of cleanly memory; but I will

(55) answer for it, the last gigot, the last tight and scanty petticoat in wear in England, was seen in Cranford—and seen without a smile.

1. The passage can best be described as

    (A) an argument in favor of the supremacy of women
    (B) a laudatory depiction of a vanishing way of life
    (C) an illustration of the virtues of female independence
    (D) an analysis of the reasons for the dearth of males
    (E) a humorous portrait of the residents of a town

2. According to the passage, the men of Cranford are primarily distinguished by their

    (A) docility
    (B) awkwardness
    (C) absence
    (D) cowardice
    (E) aloofness

3. In line 29, "offices" most likely means

    (A) places of employment
    (B) daily religious ceremonies
    (C) rooms in which household work is performed
    (D) acts done on behalf of others
    (E) positions of authority

4. The narrator's attitude toward the ladies of Cranford is primarily one of

    (A) abiding suspicion
    (B) wistful nostalgia
    (C) bitter sarcasm
    (D) gentle mockery
    (E) fervent enthusiasm

5. The scrupulous Miss Tyler (lines 53 and 54) most likely was noted for her

 (A) chaste behavior
 (B) spotless attire
 (C) wholesome outlook
 (D) precise memory
 (E) humorless disposition

6. Lines 55 and 56 suggest that "the last gigot" is

 (A) a type of covered carriage
 (B) an outmoded article of apparel
 (C) a modish kind of fabric
 (D) a subject too grave to evoke a smile
 (E) a meticulous elderly woman

7. To the narrator, the ladies of Cranford seem to be all of the following EXCEPT

 (A) idiosyncratic
 (B) benevolent
 (C) overbearing
 (D) submissive
 (E) inquisitive

Questions 8–15 are based on the following passage.

The following passage from a 1984 Scientific American *article reveals the ocean depths to be the home of strong, tumultuous currents. This theory challenges the once widely held view of the abyss as "a region as calm as it was dark."*

The notion of a tranquil abyss had been so generally held that many investigators were initially reluctant to accept the evidence for
Line strong currents and storms in the deep sea.
(5) The first argument for the existence of such currents came from theory. Cold water is denser than warm water, and models of ocean circulation showed that the sinking of cold water near the poles should generate strong,
(10) deep and steady currents flowing toward the Equator. Subsequent observations not only confirmed the presence of the deep currents but also disclosed the existence of eddies on the western side of ocean basins that can be

(15) some 300 times as energetic as the mean current. Photographs of the sea floor underlying the deep currents also revealed extensive graded beds indicative of the active transport of sediment. The final evidence for dynamic
(20) activity at great depths came from direct measurements of currents and sediments in the North Atlantic carried out in the HEBBLE[1] program.

Before we describe the HEBBLE find-
(25) ings in some detail let us briefly review the sources and sinks of deep-sea sediments and the forces that activate the global patterns of ocean circulation. The sediments that end up on the ocean floor are of two main types.
(30) One component is the detritus[2] whose source is the weathering of rocks on continents and islands. This detritus, together with decaying vegetable matter from land plants, is carried by rivers to the edge of the continent and out
(35) onto the continental shelf, where it is picked up by marine currents. Once the detritus reaches the edge of the shelf it is carried to the base of the continental rise by gravitational processes. A significant amount of ter-
(40) restrial material is also blown out to sea in subtropical regions by strong desert winds. Every year some 15 billion tons of continental material reaches the outlets of streams and rivers. Most of it is trapped there or on
(45) the continental shelves; only a few billion tons escapes into the deep sea.

The second major component arriving at the sea floor consists of the shells and skeletons of dead microscopic organisms that
(50) flourish and die in the sunlit waters of the top 100 meters of the world's oceans. Such biological material contributes to the total inventory at the bottom about three billion tons per year. Rates of accumulation are
(55) governed by rates of biological productivity, which are controlled in part by surface currents. Where surface currents meet they are said to converge, and where they part they are said to diverge. Zones of divergence of
(60) major water masses allow nutrient-rich deeper water to "outcrop" at the sunlit zone

where photosynthesis and the resulting fixa-
tion of organic carbon take place. Such belts
of high productivity and high rates of accu-
(65) mulation are normally around the major
oceanic fronts (such as the region around the
Antarctic) and along the edges of major
currents (such as the Gulf Stream off New
England and the Kuroshio currents off
(70) Japan). Nutrient-rich water also outcrops in a
zone along the Equator, where there is a
divergence of two major, wind-driven gyres.

_____

[1] Naval research program known as the High-Energy Benthic
Boundary-Layer Experiment.
[2] Debris; fragmented rock particles.

8. The primary purpose of the passage
   is to

   (A) contrast surface currents with marine
       currents
   (B) question the methods of earlier
       investigators
   (C) demonstrate the benefits of the
       HEBBLE program
   (D) describe a replicable laboratory
       experiment
   (E) summarize evidence supporting
       oceanic circulation

9. Which of the following best describes
   the attitude of many scientists when
   they first encountered the theory that
   strong currents are at work in the deeps?

   (A) Somber resignation
   (B) Measured approbation
   (C) Marked skepticism
   (D) Academic detachment
   (E) Active espousal

10. According to the passage, the earliest data
    supporting the idea that the sea depths are
    dynamic rather than placid came from
    theory based on

    (A) underwater photographic surveys
    (B) the activities of the HEBBLE
        program
    (C) analysis of North Atlantic sea-bed
        sediments
    (D) direct measurement of undersea
        currents
    (E) models showing how hot and cold
        water interact

11. The phrase "the weathering of rocks" (line
    31) refers to their

    (A) moisture content
    (B) ability to withstand meteorological
        phenomena
    (C) wearing away from exposure to the
        elements
    (D) gradual hardening into geological
        strata
    (E) rugged foundation

12. As defined in the passage, the second type
    of deep-sea sediment consists of which of
    the following?

    I. Minute particles of rock
    II. Fragmentary shells
    III. Wind-blown soil

    (A) I only
    (B) II only
    (C) I and II only
    (D) I and III only
    (E) I, II, and III

13. This passage most likely would be of
    particular interest to

    (A) navigators of sailing vessels
    (B) students of global weather patterns
    (C) current passengers on ocean liners
    (D) designers of sea-floor structures
    (E) researchers into photosynthesis

14. In the passage the authors do all of the following EXCEPT

    (A) approximate an amount
    (B) refer to a model
    (C) give an example
    (D) propose a solution
    (E) support a theory

15. The style of the passage can best be described as

    (A) oratorical
    (B) epigrammatic
    (C) expository
    (D) digressive
    (E) metaphorical

Questions 16–27 are based on the following passage.

The following passage, written by a university professor, is from a scholarly book describing how international monetary policy contributes to the world's problems.

What is money? That is not so simple a question as might appear. In fact, money can only be defined in terms of the functions it
Line performs—that is, by the need it fulfills. As
(5) Sir Ralph Hawtrey once noted, "Money is one of those concepts which, like a teaspoon or an umbrella, but unlike an earthquake or a buttercup, are definable primarily by the use or purpose which they serve." Money is anything,
(10) regardless of its physical or legal characteristics, that customarily and principally performs certain functions.

Three such functions are usually specified, corresponding to the three basic needs served
(15) by money—the need for a *medium of exchange*, the need for a *unit of account*, and the need for a *store of value*. Most familiar is the first, the function of a medium of exchange, whereby goods and services are
(20) paid for and contractual obligations discharged. In performing this role the key attribute of money is general acceptability in the settlement of debt. The second function of money, that of a unit of account, is to provide
(25) a medium of information—a common denominator or *numeraire* in which goods and services may be valued and debts expressed. In performing this role, money is said to be a "standard of value" or "measure of value" in
(30) valuing goods and services and a "standard of deferred payment" in expressing debts. The third function of money, that of a store of value, is to provide a means of holding wealth.

The development of money was one of the
(35) most important steps in the evolution of human society, comparable, in the words of one writer, "with the domestication of animals, the cultivation of the land, and the harnessing of power." Before money there was
(40) only barter, the archetypical economic transaction, which required an inverse double coincidence of wants in order for exchange to occur. The two parties to any transaction each had to desire what the other was prepared to offer.
(45) This was an obviously inefficient system of exchange, since large amounts of time had to be devoted to the necessary process of search and bargaining. Under even the most elemental circumstances, barter was unlikely to
(50) exhaust all opportunities for advantageous trade:

Bartering is costly in ways too numerous to discuss. Among others, bartering requires an expenditure of time and the
(55) use of specialized skills necessary for judging the commodities that are being exchanged. The more advanced the specialization in production and the more complex the economy, the costlier it will
(60) be to undertake all the transactions necessary to make any given good reach its ultimate user by using barter.

The introduction of generalized exchange intermediaries cut the Gordian knot of barter
(65) by decomposing the single transaction of barter into separate transactions of sale and purchase, thereby obviating the need for a double coincidence of wants. This served to facilitate multilateral exchange; the costs of

(70) transactions reduced, exchange ratios could be more efficiently equated with the demand and supply of goods and services. Consequently, specialization in production was promoted and the advantages of economic division of labor (75) became attainable—all because of the development of money.

The usefulness of money is inversely proportional to the number of currencies in circulation. The greater the number of currencies, (80) the less is any single money able to perform efficiently as a lubricant to improve resource allocation and reduce transactions costs. Diseconomies remain because of the need for multiple price quotations (diminishing the (85) information savings derived from money's role as unit of account) and for frequent currency conversions (diminishing the stability and predictability of purchasing power derived from money's roles as medium of exchange (90) and store of value). In all national societies, there has been a clear historical tendency to limit the number of currencies, and eventually to standardize the domestic money on just a single currency issued and managed by the (95) national authorities. The result has been a minimization of total transaction costs within nation-states.

Between nation-states, however, costs of transactions remain relatively high, because (100) the number of currencies remains high. Does this suggest that global efficiency would be maximized if the number of currencies in the world were minimized? Is this the optimal organizational principle for international mon-(105) etary relations? Not necessarily. It is true that total transactions costs, other things being equal, could be minimized by standardizing on just a single global money. "On the basis of the criterion of maximizing the usefulness of (110) money, we should have a single world currency." But there are other criteria of judgment as well; economic efficiency, as I have indicated, is a multi-variate concept. And we shall soon see that the costs of a single world currency or (115) its equivalent, taking full account of both the microeconomic and macroeconomic dimen-

sions of efficiency, could easily outweigh the single microeconomic benefit of lower transaction costs. As Charles Kindleberger has (120) written: "The case for international money is the general case for money. [But] it may well be that the costs of an international money are so great that the world cannot afford it."

16. The author of the passage asks the reader, "What is money?" in order to

(A) challenge the reader by asking an unanswerable question
(B) make the reader feel uncomfortable
(C) test the reader's intelligence
(D) introduce an unfamiliar definition of the word
(E) feign ignorance

17. The explanation of the three functions of money (lines 13–33)

(A) is a section of a controversial economic theory
(B) is common knowledge among informed people
(C) breaks new ground in economic thinking
(D) is a comprehensive analysis of monetary policy
(E) is valid for only some kinds of money

18. According to the passage, money meets three needs:

I. medium of exchange
II. unit of account
III. store of value

The sticker price of a new car in the dealer's showroom is an example of

(A) II only
(B) III only
(C) I and III
(D) II and III
(E) I and II

19. By calling barter "the archetypical economic transaction," the author is saying that barter

    (A) is obsolete
    (B) is both a theory and a real-life activity
    (C) is a model for economic exchanges
    (D) is a primitive form of exchange
    (E) usually satisfies all the parties involved in a deal

20. According to the passage, the chief shortcoming of barter is that

    (A) making deals is too time-consuming
    (B) three- or four-way deals are virtually impossible
    (C) down payments cannot be used
    (D) neither party to a bartering agreement is ever fully satisfied
    (E) no one could ever make a profit

21. The reference to the "Gordian knot" (line 64) suggests that the author thinks that

    (A) barter was inherently too slow
    (B) it was difficult to change the barter system to a monetary system
    (C) the economist Gordon deserves credit for introducing the monetary system
    (D) most people lack the skill to accurately determine the value of commodities
    (E) barter restricts the free exchange of goods and services

22. Based on the passage, a monetary system has all of the following advantages over barter EXCEPT

    (A) a double coincidence of wants is eliminated
    (B) the cost of doing business is lower
    (C) supply and demand determine the cost of goods and services
    (D) a greater division of labor is possible
    (E) opportunities of profitable trade are reduced

23. The author believes that having a large number of currencies in circulation

    (A) leads to an unstable money supply
    (B) reduces the efficiency of the international economy
    (C) makes international travel more complex
    (D) requires the creation of a central monetary authority
    (E) widens the gap between rich nations and poor nations

24. According to the passage, standardizing the currency of a nation is likely to result in

    (A) a reduction in the cost of monetary transactions
    (B) a short period of inflation
    (C) an increase of money in circulation
    (D) greater confidence in the banking system
    (E) increased international stature

25. By responding "Not necessarily" to the questions posed in lines 100–105, the author is suggesting that

    (A) a solution to the problem is still years away
    (B) advocates of minimizing the number of currencies have no grounds for their viewpoint
    (C) many nations resist the creation of a single world currency
    (D) the most obvious solution may not be the best solution
    (E) the simplest solution is the one that will work

26. To improve the efficiency of the international monetary system, the author supports

    (A) increasing the world's gold supply
    (B) setting limits on the amount of money being exchanged
    (C) lowering tariffs between nations
    (D) creating a single worldwide currency
    (E) reducing transaction costs

27. The author of the passage draws which of the following conclusions about the creation of a worldwide currency?

    (A) It may cause more problems than it will solve.
    (B) Discussing it further is pointless.
    (C) Reducing transaction costs must precede the creation of a worldwide currency.
    (D) Proposals for such a currency must provide for a reduction of transaction costs.
    (E) It is an ideal never to be attained.

Questions 28–40 are based on the following pair of passages.

The following passages discuss This Side of Paradise, *F. Scott Fitzgerald's autobiographical first novel, written when the author was in his early twenties. Both passages are excerpts from essays by literary critics.*

Passage 1

The defects of *This Side of Paradise* should not blind the reader to its importance in Fitzgerald's career. It marked his movement,
Line clumsy and pasted together as the novel often
(5) is, from a clever short-story writer and would-be poet to an ambitious novelist. All his life he was to think of himself primarily as a novelist, to save his best work for his novels, to plunder his published short stories for usable
(10) material for them. If he achieved nothing else in this first novel, he had at least taken his scattered literary effusions and his undescribed experi-

ences, sifted them, shaped and reshaped them, often looked at them ironically, and fashioned
(15) them into a sustained narrative. Compared with the material he took directly from his *Nassau Lit* stories, the writing had improved greatly. In many rewritten passages, *This Side of Paradise* shows Fitzgerald moving to that freshness of
(20) language which became his identifying mark.

The novel took the bold step that Fitzgerald needed: it confirmed his ideas about the importance of his feelings and about his ability to put them down. It helped Fitzgerald thrash out
(25) those "ideas still in riot" that he attributes to Amory [the novel's main character] at the close of the book: his ideas about love and women, about the Church, about his past, about the importance of *being* as contrasted with *doing*.
(30) Though it borrowed heavily from the many writers to whom he was attracted, the book still has Fitzgerald's own stamp: the naiveté and honesty that is part of "the stamp that goes into [each of] my books so that people can read it
(35) blind like Braille." If Amory is not as honest with himself as Fitzgerald's later characters can be, it is chiefly from a lack of perception rather than from a deliberate desire to deceive.

Finally, though Fitzgerald placed his twin
(40) hopes of money and the girl in the book's great success, the book is not merely contrived to achieve these aims. The badness in it is not that of the professional who shrewdly calculates his effects; it is that of the ambitious amateur writer
(45) who produces what seems to him to be witty, fresh, and powerful prose. It is a much better book than *The Romantic Egotist*, the version he finished before he left Princeton. For Fitzgerald at twenty-three, it was the book he wanted to
(50) write, the book he could write, and the book that did get written. Before it even reached its audience, Fitzgerald had found his craft.

Passage 2

It has been said by a celebrated person that to meet F. Scott Fitzgerald is to think of a stu-
(55) pid old woman with whom someone has left a diamond; she is extremely proud of the diamond and shows it to everyone who comes by,

talks in an unrestraint manner

and everyone is surprised that such an ignorant old woman should possess so valuable a jewel;
(60) for in nothing does she appear so inept as in the remarks she makes about the diamond.

The person who invented this simile did not know Fitzgerald very well and can only have seen him, I think, in his more diffident or ~~modest shy~~
(65) uninspired moods. The reader must not suppose that there is any literal truth in the image. Scott Fitzgerald is, in fact, no old woman, but a very good-looking young man, nor is he in the least stupid, but, on the contrary, exhilarat-
(70) ingly clever. Yet there *is* a symbolic truth in the description quoted above; it is true that Fitzgerald has been left with a jewel which he doesn't know quite what to do with. For he has been given imagination without intellectu-
(75) al control of it; he has been given the desire for beauty without an aesthetic ideal; and he ~~beautiful~~ has been given a gift for expression without very many ideas to express.

Consider, for example, the novel—*This*
(80) *Side of Paradise*—with which he founded his reputation. It has almost every fault and deficiency that a novel can possibly have. It is not only highly imitative but it imitates an inferior model. Fitzgerald, when he wrote the book,
(85) was drunk with Compton Mackenzie, and it sounds like an American attempt to rewrite *Sinister Street.* Now, Mackenzie, in spite of his gift for picturesque and comic invention and the capacity for pretty writing that he says he
(90) learned from Keats, lacks both the intellectual force and the emotional imagination to give body and outline to the material which he secretes in such enormous abundance. With the seeds he took from Keats's garden, one of the
(95) best-arranged gardens in England, he enflore-ated [generated flowers] so profusely that he blotted out the path of his own. Michael Fane, the hero of *Sinister Street,* was swamped in the forest of descriptions; he was smothered by
(100) creepers and columbines. From the time he went up to Oxford, his personality began to grow dimmer, and, when he last turned up (in Belgrade) he seemed quite to have lost his identity. As a consequence, Amory Blaine, the

(105) hero of *This Side of Paradise,* had a very poor chance of coherence: Fitzgerald did endow him, to be sure, with a certain emotional life which the phantom Michael Fane lacks; but he was quite as much a wavering quantity in a
(110) phantasmagoria of incident that had no dominating intention to endow it with unity and force. In short, one of the chief weaknesses of *This Side of Paradise* is that it is really not *about* anything: its intellectual and moral con-
(115) tent amounts to little more than a gesture—a gesture of indefinite revolt. The story itself, furthermore, is very immaturely imagined: it is always just verging on the ludicrous. And finally, *This Side of Paradise* is one of the most
(120) illiterate books of any merit ever published (a fault which the publisher's proofreader seems to have made no effort to remedy). Not only is it ornamented with bogus ideas and faked literary references, but it is full of literary words
(125) tossed about with the most reckless inaccuracy.

28. The author of Passage 1 thinks that *This Side of Paradise* demonstrates Fitzgerald's ability to

    (A) compose both long stories and short novels
    (B) write short stories
    (C) include poetic language in his prose
    (D) create an extended tale
    (E) manipulate the reader's emotions

29. The author of Passage 1 believes that Fitzgerald's reputation as a writer rests on

    (A) his original use of words
    (B) his compelling narratives
    (C) the suspensefulness of his plots
    (D) his use of irony
    (E) using bits and pieces to create coherent stories

30. Passage 1 suggests that Amory, the main character of *This Side of Paradise*,

    (A) is a serious and responsible person
    (B) is a thinly disguised version of Fitzgerald
    (C) represents all that Fitzgerald admired
    (D) symbolizes what Fitzgerald wanted to be
    (E) is a composite of people that Fitzgerald knew

31. By hoping that people could read his books "blind like Braille" (lines 34 and 35), Fitzgerald meant that his writing was

    (A) vivid and sensual
    (B) deep and full of meaning
    (C) sophisticated and subtle
    (D) impressive and forceful
    (E) truthful and innocent

32. Throughout Passage 1, the writing of Fitzgerald is characterized as

    (A) egotistical
    (B) immature
    (C) phony
    (D) optimistic
    (E) deceptively easy to read

33. The author of Passage 2 relates the anecdote of the old woman and the diamond in order to

    (A) disturb Fitzgerald's readers
    (B) belittle Fitzgerald as a writer
    (C) clarify a mistaken view of Fitzgerald
    (D) suggest that Fitzgerald is preoccupied with wealth
    (E) explain an aspect of Fitzgerald's personality

34. The author's assertion that "Fitzgerald has been left with a jewel which he doesn't know quite what to do with" (lines 72 and 73) most nearly means that

    (A) Fitzgerald's exceptional talent as a writer needs polishing
    (B) Fitzgerald should take more writing courses
    (C) Fitzgerald's writing needs better editing
    (D) Fitzgerald will probably become a best-selling author
    (E) Fitzgerald is destined to become one of the great American writers

35. According to the author of Passage 2, *Sinister Street* can best be described as

    (A) highly inferior to *This Side of Paradise*
    (B) more engrossing than *This Side of Paradise*
    (C) a pale imitation of *This Side of Paradise*
    (D) an unfortunate model for *This Side of Paradise*
    (E) more realistic than *This Side of Paradise*

36. The author of Passage 2 bases much of his criticism of *Sinister Street* on the grounds that

    (A) the book's hero is sadly overemotional
    (B) its flowery prose overshadows its hero's story
    (C) it deals with a conventional subject
    (D) the book lacks a sense of the picturesque
    (E) the novel will fail to interest most readers

37. *This Side of Paradise* is called "illiterate" (line 120) because it

    (A) is incoherent
    (B) uses slang
    (C) lacks substance
    (D) contains many errors
    (E) is trite

38. The authors of Passage 1 and Passage 2
     agree that *This Side of Paradise*

     (A) suggests that Fitzgerald is a talented
         writer
     (B) is the worst of Fitzgerald's novels
     (C) is a blot on Fitzgerald's career
     (D) should have been rewritten
     (E) will have a wide audience despite its
         flaws

39. According to both Passage 1 and Passage
     2, a major flaw of *This Side of Paradise*
     is its

     (A) one-dimensional characters
     (B) long-winded descriptions
     (C) moralizing
     (D) excessive wordiness
     (E) lack of artistic focus

40. Based on evidence found in Passage 1 and
     Passage 2, when were the two passages
     apparently written?

     (A) Both passages were written at about
         the same time, immediately after the
         publication of *This Side of Paradise*.
     (B) Both passages were written long after
         the publication of *This Side of
         Paradise*.
     (C) Both passages were written sometime
         between the publication of *This Side
         of Paradise* and the publication of
         Fitzgerald's next novel.
     (D) Passage 1 was written long after the
         publication of *This Side of Paradise*;
         Passage 2 was written shortly
         afterward.
     (E) Passage 1 was written shortly after the
         publication of *This Side of Paradise*;
         Passage 2 was written long afterward.

Answers to Passage-Based Reading Exercises

Level A

Exercise 1

1. C	5. E	9. C	13. D	17. B	21. A	25. D	29. C	33. E	37. C
2. D	6. D	10. D	14. B	18. C	22. B	26. E	30. B	34. D	38. C
3. C	7. C	11. B	15. E	19. D	23. A	27. D	31. C	35. D	39. B
4. C	8. D	12. D	16. E	20. C	24. B	28. E	32. A	36. D	40. A

Exercise 2

1. E	5. C	9. A	13. E	17. B	21. B	25. C	29. B	33. C	37. D
2. D	6. E	10. D	14. E	18. B	22. D	26. A	30. D	34. D	38. C
3. A	7. E	11. B	15. C	19. A	23. E	27. C	31. B	35. B	39. B
4. B	8. E	12. D	16. D	20. C	24. C	28. D	32. A	36. A	40. A

Level B

Exercise 1

1. D	5. C	9. A	13. D	17. E	21. A	25. B	29. B	33. C	37. C
2. D	6. A	10. A	14. D	18. D	22. E	26. E	30. C	34. D	38. B
3. B	7. B	11. C	15. E	19. D	23. B	27. C	31. B	35. A	39. B
4. A	8. D	12. C	16. B	20. C	24. C	28. C	32. A	36. E	40. C

Level C

Exercise 1

1. E	5. B	9. C	13. D	17. B	21. B	25. D	29. A	33. C	37. D
2. C	6. B	10. E	14. D	18. A	22. E	26. E	30. B	34. A	38. A
3. D	7. D	11. C	15. C	19. C	23. B	27. A	31. E	35. D	39. E
4. D	8. E	12. B	16. D	20. A	24. A	28. D	32. B	36. B	40. D

Answer Explanations

Level A

Exercise 1

1. (**C**) Ovenden clearly approves of speculation (pondering; evolving theories by taking a fresh look at a subject or concept). However, he approves of purposeful speculation, speculation that has as its goal the discovery of new ways of looking at the universe. Pointless, idle, *empty* speculation or woolgathering he finds unscientific.

2. (**D**) By asserting that "Speculation is its [science's] very lifeblood," Ovenden says that science cannot exist without speculation. Scientists must speculate, must evolve theories, must *form opinions about the data they gather*.

3. (**C**) A mature science tries "to see relationships between previously unrelated aspects of the universe," that is, to *connect hitherto unlinked phenomena in* significant patterns or *meaningful ways*.

4. (**C**) The similarities of the spectrums suggest the *possibility of vegetation* on Mars.

5. (**E**) Use the process of elimination to find the correct answer to this question.

    • The author *makes an approximation*: he indicates the temperature zone in which life can exist is "about [*approximately*] 75,000,000 miles wide." Therefore, you can eliminate (A).

    • The author *uses a metaphor*: he implicitly compares speculation to blood. Therefore, you can eliminate (B).

    • The author *states a resemblance*: in the last sentence of the passage, he says "the infrared spectrum of the Martian markings has been found to be very similar to the spectrum of Earth vegetation." Therefore, you can eliminate (C).

    • The author *makes a conjecture* about the sort of life-forms "without a built-in temperature control" that might exist on Mars: in the last sentence of the next-to-last paragraph, he conjectures (guesses; speculates) they "may be a form of vegetation" that closes its leaves at night. Therefore, you can eliminate (D).

    • Only (E) is left. At no time does the author *deny a contradiction*. The correct answer is (E).

6. (**D**) As the comment "I shall not soon forget that summer" (line 9) suggests, in this passage Du Bois shares his memories or *reminiscences* of what was *a memorable time* in his life.

7. (**C**) To "learn from hearsay" is to learn not from one's own personal experience but from the comments of others. Why did Du Bois have to learn about hunting from hearsay and not from experiences? The comment in parentheses suggests the reason: his mother was terrified of guns. Therefore, we can assume that he had no chance to learn about hunting because *small arms weapons had been forbidden in his home*.

8. (**D**) Use the process of elimination to answer this question.

    • Is Du Bois's journey through the countryside *gratifying* to him? Yes; he enjoys "the pleasures of the chase." Therefore, you can eliminate (A).

- Does his journey seem *interminable* to him? Yes; the "miles stretch relentlessly ahead," never letting up. Therefore, you can eliminate (B).
- Is his journey *tiring* to him? Yes; he feels "deep weariness of heart and limb." Therefore, you can eliminate (C).
- Does his hunt for a school feel *discouraging* to him? Yes; he feels "his heart sink heavily" as he hears there is no job opening. Therefore, you can eliminate (E).
- Is his journey a *carefree* one? No; throughout his journey he has the ongoing anxiety about when and where he will find a job. The correct answer is (D).

9. **(C)** Note the context in which "stage lines" appears. Du Bois has "wandered beyond railways, beyond stage lines" to the back country. The parallel structure suggests that stage lines, like railways, has to do with *transportation*, in this case with the *horse-drawn* form of transportation that took over when travelers went beyond the railroad's extent.

10. **(D)** To indicate he finds himself way out in the back country, Du Bois adopts a *colloquial*, down-home manner of speech. For example, he refers to pests or vermin as *varmints*, a term he would not customarily use.

11. **(B)** Looking back on those memorable "pleasures of the chase" (line 26), Du Bois clearly feels *nostalgia* for days gone by.

12. **(D)** Immediately on learning why Du Bois is in the vicinity, Josie "anxiously," eagerly tells him all about a potential school, stressing how "she herself longed to learn." Living in the backwoods, Josie would have been interested in meeting any stranger. However, her interest in meeting this stranger was increased when she learned his errand; that is, it was *intensified by her desire to gain an education.*

13. **(D)** Making "honest efforts to be decent and comfortable," scolding her husband and children if they do not work to improve their lot and live "like folks," Josie's mother shows her *longing for her entire family to better themselves.*

14. **(B)** According to the author, Josie was both "a little nervous and inclined to scold, like her mother" (lines 68–69) and "faithful . . . like her father (lines 69–70). Thus, she *possessed traits of both her parents.* Choice A is incorrect: the author describes both Josie and her mother as energetic; he does not portray Josie as more energetic than her mother. Choice C is incorrect: although the author comments on Josie's scolding her brothers, he does not indicate that she does so excessively. Choice D is incorrect: although Josie longs to learn, nothing in the passage suggests she looks down on her parents because they are ignorant. Choice E is incorrect: Josie's father is calm; she, in contrast, is "a little nervous and inclined to scold."

15. **(E)** The author "grew to love" this family. Clearly, he regards them with *distinct affection.*

16. **(E)** The ancient Chinese view of life is described in the opening lines of the passage. People believed in the "mathematically precise order of the universe" and in the "forces that were harmoniously connected." In other words, life was structured *according to a well-defined philosophy.*

17. **(B)** By defining *feng-shui* as a "kind of cosmic surveying tool" (line 15), the author is saying that it *is used to locate building sites.*

18. **(C)** As described in lines 1–9 of the passage, the Tao *is a way of viewing the world.*

19. **(D)** The main reason for the development of *feng-shui* is to "affect an individual and his family for generations to come" (lines 12 and 13). Evidently, the Chinese believed in *providing for future generations.*

20. **(C)** The function of a geomancer, according to lines 43–46, was to *read and interpret the terrain.*

21. **(A)** According to lines 47–57, the best building sites were located between the Dragon (hilly ground) and the Tiger (low ground), that is, on terrain that is *partly flat and partly hilly.*

22. **(B)** Because the *feng-shui* compass is an elaborate instrument with a complicated design, the author compares its center to the bull's-eye of a familiar dartboard in order to *clarify its appearance* for the reader.

23. **(A)** Lines 54–57 of the passage describe the setting of Beijing. The city is located where the valley floor begins to slope upward to the *mountains.*

24. **(B)** The use of *feng-shui* in selecting a homesite is intended to protect the residents from misfortune. However, the family, according to lines 77–83, must also be moral and upright because an ideally situated home *is no guarantee of good fortune.*

25. **(D)** Believers in *feng-shui* attentively care for the gardens surrounding their homes, since the various features of the gardens contribute to the well-being of the home and *contain symbolic meanings.*

26. **(E)** The author describes *feng-shui* objectively, as though the concept has aroused his *intellectual curiosity.*

27. **(D)** Adherents of *feng-shui* heed the presence of boulders (lines 58 and 59), design proper access to the main entrance of the house (lines 100–108), consider the placement of trees (line 86) and the shape of nearby mountains (line 58). Only *the color of the house* is not mentioned.

28. **(E)** The passage states that the condition of poor people reduces the "possibility of . . . participation in the larger economic system," made up, for example, of labor unions, political parties, and welfare agencies. Nonparticipation *isolates* the poor *from the mainstream of society.*

29. **(C)** A "culture" may be defined as a group of people sharing a specific set of beliefs and values, customs, and traditions. The phrase "culture of poverty," therefore, signifies a group for whom poverty *has become a prevailing way of life.*

30. **(B)** By pointing out that the potential for protest and for being used in political movements resides in the culture of poverty, the author is indirectly citing *a reason for eliminating poverty* from our society.

31. **(C)** People in the culture of poverty, despite their intentions, cannot live up to the middle-class values they espouse mainly because they are *unable to change the conditions of their lives* as much as they may wish to.

32. **(A)** The discussion of marriage contains several *practical and economic* reasons why poor men and women avoid legal marriages. Men, for one, don't want "expense and legal difficulties." Women want to maintain "exclusive rights to a house or any other property."

33. **(E)** The metaphor suggests the similarity between *poverty and imprisonment.*

34. **(D)** Because the speaker talks about the smell of the outdoor privy and about burying the garbage in the ground, she appears to live *in the country*. However, she worries about her sons being influenced by bad companions. Thus, she is unlikely to live on an isolated farm (where her sons would not have other boys living nearby to influence them).

35. **(D)** Although all the listed emotions are evident in the passage, *hopelessness* and despair are prevalent. Near the end, the speaker actually says, "I have come out of my despair to tell you this."

36. **(D)** The silence of the poor reaffirms their sense of despair. They feel *powerless* to alter their condition. Therefore, they listen but don't say anything.

37. **(C)** The last paragraph summarizes the speaker's intent—to *arouse the audience into action:* "Look at us with an angry heart, anger that will help you help me."

38. **(C)** Each of the choices describes Passage 2. The quality of the passage to which the audience is most likely to respond, however, is that the speaker herself *shows intense emotion.*

39. **(B)** Both authors show that poverty *means more than lack of money.* Passage 1 stresses the whole "culture of poverty." Passage 2 highlights the smells, the weariness, and the hopelessness that accompany poverty.

40. **(A)** The speaker in Passage 2 says she has had no money to fix the refrigerator, to buy a shovel, to purchase iron pills, and so forth. Each of these examples indicate a *chronic shortage of cash.*

Exercise 2

1. **(E)** Her father scorned her successes in the world outside the home because he felt "undermined by" her clear surrender or "capitulation to the ways of the West." She had given in to Western ways, disobeying his wishes. Thus, *he felt her Westernization was costing him his authority over her.*

2. **(D)** In her Japanese home, *her immediate family* (including her Westernized brothers) customarily *referred to* Caucasians by using the Japanese term *Hakujin.* In explaining the conflicts she experienced as someone caught between two cultures, she uses the Japanese term for its authenticity.

3. **(A)** The author was careful not to show her aggressiveness and assertiveness to her father because these traits were unacceptable to him. Rather, he expected his daughter to be *tranquil* (calm; serene) *and passive* (submissive; not initiating action).

4. **(B)** "Not seeing" refers to the white boys' inability to see the author as she truly was. Instead of seeing the actual Japanese-American adolescent girl, with her worries about fitting in with her friends and her embarrassment about her father's conservatism, they saw a stereotypical Oriental *geisha,* someone straight out of a paperback fantasy. Clearly, *they had no idea what she was like as an individual human being.*

5. **(C)** The term "double standard" generally refers to male-female roles, and to the different expectations society has for male and female behavior. In referring to her "double identity within a 'double standard,'" the author indicates that she was *Japanese at home* and Hakujin *outside the home.*

6. **(E)** *Madame Butterfly*, the heroine of the opera of that name, is a classic example of submissive, obedient Japanese womanhood. Thus, over the years, she has grown from a simple literary figure to become (like Stowe's Uncle Tom or Puzo's Godfather) *an ethnic stereotype.*

7. **(E)** The last sentence of the passage states that the author "was not comfortable in either role" she had to play. In other words, her reaction to these roles was primarily one of discomfort or *unease.*

8. **(E)** To be riddled with lacunae (that is, gaps or holes) is to be permeated with holes, *filled* with holes, the way a sieve is full of holes.

9. **(A)** There are major gaps in our knowledge of pre-Spanish history in Mexico. Thus, our knowledge is *incomplete.*

10. **(D)** Use the process of elimination to answer this question.

   - While the passage states art in the period "served a religious function," the passage stresses the art itself, not the religious basis for the art. Therefore, you can eliminate (A).
   - Though the early Mexican artists excelled in decorative composition, they created sculptures that went far beyond mere decoration. Therefore, you can eliminate (B).
   - The author states that Mexican art "is comparable to" great Chinese art, rivals Egyptian art, foreshadows modern European art. He does not say it exceeds or surpasses European and Asian art. Therefore, you can eliminate (C).
   - The author never discusses modern Mexican art. Therefore, you can eliminate (E).
   - Throughout the passage, particularly in the final two paragraphs, the author cites masterpiece after masterpiece of pre-Spanish Mexican art. The correct answer is (D).

11. **(B)** The author insists that the "bold simplifications or wayward conceptions" of early Mexican art were the result of creative decisions made by skilled artists and not the unfortunate consequences of sloppy technique. Thus, these supposed distortions were *deliberate* (intentional).

12. **(D)** In marveling at the artist's plastic feeling, the author is awed by the sculptor's feel for carving and shaping works of art. In other words, the author feels *admiration for both the artist's technical expertise and artistic sensibility.*

13. **(E)** The passage is discussing the Mexican artists' gift for sculpture, for fashioning or *shaping objects* into works or art. That is the sense in which "modeling" is used here.

14. **(E)** The author refers to the "surprising . . . modernity" of early Mexican sculpture. He indicates these works "anticipate" more modern, and therefore *more familiar* to the reader, works by Brancusi, Lehmbruck, and Moore.

15. **(C)** The emphasis on sculpture (masks, reclining figures, statuettes) suggests that much of Mexican art depicted *people.*

16. **(D)** The first paragraph of the passage says that the administration of every president has ended with "recriminations and mistrust." Presidents, like everyone else, hate to be criticized in public. Therefore, they all have experienced *hostility between themselves and the press.*

17. **(B)** Conflict between the president and the press is the "best proof" (line 11) that *freedom of the press is alive and well in the United States.*

18. **(B)** In the days of the Founding Fathers, there was an expectation that the press would act "like a watchdog" (lines 20 and 21) that would *carefully observe and report on the work of all elected officials.*

19. **(A)** The relationship between the press and the presidency has become increasingly complicated by changes in the nature of the presidency (lines 26–36), including the creation of the position of Press Secretary and the fact that the president is a world leader. The press itself now includes television, and reporters from all over the world cover the president. What hasn't altered the relationship between the press and the president is the fact that *the president's term of office has remained four years.*

20. **(C)** The author advises the reader (lines 40 and 41) "not to view the past in terms of our own times" because to do so violates the historical context. In other words, *we can't fully grasp the context of the past.*

21. **(B)** Basic to the beliefs of the colonists was that "whoever controlled the printing press was in the best position to control the minds of men" (lines 59–61), which meant that *the press influenced what people thought and did.*

22. **(D)** Early on, both the church and the state realized the power inherent in the printing press. It was to their mutual advantage to have a printing press set up in South America as quickly as possible. Using the printing press, the state gained control of territory, and the church *spread the word of God.*

23. **(E)** The passage says that in North America secular publishing "was soon dominant" (line 96). In other words, printing *quickly became less religious in nature.*

24. **(C)** The opening sentence of the final paragraph concludes with the clause "but the facts are quite different." Many Americans believe that the colonists immediately established a free society. The author says that this belief is incorrect. Thus, he is trying to *correct a misconception* or mistaken idea.

25. **(C)** The quotation by Berkeley suggests that the governor of Virginia took a dim view of antiestablishment activities, including printing anything that criticized the church. Evidently, he *viewed the press as a tool for spreading heresy.*

26. **(A)** Those who agree with Berkeley would support his general view *that limits should be set on freedom of the press.*

27. **(C)** The passage says that some twentieth-century people agree with Berkeley's sentiments about the free press. Issues of free press, even today *raise controversy in the United States.*

28. **(D)** In the last sentence of the first paragraph the author explains why the Grand Canyon is the "sublimest thing on earth." It is sublime "by virtue of the whole—its *ensemble,*" or its *overall appearance.*

29. **(B)** The first paragraph implies that the *Grand Canyon's incomparable size* is what is likely to impress a visitor. Only after long and careful study do observers begin to understand that the canyon has more to offer than magnitude. The distinctive quality of its overall appearance—its *ensemble,* in the author's words—lends it majesty.

30. **(D)** Lines 16–39 explain the author's view that *the Grand Canyon transcends the common notion of the word* canyon. The Grand Canyon is markedly different from other places we call *canyons.*

31. **(B)** To heighten the contrast between the Grand Canyon and ordinary canyons, the author makes a contrast between St. Mark's and a "rude (that is, crude)

dwelling" on the frontier. Since a frontier dwelling is apt to be primitive and unadorned, this suggests that St. Mark's must be a refined, *ornate structure.*

32. (**A**) The passage calls the Grand Canyon an "expansion of the simple type of drainage channels peculiar to Plateau Country," implying that *large canyons at one time were very small.* Earlier in the passage the author cited the example of a huge building. It, too, is an expansion—an enlargement of a small house.

33. (**C**) As described in the third paragraph, the rain *promotes the growth of vegetation,* described as "a veil of green." The rain also prepares the ground "for another planting."

34. (**D**) The last of the sun's light dissipates or *vanishes* as darkness falls.

35. (**B**) To the author, the coming of the rains changes the world, transforming the desert into a *revitalized* landscape filled with creatures mating and giving birth. This transformation fills him with *awe.*

36. (**A**) Several distinctive qualities of the spadefoot toad are mentioned. The toads chant throughout the night. The female toads "spew out egg masses" as they reproduce. The male toads "bellow," in their characteristic mating call, and their "burnt-peanut-like" odor fills the air. Only the *relative size* of the toad is not mentioned in the passage.

37. (**D**) To most people, the youngster's reply "is a contradiction." In other words, it seems *paradoxical* to them that a desert could smell like rain.

38. (**C**) In describing the Grand Canyon, the author uses only his sense of *sight.*

39. (**B**) The author of Passage 2 writes in the first person. He recounts his *personal experiences* with rainshowers, with toads and turtles, and with members of the Papago tribe. The author of Passage 1, on the other hand, while equally passionate about his subject, removes himself from the writing. Both authors write poetically, using figures of speech, and both respect nature's wonders. The author of Passage 2 clearly includes far less geological data than does the author of Passage 1.

40. (**A**) Except for the facts and figures of the first paragraph, Passage 1 lacks the *concrete* details of Passage 2. The author of Passage 1 writes in more *abstract* language about the nature of canyons and the uniqueness of the Grand Canyon. Passage 2, in contrast, is filled with specific down-to-earth images of the sights and sounds of the desert, from the "veil of green" of nascent vegetation to the incessant chanting of the spadefoot toads.

Level B

Exercise 1

1. (**D**) To pretend that Indians are a primitive people is to choose to see them as unlettered and barbaric. To view them as a "first" or primal people is to choose to see them as linked to ancient truths. Thus, to the author, the distinction between "primitive" and "primal" is that, *while the former has some negative connotations, the latter has neutral or positive ones.*

2. (**D**) Matthiessen rejects those who would patronizingly dismiss Indian spirituality as simple hearted (or simpleminded) in any way. Thus, he puts *animism* and *naturalism* in quotes because *he disagrees with their being applied* to something as profound as the Indian concept of earth and spirit.

3. **(B)** In the first and third paragraphs, Matthiessen is making assertions about the nature of Indian spirituality. In the second paragraph, however, he moves away from the subject of religion to exploring various theories of Indian origins in North America. Thus, the second paragraph is a *digression from the argument* made in the opening and closing paragraphs of the passage.

4. **(A)** Refusing to adopt a patronizing or condescending attitude toward Indian religion, comparing it to the most venerated or revered religions of the world, Matthiessen clearly views Indian religion with *respect.*

   (B) is incorrect. Though Matthiessen has great respect for Indian religion, his attachment to it is not so immoderate as to be termed *idolatry* (giving absolute religious devotion to something that is not actually God, for example, a physical object or man-made image).

5. **(C)** Sages in their wisdom *understand* or apprehend the universe's true nature.

6. **(A)** A miracle is by definition an act or event so extraordinary that it seems a manifestation of God's supernatural power. Thus, to call the ordinary, common acts of every day miraculous is to be self-contradictory or *paradoxical.*

7. **(B)** Lines 4 and 5 of the passage say that the hierarchy consists of the troop's *males.*

8. **(D)** Lines 9–11 of the passage say that, in primate troops, males "defend, control, and lead the troop." Therefore, the troops are *dominated by adult males.*

9. **(A)** The passage says that the strong social bond in the troop is maintained for safety (line 12). Therefore, it is meant to *protect the members of the troop.*

10. **(A)** According to lines 13 and 14, "chimpanzees lack a stable social troop." Rather, they form temporary groups (lines 16 and 17). Therefore, unlike other primates, chimpanzees *are not bound to troops.*

11. **(C)** The second paragraph of the passage contrasts the social organization of chimpanzees and the social organization of other primates. Clearly, *chimpanzees are different.*

12. **(C)** The discussion of chimpanzee social organization (lines 21–24) implies that each chimpanzee develops *a distinct personality.*

13. **(D)** The two social structures differ markedly in *the amount of individual freedom afforded to members.* In a rigidly hierarchical society, individuals must adjust their behaviors to those of the troop. In a flexible society, individuals have more freedom to follow their personal desires.

14. **(D)** Population size, according to lines 72–76, is partly controlled by *the size of the food supply.*

15. **(E)** The Budongo Forest is called a "continuous habitat" (lines 80 and 81) in which several *regional populations of chimpanzees have developed.*

16. **(B)** The opening paragraph of the passage describes the goal of the project. The project's objective is not to use a new research method but to use a different technique in order to *develop a superior theory to explain the causes of war.*

17. **(E)** The reason given in lines 2–6 for reversing the customary research method is that *existing theories fail to coincide with facts.*

18. **(D)** Although the phrase has a negative ring, the author explains that all definitions are "somewhat arbitrary." Therefore, *the scholars had no better alternatives.*

19. **(D)** The author takes pains to describe the care with which the researchers defined the terms of the study. Of particular note is that the researchers drew

up their definitions "before arriving at their conclusions" (lines 21 and 22) so that they would not define events in a way to support their hypotheses. Instead, they defined their terms as objectively as possible.

20. **(C)** By looking up the assertions of the street corner preacher in *The Wages of War*, one can check the facts. Ultimately, the author is suggesting, *facts speak louder than opinions.*

21. **(A)** The next step taken by the researchers was "to identify conditions or events... associated with wars" (lines 45–47) because of the assumption that there have been certain *political and social conditions that have often led to war.*

22. **(E)** The basic premise of the study is that there may be correlations of conditions or events that often lead to war. Seeking correlations is the basic *research method used by the participants* in the study.

23. **(B)** The author argues that correlations do not necessarily constitute proof (lines 66–69). With so many variables at play in the conditions and events leading to war, *correlations may be misinterpreted.*

24. **(C)** Lines 74–77 raise the possibility that the project may find that there is insufficient evidence to warrant a final theory of war. In other words, in spite of the participants' best intentions, the findings *may fail to produce definitive results.*

25. **(B)** The discussion of Bismarck and Hitler (lines 83–94) is presented as an example of a potential problem. Because of faulty design (e.g., a definition of *war*), one or more conclusions can be dead wrong. Consequently, the *research design and procedure may invalidate the findings.*

26. **(E)** Despite problems and flaws in "The Correlates of War" project, the author still maintains—in the last lines of the passage—that the study is *the best of its kind.*

27. **(C)** Regardless of his doubts about some research techniques being used by the scholars engaged in the project, the author takes a generally positive position regarding the outcomes of the project. He is largely *optimistic and hopeful.*

28. **(C)** The man "with his eyes fixed on the ground" is the artist who "searches." To Picasso, the search means nothing in painting. *Artists who contemplate their subjects too much* before painting may have good intentions, but they are likely to fail. After all, results, not intentions, count.

29. **(B)** Picasso's statement is a *denial of the accusation* that the principal objective of his work is "the spirit of research," discussed in lines 12–15.

30. **(C)** The idea that art *gives us more than truth; it gives us understanding* is made clear by the statement "Art is a lie that makes us realize truth, at least the truth that is given us to understand" (lines 22–24).

31. **(B)** Picasso says that his object in art is to show what he has found, not what he was looking for. Therefore, in Picasso's opinion a successful piece of art *reveals what the artist has found.*

32. **(A)** The word "naturalism" in this context means *realism.* Realists in art, as the name suggests, try to recreate as accurately as they can three-dimensional objects on a two-dimensional surface, an impossible undertaking in Picasso's view. As he writes, "Nature and art . . . cannot be the same thing."

33. **(C)** Much of the passage describes Picasso's *innovations,* his new notions, such as "freeing the technique of painting from its slavish adherence to the description of nature" and making the painter "a free creator, a poet."

34. (**D**) The passage explains that, once Picasso burst onto the art scene, the *strict rules of art* no longer applied. Among other things, Picasso broke with such past traditions as painting with "slavish adherence to the description of nature."

35. (**A**) Picasso gave painting "new laws of harmony and balance," but he was careful not to *ignore the need for harmony and balance.*

36. (**E**) The notion that *patching up a picture restricts artists' freedom of expression* is supported by the paragraph beginning on line 95. When an artist has "no regard for the nature of anything he has painted before," he has the "freedom to move at will in the boundless spaces of free expression."

37. (**C**) Throughout Passage 2, but particularly in the last paragraph, Picasso is portrayed as a *bold experimenter.* For example, the author says Picasso tested the foundations on which his own art rested.

38. (**B**) Eluard's phrase reminds us of Picasso's statement in Passage 1 that "*my object is to show what I have found.*" In other words, Picasso wants to see objects anew, with fresh eyes, or to "attain sight."

39. (**B**) Both passages allude to Picasso's "aphorism," that the artist "*does not seek, but finds*": In Passage 1, see the first paragraph; in Passage 2, see lines 86 and 87.

40. (**C**) Passage 2 is an appreciation of Picasso as artist. Throughout Passage 1, Picasso defends himself from false accusations and clarifies misconceptions about art. The tone of Passage 1, therefore, is more contentious, *more argumentative* than the tone of Passage 2.

Level C

Exercise 1

1. (**E**) Both paragraphs *humorously portray the female residents* of Cranford, describing at length their idiosyncrasies of dress and behavior.

2. (**C**) In stating that "whatever does become of the gentlemen, they are not at Cranford," the author indicates that the men are distinguished chiefly by their *absence.*

3. (**D**) The "tender good offices [performed for] each other whenever they are in distress" are the kind *acts done* by the good ladies of Cranford *on behalf of others* needing their help.

4. (**D**) In showing both the eccentricities and the virtues that characterize the ladies of Cranford, the author exhibits an attitude that is *mocking,* but only *gently* so.

5. (**B**) Note the context in which the author refers to "Miss Tyler, of cleanly memory." The author has just been talking about the unfashionable attire of Cranford ladies, emphasizing that their clothes are made of good (that is, long-lasting) material. The Cranford ladies wear their clothes for years, but they are scrupulous about keeping them clean. In this they resemble Miss Tyler, known for her *spotless attire.*

6. (**B**) Since the bulk of the last paragraph concerns the ladies' eccentricities of dress and indifference to current fashion, it can be inferred that "the last gigot" most likely is *an outmoded article of apparel* (leg-of-mutton sleeve) worn well after its time by the unfashionable ladies of Cranford.

7. **(D)** Arbitrarily ready to decide issues "without troubling themselves with unnecessary reasons," dictatorial or overbearing to their dependents, and quite able to do without men, the ladies of Cranford do not seem in the least *submissive* (yielding).

8. **(E)** By providing background on how the theory of a dynamic abyss came to take hold in the scientific community and on how the forces that activate the global patterns of ocean currents actually work, the passage serves to *summarize evidence supporting oceanic circulation.*

9. **(C)** The opening sentence states that "many investigators were initially reluctant" to accept the evidence in favor of this controversial hypothesis. Committed to the belief that the depths of the ocean were calm ("the notion of a tranquil abyss"), these scientists at first viewed the idea that the abyss could be dynamic with *marked skepticism* (distinct doubt).

10. **(E)** The passage states that the *first* argument for the existence of dynamic currents in the deeps came from theory, based on "*models* of ocean circulation" involving the tendency of cold water to sink.

11. **(C)** The weathering of rocks is the source of detritus (debris; fragmented rock particles). These bits of debris are produced by the elements' gradual *wearing away* of the rocks, which disintegrates them over time.

12. **(B)** Both minute particles of rock and grains of wind-blown soil belong to the first type of sediment discussed ("detritus whose source is the weathering of rocks on continents and islands"). Only the *fragmentary shells* of dead microscopic organisms belong to the second type.

13. **(D)** Because they need to take into account the effects of strong sea-floor currents on the structures they plan to build, *designers of sea-floor structures* are most likely to be interested in this particular article.

14. **(D)** The authors approximate an amount ("about three billion tons per year"), refer to a model of ocean circulation, give several examples ("such as the..."), and list evidence to support a theory. They never *propose a solution* to a problem.

15. **(C)** The authors are objective and factual. Their style can best be described as *espository* (explanatory).

16. **(D)** The author asks this question, not because readers don't know what money is, but because he wishes them to consider a definition different from the usual one. By the end of the paragraph the author *introduces an unfamiliar* (to most readers) *definition of the word.*

17. **(B)** At the beginning of the second paragraph the author writes that "Three such functions are usually specified," which amounts to saying that these three functions are *common knowledge among informed people.*

18. **(A)** The sticker price on a car informs prospective buyers of the cost, or value, of the car. Therefore, the sticker price qualifies as *a unit of account,* as defined in lines 23–27.

19. **(C)** The definition of "archetype" is a pattern or model on which others are based. Consequently, barter *is a model for economic exchanges.*

20. **(A)** In line 46 the author says that bartering required "large amounts of time." The expenditure of time is reiterated in lines 53 and 54. Clearly, the chief shortcoming of barter is that *making deals is too time-consuming.*

21. (**B**) A Gordian knot, an allusion to an ancient Greek myth, has come to refer to anything that is difficult to untie or unravel. Hence, *it was difficult to change the barter system to a monetary system.*

22. (**E**) The passage cites several advantages of money over barter: the double coincidence of wants is eliminated by a monetary system (lines 63–68); when money is the medium of exchange, the cost of doing business is lower (lines 68–70); supply and demand determine the cost of goods and services (70–72)—a basic principle of economics; and in a monetary system a greater division of labor is possible (72–75), which increases efficiency.

    Only (E), *opportunities of advantageous trade are reduced,* is not mentioned in the passage.

23. (**B**) According to the passage, "The usefulness of money is inversely proportional to the number of currencies in circulation" (lines 77–79). In other words, the presence of a large number of currencies *reduces the efficiency of the international economy.*

24. (**A**) Line 96 of the passage indicates that one of the benefits of a single national currency is a *reduction in the cost of monetary transactions.*

25. (**D**) After citing several reasons for streamlining the international economy by reducing the number of currencies, the next logical step is to create a single world currency. The author, however, demurs from proposing that step because, as the remainder of the passage explains, *the most obvious solution may not be the best solution.*

26. (**E**) The one most desirable benefit to be derived from a single world currency, which the author reiterates throughout the discussion, is *reducing transaction costs.*

27. (**A**) The conclusion to be drawn from all the arguments about a single world currency, particularly the high cost of introducing a single standard, is that *it may cause more problems than it will solve.*

28. (**D**) Passage 1 says that in *This Side of Paradise*, Fitzgerald managed to turn a mass of diverse material "into a sustained narrative" (line 15), indicating that Fitzgerald knew how to *create an extended tale.*

29. (**A**) Passage 1 says that "freshness of language" (lines 19 and 20) is Fitzgerald's "identifying mark." In other words, Fitzgerald built his reputation on *his original use of words.*

30. (**B**) The author of Passage 1 claims that *This Side of Paradise* helped "Fitzgerald thrash out those 'ideas still in riot' that he attributes to Amory" (lines 24–27). Amory, therefore, seems to be a *thinly disguised version of Fitzgerald* himself—a young man trying to find himself and make sense of life.

31. (**E**) In Passage 1, Fitzgerald's words are quoted in the context of a discussion of the "naiveté and honesty" of his work. The quotation confirms that Fitzgerald's writing is characteristically *truthful and innocent.*

32. (**B**) The entire passage describes the problems of Fitzgerald's *immature* writing. In comparison to the writing in Fitzgerald's earlier work, the writing in *This Side of Paradise* had "improved greatly" (line 17). Nevertheless, the author of the passage still regarded Fitzgerald as an "ambitious amateur" (line 44).

33. (**C**) The paragraph following the anecdote rebuts *a mistaken view of Fitzgerald.* Lines 63–70 portray Fitzgerald as anything but a "stupid old woman."

34. (**A**) The "jewel" refers to Fitzgerald's exceptional talent with words. Talent is not enough, however. *Fitzgerald's talent needed polishing.*

35. (**D**) Stating that *This Side of Paradise* "is not only highly imitative but... imitates an inferior model" (lines 82–84), the author indicates that *Sinister Street* was an *unfortunate* choice for a *model* on which Fitzgerald might base his book.

36. (**B**) The author describes how the hero of *Sinister Street* is "swamped in the forest of descriptions" (lines 98 and 99). The author of the novel uses so many flowery descriptive phrases that the reader cannot keep track of the novel's plot. In other words, his pretty writing or *flowery prose overshadows* the *hero's story.*

37. (**D**) One reason, among others explained in lines 121–125, that the author calls Fitzgerald's novel "illiterate" is that it *contains many errors* that should have been caught by the publisher's proofreader.

38. (**A**) Despite the flaws of *This Side of Paradise*, the authors of both passages apparently recognize *Fitzgerald's talent as a writer.* More specifically, Passage 1 concludes with the words "Fitzgerald had found his craft." Passage 2 says that Fitzgerald has "imagination" (line 74) and a "gift for expression" (line 77).

39. (**E**) Passage 1 describes *This Side of Paradise* as "clumsy and pasted together" (line 4). Passage 2 says the book has "no dominating intention to endow it with unity and force" (lines 110–112). Both criticisms refer to the book's *lack of artistic focus.*

40. (**D**) Passage 1 was written long after Fitzgerald became an important literary figure, long after his death, in fact. The author speaks of Fitzgerald in the past tense: "All his life he was to think of himself . . ." (lines 6–10), etc. Passage 2 discusses Fitzgerald as a figure on the contemporary scene: "Scott Fitzgerald is, in fact, . . . a very good-looking young man . . ." (lines 67 and 68). It also suggests that *This Side of Paradise* illustrates Fitzgerald's talent as a writer, but that his work still needs improvement. The evidence in both passages shows that *Passage 1 was written long after the publication of* This Side of Paradise; *Passage 2 was written shortly afterward.*

PART 5

BUILDING YOUR VOCABULARY

Overview

Tips on Building Your Vocabulary

SAT High-Frequency Word List

Basic Word Parts

Overview

Recognizing the meaning of words is essential to comprehending what you read. The more you stumble over unfamiliar words in a text, the more you have to take time out to look up words in your dictionary, the more likely you are to wind up losing track of what the author has to say.

To succeed in college, you must develop a college-level vocabulary. You must familiarize yourself with technical words in a wide variety of fields, mastering each field's special vocabulary. You must learn to use these words, and re-use them until they become second nature to you. The time you put in now learning vocabulary-building techniques for this exam will pay off later on, and not just on the SAT.

This section provides you with a fundamental tool that will help you build your vocabulary: Barron's SAT High-Frequency Word List.

No matter how little time you have before you take the SAT, you can familiarize yourself with the sort of vocabulary you will be facing on the test. Look over the words on our SAT High-Frequency Word List: each of these words, ranging from everyday words such as *abstract* and *objective* to less common ones such as *abstruse* and *iconoclast*, has appeared (as answer choices or as question words) from five to thirty times on SAT and SAT I tests published through 2008. Notice that the words have been divided into groups of ten so you won't be overwhelmed.

Not only will looking over the SAT High-Frequency Word List reassure you that you do know some SAT-type words, but also it will help you on the actual day of the test. These words have turned up on recent tests: some of them may turn up on the test you take. Look over these words. Review any of them that are unfamiliar to you. Try using these words on your parents and friends. Then, if the words do turn up on your test, feel confident: your knowledge of them will help you come up with the correct answers or eliminate incorrect answer choices.

Tips on Building Your Vocabulary

TIP

1

Read Widely to Develop Your Feeling for Words

There is only one effective long-range strategy for vocabulary building: READ.

Read—widely and well. Sample different fields—physics, art history, political science, geology—and different styles. Extensive reading is the one sure way to make your vocabulary grow and to develop your feeling for words.

The Sunday edition of *The New York Times* contains special sections on travel, literature, and the arts. Tuesday's edition contains a special science section. *The Washington Post* and *The Wall Street Journal* offer excellent coverage of the arts and sciences, as well as current events.

Try to develop an interest in as many fields as you can. Sample some of the quality magazines: *The New Yorker, Smithsonian, Scientific American, Natural History, Harper's, Newsweek, Time.* In these magazines, you'll find articles on the whole range of fields touched on by the SAT. If you take time to acquaint yourself with the contents of these magazines, you'll soon be in command of an expanding vocabulary.

TIP

2   Use Memory Tricks to Keep New Words in Your Active Vocabulary

Reading widely does not always help you remember the words you read. You may have the words in your passive vocabulary and be able to recognize them when you see them in a particular context and yet be unable to define them clearly or think of additional contexts for them.

Remembering words takes work. It also takes wit. You can spend hours memorizing dictionary definitions and get no place. Try capitalizing on your native intelligence by thinking up mnemonic devices—memory tricks—to help you remember new words.

Consider the word *hovel*. A hovel is a dirty, mean house. How can you remember that? *Hovel* rhymes with *shovel*. You need to shovel out the hovel to live in it. Rhymes can help you remember what words mean.

Now consider the word *hover*. To hover is to hang fluttering in the air or to wait around. Can rhyme help you here? *Hover* rhymes with *cover*. That doesn't seem to work. However, take another look at *hover*. Cut off the letter *h* and you're left with the word *over*. If a helicopter hovers over an accident, it hangs in the air; if a mother hovers over a sick child, she waits around to care for it. Hidden little words can help you remember bigger words.

Try the hidden word trick with a less familiar word than hover. Take the word *credulous*, which means gullible or easily fooled. A credulous person will give money to someone who wants to sell him the Brooklyn Bridge. Now look closely at *credulous*. What little word is hidden within it? The hidden word is *red*. What happens when a person finds out he's been taken for a fool? Often, the poor fool turns red. *Credulous, red* in the face. There's your memory trick.

TIP

3   Create Your Own Unique Flash Cards

Here's how to make memorable, masterable flash cards. Be brief, but include all the information you need. On one side write the word. On the other side write *concise* definitions—two or three words at most—for each major meaning of the word you want to learn. Include an antonym, if you can; the synonym–antonym associations can help you remember both words. To fix the word in your mind, use it in a short phrase. Then write down that phrase.

Sample Flash Card:

| ABSTRACT | theoretical; nonrepresentational

(ANT. concrete)

"abstract notion" |

You can pack an enormous amount of information onto a flash card in only a few words. Use symbols and simple sketches; you may discover you remember pictures better than phrases.

Consider This Flash Card:

| | extremely poisonous
bitterly hateful

(ANT. benign)

"virulent poison" |

The skull-and-crossbones symbol means poison all around the world.

Consider This Card as Well:

insolvent

| | bankrupt;
impoverished

(ANT. financially sound)

"insolvent debtor" |

Anyone can draw a dollar sign. What makes the dollar sign useful on this card is that it's something you added personally. You didn't just copy down definitions straight off the list—you translated the word insolvent into symbols with which you're comfortable.

Work up your own personal set of symbols and abbreviations. You can use simple plus and minus signs to clarify a word's connotations. The word *thrifty*, for example, has positive connotations; it's good to be a thrifty person, a person who has sense enough to save. Thrifty, + . The word *parsimonious*, however, has negative connotations. Though saving money is good, it's bad to carry thrift to an extreme; when old Scrooge wouldn't let his shivering clerk light a fire on the coldest day in winter, he showed just how stingy and parsimonious he was. Parsimonious, –.

| dis joint ed | disconnected;
incoherent

(ANT. Connected)

"disjointed phrases" |

Visual cues can reinforce your sense of what a word means. Consider the word *disjointed*. You can take it apart.

| precipitous | steep; headlong

(ANT. flat; gradual)

"a precipitous cliff"
prē - SIP - it - us |

You can also write words at odd angles.

| circuitous | roundabout,
winding

(ANT. direct)

"a circuitous route"
sur - KYOO - it - us |

Or you can write them in odd shapes.
If you personalize your flash cards, you'll create something uniquely memorable, something that will stick in your mind because you thought it up yourself. That's the sort of flash card that will be most valuable to you.

TIP

4   Acquaint Yourself with Word Parts—Prefixes, Suffixes, Roots—to Expand Your Vocabulary

One good approach to expanding your vocabulary is to learn how to build up (and tear apart) words. A basic knowledge of roots, prefixes, and suffixes and their meanings can help you determine the meanings of unfamiliar words.

Consider the word *magnanimity*, a correct answer choice on a published SAT. It comes from two Latin words—*magnus* (great) and *anima* (spirit). Magnanimity is greatness of spirit, openhearted generosity.

Most modern English words are derived from Latin, Greek, and Anglo-Saxon (Old English). Because few students nowadays study Latin and Greek (and even fewer study Anglo-Saxon!), the majority of high school seniors and juniors lack an important tool for unlocking the meanings of unfamiliar words.

Build your vocabulary by mastering basic word parts. Learning 30 key word parts can help you determine the meanings of over 10,000 words. Learning 50 key word parts gives you access to the meanings of over 100,000!

A list of basic word parts begins on page 203.

TIP

5   Work Through the SAT High-Frequency Word List to Expand Your College-Level Vocabulary

Take time to acquaint yourself specifically with the sorts of words you must know to do well on the SAT. Follow the procedures outlined below in order to work through the SAT High-Frequency List most profitably.

1. Select a list of 10 words.
2. Allot a definite time each day to study the list.
3. Devote at least half an hour to the list.
4. First go through the list looking at the short, simple-looking words (7 letters at most). Mark those you don't know. In studying, pay particular attention to them.
5. Go through the list again, looking at the longer words. Pay particular attention to words with more than one meaning and to familiar-looking words that turn out to have unusual definitions that surprise you. Study these secondary definitions.
6. Using the techniques shown in Tip 3, list unusual words on index cards that you can shuffle and review from time to time. (Study no more than 5 cards at a time.)
7. Use the illustrative sentences as models and make up new sentences of your own.
8. In making up new sentences, use familiar examples and be concrete: the junior high school band tuning up sounds *discordant*; in *Beauty and the Beast*, until Belle tames him, the Beast has a *volatile* temper.

For each word in the SAT High-Frequency List, the following is provided:

1. The word (printed in heavy type).
2. Its part of speech (abbreviated).
3. A brief definition.
4. A sentence illustrating the word's use.
5. Whenever appropriate, related words, together with their parts of speech.

The word list is arranged in alphabetical order.

SAT High-Frequency Word List

Word List 1

abate V. subside or moderate. Rather than leaving immediately, they waited for the storm to *abate*. abatement, N.

aberrant ADJ. abnormal or deviant. Given the *aberrant* nature of the data, we came to doubt the validity of the entire experiment.

abrasive ADJ. rubbing away; tending to grind down. Just as *abrasive* cleaning powders can wear away a shiny finish, *abrasive* remarks can wear away a listener's patience. abrade, V.

abridge V. condense or shorten. Because the publishers felt the public wanted a shorter version of *War and Peace*, they proceeded to *abridge* the novel.

absolute ADJ. complete; totally unlimited; certain. Although the King of Siam was an *absolute* monarch, he did not want to behead his unfaithful wife without *absolute* evidence of her infidelity.

abstemious ADJ. sparing in eating and drinking; temperate. Concerned whether her vegetarian son's *abstemious* diet provided him with sufficient protein, the worried mother pressed food on him.

abstract ADJ. theoretical; not concrete; non-representational. To him, hunger was an *abstract* concept; he had never missed a meal.

abstruse ADJ. obscure; profound; difficult to understand. Baffled by the *abstruse* philosophical texts assigned in class, Dave asked Lexy to explain Kant's *Critique of Pure Reason*.

accessible ADJ. easy to approach; obtainable. We asked our guide whether the ruins were *accessible* on foot.

acclaim V. applaud; announce with great approval. The NBC sportscasters *acclaimed* every American victory in the Olympics and lamented every American defeat. acclamation, acclaim, N.

Word List 2

accolade N. award of merit. In the world of public relations, a "Clio" is the highest *accolade* an advertising campaign can receive.

acknowledge V. recognize; admit. Although Iris *acknowledged* that the Beatles' tunes sounded pretty dated nowadays, she still preferred them to the hip-hop songs her brothers played.

acquiesce V. assent; agree without protesting. When we asked her to participate in the play, she immediately *acquiesced*. acquiescence, N.; acquiescent, ADJ.

acrimonious ADJ. bitter in words or manner. The candidate attacked his opponent in highly *acrimonious* terms. acrimony, N.

acute ADJ. quickly perceptive; keen; brief and severe. The *acute* young doctor realized immediately that the gradual deterioration of her patient's once-*acute* hearing was due to a chronic illness, not an *acute* one.

address V. direct a speech to; deal with or discuss. Due to *address* the convention in July, Brown planned to *address* the issue of low-income housing in his speech.

adherent N. supporter; follower. In the wake of the scandal, the senator's one-time *adherents* quietly deserted him.

adjacent ADJ. neighboring; adjoining. You will find questions based on this reading passage located on the *adjacent* page.

adroit ADJ. skillful; nimble. The juggler's admirers particularly enjoyed his *adroit* handling of difficult balancing tricks.

adulation N. flattery; admiration. The rock star relished the *adulation* she received from her groupies and yes-men.

Word List 3

adversary N. opponent. The young wrestler struggled to overcome his *adversary*.

adverse ADJ. unfavorable; hostile. The recession had a highly *adverse* effect on

Father's investment portfolio: he lost so much money that he could no longer afford the butler and the upstairs maid. adversity, N.

advocate V. urge; plead for. Noted abolitionists such as Frederick Douglass and Sojourner Truth *advocated* the eradication of the Southern institution of slavery. also N.

aesthetic ADJ. artistic; dealing with or capable of appreciation of the beautiful. The beauty of Tiffany's stained glass appealed to Esther's *aesthetic* sense. aesthete, N.

affable ADJ. easily approachable; warmly friendly. Accustomed to cold, aloof supervisors, Nicholas was amazed at how *affable* his new employer was.

affinity N. natural liking; kinship; similarity. Octavia felt an immediate *affinity* for the folk dancers she met; their love of dance was hers as well.

affirmation N. positive assertion; confirmation; solemn pledge by one who refuses to take an oath. Despite Tom's *affirmations* of innocence, Aunt Polly still suspected he had eaten the pie.

aggressor N. attacker. Before you punish both boys for fighting, see whether you can determine which one was the *aggressor*.

alienate V. make hostile; separate. Heather's attempts to *alienate* Amy from Ellen failed because the two friends had complete faith in one another.

alleviate V. relieve. The doctor's reassuring remarks *alleviated* June's fears for the baby; though he'd been born prematurely, he was rapidly gaining weight and could go home in a couple of weeks.

Word List 4

aloof ADJ. apart; reserved; standoffish. His classmates thought James was a snob because, instead of joining in their conversations, he remained silent and *aloof*.

altruistic ADJ. unselfishly generous; concerned for others. In providing tutorial assistance and college scholarships for hundreds of economically disadvantaged youths, Eugene

Lang performed a truly *altruistic* deed. altruism, N.

ambiguous ADJ. unclear or doubtful in meaning. The proctor's *ambiguous* instructions thoroughly confused us; we didn't know which columns we should mark and which we should leave blank. ambiguity, N.

ambivalence N. the state of having contradictory or conflicting emotional attitudes. Torn between loving her parents one minute and hating them the next, she was confused by the *ambivalence* of her feelings. ambivalent, ADJ.

ameliorate V. improve; make more satisfactory. Carl became a union organizer because he wanted to join the fight to *ameliorate* the working conditions in the factory.

amend V. correct; change, generally for the better. Hoping to *amend* his circumstances, Luong left Vietnam for the United States.

amorphous ADJ. formless; lacking shape or definition. As soon as we have decided on our itinerary, we shall send you a copy; right now, our plans are still *amorphous*.

ample ADJ. abundant. Bond had *ample* opportunity to escape. Why did he let us catch him?

analogy N. similarity; parallelism. A well-known *analogy* compares the body's immune system to an army whose defending troops are the lymphocytes or white blood cells. analogous, ADJ.

anarchist N. person who seeks to overturn the established government; advocate of abolishing authority. Denying she was an *anarchist*, Katya maintained she wished only to make changes in our government, not to destroy it entirely. anarchy, N.

Word List 5

anecdote N. short account of an amusing or interesting event. Rather than make concrete proposals for welfare reform, President Ronald Reagan told *anecdotes* about poor people who became wealthy despite their impoverished backgrounds. anecdotal, ADJ.

animosity N. active enmity. By advocating cuts in campaign spending and limits on congressional powers, the reform candidate seemed almost to invite the *animosity* of the party's leaders.

antagonism N. hostility; active resistance. Barry showed his *antagonism* toward his new stepmother by ignoring her whenever she tried talking to him. antagonistic, ADJ.

antidote N. medicine to counteract a poison or disease. When Marge's child accidentally swallowed some cleaning fluid, the local poison control hotline told Marge how to administer the *antidote*.

antiquated ADJ. old-fashioned; obsolete. Philip had grown so accustomed to editing his articles on word processors that he thought typewriters were too *antiquated* for him to use. antiquity, N.

antithesis N. contrast; direct opposite of or to. Good is the *antithesis* of evil, innocence the *antithesis* of guilt.

apathy N. lack of caring; indifference. A firm believer in democratic government, she could not understand the *apathy* of people who never bothered to vote. apathetic, ADJ.

apocryphal ADJ. untrue; made up; not genuine. To impress his friends, Ted invented *apocryphal* tales of his adventures in the big city.

appease V. pacify or soothe; relieve. Tom and Jody tried to *appease* their crying baby by offering him one toy after another. However, they couldn't calm him down until they *appeased* his hunger by giving him a bottle.

appreciate V. be thankful for; increase in worth; be thoroughly conscious of. Little Orphan Annie truly *appreciated* the stocks Daddy Warbucks gave her, which *appreciated* in value considerably over the years.

Word List 6

apprehension N. fear; discernment; capture. The tourist refused to drive his rental car through downtown Miami because he felt some *apprehension* that he might be carjacked. apprehensive, ADJ.

arable ADJ. fit for growing crops. The first settlers wrote home glowing reports of the New World, praising its vast acres of *arable* land ready for the plow.

arbitrary ADJ. unreasonable or capricious; randomly selected without any reason; based solely on one's unrestricted will or judgment. The coach claimed the team lost because the umpire made some *arbitrary* calls.

archaic ADJ. antiquated. "Methinks," "thee," and "thou" are *archaic* words that are no longer part of our standard vocabulary.

ardor N. heat; passion; zeal. Katya's *ardor* was catching; soon all her fellow demonstrators were busily making posters and handing out flyers, inspired by her enthusiasm for the cause. ardent, ADJ.

arid ADJ. dry; barren. The cactus has adapted to survive in an *arid* environment.

arrogance N. pride; haughtiness. Convinced that Emma thought she was better than anyone else in the class, Ed rebuked her for her *arrogance*. arrogant, ADJ.

articulate ADJ. effective; distinct. Her *articulate* presentation of the advertising campaign impressed her employers so much that they put her in charge of the project. also V.

artifact N. object made by human beings, either handmade or mass-produced. Archaeologists debated the significance of the *artifacts* discovered in the ruins of Asia Minor but came to no conclusion about the culture they represented.

artisan N. manually skilled worker; craftsman, as opposed to artist. Elderly *artisans* from Italy trained Harlem teenagers to carve the stone figures that would decorate the new wing of the cathedral.

Word List 7

ascendancy N. controlling influence. Leaders of religious cults maintain *ascendancy* over their followers by methods that can verge on brainwashing.

ascetic ADJ. practicing self-denial; austere. The wealthy, self-indulgent young man felt oddly drawn to the *ascetic* life led by members of some monastic orders. also N.

aspire V. seek to attain; long for. Because he *aspired* to a career in professional sports, Philip enrolled in a graduate program in sports management. aspiration, N.

assuage V. ease or lessen (pain); satisfy (hunger); soothe (anger). Jilted by Jane, Dick tried to *assuage* his heartache by indulging in ice cream. One gallon later, he had *assuaged* his appetite but not his grief.

astute ADJ. wise; shrewd. Expecting Miss Marple to be a woolly-headed old lady, Inspector Craddock was startled by the *astute* observations she made.

atrophy V. waste away. After three months in a cast, Stan's biceps had *atrophied* somewhat; however, he was sure that if he pumped iron for a while he would soon build them up. also, N.

attentive ADJ. considerate; thoughtful; paying attention. Thuy is very *attentive* to her Vietnamese-speaking parents, acting as their interpreter and helping them deal with American society.

attribute V. ascribe; explain. I *attribute* her success in science to the encouragement she received from her parents.

audacious ADJ. daring; bold. Audiences cheered as Luke Skywalker and Princess Leia made their *audacious*, death-defying leap to freedom, escaping Darth Vader's troops. audacity, N.

augment V. increase; add to. Beth *augmented* her inadequate salary by selling Tupperware at parties at friends' homes.

Word List 8

austerity N. sternness; severity; strict economy; lack of luxuries. The bishops charged with conducting the heresy inquiry were a solemn, somewhat forbidding group; their demeanor reflected their *austerity*. austere, ADJ.

authentic ADJ. genuine. The art expert was able to distinguish the *authentic* Van Gogh painting from the forged copy. authenticate, V.

authoritarian ADJ. subordinating the individual to the state; completely dominating another's will. The leaders of the *authoritarian* regime ordered the suppression of the democratic protest movement. After years of submitting to the will of her *authoritarian* father, Elizabeth Barrett ran away from home with the poet Robert Browning.

autonomous ADJ. self-governing. Although the University of California at Berkeley is just one part of the state university system, in many ways Cal Berkeley is *autonomous*, for it runs several programs that are not subject to outside control. autonomy, N.

aversion N. firm dislike. Their mutual *aversion* was so great that they refused to speak to one another.

banal ADJ. hackneyed; commonplace; trite. Was it Pendleton's stale plot or his cliché-ridden dialogue that made his play seem so *banal*? banality, N.

bane N. cause of ruin; curse. Lucy's little brother was the *bane* of her existence; he made her life a total misery.

belie V. contradict; give a false impression. His coarse, hard-bitten exterior *belied* his inner sensitivity.

belittle V. disparage; make fun of. Parents should not *belittle* their children's early attempts at drawing, but should encourage their efforts.

belligerent ADJ. quarrelsome. Whenever he had too much to drink, he became *belligerent* and tried to pick fights with strangers.

Word List 9

benevolent ADJ. generous; charitable. Mr. Fezziwig was a *benevolent* employer who wished to make Christmas merrier for young Scrooge and his other employees.

benign ADJ. kindly; favorable; not malignant. Though her *benign* smile and gentle bearing made Miss Marple seem a sweet little old lady, in reality she was a tough-minded, shrewd observer of human nature.

bequeath V. leave to someone by a will; hand down. Although Maud had intended to *bequeath* the family home to her nephew, she died before changing her will. bequest, N.

biased ADJ. slanted; prejudiced. Because the judge played golf regularly with the district attorney's father, we feared he might be *biased* in the prosecution's favor. bias, N.

bland ADJ. soothing; mild; dull. Unless you want your stomach lining to be eaten away, stick to a *bland* diet. blandness, N.

blasphemy N. irreverence; sacrilege; cursing. In my father's house, the Dodgers were the holiest of holies; to cheer for another team was to utter words of *blasphemy*. blasphemous, ADJ.

bolster V. support; reinforce. The debaters amassed file boxes full of evidence to *bolster* their arguments.

braggart N. boastful person. I wouldn't mind Bob's being such a *braggart* if I felt he'd done anything worth bragging about.

brawn N. muscular strength; sturdiness. It takes *brawn* to become a champion weight-lifter. brawny, ADJ.

brevity N. conciseness; briefness. *Brevity* is essential when you send a telegram or cablegram; you are charged for every word.

Word List 10

buttress V. support; prop up. The attorney came up with several far-fetched arguments in a vain attempt to *buttress* his weak case. also N.

cacophonous ADJ. discordant; inharmonious. Do the students in the orchestra enjoy the *cacophonous* sounds they make when they're tuning up? I don't know how they can stand the racket. cacophony, N.

cajole V. coax; wheedle. Diane tried to *cajole* her father into letting her drive the family car. cajolery, N.

calculated ADJ. deliberately planned; likely. Lexy's choice of clothes to wear to the debate tournament was carefully *calculated*. Her conventional suit was one *calculated* to appeal to the conservative judges.

candor N. frankness. Jack can carry *candor* too far: when he told Jill his honest opinion of her, she felt like slapping his face. candid, ADJ.

capricious ADJ. unpredictable; fickle. The storm was *capricious*: it changed course constantly. Jill was *capricious*, too; she changed boyfriends almost as often as she changed clothes.

caricature N. distortion; burlesque. The cartoonist's *caricature* of President Bush grossly exaggerated the size of the president's ears. also V.

censorious ADJ. critical. *Censorious* people delight in casting blame.

censure V. blame; criticize. The senator was *censured* for behavior inappropriate to a member of Congress. also N.

certitude N. certainty. Though there was no *certitude* of his getting the job, Lou thought he had a good chance of doing so.

Word List 11

charlatan N. quack; pretender to knowledge. When they realized that the Wizard didn't know how to get them back to Kansas, Dorothy and her companions were indignant that they'd been duped by a *charlatan*.

chronicle V. report; record (in chronological order). The gossip columnist was paid to *chronicle* the latest escapades of socially prominent celebrities. also N.

civil ADJ. having to do with citizens or the state; courteous and polite. Although Internal Revenue Service agents are *civil* servants, they are not always *civil* to suspected tax cheats. civility, N.

clamor N. noise. The *clamor* of the children at play outside made it impossible for her to take a nap. also V.

clemency N. disposition to be lenient; mildness, as of the weather. Why did the defense lawyer look pleased when his case was sent to Judge Bland's chambers? Bland was known for her *clemency* toward first offenders. clement, ADJ.

coercion N. use of force to get someone to obey. The inquisitors used both physical and psychological *coercion* to force Joan of Arc to deny that her visions were sent by God. coerce, V.

commemorate V. honor the memory of. The statue of the Minuteman *commemorates* the valiant soldiers who fought in the Revolutionary War.

compelling ADJ. overpowering; irresistible in effect. The prosecutor presented a well-reasoned case, but the defense attorney's *compelling* arguments for leniency won over the jury.

compile V. assemble; gather; accumulate. We planned to *compile* a list of the words most frequently used on the SAT examinations.

compliance N. readiness to yield; conformity in fulfilling requirements. When I give an order, I expect *compliance*, not defiance. The design for the new school had to be in *compliance* with the local building code. comply, V.

Word List 12

composure N. mental calmness. Even the latest crisis at work failed to shake Nancy's *composure*.

comprehensive ADJ. thorough; inclusive. This book provides a *comprehensive* review of critical reading skills for the SAT.

concede V. admit; yield. Despite all the evidence Monica had assembled, Mark refused to *concede* that she was right. concession, N.

conciliatory ADJ. reconciling; appeasing; amiable. Hoping to end the coldness that had grown between them, he wrote a *conciliatory* note. conciliate, V.

concise ADJ. brief and compact. When you define a new word, be *concise*: the shorter the definition, the easier it is to remember.

conclusive ADJ. convincing; decisive. We have *conclusive* evidence that proves her innocence.

concur V. agree in opinion. Justice O'Connor wrote a minority opinion because she did not *concur* with the reasoning of her fellow justices.

condone V. overlook voluntarily; forgive. Unlike the frail widow, who indulged her only son and *condoned* his minor offenses, the boy's stern uncle did nothing but scold him.

confirm V. corroborate; verify; support. I have several witnesses who will *confirm* my account of what happened.

conflagration N. great fire. In the *conflagration* that followed the 1906 earthquake, much of San Francisco burned to the ground.

Word List 13

confound V. confuse; puzzle. No mystery could *confound* Sherlock Holmes for long.

confront V. face; challenge. All I ask is the chance to *confront* my accusers face to face.

conscientious ADJ. scrupulous; careful. A *conscientious* editor, she checked every definition for its accuracy.

consensus N. general agreement. Every time the garden club members had nearly reached a *consensus* about what to plant, Mistress Mary, quite contrary, disagreed.

consistency N. absence of contradictions; dependability; uniformity; degree of thickness. Holmes judged puddings and explanations on their *consistency*: he liked his puddings without lumps and his explanations without improbabilities.

constraint N. compulsion; repression of feelings. Because he trusted his therapist completely, he discussed his feelings openly with her without feeling the least *constraint*. constrain, V.

contagion N. infection. Fearing *contagion*, they took great steps to prevent the spread of the disease.

contemporary N. person belonging to the same period. Though Charlotte Bronte and George Eliot were *contemporaries*, the two novelists depicted their Victorian world in markedly different ways. also ADJ.

contend V. struggle; compete; assert earnestly. Sociologist Harry Edwards *contends* that young African-American athletes are exploited by some college recruiters. contention, N.

contentious ADJ. quarrelsome. Disagreeing violently with the referees' ruling, the coach became so *contentious* that they threw him out of the game.

Word List 14

contract V. compress or shrink; make a pledge; catch a disease. Warm metal expands; cold metal *contracts*.

converge V. approach; tend to meet; come together. African-American men from all over the United States *converged* on Washington to take part in the historic Million Man march.

conviction N. strongly held belief. Nothing could shake his *conviction* that she was innocent. (secondary meaning)

cordial ADJ. gracious; heartfelt. Our hosts greeted us at the airport with a *cordial* welcome and a hearty hug.

corroborate V. confirm; support. Though Huck was quite willing to *corroborate* Tom's story, Aunt Polly knew better than to believe either of them.

corrosion N. destruction by chemical action. The *corrosion* of the girders supporting the bridge took place so gradually that no one suspected any danger until the bridge suddenly collapsed. corrode, V.

credibility N. believability. Because the candidate had made some pretty unbelievable promises, we began to question the *credibility* of everything he said.

credulity N. belief on slight evidence; gullibility; naivete. Con artists take advantage of the *credulity* of inexperienced investors to swindle them out of their savings. credulous, ADJ.

criterion N. standard used in judging. What *criterion* did you use when you selected this essay as the prize winner? criteria, PL.

cryptic ADJ. mysterious; hidden; secret. Thoroughly baffled by Holmes's *cryptic* remarks, Watson wondered whether Holmes was intentionally concealing his thoughts about the crime.

Word List 15

cursory ADJ. casual; hastily done. Because a *cursory* examination of the ruins indicates the possibility of arson, we believe the insurance agency should undertake a more extensive investigation of the fire's cause.

curtail V. shorten; reduce. Barbie declined Ken's invitation to go to the movies, saying her father had ordered her to *curtail* her social life.

cynic N. one who is skeptical or distrustful of human motives. A born *cynic*, Sidney was suspicious whenever anyone gave him a gift "with no strings attached." cynical, ADJ.

daunt V. intimidate; frighten. "Boast all you like of your prowess. Mere words cannot *daunt* me," the hero answered the villain.

dawdle V. loiter; waste time. We have to meet a deadline so don't *dawdle*; just get down to work.

debilitate V. weaken; enfeeble. Michael's severe bout of the flu *debilitated* him so much that he was too tired to go to work for a week.

debunk V. expose something as nonsensical or false. I have gathered enough evidence to *debunk* the legend that Billy the Kid was a heroic, Robin Hood-like figure.

decorum N. propriety; orderliness and good taste in manners. Even the best-mannered students have trouble behaving with *decorum* on the last day of school. decorous, ADJ.

defame V. harm someone's reputation; malign. If you try to *defame* my good name, my lawyers will see you in court. defamation, N.

deference N. courteous regard for another's wish. In *deference* to the minister's request, please do not take photographs during the wedding service.

Word List 16

defiance N. refusal to yield; resistance. When John reached the "terrible two's," he responded to every parental request with howls of *defiance*. defy, V. defiant, ADJ.

degenerate V. become worse; deteriorate. As the fight dragged on, the champion's stamina *degenerated* until he could barely keep on his feet.

degrade V. lower in rank or dignity; debase. Some secretaries object to fetching the boss a cup of coffee because they feel it *degrades* them to do such lowly tasks.

deliberate V. consider; ponder. Offered the new job, she asked for time to *deliberate* before she told them her decision.

delineate V. portray; depict; sketch. Using only a few descriptive phrases, Austen *delineates* the character of Mr. Collins so well that we can predict his every move. delineation, N.

denounce V. condemn; criticize. The reform candidate *denounced* the corrupt city officers for having betrayed the public's trust. denunciation, N.

deny V. contradict; refuse. Do you *deny* his story, or do you support what he says? denial, N.

depict V. portray; describe. Some newspaper accounts *depicted* the movie star as a reclusive prima donna; others portrayed her as a sensitive artist harassed by the media. depiction, N.

deplore V. regret strongly; express grief over. Although Ann Landers *deplored* the disintegration of the modern family, she recognized that not every marriage could be saved.

depravity N. corruption; wickedness. Even Romans who had grown accustomed to perversions and immorality during Tiberius's reign were shocked by the *depravity* of the emperor Caligula.

Word List 17

deprecate V. express disapproval of; protest against; belittle. A firm believer in old-fashioned courtesy, Miss Post *deprecated* the modern tendency to address new acquaintances by their first names. deprecatory, ADJ.

deride V. ridicule; make fun of. The critics *derided* his pretentious dialogue and refused to consider his play seriously. derision, N.

derivative ADJ. unoriginal; derived from another source. Although her early poetry was clearly *derivative* in nature, the critics felt she had promise and eventually would find her own voice.

despondent ADJ. depressed; gloomy. To the concern of his parents, William became seriously *despondent* after he broke up with Jan. despondency, N.

despot N. tyrant; harsh, authoritarian ruler. How could a benevolent king turn overnight into a *despot*?

detached ADJ. emotionally removed; calm and objective; indifferent. A psychoanalyst must maintain a *detached* point of view and stay uninvolved with her patients' personal lives. detachment, N. (secondary meaning)

deterrent N. something that discourages; hindrance. Does the threat of capital punishment serve as a *deterrent* to potential killers? deter, V.

detrimental ADJ. harmful; damaging. Journalists wondered whether Senator Obama's relationship with his controversial minister would eventually prove *detrimental* to his chances of being elected president. detriment, N.

devious ADJ. roundabout; erratic; not straightforward. His plan was so *devious* that it was only with great difficulty we could follow its shifts and dodges.

devise V. think up; invent; plan. How clever he must be to have *devised* such a devious plan! What ingenious inventions might he have *devised* if he had turned his mind to science and not to crime!

Word List 18

didactic ADJ. teaching; instructional. Pope's lengthy poem *An Essay on Man* is too *didactic* for my taste: I dislike it when poets turn preachy and moralize.

diffuse ADJ. wordy; rambling; spread out. If you pay authors by the word, you tempt them to produce *diffuse* manuscripts rather than concise ones.

digression N. wandering away from the subject. Nobody minded when Professor Renoir's lectures wandered away from their official themes; his *digressions* were always more fascinating than the topic of the day. digress, V.

diligence N. steadiness of effort; persistent hard work. Her employers were greatly impressed by her *diligence* and offered her a partnership in the firm. diligent, ADJ.

diminution N. lessening; reduction in size. Old Jack was as sharp at eighty as he had been at fifty; increasing age led to no *diminution* of his mental acuity.

disband V. dissolve; disperse. The chess club *disbanded* after its disastrous initial season.

discerning ADJ. mentally quick and observant; having insight. Though no genius, the star was sufficiently *discerning* to tell her true friends from the countless phonies who flattered her. discernment, N.

disclose V. reveal. Although competitors offered him bribes, he refused to *disclose* any information about his company's forthcoming product. disclosure, N.

discordant ADJ. not harmonious; conflicting. Nothing is quite so *discordant* as the sound of a junior high school orchestra tuning up. discord, N.

discount V. disregard. Be prepared to *discount* what he has to say about his ex-wife; he is still very bitter about the divorce.

Word List 19

discredit V. defame; destroy confidence in; disbelieve. The campaign was highly negative in tone; each candidate tried to *discredit* the others.

discrepancy N. lack of consistency; difference; contradiction. "Observe, Watson, the significant *discrepancies* between Sir Percy's original description of the crime and his most recent testimony. What do these contradictions suggest?"

discriminating ADJ. able to see differences; prejudiced. A superb interpreter of Picasso, she was sufficiently *discriminating* to judge the most complex works of modern art. (secondary meaning) discrimination, N.

discursive ADJ. digressing; rambling. As the lecturer wandered from topic to topic, we wondered what if any point there was to his *discursive* remarks.

disdain V. view with scorn or contempt. In the film *Funny Face*, the bookish heroine *disdained* fashion models for their lack of intellectual interests. also N.

disinclination N. unwillingness. Some mornings I feel a great *disinclination* to get out of bed.

disinterested ADJ. unprejudiced. In view of the judge's political ambitions and the lawyers' financial interest in the case, the only *disinterested* person in the courtroom may have been the court reporter.

dismantle V. take apart. When the show closed, they *dismantled* the scenery before storing it.

dismiss V. put away from consideration; reject. Believing in John's love for her, she *dismissed* the notion that he might be unfaithful. (secondary meaning)

disparage V. belittle. A doting mother, Emma was far more likely to praise her son's crude attempts at art than to *disparage* them.

Word List 20

disparity N. difference; condition of inequality. Their *disparity* in rank made no difference at all to the prince and Cinderella.

dispassionate ADJ. calm; impartial. Known in the company for his cool judgment, Bill could impartially examine the causes of a problem, giving a *dispassionate* analysis of what had gone wrong, and go on to suggest how to correct the mess.

dispel V. drive away; scatter; cause to vanish. The bright sunlight eventually *dispelled* the morning mist.

disperse V. cause to break up; scatter. The police fired tear gas into the crowd to *disperse* the protesters.

disputatious ADJ. argumentative; fond of arguing. Convinced he knew more than his lawyers, Alan was a *disputatious* client, ready to argue about the best way to conduct the case.

disseminate V. distribute; spread; scatter (like seeds). By their use of the Internet, propagandists have been able to *disseminate* their pet doctrines to new audiences around the globe.

dissent V. disagree. In a recent Supreme Court decision, Justice Ginsburg *dissented* from the majority opinion. also N.

dissipate V. squander; waste; scatter. Although Jon had the potential to become a fine actor, he seemed content to *dissipate* his talents by appearing in burlesque shows and soap operas.

dissonance N. discord; disagreement. Composer Charles Ives often used *dissonance*—clashing or unresolved chords—for special effects in his musical works.

dissuade V. persuade not to do; discourage. Since Tom could not *dissuade* Huck from running away from home, he decided to accompany his friend. dissuasion, N.

Word List 21

distant ADJ. reserved or aloof; cold in manner. His *distant* greeting made me feel unwelcome from the start. (secondary meaning)

divergent ADJ. differing; deviating. Since graduating from medical school, the two doctors have taken *divergent* paths, one going on to become a nationally prominent surgeon, the other dedicating himself to a small family practice in his home town. divergence, N.

diverse ADJ. many and different; distinctly unlike. San Francisco offers tourists *diverse* pleasures, some as simple as a ride on a cable car, others as sophisticated as a night at the opera. diversity, N.

divulge V. reveal. No lover of gossip, Charlotte would never *divulge* anything that a friend told her in confidence.

doctrine N. teachings, in general; particular principle (religious, legal, and so on) taught. He was so committed to the *doctrines* of his faith that he was unable to evaluate them impartially.

document V. provide written evidence. She kept all the receipts from her business trip in order to *document* her expenses for the firm. also N.

dogmatic ADJ. opinionated; arbitrary; doctrinal. We tried to discourage Doug from being so *dogmatic*, but never could convince him that his opinions might be wrong.

dormant ADJ. sleeping; lethargic; latent. At fifty her long-*dormant* ambition to write flared up once more; within a year she had completed the first of her great historical novels.

dubious ADJ. questionable; filled with doubt. Many critics of the SAT contend that the test is of *dubious* worth. Jack claimed he could get a perfect 2400 on the SAT, but Ellen was *dubious*: she knew he hadn't cracked a book in three years.

duplicity N. double-dealing; hypocrisy. When Tanya learned that Mark had been two-timing her, she was furious at his *duplicity*. duplicitous, ADJ.

Word List 22

duration N. length of time something lasts. Because she wanted the children to make a good impression on the dinner guests, Mother promised them a treat if they would behave for the *duration* of the meal.

dutiful ADJ. respectful; obedient. The *dutiful* child grew up to be a conscientious adult, aware of her civic obligations.

ebb V. recede; lessen. Sitting on the beach, Mrs. Dalloway watched the waters recede as the tide slowly *ebbed*. also, N.

eccentric ADJ. odd; whimsical; irregular. The comet veered dangerously close to Earth in its *eccentric* orbit.

eclectic ADJ. selective in choosing from a variety of sources. The reviewers praised the new restaurant's *eclectic* selection of dishes, which ranged from Oriental stir fries to French ragouts and stews.

eclipse V. darken; extinguish; surpass. The new stock market high *eclipsed* the previous record set in 1995.

effervescent ADJ. exuberant; bubbly and excited. Nothing depressed Amy for long; she was so naturally *effervescent* that she was soon as high-spirited as ever. effervesce, V.

egotistical ADJ. excessively self-centered; self-important; conceited. Typical *egotistical* remark: "But enough of this chit-chat about you and your little problems. Let's talk about what's really important: *me!*" egotism, N.

elated ADJ. overjoyed; in high spirits. Grinning from ear to ear, Bonnie Blair was clearly *elated* by her fifth Olympic gold medal. elation, N.

eloquence N. expressiveness; persuasive speech. The crowds were stirred by Martin Luther King's *eloquence*. eloquent, ADJ.

Word List 23

elusive ADJ. evasive; baffling; hard to grasp. No matter how hard Tom tried to lure the trout into taking the bait, the fish was too *elusive* for him to catch. elude, V.

embellish V. adorn; ornament. The costume designer *embellished* the leading lady's ball gown with yards and yards of ribbon and lace.

emulate V. imitate; rival. In a brief essay, describe a person you admire, someone whose virtues you would like to *emulate*.

endorse V. approve; support. Everyone waited to see which one of the rival candidates for the city council the mayor would *endorse*. endorsement, N. (secondary meaning)

enduring ADJ. lasting; surviving. Keats believed in the *enduring* power of great art, which would outlast its creators' brief lives.

enervate V. weaken. She was slow to recover from her illness; even a short walk to the window would *enervate* her. enervation, N.

engender V. cause; produce. To receive praise for real accomplishments *engenders* self-confidence in a child.

enhance V. advance; improve. You can *enhance* your chances of being admitted to the college of your choice by learning to write well; an excellent essay can *enhance* any application.

enigma N. puzzle; mystery. "What *do* women want?" asked Dr. Sigmund Freud. Their behavior was an *enigma* to him.

enmity N. ill will; hatred. At Camp David President Carter labored to bring an end to the *enmity* that prevented Egypt and Israel from living in peace.

Word List 24

enumerate V. list; mention one by one. Huck hung his head in shame as Miss Watson *enumerated* his many flaws.

ephemeral ADJ. short-lived; fleeting. With its adult stage lasting less than two days, the mayfly is by definition an *ephemeral* creature.

epic N. long heroic poem, or similar work of art. Kurosawa's film *Seven Samurai* is an *epic* that portrays the struggle of seven warriors to destroy a band of robbers. also ADJ.

epicure N. connoisseur of food and drink. *Epicures* patronize this restaurant because it features exotic wines and dishes. epicurean, ADJ.

episodic ADJ. loosely connected; divided into incidents; occurring at intervals. Though he tried to follow the plot of *Gravity's Rainbow*, John found the novel too *episodic*; he enjoyed individual passages, but had trouble following the work as a whole.

equanimity N. calmness of temperament; composure. Even the inevitable strains of caring for an ailing mother did not disturb Bea's *equanimity*.

equivocal ADJ. ambiguous; intentionally misleading. Rejecting the candidate's *equivocal* comments on tax reform, the reporters pressed him to say where he stood on the issue. equivocate, V.

erratic ADJ. odd; unpredictable; wandering. Investors become anxious when the stock market appears *erratic*.

erroneous ADJ. mistaken; wrong. I thought my answer was correct, but it was *erroneous*.

erudite ADJ. learned; scholarly. Unlike much scholarly writing, Huizinga's prose was entertaining as well as *erudite*, lively as well as learned. erudition, N.

Word List 25

esoteric ADJ. hard to understand; known only to the chosen few. Stories in *The New Yorker* often include allusions to obscure people and events, references so *esoteric* that only true New Yorkers can understand them.

espouse V. adopt; support. She was always ready to *espouse* a worthy cause.

esteem V. respect; value; judge. Jill *esteemed* Jack's taste in music, but she deplored his taste in clothes.

ethereal ADJ. light; heavenly; unusually refined. In Shakespeare's *The Tempest*, the spirit Ariel is an *ethereal* creature, too airy and unearthly for our mortal world.

eulogy N. expression of praise, often on the occasion of someone's death. Instead of delivering a spoken *eulogy* at Genny's memorial service, Jeff sang a song he had written in her honor.

euphemism N. mild expression used in place of an unpleasant one. The Nazis did not describe their slaughter of the Jews as genocide; instead, they used a *euphemism,* calling it "the final solution."

euphonious ADJ. pleasing in sound. *Euphonious* even when spoken, the Italian language is particularly pleasing to the ear when sung. euphony, N.

euphoria N. feeling of great happiness and well-being (sometimes exaggerated). Delighted with her SAT scores, sure that the university would accept her, Allison was filled with *euphoria.* euphoric, ADJ.

evanescent ADJ. fleeting; vanishing. Brandon's satisfaction in his new job was *evanescent,* for he immediately began to notice its many drawbacks. evanescence, N.

exacerbate V. worsen; embitter; aggravate. When acacias are in bloom, the increase of pollen in the air *exacerbates* Richard's asthma.

Word List 26

exacting ADJ. extremely demanding. Cleaning the ceiling of the Sistine Chapel was an *exacting* task, one that demanded extremely meticulous care on the part of the restorers. exaction, N.

exalt V. raise in rank or dignity; praise. The rock star Mick Jagger was *exalted* to the rank

of knighthood by the Queen; he now is known as Sir Mick Jagger.

execute V. put into effect; carry out. The choreographer wanted to see how well Margaret could *execute* a pirouette. (secondary meaning) execution, N.

exemplary ADJ. serving as a model; outstanding. At commencement the dean praised Ellen for her *exemplary* behavior as class president.

exemplify V. serve as an example of; embody. For a generation of balletgoers, Rudolf Nureyev *exemplified* the ideal of masculine grace.

exhaustive ADJ. thorough; comprehensive. We have made an *exhaustive* study of all published SAT tests and are happy to share our research with you.

exhilarating ADJ. invigorating and refreshing; cheering. Though some of the hikers found tramping through the snow tiring, Jeffrey found the walk on the cold, crisp day *exhilarating.*

exonerate V. acquit; exculpate. The defense team feverishly sought fresh evidence that might *exonerate* their client.

expedient ADJ. suitable to achieve a particular end; practical; politic. A pragmatic politician, he was guided by what was *expedient* rather than by what was ethical. expediency, N.

expedite V. hasten. Because we are on a tight schedule, we hope you will be able to *expedite* the delivery of our order.

Word List 27

expertise N. specialized knowledge; expert skill. Although she is knowledgeable in a number of fields, she was hired for her special *expertise* in computer programming.

explicit ADJ. totally clear; definite; outspoken. Don't just hint around that you're dissatisfied: be *explicit* about what's bothering you.

exploit N. deed or action, particularly a brave deed. Raoul Wallenberg was noted for his *exploits* in rescuing Jews from Hitler's forces.

exploit V. make use of, sometimes unjustly. Cesar Chavez fought attempts to *exploit* migrant farmworkers in California. exploitation, N.

expository ADJ. explanatory; intended to explain. The manual that came with my DVR was no masterpiece of *expository* prose: its explanations were so garbled that I couldn't even figure out how to rewind a program. exposition, N.

extant ADJ. still in existence. I'd hoped to buy a copy of Margaret Dean Smith's facsimile of *The Dancing Master*. Unfortunately, all the copies *extant* are in libraries or private collections; none is for sale.

extol V. praise; glorify. The president *extolled* the astronauts, calling them the pioneers of the Space Age.

extraneous ADJ. not essential; superfluous. No wonder Ted can't think straight! His mind is so cluttered up with *extraneous* trivia that he can't concentrate on the essentials.

extricate V. free; disentangle. The fox could not *extricate* itself from the trap.

exuberance N. overflowing abundance; joyful enthusiasm; flamboyance; lavishness. I was bowled over by the *exuberance* of Amy's welcome. What an enthusiastic greeting!

Word List 28

facile ADJ. easily accomplished; ready or fluent; superficial. Words came easily to Jonathan: he was a *facile* speaker and prided himself on being ready to make a speech at a moment's notice.

facilitate V. help bring about; make less difficult. Rest and proper nourishment should *facilitate* the patient's recovery.

fallacious ADJ. false; misleading. Paradoxically, *fallacious* reasoning does not always yield erroneous results: even though your logic may be faulty, the answer you get may nevertheless be correct. fallacy, N.

fanaticism N. excessive zeal; extreme devotion to a belief or cause. When Islamic fundamentalists demanded the death of Salman Rushdie because his novel questioned their faith, world opinion condemned them for their *fanaticism*.

fastidious ADJ. difficult to please; squeamish. Bobby was such a *fastidious* eater that he would eat a sandwich only if his mother first cut off every scrap of crust.

feasible ADJ. practical. Without additional funding, it may not be *feasible* to build a new stadium for the team on the highly developed west side of the city.

fervor N. glowing ardor; intensity of feeling. At the protest rally, the students cheered the strikers and booed the dean with equal *fervor*.

fickle ADJ. changeable; faithless. As soon as Romeo saw Juliet, he forgot all about his old girlfriend Rosaline. Was Romeo *fickle*?

figurative ADJ. not literal, but metaphorical; using a figure of speech. "To lose one's marbles" is a *figurative* expression; if you're told that Jack has lost his marbles, no one expects you to rush out to buy him a replacement set.

flagrant ADJ. conspicuously wicked; blatant; outrageous. The governor's appointment of his brother-in-law to the State Supreme Court was a *flagrant* violation of the state laws against nepotism (favoritism based on kinship).

Word List 29

flippant ADJ. lacking proper seriousness. When Mark told Mona he loved her, she dismissed his earnest declaration with a *flippant* "Oh, you say that to all the girls!" flippancy, N.

florid ADJ. excessively ornate; flowery; reddish. He was an old-fashioned orator, known for his overblown rhetoric and his *florid* prose.

fluctuate V. waver; shift. The water pressure in our shower *fluctuates* wildly; you start rinsing yourself off with a trickle, and two minutes later, you think you're going to drown.

foolhardy ADJ. rash; heedless. Don't be *foolhardy*. Get some advice from experienced people before you strike out on your own.

foresight N. ability to foresee future happenings; prudence. A wise investor, she had the *foresight* to buy land just before the current real estate boom.

forestall V. prevent by taking action in advance. By setting up a prenuptial agreement, the prospective bride and groom hoped to *forestall* any potential arguments about money in the event of a divorce.

forsake V. desert; abandon; renounce. No one expected Gauguin to *forsake* his wife and children and run off to Tahiti.

forthright ADJ. outspoken; frank. Never afraid to call a spade a spade, she was perhaps too *forthright* to be a successful party politician.

fortuitous ADJ. accidental; by chance. Though he pretended their encounter was *fortuitous*, he'd actually been hanging around her usual haunts for the past two weeks.

foster V. rear; encourage; nurture. According to the legend, Romulus and Remus were *fostered* by a she-wolf who raised them as if they were her cubs. also ADJ.

Word List 30

founder V. fail completely; sink. After hitting the submerged iceberg, the *Titanic* started taking in water rapidly and soon *foundered*.

founder N. person who establishes (an organization, business). Among those drowned when the *Titanic* sank was the *founder* of the Abraham & Straus department store.

frail ADJ. weak. The delicate child seemed too *frail* to lift the heavy carton. frailty, N.

frivolous ADJ. lacking in seriousness; self-indulgently carefree; relatively unimportant. Though Nancy enjoyed Bill's *frivolous*, lighthearted companionship, she sometimes wondered whether he could ever be serious. frivolity, N.

frugality N. thrift; economy. In economically hard times, those who do not learn to practice *frugality* risk bankruptcy. frugal, ADJ.

fundamental V. basic; primary; essential. The committee discussed all sorts of side issues without ever getting down to addressing the *fundamental* problem.

furtive ADJ. stealthy; sneaky. Noticing the *furtive* glance the customer gave the diamond bracelet on the counter, the jeweler wondered whether he had a potential shoplifter on his hands.

futile ADJ. ineffective; fruitless. It is *futile* for me to try to get any work done around here while the telephone is ringing every 30 seconds.

galvanize V. stimulate by shock; stir up; revitalize. News that the prince was almost at their door *galvanized* the ugly stepsisters into a frenzy of combing and primping.

garbled ADJ. mixed up; jumbled; distorted. A favorite party game involves passing a whispered message from one person to another, till, by the time it reaches the last player, the message is totally *garbled*.

Word List 31

garrulous ADJ. loquacious; wordy; talkative. My Uncle Henry can out-talk any three people I know. He is the most *garrulous* person in Cayuga County.

genre N. particular variety of art or literature. Both a short-story writer and a poet, Langston Hughes proved himself equally skilled in either *genre*.

germane ADJ. pertinent; bearing upon the case at hand. The judge would not allow the testimony to be heard by the jury because it was not *germane* to the case.

glacial ADJ. like a glacier; extremely cold. Never a warm person, John, when offended, could seem positively *glacial*.

glib ADJ. fluent; facile; slick. Keeping up a steady patter to entertain his customers, the kitchen gadget salesman was a *glib* speaker, never at a loss for a word.

glutton N. someone who eats too much; greedy person. Who is the *glutton* who ate up all the chocolate chip cookies I made for dessert? gluttonous, ADJ.

gorge N. small, steep-walled canyon. The white-water rafting guide warned us about the rapids farther downstream, where the river cut through a narrow *gorge*.

grandiose ADJ. pretentious; high-flown; ridiculously exaggerated; impressive. The aged matinee idol still had *grandiose* notions of his supposed importance in the theatrical world.

gratify V. please. Serena's parents were *gratified* by her successful performance at Wimbledon.

gratuitous ADJ. given freely; unwarranted; unprovoked; uncalled for. Quit making *gratuitous* comments about my driving; no one asked you for your opinion.

Word List 32

gravity N. seriousness. We could tell we were in serious trouble from the *gravity* of the principal's expression. (secondary meaning) grave, ADJ.

gregarious ADJ. sociable. Typically, partygoers are *gregarious*; hermits are not.

grievance N. cause of complaint. When her supervisor ignored her complaint, she took her *grievance* to the union.

grudging ADJ. unwilling; reluctant; stingy. We received only *grudging* support from the mayor despite his earlier promises of aid.

guile N. deceit; duplicity; wiliness; cunning. Iago uses considerable *guile* to trick Othello into believing that Desdemona has been unfaithful.

gullible ADJ. easily deceived. *Gullible* people have only themselves to blame if they fall for scams repeatedly. As the saying goes, "Fool me once, shame on you. Fool me twice, shame on *me*."

hackneyed ADJ. commonplace; trite. When the reviewer criticized the movie for its *hackneyed* plot, we agreed; we had seen similar stories hundreds of times before.

hallowed ADJ. blessed; consecrated; venerated. General Douglas MacArthur wrote, "Duty, honor, country: those three *hallowed* words reverently dictate what you ought to be, what you can be, what you will be."

hamper V. obstruct. The new mother didn't realize how much the effort of caring for an infant would *hamper* her ability to keep an immaculate house.

harass V. annoy by repeated attacks; torment. When he could not pay his bills as quickly as he had promised, he was *harassed* by his creditors.

Word List 33

hardy ADJ. sturdy; robust; able to stand inclement weather. We asked the gardening expert to recommend particularly *hardy* plants that could withstand our harsh New England winters.

haughtiness N. pride; arrogance. When she realized that Darcy believed himself too good to dance with his inferiors, Elizabeth took great offense at his *haughtiness*.

hedonist N. one who believes that pleasure is the sole aim in life. A thoroughgoing *hedonist*, he considered only his own pleasure and ignored any claims others had on his money or time.

heed V. pay attention to; consider. We hope you *heed* our advice and get a good night's sleep before the test. also N.

heresy N. opinion contrary to popular belief; opinion contrary to accepted religion. Galileo's assertion that Earth moves around the sun directly contradicted the religious teachings of his day; as a result, he was tried for *heresy*. heretic, N.

heterodox ADJ. unorthodox; unconventional. To those who upheld the belief that Earth did not move, Galileo's theory that Earth circles the sun was disturbingly *heterodox*.

heterogeneous ADJ. dissimilar; mixed. This year's entering class is a remarkably *heterogeneous* body: it includes students from 40 different states and 26 foreign countries, some the children of billionaires, others the offspring of welfare families.

heyday N. time of greatest success; prime. In their *heyday*, the San Francisco Forty-Niners won the Super Bowl two years running.

hiatus N. gap; interruption in duration or continuity; pause. During the summer *hiatus*, many students try to earn enough money to pay their tuition for the next school year.

hierarchy N. arrangement by rank or standing; authoritarian body divided into ranks. To be low man on the totem pole is to have an inferior place in the *hierarchy*.

Word List 34

hindrance   N. block; obstacle. Stalled cars along the highway present a *hindrance* to traffic that tow trucks should remove without delay. hinder, V.

hoard   V. stockpile; accumulate for future use. Whenever there are rumors of a food shortage, many people are tempted to *hoard* food. also N.

homogeneous   ADJ. of the same kind. Because the student body at Elite Prep was so *homogeneous*, Sara and James decided to send their daughter to a school that offered greater cultural diversity.

hone   V. sharpen. Determined to get a good shave, Ed *honed* his razor with great care.

hostility   N. unfriendliness; hatred. Children often feel *hostility* toward the new baby in the family.

humane   ADJ. marked by kindness or consideration. It is ironic that the *Humane* Society sometimes must show its compassion toward mistreated animals by killing them to put them out of their misery.

husband   V. use sparingly; conserve; save. Marathon runners must *husband* their energy so that they can keep going for the entire distance.

hyperbole   N. exaggeration; overstatement. As far as I'm concerned, Apple's claims about the new computer are pure *hyperbole*: no machine is that good!

hypocritical   ADJ. pretending to be virtuous; deceiving. Believing Eddie to be interested only in his own advancement, Greg resented his *hypocritical* posing as a friend. hypocrisy, N.

hypothetical   ADJ. based on assumptions or hypotheses; supposed. Suppose you are accepted by Harvard, Stanford, and Brown. Which one would you choose to attend? Remember: this is only a *hypothetical* situation. hypothesis, N.

Word List 35

iconoclast   N. one who attacks cherished traditions. A born *iconoclast*, Jean Genet deliberately set out to shock conventional theatergoers with his radical plays.

idiosyncrasy   N. individual trait, usually odd in nature; eccentricity. One of Richard Nixon's little *idiosyncracies* was his liking for ketchup on cottage cheese. One of Hannibal Lecter's little *idiosyncrasies* was his liking for human flesh.

ignominy   N. deep disgrace; shame or dishonor. To lose the Ping-Pong match to a trained chimpanzee! How could Rollo stand the *ignominy* of his defeat?

illicit   ADJ. illegal. The defense attorney maintained that her client had never performed any *illicit* action.

illuminate   V. brighten; clear up or make understandable; enlighten. Just as a lamp can *illuminate* a dark room, a perceptive comment can *illuminate* a knotty problem.

illusory   ADJ. deceptive; not real. Unfortunately, the costs of running the lemonade stand were so high that Tom's profits proved *illusory*.

imbalance   N. lack of balance or symmetry; disproportion. Because of the great *imbalance* between the number of males and females invited, the dance was unsuccessful.

immaculate   ADJ. spotless; flawless; absolutely clean. Ken and Jessica were wonderful tenants and left the apartment in *immaculate* condition when they moved out.

immune   ADJ. resistant to; free or exempt from. Fortunately, Florence had contracted chicken pox as a child and was *immune* to it when her baby broke out in spots. immunity, N.

immutable   ADJ. unchangeable. All things change over time; nothing is *immutable*.

Word List 36

impair   V. injure; hurt. Drinking alcohol can *impair* your ability to drive safely; if you're going to drink, don't drive.

impartial   ADJ. not biased; fair. Knowing that she could not be *impartial* about her own child, Jo refused to judge any match in which Billy was competing.

impassive   ADJ. without feeling; imperturbable; stoical. Refusing to let the enemy see how deeply shaken he was by his capture, the prisoner kept his face *impassive*.

impeccable ADJ. faultless. The uncrowned queen of the fashion industry, Diana was acclaimed for her *impeccable* taste.

impecunious ADJ. without money. Though Scrooge claimed he was too *impecunious* to give alms, he easily could have afforded to be charitable.

impede V. hinder; block; delay. The special prosecutor determined that the attorney general, though inept, had not intentionally set out to *impede* the progress of the investigation.

impel V. drive or force onward. A strong feeling of urgency *impelled* her; if she failed to finish the project right then, she knew that she would never get it done.

imperceptible ADJ. unnoticeable; undetectable. Fortunately, the stain on the blouse was *imperceptible* after the blouse had gone through the wash.

imperious ADJ. domineering; haughty. Jane rather liked a man to be masterful, but Mr. Rochester seemed so bent on getting his own way that he was actually *imperious*!

impervious ADJ. impenetrable; incapable of being damaged or distressed. The carpet salesman told Simone that his most expensive brand of floor covering was warranted to be *impervious* to ordinary wear and tear.

Word List 37

impetuous ADJ. violent; hasty; rash. "Leap before you look" was the motto suggested by one particularly *impetuous* young man.

implausible ADJ. unlikely; unbelievable. Though her alibi seemed *implausible*, it in fact turned out to be true.

implement V. put into effect; supply with tools. The mayor was unwilling to *implement* the plan until she was sure it had the governor's backing. implementation, N.

implication N. something hinted at or suggested. When Miss Watson said she hadn't seen her purse since the last time Jim was in the house, the *implication* was that she suspected Jim had taken it. imply, V.

implicit ADJ. understood but not stated. Jack never told Jill he adored her; he believed his love was *implicit* in his actions.

impoverished ADJ. poor. The typical "rags to riches" story tells the tale of an *impoverished* youth who through his own efforts rises to a position of wealth and prosperity.

impromptu ADJ. without previous preparation; off the cuff; on the spur of the moment. The judges were amazed that she could make such a thorough, well-supported presentation in an *impromptu* speech.

impudence N. impertinence; insolence. When kissed on the cheek by a perfect stranger, Lady Catherine exclaimed, "Of all the nerve! Young man, I should have you horsewhipped for your *impudence*."

inadvertently ADV. by oversight; carelessly or unintentionally. Judy's great fear was that she might *inadvertently* omit a question on the exam and mismark her whole answer sheet.

inane ADJ. silly; senseless. There's no point to what you're saying. Why are you bothering to make such *inane* remarks?

Word List 38

inaugurate V. start; initiate; install in office. The airline decided to *inaugurate* its new route to the Far East with a special reduced fare offer. inaugural, ADJ.

incense V. enrage; infuriate. Cruelty to defenseless animals *incensed* Kit.

incentive N. spur; motive. Mike's strong desire to outshine his big sister was all the *incentive* he needed to do well in school.

incessant ADJ. uninterrupted; unceasing. We could not fall asleep because of the crickets' *incessant* chirping, which seemed to go on all night long.

incidental ADJ. not essential; minor. The scholarship covered his major expenses at college and some of his *incidental* expenses as well.

incisive ADJ. cutting; sharp. Her *incisive* commentary cut through the tangle of arguments, exposing fallacies and logical flaws.

incite V. arouse to action; goad; motivate; induce to exist. In a fiery speech, Mario *incited* his fellow students to go out on strike to protest the university's anti-affirmative-action stand.

incline N. slope; slant. The architect recommended that the nursing home's ramp be rebuilt because its *incline* was too steep for wheelchairs.

inclined ADJ. tending or leaning toward; bent. Though I am *inclined* to be skeptical, the witness's manner *inclines* me to believe his story. also V.

inclusive ADJ. tending to include all. The comedian turned down the invitation to join the Players' Club, saying any club that would let him in was too *inclusive* for him.

Word List 39

incoherent ADJ. unintelligible; muddled; illogical. The bereaved father sobbed and stammered, his words becoming almost *incoherent* in his grief. incoherence, N.

incongruous ADJ. not fitting; absurd. Towering over the nearby houses, the McMansion looked wholly *incongruous* in the historic neighborhood of small Craftsman-style bungalows. incongruity, N.

inconsequential ADJ. insignificant; unimportant. Brushing off Ali's apologies for having broken the wineglass, Tamara said, "Don't worry about it; it's *inconsequential.*"

incontrovertible ADJ. indisputable; not open to question. Unless you find the evidence against my client absolutely *incontrovertible*, you must declare her not guilty of this charge.

incorrigible ADJ. uncorrectable. Though Widow Douglass hoped to reform Huck, Miss Watson called him *incorrigible* and said he would come to no good end.

indefatigable ADJ. tireless. Although the effort of taking out the garbage tired Wayne out for the entire morning, when it came to partying, he was *indefatigable.*

indict V. charge. The district attorney didn't want to *indict* the suspect until she was sure she had a strong enough case to convince a jury. indictment, N.

indifferent ADJ. unmoved; lacking concern. Because she felt no desire to marry, she was *indifferent* to his constant proposals.

indigenous ADJ. native. Cigarettes are made of tobacco, one of the *indigenous* plants the early explorers found in the New World.

indigent ADJ. poor; destitute. Someone who is truly *indigent* can't even afford to buy a pack of cigarettes. (Don't mix up *indigent* and *indigenous.* See preceding example.)

Word List 40

indiscriminate ADJ. choosing at random; confused. Disapproving of her son's *indiscriminate* television viewing, Shirley decided to restrict him to watching educational programs.

indolent ADJ. lazy. Couch potatoes who lie back on their sofas watching television are by definition *indolent.* indolence, N.

indomitable ADJ. unconquerable; unyielding. Focusing on her game despite all her personal problems, tennis champion Steffi Graf proved she had an *indomitable* will to win.

indubitable ADJ. unable to be doubted; unquestionable. Auditioning for the chorus line, Molly was an *indubitable* hit: the director fired the leading lady and hired Molly in her place!

induce V. persuade; bring about. After the quarrel, Tina said nothing could *induce* her to talk to Tony again. inducement, N.

indulge V. humor; treat leniently. Parents who constantly *indulge* their children by giving in to their every whim may thoroughly spoil them.

industrious ADJ. diligent; hard-working. If you are *industrious* and apply yourself to your assignments, you will do well in college. industry, N.

ineffectual ADJ. not effective; weak. Because the candidate failed to get across his message to the public, his campaign was *ineffectual.*

inept ADJ. unsuited; absurd; incompetent. The *inept* glovemaker was all thumbs.

inequity N. unfairness. In demanding equal pay for equal work, women protest the basic *inequity* of a system that gives greater financial rewards to men.

Word List 41

inert ADJ. inactive; lacking power to move. "Get up, you lazybones," Tina cried to Tony, who lay in bed *inert*.

inexorable ADJ. relentless; unyielding; implacable. Ignoring the defense attorney's pleas for clemency, the judge was *inexorable*, giving the convicted felon the maximum punishment allowed by law.

infamous ADJ. notoriously bad. Charles Manson and Jeffrey Dahmer are both *infamous* killers.

infer V. deduce; conclude. From the students' glazed looks, it was easy for me to *infer* that they were bored out of their minds.

infiltrate V. pass into or through; penetrate (an organization) sneakily. In order to be able to *infiltrate* enemy lines at night without being seen, the scouts darkened their faces and wore black coveralls. infiltrator, N.

infinitesimal ADJ. exceedingly small; so small as to be almost nonexistent. Making sure everyone was aware she was on an extremely strict diet, Melanie said she would have only an *infinitesimal* sliver of pie.

infraction N. violation (of a rule or regulation); breach. When Dennis Rodman butted heads with a referee, he committed a clear *infraction* of NBA rules.

ingenious ADJ. clever; resourceful. Kit admired the *ingenious* way her iPod shuffled the songs on her playlist. ingenuity, N.

ingrate N. ungrateful person. That *ingrate* Bob sneered at the tie I gave him.

inherent ADJ. firmly established by nature or habit; intrinsic. Elaine's *inherent* love of justice caused her to champion people whom she thought society had treated unfairly.

Word List 42

inimical ADJ. unfriendly; hostile; harmful; detrimental. I've always been friendly to Martha. Why is she so *inimical* to me?

initiate V. begin; originate; receive into a group. The college is about to *initiate* a program to reduce math anxiety among students.

injurious ADJ. harmful. Smoking cigarettes can be *injurious* to your health.

innate ADJ. inborn. Mozart's parents soon recognized young Wolfgang's *innate* talent for music.

innocuous ADJ. harmless. An occasional glass of wine with dinner is relatively *innocuous* and should have no ill effect.

innovation N. change; introduction of something new. Although Richard liked to keep up with all the latest technological *innovations*, he didn't always abandon tried and true techniques in favor of something new. innovate, V.

inopportune ADJ. untimely; poorly chosen. A rock concert is an *inopportune* setting for a quiet conversation.

insatiable ADJ. not easily satisfied; greedy. Lexy's passion for new clothes is *insatiable*; she can shop till she literally drops.

insightful ADJ. discerning; perceptive. Sol thought he was very *insightful* about human behavior, but he hadn't a clue why people acted the way they did.

insinuate V. hint; imply; creep in. When you said I looked robust, were you trying to *insinuate* I'm getting fat?

Word List 43

insipid ADJ. lacking in flavor; dull. Flat prose and flat ginger ale are equally *insipid*: both lack sparkle.

insolvent ADJ. bankrupt; unable to repay one's debts. Although young Lord Widgeon was *insolvent*, he had no fear of being thrown into debtors' prison; he was sure that, if his creditors pressed him for payment, his wealthy parents would repay what he owed.

instigate V. urge; start; provoke. Rumors of police corruption led the mayor to *instigate* an investigation into the department's activities.

insularity N. narrow-mindedness; isolation. The *insularity* of the islanders manifested itself in their suspicion of anything foreign. insular, ADJ.

insuperable ADJ. insurmountable; unbeatable. Though the odds against their survival seemed *insuperable*, the Apollo 13 astronauts reached Earth safely.

insurgent ADJ. rebellious. Because the *insurgent* forces had occupied the capital and had gained control of the railway lines, several of the war correspondents covering the uprising predicted a rebel victory.

intangible ADJ. not material; not able to be perceived by touch; vague; elusive. Emotions are *intangible*, and yet we know that we feel love and hate, though we cannot grasp these feelings in our hands.

integral ADJ. complete; necessary for completeness. Physical education is an *integral* part of our curriculum; a sound mind and a sound body are complementary.

integrity N. uprightness; wholeness. Lincoln, whose personal *integrity* has inspired millions, fought a civil war to maintain the *integrity* of the republic, that these United States might remain undivided for all time.

intermittent ADJ. periodic; on and off. The outdoor wedding reception had to be moved indoors to avoid the *intermittent* showers that fell on and off all afternoon.

Word List 44

intervene V. come between. Rachel tried to *intervene* in the quarrel between her two sons.

intimidate V. frighten. I'll learn karate and then those big bullies won't be able to *intimidate* me any more.

intractable ADJ. unruly; stubborn; unyielding. Charlie Brown's friend Pigpen was *intractable*: he absolutely refused to take a bath.

intransigence N. refusal of any compromise; stubbornness. When I predicted that the strike would be over in a week, I didn't expect to encounter such *intransigence* from both sides. intransigent, ADJ.

intrepid ADJ. fearless. For her *intrepid* conduct in nursing the wounded during the war,

Florence Nightingale was honored by Queen Victoria.

intricate ADJ. complex; knotty; tangled. Eric spent many hours designing mazes so *intricate* that none of his classmates could solve them. intricacy, N.

intrinsic ADJ. essential; inherent; built-in; natural. Although my grandmother's china has little *intrinsic* value, I shall always treasure it for the memories it evokes.

introspective ADJ. looking within oneself. Though young Francis of Assisi led a wild and worldly life, even he had *introspective* moments during which he examined his soul.

intuition N. immediate insight; power of knowing without reasoning. Even though Tony denied that anything was wrong, Tina trusted her *intuition* that something was bothering him. intuitive, ADJ.

inundate V. overwhelm; flood; submerge. This semester I am *inundated* with work. You should see the piles of paperwork flooding my desk.

Word List 45

invert V. turn upside down or inside out. When he *inverted* his body in a handstand, he felt the blood rush to his head.

irascible ADJ. irritable; easily angered. Pop had what people call a hair-trigger temper: he was a hot-tempered, *irascible* guy.

ironic ADJ. relating to a contradiction between an event's expected result and its actual outcome; sarcastic. It is *ironic* that his success came when he least wanted it. irony, N.

irrational ADJ. illogical; lacking reason; insane. Many people have such an *irrational* fear of snakes that they panic at the sight of a harmless garter snake.

irrelevant ADJ. not applicable; unrelated. No matter how *irrelevant* the patient's mumblings may seem, they give us some indications of what he has on his mind.

irreproachable ADJ. blameless; impeccable. Homer's conduct at the office party was *irreproachable*; even Marge didn't have anything bad to say about how he behaved.

irresolute ADJ. uncertain how to act; weak. Once you have made your decision, don't waver: a leader should never appear *irresolute*.

irreverence N. lack of proper respect. Some audience members were amused by the *irreverence* of the comedian's jokes about the Pope; others felt offended by his lack of respect for their faith. irreverent, ADJ.

jargon N. language used by a special group; technical terminology; gibberish. The computer salesmen at the store used a *jargon* of their own that we simply couldn't follow; we had no idea what they were jabbering about.

jocular ADJ. said or done in jest; joking. Although Bill knew the boss hated jokes, he couldn't resist making one *jocular* remark.

Word List 46

judicious ADJ. sound in judgment; wise. At a key moment in his life, Tom made a *judicious* investment that was the foundation of his later wealth.

justification N. good or just reason; defense; excuse. The jury found him guilty of the more serious charge because they could see no possible *justification* for his actions.

kindle V. start a fire; inspire. Her teacher's praise *kindled* a spark of hope inside Maya.

labyrinth N. maze. Hiding from Indian Joe, Tom and Becky soon lost themselves in the *labyrinth* of secret underground caves.

laconic ADJ. brief and to the point. Many of the characters portrayed by Clint Eastwood are *laconic* types: strong men of few words.

lament V. grieve; express sorrow. Even advocates of the war *lamented* the loss of so many lives in combat. also N. lamentation, N.

lassitude N. languor; weariness. After a massage and a long soak in the hot tub, I gave in to my growing *lassitude* and lay down for a nap.

laud V. praise. The NFL *lauded* Boomer Esiason's efforts to raise money to combat cystic fibrosis. laudable, laudatory, ADJ.

lavish ADJ. liberal; wasteful; extravagant. Her wealthy suitors wooed her with *lavish* gifts. also V.

legacy N. a gift made by a will. Part of my *legacy* from my parents is an album of family photographs.

Word List 47

lethargic ADJ. drowsy; dull. The stifling classroom made Sarah *lethargic*: she felt as if she were about to nod off. lethargy, N.

levity N. lack of seriousness; lightness. Stop giggling and wriggling around in your seats: such *levity* is inappropriate in church.

linger V. loiter or dawdle; continue or persist. Hoping to see Juliet pass by, Romeo *lingered* outside the Capulet house for hours. Though Mother made stuffed cabbage on Monday, the smell *lingered* around the house for days.

list V. tilt; lean over. That flagpole should be absolutely vertical; instead, it *lists* to one side. (secondary meaning)

listlessness N. lack in spirit or energy. We had expected him to be full of enthusiasm and were surprised by his *listlessness*.

loathe V. detest. Booing and hissing, the audience showed how much they *loathed* the wicked villain.

lofty ADJ. very high. Though Barbara Jordan's fellow students used to tease her about her *lofty* ambitions, she rose to hold one of the highest positions in the land.

loquacious ADJ. talkative. Though our daughter barely says a word to us these days, put a cell phone in her hand and you'll see how *loquacious* she is: our phone bills are out of sight!

lucid ADJ. easily understood; clear; intelligible. Ellen made an excellent teacher: her explanations of technical points were *lucid* enough for a child to grasp. lucidity, N.

lurid ADJ. wild; sensational; graphic; gruesome. Do the *lurid* cover stories in the *Enquirer* actually attract people to buy that trashy tabloid?

Word List 48

magnanimous ADJ. generous. Philanthropists by definition are *magnanimous*; misers, by definition, are not. magnanimity, N.

magnate N. person of prominence or influence. Growing up in Pittsburgh, Annie Dillard was surrounded by the mansions of the great steel and coal *magnates* who set their mark on that city.

maladroit ADJ. clumsy; bungling. "Oh! My stupid tongue!" exclaimed Jane, embarrassed at having said anything so *maladroit*.

malevolent ADJ. wishing evil. Iago is a *malevolent* villain who takes pleasure in ruining Othello.

malice N. hatred; spite. Jealous of Cinderella's beauty, her wicked stepsisters expressed their *malice* by forcing her to do menial tasks. malicious, ADJ.

malign V. speak evil of; bad-mouth; defame. Putting her hands over her ears, Rose refused to listen to Betty *malign* her friend Susan.

marred ADJ. damaged; disfigured. She had to refinish the *marred* surface of the table. mar, V.

martinet N. rigid disciplinarian; strict military officer. No talking at meals! No mingling with the servants! Miss Minchin was a *martinet* who insisted that the schoolgirls in her charge observe each regulation to the letter.

materialism N. preoccupation with physical comforts and things. By its nature, *materialism* is opposed to idealism, for where the materialist emphasizes the needs of the body, the idealist emphasizes the needs of the soul.

meager ADJ. scanty; inadequate. Still hungry after his *meager* serving of porridge, Oliver Twist asked for a second helping.

Word List 49

meander V. wind or turn in a course. Needing to stay close to a source of water, he followed every twist and turn of the stream as it *meandered* through the countryside.

medley N. mixture. To avoid boring listeners by playing any one tune for too long, bands may combine three or four tunes into a *medley*.

meek ADJ. quiet and obedient; spiritless. Can Lois Lane see through Superman's disguise and spot the superhero hiding behind the guise of *meek*, timorous Clark Kent?

melancholy ADJ. gloomy; morose; blue. To Eugene, stuck in his small town, a train whistle was a *melancholy* sound, for it made him think of all the places he would never get to see.

mercenary ADJ. interested in money or gain. Andy's every act was prompted by *mercenary* motives: his first question was always "What's in it for me?" also N.

mercurial ADJ. capricious; changing; fickle. Quick as quicksilver to change his moods, he was a *mercurial* creature, whose reactions were impossible to predict.

merger N. combination (of two business corporations). When the firm's president married the director of financial planning, the office joke was that it wasn't a marriage, it was a *merger*.

methodical ADJ. systematic. An accountant must be *methodical* and maintain order among his financial records.

meticulous ADJ. excessively careful; painstaking; scrupulous. Martha Stewart was a *meticulous* housekeeper, fussing about each and every detail that went into making up her perfect home.

minute ADJ. extremely small. The twins resembled one another closely; only *minute* differences set them apart.

Word List 50

misanthrope N. one who hates mankind. In *Gulliver's Travels*, Swift portrays an image of humanity as vile, degraded beasts; for this reason, some critics consider him a *misanthrope*.

miserly ADJ. stingy; mean. The *miserly* old man greedily counted the gold coins he had hoarded over the years.

misnomer N. wrong name; incorrect designation. His tyrannical conduct proved to us all that his nickname, King Eric the Just, was a *misnomer*.

mitigate V. appease; moderate. Because solar energy has the power to reduce greenhouse gases, conversion to the use of solar energy may help *mitigate* global warming.

mock V. ridicule; imitate, often in derision. It is unkind to mock anyone; it is stupid to *mock* anyone significantly bigger than you. mockery, N.

mollify V. soothe. The airline customer service representative tried to *mollify* the angry passenger by offering her a seat in first class.

momentous ADJ. very important. When Marie and Pierre Curie discovered radium, they had no idea of the *momentous* impact their discovery would have upon society.

monotony N. sameness leading to boredom. What could be more deadly dull than the *monotony* of punching numbers into a computer hour after hour? monotonous, ADJ.

morbid ADJ. given to unwholesome thought; moody; characteristic of disease. People who visit disaster sites in order to peer at the grisly wreckage are indulging their *morbid* curiosity.

morose ADJ. ill-humored; sullen; melancholy. Forced to take early retirement, Bill acted *morose* for months; then, all of a sudden, he shook off his sullen mood and was his usual cheerful self.

Word List 51

mundane ADJ. worldly as opposed to spiritual. Uninterested in philosophical or spiritual discussions, Tom talked only of *mundane* matters such as the daily weather forecast or the latest basketball results.

munificent ADJ. very generous. The Annenberg Trust made a *munificent* gift that supported art programs in the public schools. munificence, N.

mutability N. ability to change in form; fickleness. Going from rags to riches, and then back to rags again, the bankrupt financier was a victim of the *mutability* of fortune.

muted ADJ. silent; muffled; toned down. In the funeral parlor, the mourners' voices had a *muted* quality. mute, V.

naivete N. quality of being unsophisticated; simplicity; artlessness; gullibility. Touched by

the *naivete* of sweet, convent-trained Cosette, Marius pledges himself to protect her innocence. naive, ADJ.

nefarious ADJ. very wicked. The villain's crimes, though various, were one and all *nefarious*.

negate V. cancel out; nullify; deny. A sudden surge of adrenaline can *negate* the effects of fatigue; there's nothing like a good shock to wake you up.

nonchalance N. indifference; lack of concern; composure. Cool, calm, and collected under fire, James Bond shows remarkable *nonchalance* in the face of danger. nonchalant, ADJ.

nonentity N. person of no importance; nonexistence. Because the two older princes dismissed their youngest brother as a *nonentity*, they never suspected that he was quietly plotting to seize the throne.

nostalgia N. homesickness; longing for the past. My grandfather seldom spoke of life in the old country; he had little patience with *nostalgia*. nostalgic, ADJ.

Word List 52

notoriety N. disrepute; ill fame. To the starlet, any publicity was good publicity: if she couldn't have a good reputation, she'd settle for *notoriety*. notorious, ADJ.

novelty N. something new; newness. GPS receivers are no longer a *novelty* in automobiles; every rental car we drive these days has one. novel, ADJ.

novice N. beginner. When Grandma got her first cell phone, she was such a complete *novice* that she couldn't even change her ringtone.

nuance N. shade of difference in meaning or color. Jody gazed at the Monet landscape for an hour, appreciating every subtle *nuance* of color in the painting.

nullify V. to make invalid; void; abolish. Once the contract was *nullified*, it no longer had any legal force.

nurture V. nourish; educate; foster. The Head Start program attempts to *nurture* pre-kindergarten children so that they will do well when they enter public school. also N.

obdurate ADJ. stubborn. Although defeat appeared inevitable, the general was *obdurate* in his refusal to surrender.

objective ADJ. not influenced by emotions; fair. Even though he was her son, she tried to be *objective* about his behavior. objectivity, N.

objective N. goal; aim. A degree in medicine was her ultimate *objective*.

obliterate V. destroy completely. In the film *Independence Day*, the explosion *obliterated* the White House, vaporizing it completely.

Word List 53

oblivion N. obscurity; forgetfulness. After a brief period of popularity, Hurston's works fell into *oblivion*; no one bothered to reprint them, or even to read them any more.

oblivious ADJ. inattentive or unmindful; wholly absorbed. Deep in her book, Nancy was *oblivious* to the noisy squabbles of her brother and his friends.

obscure ADJ. dark; vague; unclear. Even after I read the poem a fourth time, its meaning was still *obscure*. obscurity, N.

obscure V. darken; make unclear. At times he seemed purposely to *obscure* his meaning, preferring mystery to clarity.

obsequious ADJ. slavishly attentive; servile; fawning; sycophantic. Helen valued people who acted as if they respected themselves; nothing irritated her more than an *obsequious* waiter or a fawning salesclerk.

obsessive ADJ. related to thinking about something constantly; preoccupying. Ballet, which had been a hobby, began to dominate his life; his love of dancing became *obsessive*. obsession, N.

obstinate ADJ. stubborn; hard to control or treat. We tried to persuade him to give up smoking, but he was *obstinate* and refused to change. obstinacy, N.

obtuse ADJ. blunt; stupid. What can you do with somebody who's so *obtuse* that he can't even tell that you're insulting him?

officious ADJ. meddlesome; excessively pushy in offering one's services. After the long flight, Jill just wanted to nap, but the *officious* bellboy was intent on showing her all the special features of the deluxe suite.

ominous ADJ. threatening. Those clouds are *ominous*; they suggest a severe storm is on the way.

Word List 54

opaque ADJ. dark; not transparent. The *opaque* window shade kept the sunlight out of the room. opacity, N.

opportunist N. individual who sacrifices principles for expediency by taking advantage of circumstances. A born *opportunist*, the vicar of Bray changed his political convictions to suit whoever was in power, switching from fervent monarchist to puritan reformer in order to retain his ecclesiastical living.

optimist N. person who looks on the good side. The pessimist says the glass is half-empty; the *optimist* says it is half-full.

optional ADJ. not compulsory; left to one's choice. I was amazed by the range of *optional* accessories available for my iPod. option, N.

opulence N. extreme wealth; luxuriousness; abundance. The glitter and *opulence* of the ballroom took Cinderella's breath away. opulent, ADJ.

orator N. public speaker. The abolitionist Frederick Douglass was a brilliant *orator* whose speeches brought home to his audience the evils of slavery.

ornate ADJ. excessively or elaborately decorated. The furnishings of homes shown on *Lifestyles of the Rich and Famous* tend to be highly *ornate*.

ostentatious ADJ. showy; pretentious; trying to attract attention. Trump's latest casino in Atlantic City is the most *ostentatious* gambling palace in the East: it easily outglitters its competitors. ostentation, N.

pacifist N. one opposed to force; anti-militarist. Shooting his way through the jungle, Rambo was clearly no *pacifist*.

painstaking ADJ. showing hard work; taking great care. The new high-frequency word list is the result of *painstaking* efforts on the part of our research staff.

Word List 55

paltry ADJ. insignificant; petty; trifling. While NBA stars make an annual average salary of more than $5 million, a player in basketball's minor league may make as little as a *paltry* $15,000.

paradigm N. model; example; pattern. Pavlov's experiment in which he trains a dog to salivate on hearing a bell is a *paradigm* of the conditioned-response experiment in behavioral psychology.

paradox N. something apparently contradictory in nature; statement that looks false but is actually correct. Richard presents a bit of a *paradox*, for he is a card-carrying member of both the National Rifle Association and the relatively pacifist American Civil Liberties Union. paradoxical, ADJ.

paragon N. model of perfection. Her fellow students disliked Lavinia because Miss Minchin always pointed her out as a *paragon* of virtue.

parochial ADJ. narrow in outlook; provincial; related to parishes. Although Jane Austen's novels are set in small rural communities, her concerns are universal, not *parochial*.

parody N. humorous imitation; spoof; takeoff; travesty. The show *Forbidden Broadway* presents *parodies* spoofing the year's new productions playing on Broadway.

parry V. ward off a blow; deflect. Unwilling to injure his opponent in such a pointless clash, Dartagnan simply tried to *parry* his rival's thrusts.

parsimony N. stinginess; excessive frugality. Silas Marner's *parsimony* did not allow him to indulge himself in any luxuries.

partial ADJ. incomplete. In this issue we have published only a *partial* list of contributors because we lack space to acknowledge everyone.

partial ADJ. biased; having a liking for something. I am extremely *partial* to chocolate eclairs. partiality, N.

partisan ADJ. one-sided; prejudiced; committed to a party. On certain issues of principle, she refused to take a *partisan* stand, but let her conscience, not her political affiliation, be her guide. also N.

Word List 56

passive ADJ. not active; acted upon. Mahatma Gandhi urged his followers to pursue a program of *passive* resistance rather than resorting to violence and acts of terrorism.

paucity N. scarcity; lack. They closed the restaurant because the *paucity* of customers meant that it was a losing proposition to operate.

pedantic ADJ. showing off learning; bookish. Leavening his decisions with humorous, down-to-earth anecdotes, Judge Wapner was a pleasant contrast to the typical *pedantic* legal scholar. pedant, pedantry, N.

penchant N. strong inclination; liking. Dave has a *penchant* for taking risks: one semester he went steady with three girls, two of whom were stars on the school karate team.

pensive ADJ. dreamily thoughtful; thoughtful with a hint of sadness; contemplative. Michelangelo's statue of Lorenzo de Medici presents the duke in a *pensive* attitude, as if deep in thought.

perceptive ADJ. insightful; aware; wise. Although Maud was a generally *perceptive* critic, she had her blind spots: she could never see flaws in the work of her friends.

perfunctory ADJ. superficial; not thorough; lacking interest, care, or enthusiasm. Giving the tabletop only a *perfunctory* swipe with her dust cloth, Betty promised herself she'd do a more thorough job tomorrow.

peripheral ADJ. marginal; outer. We lived, not in central London, but in one of those *peripheral* suburbs that spring up on the outskirts of a great city. periphery, N.

perjury N. false testimony while under oath. Rather than lie under oath and perhaps be indicted for *perjury*, the witness chose to take the Fifth Amendment, refusing to answer any questions on the grounds that he might incriminate himself.

pernicious ADJ. very destructive. Crack cocaine has had a *pernicious* effect on urban society: It has destroyed families, turned children into drug dealers, and increased the spread of violent crime.

Word List 57

perpetuate V. make something last; preserve from extinction. Some critics attack *The Adventures of Huckleberry Finn* because they believe Twain's book *perpetuates* a false image of African-Americans in this country.

perturb V. disturb greatly. The thought that electricity might be leaking out of the empty light bulb sockets *perturbed* my aunt so much that at night she crept about the house screwing fresh bulbs in the vacant spots.

pervasive ADJ. pervading; spread throughout every part. Despite airing them for several hours, Martha could not rid her clothes of the *pervasive* odor of mothballs that clung to them. pervade, V.

pessimism N. belief that life is basically bad or evil; gloominess. People inclined to *pessimism* view the wineglass as half-empty; people inclined to optimism view it as half-full.

petty ADJ. trivial; unimportant; very small. She had no major complaints about his work, only a few *petty* quibbles that were almost too minor to state.

petulant ADJ. touchy; peevish. If you'd had hardly any sleep for three nights and people kept phoning and waking you up, you'd sound *petulant*, too.

phenomena N. PL. observable facts; subjects of scientific investigation. We kept careful records of the *phenomena* we noted in the course of these experiments. phenomenon, SING.

philanthropist N. lover of mankind; doer of good. In his role as *philanthropist* and public benefactor, John D. Rockefeller, Sr., donated millions to charity; as an individual, however, he was a tight-fisted old man.

pious ADJ. devout; religious. The challenge for church people today is how to be *pious* in the best sense, that is, to be devout without becoming hypocritical or sanctimonious. piety, N.

pitfall N. hidden danger; concealed trap. Her parents warned young Sophie against the many *pitfalls* that lay in wait for her in the dangerous big city.

Word List 58

pithy ADJ. concise; meaningful; substantial; meaty. While other girls might have gone on and on about how uncool Elton was, Liz summed him up in one *pithy* remark: "He's bogus!"

pivotal ADJ. crucial; key; vital. The new "smart weapons" technology played a *pivotal* role in the quick resolution of the war.

placate V. pacify; conciliate. The store manager tried to *placate* the angry customer, offering to replace the damaged merchandise or to give back her money right away.

plagiarize V. steal another's ideas and pass them off as one's own. The teacher could tell that the student had *plagiarized* parts of his essay; she recognized whole paragraphs straight from *Barron's Book Notes*.

platitude N. trite remark; commonplace statement. In giving advice to his son, old Polonius expressed himself only *in platitudes*; every word out of his mouth was a commonplace.

plausible ADJ. having a show of truth but open to doubt; specious. Your mother made you stay home from school because she needed you to program the VCR? I'm sorry, you'll have to come up with a more *plausible* excuse than that.

pliant ADJ. flexible; easily influenced. Pinocchio's disposition was *pliant*; he was like putty in his tempters' hands.

plight N. condition, state (especially a bad state or condition); predicament. Many people feel that the federal government should do more to alleviate the *plight* of the homeless.

poignancy N. quality of being deeply moving; keenness of emotion. Watching the tearful reunion of the long-separated mother and child, the social worker was touched by the *poignancy* of the scene. poignant, ADJ.

polemical ADJ. aggressive in verbal attack; disputatious. Alexis was a master of *polemical* rhetoric; she should have worn a T-shirt with the slogan "Born to Debate." polemic, N.

precipitous ADJ. steep; overhasty. This hill is difficult to climb because it is so *precipitous*; one slip, and our descent will be *precipitous* as well.

Word List 59

pomposity N. exaggerated self-esteem; excessive grandness in manner or speech. Although the commencement speaker had some good things to say, we had to laugh at his *pomposity* and general air of self-importance. pompous, ADJ.

ponderous ADJ. weighty; unwieldy. Sol's humor lacked the light touch; his jokes were always *ponderous*.

porous ADJ. full of pores; like a sieve. Dancers like to wear *porous* clothing because it allows the ready passage of water and air.

potent ADJ. powerful; persuasive; greatly influential. Looking at the expiration date on the cough syrup bottle, we wondered whether the medicine would still be *potent*. potency, N.

pragmatic ADJ. practical (as opposed to idealistic); concerned with the practical worth or impact of something. This coming trip to France should provide me with a *pragmatic* test of the value of my conversational French class.

prattle V. babble. We enjoyed listening to baby Santiago happily *prattle* in English and Spanish about the night and the stars and *la luna*.

precarious ADJ. uncertain; risky. Saying the stock would be a *precarious* investment, Tom advised me against purchasing it.

precedent N. something preceding in time that may be used as an authority or guide for future action. If I buy you a car for your sixteenth birthday, your brothers will want me to buy them cars when they turn sixteen, too; I can't afford to set such an expensive *precedent*.

precipitate ADJ. rash; premature; hasty; sudden. Though I was angry enough to resign on the spot, I had enough sense to keep myself from quitting a job in such a *precipitate* fashion.

Word List 60

preclude V. make impossible; eliminate. Because the band had already signed a contract to play in Hollywood on New Year's Eve, that booking *precluded* their accepting the New Year's Eve gig in London they were offered.

precocious ADJ. advanced in development. Listening to the grown-up way the child discussed serious topics, we couldn't help remarking how *precocious* she was. precocity, N.

predator N. creature that seizes and devours another animal; person who robs or exploits others. Not just cats, but a wide variety of *predators*—owls, hawks, weasels, foxes—catch mice for dinner. A carnivore is by definition *predatory*, for it *preys* on weaker creatures. prey, V.

predecessor N. former occupant of a post. I hope I can live up to the fine example set by my late *predecessor* in this office.

predilection N. partiality; preference. Although Ogden Nash wrote all sorts of poetry over the years, he had a definite *predilection* for limericks.

preposterous ADJ. absurd; ridiculous. When he tried to downplay his youthful experiments with marijuana by saying he hadn't inhaled, we all thought, "What a *preposterous* excuse!"

prestige N. impression produced by achievements or reputation. Did Rockefeller become a philanthropist because he was innately generous or because he hoped to gain social *prestige* by donating to popular causes?

presumptuous ADJ. overconfident; impertinently bold; taking liberties. Matilda thought it was somewhat *presumptuous* of the young man to have addressed her without first having been introduced. Perhaps manners were freer here in the New World.

pretentious ADJ. ostentatious; pompous; making unjustified claims; overambitious. None of the other prize winners is wearing her medal; isn't it a bit *pretentious* of you to wear yours?

prevalent ADJ. widespread; generally accepted. A radical committed to social change, Reed had no patience with the conservative views *prevalent* in the America of his day.

Word List 61

problematic ADJ. doubtful; unsettled; questionable; perplexing. Given the many areas of conflict still awaiting resolution, the outcome of the peace talks remains *problematic*.

proclivity N. inclination; natural tendency. Watching the two-year-old voluntarily put away his toys, I was amazed by his *proclivity* for neatness.

procrastinate V. postpone; delay or put off. Looking at four years of receipts and checks he still had to sort through, Bob was truly sorry he had *procrastinated* for so long and not finished filing his taxes long ago.

prodigal ADJ. wasteful; reckless with money. Don't be so *prodigal* spending my money; when you've earned some money, you can waste it as much as you want! also N.

prodigious ADJ. marvelous; enormous. Watching the champion weight lifter heave the weighty barbell to shoulder height and then boost it overhead, we marveled at his *prodigious* strength.

prodigy N. marvel; highly gifted child. Menuhin was a *prodigy*, performing wonders on his violin when he was barely eight years old.

profane V. violate; desecrate; treat unworthily. The members of the mysterious Far Eastern cult sought to kill the British explorer because he had *profaned* the sanctity of their holy goblet by using it as an ashtray. also ADJ.

profligate ADJ. dissipated; wasteful; wildly immoral. We must reverse the *profligate* spending that has characterized this administration's fiscal policy and that has left

us with a projected deficit of almost 500 billion dollars. also N.

profound ADJ. deep; not superficial; complete. Freud's remarkable insights into human behavior caused his fellow scientists to honor him as a *profound* thinker. profundity, N.

profusion N. overabundance; lavish expenditure; excess. At the wedding feast, food and drink were served in such *profusion* that the goodies piled on the tables almost overflowed onto the floor.

Word List 62

proliferation N. rapid growth; spread; multiplication. Times of economic hardship inevitably encourage the *proliferation* of countless get-rich-quick schemes. proliferate, V.

prolific ADJ. abundantly fruitful. My editors must assume I'm a *prolific* writer: they expect me to revise six books this year!

prologue N. introduction (to a poem or play). In the *prologue* to *Romeo and Juliet*, Shakespeare introduces the audience to the feud between the Montagues and the Capulets.

prophetic ADJ. foretelling the future. I have no magical *prophetic* powers; when I predict what will happen, I base my predictions on common sense. prophesy, V.

propitious ADJ. favorable; fortunate; advantageous. Chloe consulted her horoscope to see whether Tuesday would be a *propitious* time to dump her boyfriend.

propriety N. fitness; correct conduct. Miss Manners counsels her readers so that they may behave with due *propriety* in any social situation and not embarrass themselves.

prosaic ADJ. dull and unimaginative; matter-of-fact; factual. Though the ad writers had come up with a wildly imaginative campaign to publicize the new product, the head office rejected it for a more *prosaic*, ordinary approach.

protract V. prolong. Seeking to delay the union members' vote, the management team tried to *protract* the negotiations endlessly.

provincial ADJ. pertaining to a province; limited in outlook; unsophisticated. As *provincial* governor, Sir Henry administered the Queen's law in his remote corner of Canada. Caught up in local problems, out of touch with London news, he became sadly *provincial*.

provisional ADJ. tentative. Edward's appointment was *provisional*; he needed the approval of the board of directors before it would be made permanent.

Word List 63

provocative ADJ. arousing anger or interest; annoying. In a typically *provocative* act, the bully kicked sand into the weaker man's face.

proximity N. nearness. Blind people sometimes develop a compensatory ability to sense the *proximity* of objects around them.

prudent ADJ. cautious; careful. A miser hoards money not because he is *prudent* but because he is greedy. prudence, N.

pugnacity N. combativeness; disposition to fight. "Put up your dukes!" he cried, making a fist to show his *pugnacity*. pugnacious, ADJ.

pungent ADJ. stinging; sharp in taste or smell; caustic. The *pungent* odor of ripe Limburger cheese appealed to Simone but made Stanley gag.

purse V. pucker; contract into wrinkles. Miss Watson *pursed* her lips to show her disapproval of Huck's bedraggled appearance.

qualified ADJ. limited; restricted. Unable to give the candidate full support, the mayor gave him only a *qualified* endorsement. (secondary meaning)

quandary N. dilemma. When both Harvard and Stanford accepted Laura, she was in a *quandary* as to which school she should attend.

quell V. extinguish; put down; quiet. Miss Minchin's demeanor was so stern and forbidding that she could *quell* any unrest among her students with one intimidating glance.

querulous ADJ. fretful; whining. Even the most agreeable toddlers can begin to act *querulous* if they miss their nap.

Word List 64

quiescent ADJ. at rest; dormant; temporarily inactive. After the great eruption, fear of Mount Etna was great; people did not return to cultivate its rich hillside lands until the volcano had been *quiescent* for a full two years.

ramble V. wander aimlessly (physically or mentally). Listening to the teacher *ramble*, Judy wondered whether he'd ever make his point.

rancor N. bitterness; hatred. Thirty years after the war, she could not let go of the past but was still filled with *rancor* against the foe.

rant V. rave; talk excitedly; scold; make a grandiloquent speech. When he heard that I'd totaled the family car, Dad began to *rant* at me like a complete madman.

ratify V. approve formally; verify. Party leaders doubted that they had enough votes in both houses of Congress to *ratify* the constitutional amendment.

raucous ADJ. harsh and shrill; disorderly and boisterous. The *raucous* crowd of New Year's Eve revelers got progressively noisier as midnight drew near.

raze V. destroy completely. Spelling is important: to raise a building is to put it up; to *raze* a building is to tear it down.

rebuttal N. refutation; response with contrary evidence. The defense lawyer confidently listened to the prosecutor sum up his case, sure that she could answer his arguments in her *rebuttal*.

recalcitrant ADJ. obstinately stubborn; determined to resist authority; unruly. Which animal do you think is more *recalcitrant*, a pig or a mule?

recant V. disclaim or disavow; retract a previous statement; openly confess error. Hoping to make Joan of Arc *recant* her sworn testimony, her English captors tried to convince her that her visions had been sent to her by the Devil.

Word List 65

receptive ADJ. quick or willing to receive ideas, suggestions, etc. Adventure-loving Huck Finn proved a *receptive* audience for Tom's tales of buried treasure and piracy.

recluse N. hermit; loner. Disappointed in love, Miss Emily became a *recluse*; she shut herself away in her empty mansion and refused to see another living soul. reclusive, ADJ.

recount V. narrate or tell; count over again. A born storyteller, my father loved to *recount* anecdotes about his early years in New York.

rectify V. set right; correct. You had better send a check to *rectify* your account before American Express cancels your credit card.

redundant ADJ. superfluous; repetitious; excessively wordy. In your essay, you unnecessarily repeat several points; try to be less *redundant* in the future. redundancy, N.

refute V. disprove. The defense called several respectable witnesses who were able to *refute* the false testimony of the prosecution's sole witness.

relegate V. banish to an inferior position; delegate; assign. After Ralph dropped his second tray of drinks that week, the manager swiftly *relegated* him to a minor post cleaning up behind the bar.

relevant ADJ. pertinent; referring to the case in hand. How *relevant* Virginia Woolf's essays are to women writers today! It's as if Woolf in the 1930s foresaw their current literary struggles. relevance, N. relevancy, N.

relinquish V. give up something with reluctance; yield. Denise never realized how hard it would be for her to *relinquish* her newborn son to the care of his adoptive parents.

relish V. savor; enjoy. Watching Peter enthusiastically chow down, I thought, "Now there's a man who *relishes* a good dinner!" also N.

Word List 66

remorse N. guilt; self-reproach. The murderer felt no *remorse* for his crime.

renegade N. deserter; traitor. Because he had abandoned his post and joined forces with the Indians, his fellow officers considered the hero of *Dancing with Wolves* a *renegade*. also ADJ.

renounce V. forswear; repudiate; abandon; discontinue. Joan of Arc refused to *renounce* her testimony even though she knew she would be burned at the stake as a witch.

repel V. drive away; disgust. At first, the Beast's ferocious appearance *repelled* Beauty, but she came to love the tender heart hidden behind that beastly exterior.

replete ADJ. filled to the brim or to the point of being stuffed; abundantly supplied. The movie star's memoir was *replete* with juicy details about the love life of half of Hollywood.

reprehensible ADJ. deserving blame. Shocked by the viciousness of the bombing, politicians of every party uniformly condemned the terrorists' *reprehensible* deed.

repress V. restrain; hold back; crush; suppress. Anne's parents tried to curb her impetuosity without *repressing* her boundless high spirits.

reprimand V. reprove severely; rebuke. Every time Ermengarde made a mistake in class, she was afraid that Miss Minchin would *reprimand* her and tell her father how badly she was doing in school. also N.

reproach V. express disapproval. He never could do anything wrong without imagining how the look on his mother's face would *reproach* him afterwards. also N. reproachful, ADJ.

reprove V. censure; rebuke. The principal severely *reproved* the students whenever they talked in the halls.

Word List 67

repudiate V. disown; disavow. On separating from Tony, Tina announced that she would *repudiate* all debts incurred by her soon-to-be ex-husband.

rescind V. cancel. Because of the public outcry against the new taxes, the senator proposed a bill to *rescind* the unpopular financial measure.

reserve N. self-control; formal but distant manner. Although some girls were attracted by Mark's air of *reserve*, Judy was put off by it, for she felt his aloofness indicated a lack of openness. reserved, ADJ.

resigned ADJ. unresisting; patiently submissive. *Resigned* to his downtrodden existence, Bob Cratchit was too meek to protest Scrooge's bullying.

resolution N. determination; resolve. Nothing could shake his *resolution* that his children would get the best education that money could buy. resolute, ADJ.

resolve N. determination; firmness of purpose. How dare you question my *resolve* to take up skydiving! Of course I haven't changed my mind!

resolve V. decide; settle; solve. Holmes *resolved* to travel to Bohemia to *resolve* the dispute between Irene Adler and the king.

respite N. interval of relief; time for rest; delay in punishment. After working nonstop on this project for three straight months, I need a *respite*!

resplendent ADJ. dazzling; glorious; brilliant. While all the adults were commenting how glorious the emperor looked in his *resplendent* new clothes, one little boy was heard to say, "But he's naked!"

restraint N. controlling force; control over one's emotions. Amanda dreamed of living an independent life, free of all parental *restraints*.

Word List 68

reticent ADJ. reserved; uncommunicative; inclined to be silent. Fearing his competitors might get advance word about his plans from talkative staff members, Hughes preferred *reticent* employees to loquacious ones. reticence, N.

retiring ADJ. modest; shy. Given Susan's *retiring* personality, no one expected her to take up public speaking; surprisingly enough, she became a star of the school debate team.

retract V. withdraw; take back. When I saw how Fred and his fraternity brothers had

trashed the frat house, I decided to *retract* my offer to let them use our summer cottage for the weekend. retraction, N.

reverent ADJ. respectful. The young acolyte's *reverent* attitude was appropriate in a house of worship.

rhetorical ADJ. pertaining to effective communication; insincere in language. To win his audience, the speaker used every *rhetorical* trick in the book.

rigorous ADJ. severe; harsh; demanding; exact. Disliked by his superiors, the officer candidate in *An Officer and a Gentleman* went through an extremely *rigorous* training program.

robust ADJ. vigorous; strong. After pumping iron and taking karate for six months, the little old lady was far more *robust* in health and could break a plank with her fist.

rudimentary ADJ. not developed; elementary; crude. Although my grandmother's English vocabulary was limited to a few *rudimentary* phrases, she always could make herself understood.

ruthless ADJ. pitiless; cruel. Captain Hook was a dangerous, *ruthless* villain who would stop at nothing to destroy Peter Pan.

sagacious ADJ. perceptive; shrewd; having insight. Mr. Bond, that was not a particularly *sagacious* move on your part. I had not expected such a foolish trick from a smart fellow like you. sagacity, N.

Word List 69

sage N. person celebrated for wisdom. Hearing tales of a mysterious Master of All Knowledge who lived in the hills of Tibet, Sandy was possessed with a burning desire to consult the legendary *sage*. also ADJ.

sanction V. approve; ratify. Nothing will convince me to *sanction* the engagement of my daughter to such a worthless young man.

sanctuary N. refuge; shelter; shrine; holy place. The tiny attic was Helen's *sanctuary* to which she fled when she had to get away from the rest of her family.

sarcasm N. scornful remarks; stinging rebuke. Though Ralph tried to ignore the mocking comments of his supposed friends, their *sarcasm* wounded him deeply.

satirical ADJ. mocking. The humor of cartoonist Gary Trudeau often is *satirical*; through the comments of the Doonesbury characters, Trudeau ridicules political corruption and folly.

saturate V. soak thoroughly. *Saturate* your sponge with water until it can't hold any more.

savory ADJ. tasty; pleasing, attractive, or agreeable. Julia Child's recipes enable amateur chefs to create *savory* delicacies for their guests.

scanty ADJ. meager; insufficient. Thinking his helping of food was *scanty*, Oliver Twist asked for more.

scrupulous ADJ. conscientious; extremely thorough. I'm very happy to recommend Adam as an employee because he's always been highly *scrupulous* about doing a good job whenever he's worked for me.

scrutinize V. examine closely and critically. Searching for flaws, the sergeant *scrutinized* every detail of the private's uniform.

Word List 70

seclusion N. isolation; solitude. One moment she loved crowds; the next, she sought *seclusion*. secluded, ADJ.

sectarian ADJ. relating to a religious faction or subgroup; narrow-minded; limited. Far from being broad-minded, the religious leader was intolerant of new ideas, paying attention only to purely *sectarian* interests. sect, N.

sedentary ADJ. requiring sitting. Disliking the effect of her *sedentary* occupation on her figure, Stacy decided to work out at the gym every other day.

sequester V. isolate; retire from public life; segregate; seclude. Banished from his kingdom, the wizard Prospero *sequestered* himself on a desert island.

serenity N. calmness; placidity. The sound of air raid sirens pierced the *serenity* of the quiet village of Pearl Harbor.

servile ADJ. slavishly submissive; fawning; cringing. Constantly fawning on his employer, Uriah Heep was a *servile* creature.

sever V. cut; separate. The released prisoner wanted to begin a new life and *sever* all connections with his criminal past. severance, N.

severity N. harshness; intensity; austerity; rigidity. The newspaper editorials disapproved of the *severity* of the sentence.

shrewd ADJ. clever; astute. A *shrewd* investor, he took clever advantage of the fluctuations of the stock market.

singular ADJ. unique; extraordinary; odd. Though the young man tried to understand Father William's *singular* behavior, he still found it odd that the old man incessantly stood on his head. singularity, N.

Word List 71

skeptical ADJ. doubting; suspending judgment until one has examined the evidence supporting a point of view. I am *skeptical* about the new health plan; I want some proof that it can work. skepticism, N.

slacken V. slow up; loosen. As they passed the finish line, the runners *slackened* their pace.

slander N. defamation; utterance of false and malicious statements. Considering the negative comments politicians make about each other, it's a wonder that more of them aren't sued for *slander*. also V.

slothful ADJ. lazy. The British word "layabout" is a splendid descriptive term for someone *slothful*: What did the lazy bum do? He lay about the house all day. sloth, N.

sluggish ADJ. slow; lazy; lethargic. After two nights without sleep, she felt *sluggish* and incapable of exertion.

solemnity N. seriousness; gravity. The minister was concerned that nothing should disturb the *solemnity* of the marriage service.

solicit V. request earnestly; seek. Knowing she needed to have a solid majority for the budget to pass, the mayor telephoned all the members of the city council to *solicit* their votes.

solitude N. state of being alone; seclusion. Much depends on how much you like your own company. What to one person seems fearful isolation, to another is blessed *solitude*.

soluble ADJ. able to be dissolved; able to be explained. Sherlock Holmes took the *soluble* powder and dissolved it into a seven percent solution.

somber ADJ. gloomy; depressing; dark; drab. From the doctor's grim expression, I could tell he had *somber* news.

Word List 72

sparse ADJ. not thick; thinly scattered; scanty. He had moved from the densely populated city to the remote countryside where the population was *sparse*.

spendthrift N. someone who wastes money. Easy access to credit encourages people to turn into *spendthrifts* who shop till they drop.

spontaneity N. lack of premeditation; naturalness; freedom from constraint. When Betty and Amy met, Amy impulsively hugged her roommate-to-be, but Betty drew back, unprepared for such *spontaneity*. spontaneous, ADJ.

sporadic ADJ. occurring irregularly. Although you can still hear *sporadic* outbursts of laughter and singing outside, the big Halloween parade has passed; the party's over till next year.

spurious ADJ. false; counterfeit. The antique dealer hero of Jonathan Gash's mystery novels gives the reader tips on how to tell *spurious* antiques from the real thing.

spurn V. reject; scorn. The heroine *spurned* the villain's advances.

squalor N. filth; degradation; dirty, neglected state. Rusted, broken-down cars in the yard, trash piled up on the porch, tar paper peeling from the roof, the shack was the picture of *squalor*.

squander V. waste. If you *squander* your allowance on candy and comic books, you won't have any money left to buy the new box of crayons you want.

stagnant ADJ. motionless; stale; dull. Mosquitoes commonly breed in ponds of *stagnant* water. stagnate, V.

stanza N. division of a poem. Do you know the last *stanza* of "The Star-Spangled Banner"?

Word List 73

static ADJ. unchanging; lacking development. Nothing had changed at home; life was *static*. stasis, N.

steadfast ADJ. loyal; unswerving. Penelope was *steadfast* in her affections, faithfully waiting for Ulysses to return from his wanderings.

stoic ADJ. impassive; unmoved by joy or grief. I wasn't particularly *stoic* when I had my flu shot; I squealed like a stuck pig. also N.

strident ADJ. loud and harsh; insistent. We could barely hear the speaker over the *strident* cries of the hecklers.

strut N. pompous walk; swagger. Colonel Blimp's *strut* as he marched about the parade ground revealed him for what he was: a pompous buffoon. also V.

stupefy V. make numb; stun; amaze. Disapproving of drugs in general, Laura refused to take sleeping pills or any other medicine that might *stupefy* her.

subdued ADJ. less intense; quieter. In the hospital visitors spoke in a *subdued* tone of voice for fear of disturbing the patients.

submissive ADJ. yielding; timid. Crushed by his authoritarian father, Will had no defiance left in him; he was totally *submissive* in the face of authority.

subordinate ADJ. occupying a lower rank; inferior; submissive. Bishop Proudie's wife expected all the *subordinate* clergy to behave with great deference to the wife of their superior. also N., V.

subside V. settle down; descend; grow quiet. The doctor assured us that the fever would eventually *subside*.

Word List 74

substantial ADJ. ample; solid. The scholarship represented a *substantial* sum of money.

substantiate V. establish by evidence; verify; support. These endorsements from satisfied customers *substantiate* our claim that Barron's *How to Prepare for the SAT* is the best SAT-prep book on the market.

subtlety N. perceptiveness; ingenuity; delicacy. Never obvious, she expressed herself with such *subtlety* that her remarks went right over the heads of most of her audience. subtle, ADJ.

succinct ADJ. brief; terse; compact. Don't bore your audience with excess verbiage: be *succinct.*

supercilious ADJ. arrogant; condescending; patronizing. The *supercilious* headwaiter sneered at customers who he thought did not fit in at a restaurant catering to an ultrafashionable crowd.

superficial ADJ. trivial; shallow. Since your report gave only a *superficial* analysis of the problem, I cannot give you more than a passing grade.

superfluous ADJ. excessive; overabundant; unnecessary. Please try not to include so many *superfluous* details in your report; just give me the facts. superfluity, N.

supplant V. replace; usurp. Did the other woman actually *supplant* Princess Diana in Prince Charles's affections, or did Charles never love Diana at all?

suppress V. crush; subdue; inhibit. After the armed troops had *suppressed* the rebellion, the city was placed under martial law.

surmount V. overcome. I know you can *surmount* any difficulties that may stand in the way of your getting an education.

Word List 75

surpass V. exceed. Her SAT scores *surpassed* our expectations.

surreptitious ADJ. secret; furtive; sneaky; hidden. Hoping to discover where his mom had hidden the Christmas presents, Timmy took a *surreptitious* peek into the master bedroom closet.

susceptible ADJ. impressionable; easily influenced; having little resistance, as to a disease; receptive to. Said the patent medicine man to the extremely *susceptible* customer: "Buy this new miracle drug, and you will no longer be *susceptible* to the common cold."

sustain V. experience; support; nourish. Stuart *sustained* such a severe injury that the doctors feared he would be unable to work to *sustain* his growing family.

swindler N. cheat. She was gullible and trusting, an easy victim for the first *swindler* who came along.

sycophant N. servile flatterer; bootlicker; yes man. Fed up with the toadies and brownnosers who made up his entourage, the star cried, "Get out, all of you! I'm sick to death of *sycophants!*"

symmetry N. arrangement of parts so that balance is obtained; congruity. Something lopsided by definition lacks *symmetry.*

taciturn ADJ. habitually silent; talking little. The stereotypical cowboy is a *taciturn* soul, answering lengthy questions with "Yep" or "Nope."

taint V. contaminate; cause to lose purity; modify with a trace of something bad. Fighting to preserve her good name, Desdemona wondered what had occurred to *taint* her reputation. also N.

tangential ADJ. peripheral; only slightly connected; digressing. Despite Clark's attempts to distract her with *tangential* remarks, Lois kept on coming back to her main question: why couldn't he come out to dinner with Superman and her?

Word List 76

tangible ADJ. able to be touched; real; palpable. Although Tom did not own a house, he had several *tangible* assets—a car, a television, a PC—that he could sell if he needed cash.

tantamount ADJ. equivalent in effect or value. Though Rudy claimed his wife was off visiting friends, his shriek of horror when she walked into the room was *tantamount* to a confession that he believed she was dead.

tedious ADJ. boring; tiring. The repetitious nature of work on the assembly line made Martin's job very *tedious*. tedium, N.

temper V. moderate; tone down or restrain; toughen (steel). Not even her supervisor's grumpiness could *temper* Nancy's enthusiasm for her new job.

tenacity N. firmness; persistence. Jean Valjean could not believe the *tenacity* of Inspector Javert. All Valjean had done was to steal a loaf of bread, and the inspector had pursued him doggedly for twenty years! tenacious, ADJ.

tentative ADJ. provisional; experimental; doubtful. Your *tentative* proposal sounds feasible; let me know when the final details are worked out.

termination N. end. Because of the unexpected *termination* of his contract, he urgently needed a new job.

terse ADJ. concise; abrupt; pithy. There is a fine line between speech that is *terse* and to the point and speech that is too abrupt.

threadbare ADJ. worn through till the threads show; shabby and poor. The poor adjunct professor hid the *threadbare* spots on his jacket by sewing leather patches on his sleeves.

thrive V. prosper; flourish. Despite the impact of the recession on the restaurant trade, Philip's cafe *thrived*.

Word List 77

tirade N. extended scolding; denunciation; harangue. The cigar smoker went into a bitter *tirade* denouncing the antismoking forces that had succeeded in banning smoking from most planes and restaurants.

torpor N. lethargy; sluggishness; dormancy. Throughout the winter, nothing aroused the bear from his *torpor*: he would not emerge from hibernation until spring.

tractable ADJ. docile; easily managed. Although Susan seemed a *tractable* young woman, she had a stubborn streak of independence that occasionally led her to defy the powers-that-be when she felt they were in the wrong.

tranquillity N. calmness; peace. After the commotion and excitement of the city, I appreciate the *tranquillity* of these fields and forests.

transcendent ADJ. surpassing; exceeding ordinary limits; superior. For the amateur chef, dining at the four-star restaurant was a *transcendent* experience: the meal surpassed his wildest dreams.

transient ADJ. momentary; temporary; staying for a short time. Lexy's joy at finding the perfect Christmas gift for Phil was *transient*; she still had to find presents for Roger, Laura, Allison, and Uncle Bob.

transparent ADJ. easily detected; permitting light to pass through freely. Bobby managed to put an innocent look on his face; to his mother, however, his guilt was *transparent*.

trepidation N. fear; nervous apprehension. If you've never seen an SAT test, it's natural for you to feel some *trepidation* when you take the exam; if you're familiar with the test, however, you've got a much better chance of staying calm.

trifling ADJ. trivial; unimportant. Why bother going to see a doctor for such a *trifling*, everyday cold?

trite ADJ. hackneyed; commonplace. The *trite* and predictable situations in many television programs turn off many viewers, who respond by turning off their sets.

Word List 78

trivial ADJ. unimportant; trifling. Too many magazines ignore newsworthy subjects and feature *trivial* affairs. trivia, N.

turbulence N. state of violent agitation. Warned of approaching *turbulence* in the atmosphere, the pilot told the passengers to fasten their seat belts.

turmoil N. great commotion and confusion. Lydia running off with a soldier! Mother fainting at the news! The Bennet household was in *turmoil*.

tyranny N. oppression; cruel government. Frederick Douglass fought against the *tyranny* of slavery throughout his entire life.

undermine V. weaken; sap. The recent corruption scandals have *undermined* many people's faith in the city government.

uniformity N. sameness; monotony. After a while, the *uniformity* of TV situation comedies becomes boring. uniform, ADJ.

universal ADJ. characterizing or affecting all; present everywhere. At first, no one shared Christopher's opinions; his theory that the world was round was met with *universal* disdain.

unkempt ADJ. disheveled; uncared for in appearance. Jeremy hated his neighbor's *unkempt* lawn: he thought its neglected appearance had a detrimental effect on neighborhood property values.

unprecedented ADJ. novel; unparalleled. For a first novel, Margaret Mitchell's novel *Gone with the Wind* was an *unprecedented* success.

unwarranted ADJ. unjustified; groundless; undeserved. We could not understand Martin's *unwarranted* rudeness to his mother's guests.

Word List 79

usurp V. seize another's power or rank. The revolution ended when the victorious rebel general succeeded in his attempt to *usurp* the throne.

vacillate V. waver; fluctuate. Uncertain which suitor she ought to marry, the princess *vacillated*, saying now one, now the other. vacillation, N.

venerate V. revere. In Tibet today, the common people still *venerate* their traditional spiritual leader, the Dalai Lama.

veracity N. truthfulness. Trying to prove Anita Hill a liar, Senator Specter repeatedly questioned her *veracity*.

verbose ADJ. wordy. We had to make some major cuts in Senator Foghorn's speech because it was far too *verbose*. verbosity, N.

viable ADJ. practical or workable; capable of maintaining life. The plan to build a new baseball stadium, though missing a few details, is *viable* and stands a good chance of winning popular support.

vigor N. active strength. Although he was over seventy years old, Jack had the *vigor* of a man in his prime. vigorous, ADJ.

vilify V. slander. Waging a highly negative campaign, the candidate attempted to *vilify* his opponent's reputation.

vindicate V. clear from blame; exonerate; justify or support. The lawyer's goal was to *vindicate* her client and prove him innocent on all charges. The critics' extremely favorable reviews *vindicate* my opinion that *The Madness of King George* is a brilliant movie.

vindictive ADJ. out for revenge; malicious. Divorce sometimes brings out a *vindictive* streak in people; when Tony told Tina he was getting a divorce, she poured green Jello into his aquarium and turned his tropical fish into dessert.

Word List 80

virtuoso N. highly skilled artist. The child prodigy Yehudi Menuhin grew into a *virtuoso* whose violin performances thrilled millions. virtuosity, N.

virulent ADJ. extremely poisonous; hostile; bitter. Laid up with an extremely *virulent* case of measles, he blamed his doctors because his recovery took so long. In fact, he became quite *virulent* on the subject of the quality of modern medical care. virulence, N.

volatile ADJ. changeable; explosive; evaporating rapidly. The political climate today is extremely *volatile*: no one can predict what the electorate will do next. Maria Callas's temper was extremely *volatile*: the only thing you could predict was that she would blow up. Acetone is an extremely *volatile* liquid: it evaporates instantly.

voluble ADJ. fluent; glib; talkative. An excessively *voluble* speaker suffers from logorrhea: he runs off at the mouth a lot!

voluminous ADJ. bulky; large. Despite her family burdens, she kept up a *voluminous* correspondence with her friends.

vulnerable ADJ. susceptible to wounds. His opponents could not harm Achilles, who was *vulnerable* only in his heel.

whimsical ADJ. capricious; fanciful. He dismissed his generous gift to his college as a sentimental fancy, an old man's *whimsical* gesture. whimsy, N.

willful ADJ. intentional; headstrong; stubbornly set on getting one's way. Donald had planned to kill his wife for months; clearly, her death was a case of deliberate, *willful* murder, not a crime of passion committed by a hasty, *willful* youth unable to foresee the consequences of his deeds.

withhold V. refuse to give; hold back. The NCAA may *withhold* permission for academically underprepared athletes to participate in intercollegiate sports as freshmen.

zealot N. fanatic; person who shows excessive zeal. Though Glenn was devout, he was no *zealot*; he never tried to force his beliefs on his friends.

Basic Word Parts

In addition to reviewing the SAT High-Frequency Word List, what other quick vocabulary-building tactics can you follow when you face an SAT deadline?

One good approach is to learn how to build up (and tear apart) words. You know that words are made up of other words: the *room* in which you *store* things is the *storeroom*; the person whose job is to *keep* the *books* is the *bookkeeper*.

Just as words are made up of other words, words are also made up of word parts: prefixes, suffixes, and roots. A knowledge of these word parts and their meanings can help you determine the meanings of unfamiliar words.

Most modern English words are derived from Anglo-Saxon (Old English), Latin, and Greek. Because few students nowadays study Latin and Greek (and even fewer study Anglo-Saxon!), the majority of high school juniors and seniors lack a vital tool for unlocking the meaning of unfamiliar words.

Build your vocabulary by mastering basic word parts. Learning thirty key word parts can help you unlock the meaning of over 10,000 words. Learning fifty key word parts can help you unlock the meaning of over 100,000!

Common Prefixes

Prefixes are syllables that precede the root or stem of a word and change or refine its meaning.

Prefix	Meaning	Illustration
ab, abs	from, away from	*abduct* lead away, kidnap *abjure* renounce *abject* degraded, cast down
ambi	both	*ambidextrous* skilled with both hands *ambiguous* of double meaning *ambivalent* having two conflicting emotions
an, a	without	*anarchy* lack of government *anemia* lack of blood *amoral* without moral sense
ante	before	*antecedent* preceding event or word *antediluvian* ancient (before the flood) *antenuptial* before the wedding

Prefix	Meaning	Illustration
anti	against, opposite	*antipathy* hatred *antiseptic* against infection *antithetical* exactly opposite
arch	chief, first	*archetype* original *archbishop* chief bishop *archeology* study of first or ancient times
bi	two	*bicameral* composed of two houses (Congress) *biennial* every two years *bicycle* two-wheeled vehicle
cata	down	*catastrophe* disaster *cataract* waterfall *catapult* hurl (throw down)
circum	around	*circumnavigate* sail around (the globe) *circumspect* cautious (looking around) *circumscribe* limit (place a circle around)
com (co, col, con, cor)	with, together	*combine* merge with *commerce* trade with *communicate* correspond with *coeditor* joint editor *collateral* subordinate, connected *conference* meeting *corroborate* confirm
contra, contro	against	*contravene* conflict with *controversy* dispute
de	down, away	*debase* lower in value *decadence* deterioration *decant* pour off
di	two	*dichotomy* division into two parts *dilemma* choice between two bad alternatives
dia	across	*diagonal* across a figure *diameter* distance across a circle *diagram* outline drawing
dis	not, apart	*discord* lack of harmony *disparity* condition of inequality; difference
dys	faulty, bad	*dyslexia* faulty ability to read *dyspepsia* indigestion
ex, e	out	*expel* drive out *extirpate* root out *eject* throw out
extra, extro	beyond, outside	*extracurricular* beyond the curriculum *extraterritorial* beyond a nation's bounds *extrovert* person interested chiefly in external objects and actions

Prefix	Meaning	Illustration
hyper	above; excessively	*hyperbole* exaggeration *hyperventilate* breathe at an excessive rate
hypo	beneath; lower	*hypoglycemia* low blood sugar
in (il, im, ir)	not	*inefficient* not efficient *inarticulate* not clear or distinct *illegible* not readable *impeccable* not capable of sinning; flawless *irrevocable* not able to be called back
in (il, im, ir)	in, on, upon	*invite* call in *illustration* something that makes clear *impression* effect upon mind or feelings *irradiate* shine upon
inter	between, among	*intervene* come between *international* between nations *interjection* a statement thrown in
intra, intro	within	*intramural* within a school *introvert* person who turns within himself
macro	large, long	*macrobiotic* tending to prolong life *macrocosm* the great world (the entire universe)
mega	great, million	*megalomania* delusions of grandeur *megaton* explosive force of a million tons of TNT
meta	involving change	*metamorphosis* change of form
micro	small	*microcosm* miniature universe *microbe* minute organism *microscopic* extremely small
mis	bad, improper	*misdemeanor* minor crime; bad conduct *mischance* unfortunate accident *misnomer* wrong name
mis	hatred	*misanthrope* person who hates mankind *misogynist* woman-hater
mono	one	*monarchy* government by one ruler *monotheism* belief in one god
multi	many	*multifarious* having many parts *multitudinous* numerous
neo	new	*neologism* newly coined word *neophyte* beginner; novice
non	not	*noncommittal* undecided *nonentity* person of no importance
pan	all, every	*panacea* cure-all *panorama* unobstructed view in all directions
per	through, completely	*permeable* allowing passage through *pervade* spread throughout

Prefix	Meaning	Illustration
peri	around, near	*perimeter* outer boundary *periphery* edge
poly	many	*polygamist* person with several spouses *polyglot* speaking several languages
post	after	*postpone* delay *posterity* generations that follow *posthumous* after death
pre	before	*preamble* introductory statement *prefix* word part placed before a root/stem *premonition* forewarning
prim	first	*primordial* existing at the dawn of time *primogeniture* state of being the first born
pro	forward, in favor of	*propulsive* driving forward *proponent* supporter
proto	first	*prototype* first of its kind
pseudo	false	*pseudonym* pen name
re	again, back	*reiterate* repeat *reimburse* pay back
retro	backward	*retrospect* looking back *retroactive* effective as of a past date
se	away, aside	*secede* withdraw *seclude* shut away *seduce* lead astray
semi	half, partly	*semiannual* every six months *semiconscious* partly conscious
sub (suc, suf, sug, sup, sus)	under, less	*subway* underground road *subjugate* bring under control *succumb* yield; cease to resist
super, sur	over, above	*supernatural* above natural things *supervise* oversee *surtax* additional tax
syn (sym, syl, sys)	with, together	*synchronize* time together *synthesize* combine together *sympathize* pity; identify with *syllogism* explanation of how ideas relate *system* network
tele	far	*telemetry* measurement from a distance *telegraphic* communicated over a distance
trans	across	*transport* carry across *transpose* reverse, move across
ultra	beyond, excessive	*ultramodern* excessively modern *ultracritical* exceedingly critical

Prefix	Meaning	Illustration
un	not	*unfeigned* not pretended; real *unkempt* not combed; disheveled *unwitting* not knowing; unintentional
under	below	*undergird* strengthen underneath *underling* someone inferior
uni	one	*unison* oneness of pitch; complete accord *unicycle* one-wheeled vehicle
vice	in place of	*vicarious* acting as a substitute *viceroy* governor acting in place of a king
with	away, against	*withhold* hold back; keep *withstand* stand up against; resist

Common Roots and Stems

Roots are basic word elements that have been carried over into English. *Stems* are variations of roots brought about by changes in declension or conjugation.

Root or Stem	Meaning	Illustration
ac, acr	sharp	*acrimonious* bitter; caustic *acerbity* bitterness of temper *acidulate* to make somewhat acid or sour
aev, ev	age, era	*primeval* of the first age *coeval* of the same age or era *medieval* or *mediaeval* of the middle ages
ag, act	do	*act* deed *agent* doer
agog	leader	*demagogue* false leader of people *pedagogue* teacher (leader of children)
agri, agrari	field	*agrarian* one who works in the field *agriculture* cultivation of fields *peregrination* wandering (through fields)
ali	another	*alias* assumed (another) name *alienate* estrange (turn away from another)
alt	high	*altitude* height *altimeter* instrument for measuring height
alter	other	*altruistic* unselfish, considering others *alter ego* a second self
am	love	*amorous* loving, especially sexually *amity* friendship *amicable* friendly

Root or Stem	Meaning	Illustration
anim	mind, soul	*animadvert* cast criticism upon *unanimous* of one mind *magnanimity* greatness of mind or spirit
ann, enn	year	*annuity* yearly remittance *biennial* every two years *perennial* present all year; persisting for several years
anthrop	man	*anthropology* study of man *misanthrope* hater of mankind *philanthropy* love of mankind; charity
apt	fit	*aptitude* skill *adapt* make suitable or fit
aqua	water	*aqueduct* passageway for conducting water *aquatic* living in water
arch	ruler, first	*archaeology* study of antiquities (study of first things) *monarch* sole ruler *anarchy* lack of government
aster	star	*astronomy* study of the stars *asterisk* star-like type character (*) *disaster* catastrophe (contrary star)
aud, audit	hear	*audible* able to be heard *auditorium* place where people may be heard *audience* hearers
auto	self	*autocracy* rule by one person (self) *automobile* vehicle that moves by itself *autobiography* story of one's own life
belli	war	*bellicose* inclined to fight *belligerent* inclined to wage war *rebellious* resisting authority
ben, bon	good	*benefactor* one who does good deeds *benevolence* charity (wishing good) *bonus* something extra above regular pay
biblio	book	*bibliography* list of books *bibliophile* lover of books *Bible* The Book
bio	life	*biography* writing about a person's life *biology* study of living things *biochemist* student of the chemistry of living things
breve	short	*brevity* briefness *abbreviate* shorten

Root or Stem	Meaning	Illustration
cad, cas	to fall	*decadent* deteriorating *cadence* intonation, musical movement *cascade* waterfall
cap (capt, cept, cip)	to take	*capture* seize *participate* take part *precept* wise saying (originally a command)
capit, capt	head	*decapitate* remove (cut off) someone's head *captain* chief
carn	flesh	*carnivorous* flesh-eating *carnage* destruction of life *carnal* fleshly
ced, cess	to yield, to go	*recede* go back, withdraw *antecedent* that which goes before *process* go forward
celer	swift	*celerity* swiftness *decelerate* reduce swiftness *accelerate* increase swiftness
cent	one hundred	*century* one hundred years *centennial* hundredth anniversary *centipede* many-footed, wingless animal
chron	time	*chronology* timetable of events *anachronism* a thing out of time sequence *chronicle* register events in order of time
cid, cis	to cut, to kill	*incision* a cut (surgical) *homicide* killing of a man *fratricide* killing of a brother
cit, citat	to call, to start	*incite* stir up, start up *excite* stir up *recitation* a recalling (or repeating) aloud
civi	citizen	*civilization* society of citizens, culture *civilian* member of community *civil* courteous
clam, clamat	to cry out	*clamorous* loud *declamation* speech *acclamation* shouted approval
claud (claus, clos, clud)	to close	*claustrophobia* fear of close places *enclose* close in *conclude* finish
cognosc, cognit	to learn	*agnostic* lacking knowledge, skeptical *incognito* traveling under assumed name *cognition* knowledge
cord	heart	*accord* agreement (from the heart) *cordial* friendly *discord* lack of harmony

Root or Stem	Meaning	Illustration
corpor	body	*incorporate* organize into a body *corporeal* pertaining to the body, fleshly *corpse* dead body
cred, credit	to believe	*incredulous* not believing, skeptical *credulity* gullibility *credence* belief
cur	to care	*curator* person who has the care of something *sinecure* position without responsibility *secure* safe
curr, curs	to run	*excursion* journey *cursory* brief *precursor* forerunner
deb, debit	to owe	*debt* something owed *indebtedness* debt *debenture* bond
dem	people	*democracy* rule of the people *demagogue* (false) leader of the people *epidemic* widespread (among the people)
derm	skin	*epidermis* skin *pachyderm* thick-skinned quadruped *dermatology* study of skin and its disorders
di, diurn	day	*diary* a daily record of activities, feelings, etc. *diurnal* pertaining to daytime
dic, dict	to say	*abdicate* renounce *diction* speech *verdict* statement of jury
doc, doct	to teach	*docile* obedient; easily taught *document* something that provides evidence *doctor* learned person (originally, teacher)
domin	to rule	*dominate* have power over *domain* land under rule *dominant* prevailing
duc, duct	to lead	*viaduct* arched roadway *aqueduct* artificial waterway
dynam	power, strength	*dynamic* powerful *dynamite* powerful explosive *dynamo* engine making electrical power
ego	I	*egoist* person who is self-interested *egotist* selfish person *egocentric* revolving about self
erg, urg	work	*energy* power *metallurgy* science and technology of metals

Root or Stem	Meaning	Illustration
err	to wander	*error* mistake *erratic* not reliable, wandering *knight-errant* wandering knight
eu	good, well, beautiful	*eulogize* praise *euphemism* substitution of pleasant way of saying something blunt
fall, fals	to deceive	*fallacious* misleading *infallible* not prone to error, perfect *falsify* lie
fer, lat	to bring, to bear	*transfer* bring from one place to another *translate* bring from one language to another *conifer* bearing cones, as pine trees
fid	belief, faith	*infidel* nonbeliever, heathen *confidence* assurance, belief
fin	end, limit	*confine* keep within limits *finite* having definite limits
flect, flex	bend	*flexible* able to bend *deflect* bend away, turn aside
fort	luck, chance	*fortuitous* accidental, occurring by chance *fortunate* lucky
fort	strong	*fortitude* strength, firmness of mind *fortification* strengthening *fortress* stronghold
frag, fract	break	*fragile* easily broken *infraction* breaking of a rule *fractious* unruly, tending to break rules
fug	flee	*fugitive* someone who flees *refuge* shelter, home for someone fleeing
fus	pour	*effusive* gushing, pouring out *diffuse* widespread (poured in many directions)
gam	marriage	*monogamy* marriage to one person *bigamy* marriage to two people at the same time *polygamy* having many wives or husbands at the same time
gen, gener	class, race	*genus* group of animals with similar traits *generic* characteristic of a class *gender* class organized by sex
grad, gress	go, step	*digress* go astray (from the main point) *regress* go backwards *gradual* step by step, by degrees

Root or Stem	Meaning	Illustration
graph, gram	writing	*epigram* pithy statement *telegram* instantaneous message over great distance *stenography* shorthand (writing narrowly)
greg	flock, herd	*gregarious* tending to group together as in a herd *aggregate* group, total *egregious* conspicuously bad; shocking
it, itiner	journey, road	*exit* way out *itinerary* plan of journey
jac (jact, jec)	to throw	*projectile* missile; something thrown forward *trajectory* path taken by thrown object *ejaculatory* casting or throwing out
jur, jurat	to swear	*perjure* testify falsely *jury* group of men and women sworn to seek the truth
labor, laborat	to work	*laboratory* place where work is done *collaborate* work together with others *laborious* difficult
leg (lect, lig)	to choose, to read	*election* choice *legible* able to be read *eligible* able to be selected
leg	law	*legislature* law-making body *legitimate* lawful *legal* lawful
liber, libr	book	*library* collection of books *libretto* the "book" of a musical play *libel* slander (originally found in a little book)
liber	free	*liberation* the fact of setting free *liberal* generous (giving freely); tolerant
log	word, study	*entomology* study of insects *etymology* study of word parts and derivations *monologue* speech by one person
loqu, locut	to talk	*soliloquy* speech by one individual *loquacious* talkative *elocution* speech
luc	light	*elucidate* enlighten *lucid* clear *translucent* allowing some light to pass through
magn	great	*magnify* enlarge *magnanimity* generosity, greatness of soul *magnitude* greatness, extent
mal	bad	*malevolent* wishing evil *malediction* curse *malefactor* evil-doer

Root or Stem	Meaning	Illustration
man	hand	*manufacture* create (make by hand) *manuscript* written by hand *emancipate* free (let go from the hand)
mar	sea	*maritime* connected with seafaring *submarine* undersea craft *mariner* seaman
mater, matr	mother	*maternal* pertaining to motherhood *matriarch* female ruler of a family, group, or state *matrilineal* descended on the mother's side
mit, miss	to send	*missile* projectile *dismiss* send away *transmit* send across
mob (mot, mov)	move	*mobilize* cause to move *motility* ability to move *immovable* not able to be moved
mon, monit	to warn	*admonish* warn *premonition* foreboding *monitor* watcher (warner)
mori, mort	to die	*mortuary* funeral parlor *moribund* dying *immortal* not dying
morph	shape, form	*amorphous* formless, lacking shape *metamorphosis* change of shape *anthropomorphic* in the shape of man
mut	change	*immutable* not able to be changed *mutate* undergo a great change *mutability* changeableness, inconstancy
nat	born	*innate* from birth *prenatal* before birth *nativity* birth
nav	ship	*navigate* sail a ship *circumnavigate* sail around the world *naval* pertaining to ships
neg	deny	*negation* denial *renege* deny, go back on one's word *renegade* turncoat, traitor
nomen, nomin	name	*nomenclature* act of naming, terminology *nominal* in name only (as opposed to actual) *cognomen* surname, distinguishing nickname
nov	new	*novice* beginner *renovate* make new again *novelty* newness

Root or Stem	Meaning	Illustration
omni	all	*omniscient* all knowing *omnipotent* all powerful *omnivorous* eating everything
oper	to work	*operate* work *cooperation* working together
pac	peace	*pacify* make peaceful *pacific* peaceful *pacifist* person opposed to war
pass	feel	*dispassionate* free of emotion *impassioned* emotion-filled *impassive* showing no feeling
pater, patr	father	*patriotism* love of one's country (fatherland) *patriarch* male ruler of a family, group, or state *paternity* fatherhood
path	disease, feeling	*pathology* study of diseased tissue *apathetic* lacking feeling; indifferent *antipathy* hostile feeling
ped, pod	foot	*impediment* stumbling block; hindrance *tripod* three-footed stand *quadruped* four-footed animal
ped	child	*pedagogue* teacher of children *pediatrician* children's doctor
pel, puls	to drive	*compulsion* a forcing to do *repel* drive back *expel* drive out, banish
pet, petit	to seek	*petition* request *appetite* craving, desire *compete* vie with others
phil	love	*philanthropist* benefactor, lover of humanity *Anglophile* lover of everything English *philanderer* one involved in brief love affairs
pon, posit	to place	*postpone* place after *positive* definite, unquestioned (definitely placed)
port, portat	to carry	*portable* able to be carried *transport* carry across *export* carry out (of country)
poten	able, powerful	*omnipotent* all-powerful *potentate* powerful person *impotent* powerless
psych	mind	*psychology* study of the mind *psychosis* mental disorder *psychopath* mentally ill person

Root or Stem	Meaning	Illustration
put, putat	to trim, to calculate	*putative* supposed (calculated) *computation* calculation *amputate* cut off
quer (ques, quir, quis)	to ask	*inquiry* investigation *inquisitive* questioning *query* question
reg, rect	rule	*regicide* murder of a ruler *regent* ruler *insurrection* rebellion; overthrow of a ruler
rid, ris	to laugh	*derision* scorn *ridiculous* deserving to be laughed at
rog, rogat	to ask	*interrogate* question *prerogative* privilege
rupt	to break	*interrupt* break into *bankrupt* insolvent *rupture* a break
sacr	holy	*sacred* holy *sacrilegious* impious, violating something holy *sacrament* religious act
sci	to know	*science* knowledge *omniscient* knowing all *conscious* aware
scop	watch, see	*periscope* device for seeing around corners *microscope* device for seeing small objects
scrib, script	to write	*transcribe* make a written copy *script* written text *circumscribe* write around, limit
sect	cut	*dissect* cut apart *bisect* cut into two pieces
sed, sess	to sit	*sedentary* inactive (sitting) *session* meeting
sent, sens	to think, to feel	*consent* agree *resent* show indignation *sensitive* showing feeling
sequi (secut, seque)	to follow	*consecutive* following in order *sequence* arrangement *sequel* that which follows *non sequitur* something that does not follow logically
solv, solut	to loosen	*absolve* free from blame *dissolute* morally lax *absolute* complete (not loosened)

Root or Stem	Meaning	Illustration
somn	sleep	*insomnia* inability to sleep *somnolent* sleepy *somnambulist* sleepwalker
soph	wisdom	*philosopher* lover of wisdom *sophisticated* worldly wise
spec, spect	to look at	*spectator* observer *aspect* appearance *circumspect* cautious (looking around)
spir	breathe	*respiratory* pertaining to breathing *spirited* full of life (breath)
string, strict	bind	*stringent* strict *constrict* become tight *stricture* limit, something that restrains
stru, struct	build	*constructive* helping to build *construe* analyze (how something is built)
tang (tact, ting)	to touch	*tangent* touching *contact* touching with, meeting *contingent* depending upon
tempor	time	*contemporary* at same time *extemporaneous* impromptu *temporize* delay
ten, tent	to hold	*tenable* able to be held *tenure* holding of office *retentive* holding; having a good memory
term	end	*interminable* endless *terminate* end
terr	land	*terrestrial* pertaining to earth *subterranean* underground
therm	heat	*thermostat* instrument that regulates heat *diathermy* sending heat through body tissues
tors, tort	twist	*distort* twist out of true shape or meaning *torsion* act of twisting *tortuous* twisting
tract	drag, pull	*distract* pull (one's attention) away *intractable* stubborn, unable to be dragged *attraction* pull, drawing quality
trud, trus	push, shove	*intrude* push one's way in *protrusion* something sticking out
urb	city	*urban* pertaining to a city *urbane* polished, sophisticated (pertaining to a city dweller) *suburban* outside of a city

Root or Stem	Meaning	Illustration
vac	empty	*vacuous* lacking content, empty-headed *evacuate* compel to empty an area
vad, vas	go	*invade* enter in a hostile fashion *evasive* not frank; eluding
veni (vent, ven)	to come	*intervene* come between *prevent* stop *convention* meeting
ver	true	*veracious* truthful *verify* check the truth *verisimilitude* appearance of truth
verb	word	*verbose* wordy *verbiage* excessive use of words *verbatim* word for word
vers, vert	turn	*vertigo* turning dizzy *revert* turn back (to an earlier state) *diversion* something causing one to turn aside
via	way	*deviation* departure from the way *viaduct* roadway (arched) *trivial* trifling (small talk at crossroads)
vid, vis	to see	*vision* sight *evidence* things seen *vista* view
vinc (vict, vanq)	to conquer	*invincible* unconquerable *victory* winning *vanquish* defeat
viv, vit	alive	*vivisection* operating on living animals *vivacious* full of life *vitality* liveliness
voc, vocat	to call	*avocation* calling, minor occupation *provocation* calling or rousing the anger of *invocation* calling in prayer
vol	wish	*malevolent* wishing someone ill *voluntary* of one's own will
volv, volut	to roll	*revolve* roll around *evolve* roll out, develop *convolution* coiled state

Common Suffixes

Suffixes are syllables that are added to a word. Occasionally, they change the meaning of the word; more frequently, they serve to change the grammatical form of the word (noun to adjective, adjective to noun, noun to verb).

Suffix	Meaning	Illustration
able, ible	capable of (adjective suffix)	*portable* able to be carried *interminable* not able to be limited *legible* able to be read
ac, ic	like, pertaining to (adjective suffix)	*cardiac* pertaining to the heart *aquatic* pertaining to the water *dramatic* pertaining to the drama
acious, icious	full of (adjective suffix)	*audacious* full of daring *perspicacious* full of mental perception *avaricious* full of greed
al	pertaining to (adjective or noun suffix)	*maniacal* insane *final* pertaining to the end *logical* pertaining to logic
ant, ent	full of (adjective or noun suffix)	*eloquent* pertaining to fluid, effective speech *suppliant* pleader (person full of requests) *verdant* green
ary	like, connected with (adjective or noun suffix)	*dictionary* book connected with words *honorary* with honor *luminary* celestial body
ate	to make (verb suffix)	*consecrate* to make holy *enervate* to make weary *mitigate* to make less severe
ation	that which is (noun suffix)	*exasperation* irritation *irritation* annoyance
cy	state of being (noun suffix)	*democracy* government ruled by the people *obstinacy* stubbornness *accuracy* correctness
eer (er, or)	person who (noun suffix)	*mutineer* person who rebels *lecher* person who lusts *censor* person who deletes improper remarks
escent	becoming (adjective suffix)	*evanescent* tending to vanish *pubescent* arriving at puberty
fic	making, doing (adjective suffix)	*terrific* arousing great fear *soporific* causing sleep

Suffix	Meaning	Illustration
fy	to make (verb suffix)	*magnify* enlarge *petrify* turn to stone *beautify* make beautiful
iferous	producing, bearing (adjective suffix)	*pestiferous* carrying disease *vociferous* bearing a loud voice
il, ile	pertaining to, capable of (adjective suffix)	*puerile* pertaining to a boy or child *ductile* capable of being hammered or drawn *civil* polite
ism	doctrine, belief (noun suffix)	*monotheism* belief in one god *fanaticism* excessive zeal; extreme belief
ist	dealer, doer (noun suffix)	*fascist* one who believes in a fascist state *realist* one who is realistic *artist* one who deals with art
ity	state of being (noun suffix)	*annuity* yearly grant *credulity* state of being unduly willing to believe *sagacity* wisdom
ive	like (adjective suffix)	*expensive* costly *quantitative* concerned with quantity *effusive* gushing
ize, ise	make (verb suffix)	*victimize* make a victim of *rationalize* make rational *harmonize* make harmonious *enfranchise* make free or set free
oid	resembling, like (adjective suffix)	*ovoid* like an egg *anthropoid* resembling man *spheroid* resembling a sphere
ose	full of (adjective suffix)	*verbose* full of words *lachrymose* full of tears
osis	condition (noun suffix)	*psychosis* diseased mental condition *neurosis* nervous condition *hypnosis* condition of induced sleep
ous	full of (adjective suffix)	*nauseous* full of nausea *ludicrous* foolish
tude	state of (noun suffix)	*fortitude* state of strength *beatitude* state of blessedness *certitude* state of sureness

PART 6

TESTS FOR PRACTICE

Critical Reading Test 1

Critical Reading Test 2

Critical Reading Test 3

ANSWER SHEET
CRITICAL READING TEST 1

Section 1

1. Ⓐ Ⓑ Ⓒ Ⓓ Ⓔ	8. Ⓐ Ⓑ Ⓒ Ⓓ Ⓔ	14. Ⓐ Ⓑ Ⓒ Ⓓ Ⓔ	20. Ⓐ Ⓑ Ⓒ Ⓓ Ⓔ
2. Ⓐ Ⓑ Ⓒ Ⓓ Ⓔ	9. Ⓐ Ⓑ Ⓒ Ⓓ Ⓔ	15. Ⓐ Ⓑ Ⓒ Ⓓ Ⓔ	21. Ⓐ Ⓑ Ⓒ Ⓓ Ⓔ
3. Ⓐ Ⓑ Ⓒ Ⓓ Ⓔ	10. Ⓐ Ⓑ Ⓒ Ⓓ Ⓔ	16. Ⓐ Ⓑ Ⓒ Ⓓ Ⓔ	22. Ⓐ Ⓑ Ⓒ Ⓓ Ⓔ
4. Ⓐ Ⓑ Ⓒ Ⓓ Ⓔ	11. Ⓐ Ⓑ Ⓒ Ⓓ Ⓔ	17. Ⓐ Ⓑ Ⓒ Ⓓ Ⓔ	23. Ⓐ Ⓑ Ⓒ Ⓓ Ⓔ
5. Ⓐ Ⓑ Ⓒ Ⓓ Ⓔ	12. Ⓐ Ⓑ Ⓒ Ⓓ Ⓔ	18. Ⓐ Ⓑ Ⓒ Ⓓ Ⓔ	24. Ⓐ Ⓑ Ⓒ Ⓓ Ⓔ
6. Ⓐ Ⓑ Ⓒ Ⓓ Ⓔ	13. Ⓐ Ⓑ Ⓒ Ⓓ Ⓔ	19. Ⓐ Ⓑ Ⓒ Ⓓ Ⓔ	25. Ⓐ Ⓑ Ⓒ Ⓓ Ⓔ
7. Ⓐ Ⓑ Ⓒ Ⓓ Ⓔ			

Section 2

1. Ⓐ Ⓑ Ⓒ Ⓓ Ⓔ	8. Ⓐ Ⓑ Ⓒ Ⓓ Ⓔ	14. Ⓐ Ⓑ Ⓒ Ⓓ Ⓔ	20. Ⓐ Ⓑ Ⓒ Ⓓ Ⓔ
2. Ⓐ Ⓑ Ⓒ Ⓓ Ⓔ	9. Ⓐ Ⓑ Ⓒ Ⓓ Ⓔ	15. Ⓐ Ⓑ Ⓒ Ⓓ Ⓔ	21. Ⓐ Ⓑ Ⓒ Ⓓ Ⓔ
3. Ⓐ Ⓑ Ⓒ Ⓓ Ⓔ	10. Ⓐ Ⓑ Ⓒ Ⓓ Ⓔ	16. Ⓐ Ⓑ Ⓒ Ⓓ Ⓔ	22. Ⓐ Ⓑ Ⓒ Ⓓ Ⓔ
4. Ⓐ Ⓑ Ⓒ Ⓓ Ⓔ	11. Ⓐ Ⓑ Ⓒ Ⓓ Ⓔ	17. Ⓐ Ⓑ Ⓒ Ⓓ Ⓔ	23. Ⓐ Ⓑ Ⓒ Ⓓ Ⓔ
5. Ⓐ Ⓑ Ⓒ Ⓓ Ⓔ	12. Ⓐ Ⓑ Ⓒ Ⓓ Ⓔ	18. Ⓐ Ⓑ Ⓒ Ⓓ Ⓔ	24. Ⓐ Ⓑ Ⓒ Ⓓ Ⓔ
6. Ⓐ Ⓑ Ⓒ Ⓓ Ⓔ	13. Ⓐ Ⓑ Ⓒ Ⓓ Ⓔ	19. Ⓐ Ⓑ Ⓒ Ⓓ Ⓔ	25. Ⓐ Ⓑ Ⓒ Ⓓ Ⓔ
7. Ⓐ Ⓑ Ⓒ Ⓓ Ⓔ			

Section 3

1. Ⓐ Ⓑ Ⓒ Ⓓ Ⓔ	8. Ⓐ Ⓑ Ⓒ Ⓓ Ⓔ	14. Ⓐ Ⓑ Ⓒ Ⓓ Ⓔ	20. Ⓐ Ⓑ Ⓒ Ⓓ Ⓔ
2. Ⓐ Ⓑ Ⓒ Ⓓ Ⓔ	9. Ⓐ Ⓑ Ⓒ Ⓓ Ⓔ	15. Ⓐ Ⓑ Ⓒ Ⓓ Ⓔ	21. Ⓐ Ⓑ Ⓒ Ⓓ Ⓔ
3. Ⓐ Ⓑ Ⓒ Ⓓ Ⓔ	10. Ⓐ Ⓑ Ⓒ Ⓓ Ⓔ	16. Ⓐ Ⓑ Ⓒ Ⓓ Ⓔ	22. Ⓐ Ⓑ Ⓒ Ⓓ Ⓔ
4. Ⓐ Ⓑ Ⓒ Ⓓ Ⓔ	11. Ⓐ Ⓑ Ⓒ Ⓓ Ⓔ	17. Ⓐ Ⓑ Ⓒ Ⓓ Ⓔ	23. Ⓐ Ⓑ Ⓒ Ⓓ Ⓔ
5. Ⓐ Ⓑ Ⓒ Ⓓ Ⓔ	12. Ⓐ Ⓑ Ⓒ Ⓓ Ⓔ	18. Ⓐ Ⓑ Ⓒ Ⓓ Ⓔ	24. Ⓐ Ⓑ Ⓒ Ⓓ Ⓔ
6. Ⓐ Ⓑ Ⓒ Ⓓ Ⓔ	13. Ⓐ Ⓑ Ⓒ Ⓓ Ⓔ	19. Ⓐ Ⓑ Ⓒ Ⓓ Ⓔ	25. Ⓐ Ⓑ Ⓒ Ⓓ Ⓔ
7. Ⓐ Ⓑ Ⓒ Ⓓ Ⓔ			

1 1 1 1 1 1 1 1 1 1 1 1

CRITICAL READING TEST 1

Section 1

TIME—25 MINUTES
24 QUESTIONS

For each of the following questions, select the best answer from the choices provided and fill in the appropriate circle on the answer sheet.

Each of the following sentences contains one or two blanks; each blank indicates that a word or set of words has been left out. Below the sentence are five words or phrases, lettered A through E. Select the word or set of words that best completes the sentence.

Example:

Fame is ----; today's rising star is all too soon tomorrow's washed-up has-been.

(A) rewarding   (B) gradual
(C) essential   (D) spontaneous
(E) transitory

1. Despite careful restoration and cleaning of the murals in the 1960s, the colors slowly but steadily _____.

    (A) persisted
    (B) embellished
    (C) saturated
    (D) deteriorated
    (E) stabilized

2. After the lonely rigors of writing, Mr. Doyle enjoys the _____ aspects of filmmaking.

    (A) impersonal
    (B) transitory
    (C) narrative
    (D) social
    (E) profitable

3. So _____ was the textile trade between England and America—vast quantities of indigo and raw-ginned cotton a year going in one direction, millions of yards of printed cotton fabrics in the other—that it _____ right through the American War of Independence.

    (A) negligible...endured
    (B) important...continued
    (C) illicit...collaborated
    (D) inappropriate...persisted
    (E) pervasive...ceased

4. Like doctors exploring the mysteries concealed within the human body, astronomers are finding that X rays offer an invaluable means for examining otherwise _____ structures.

    (A) inconsequential
    (B) hidden
    (C) ambivalent
    (D) diseased
    (E) ephemeral

5. When trees go dormant in winter, the procedure is anything but _____: it is an active metabolic process that changes the plant _____.

    (A) sleepy...radically
    (B) pleasant...intermittently
    (C) dynamic...majestically
    (D) overt...openly
    (E) organic...thoroughly

GO ON TO THE NEXT PAGE

1 1 1 1 1 1 1 1 1 1 1 1

6. As Reginald Machell's lavishly carved throne clearly illustrates, California craftsmen were not afraid of _____.

(A) competition
(B) embellishment
(C) imitation
(D) expediency
(E) antiquity

7. One might dispute the author's handling of particular points of Kandinsky's interaction with his artistic environment, but her main theses are _____.

(A) unaesthetic
(B) incongruous
(C) untenable
(D) undecipherable
(E) irreproachable

8. After reading numbers of biographies recounting dysfunctions and disasters, failed marriages and failed careers, Joyce Carol Oates _____ a word to _____ the genre: *pathography*, the story of diseased lives.

(A) invented…curtail
(B) reiterated…criticize
(C) hypothesized…indict
(D) dismissed…obscure
(E) coined…describe

GO ON TO THE NEXT PAGE

1   1   1   1   1   1   1   1   1   1   1

Read each of the passages below, and then answer the questions that follow the passage. The correct response may be stated outright or merely suggested in the passage.

Questions 9 and 10 are based on the following passage.

In 1846, when the three Bronte sisters, hoping for publication, sent their verses to Messrs. Aylott and Jones, they adopted mascu-
Line line pseudonyms, calling themselves Currer,
(5) Ellis, and Acton Bell. Strictly speaking, this masculine disguise was unnecessary: in England, women writers had been published since the 1670s, when the novelist and playwright Aphra Behn became the first woman to
(10) earn a living with her pen. The Brontes, however, knew the prejudice they would face, were they to publish under their own names. Even Robert Southey, then Poet Laureate of England, shared this common prejudice, writ-
(15) ing to Charlotte Bronte, "Literature cannot be the business of a woman's life, and it ought not to be."

9.   In line 3, "adopted" most nearly means

   (A) approved
   (B) altered
   (C) assumed
   (D) fostered
   (E) confiscated

10.   The passage suggests that the Brontes' decision to use masculine pseudonyms was

   (A) counterproductive
   (B) prejudicial
   (C) temporary
   (D) arbitrary
   (E) justified

Questions 11 and 12 are based on the following passage.

"What monsters these devilfish are, what vitality our Creator has given them, what vigor in their movements!" So Jules Verne
Line wrote, conjuring up the attack of the giant
(5) squid. Despite Verne's stirring words, members of genus *Architeuthis* (Greek for "chief" squid) have shown little vitality on surfacing; commonly they have been found dead or dying, caught in trawlers' nets or washed
(10) ashore. Marine biologists have long dreamed of observing these reputedly lethargic creatures of the deep in their native habitat. Now a team of Japanese scientists has managed to film a giant squid aggressively attacking its
(15) prey at a depth of 3,000 feet. The race to film the giant squid is over.

11.   The tone of lines 5–10 ("Despite…ashore") is best described as

   (A) ebullient
   (B) censorious
   (C) resentful
   (D) ironic
   (E) mournful

12.   The conclusion of the passage (lines 10–16) suggests that the giant squid

   (A) is a more active predator than previously supposed
   (B) deserves its reputation for lethargy
   (C) has abandoned its native habitat
   (D) will be featured in a horror movie
   (E) is preyed upon by other creatures of the deep

GO ON TO THE NEXT PAGE

1 1 1 1 1 1 1 1 1 1 1 1

Questions 13–24 are based on the following passage.

The following passage is an excerpt from Henry James's short story "The Pupil." In this section, Pemberton, the young British tutor, describes some of the hasty trips around Europe during which he came to know his pupil, Morgan Moreen, and Morgan's family.

A year after he had come to live with them Mr. and Mrs. Moreen suddenly gave up the villa at Nice. Pemberton had got used to sud-
Line denness, having seen it practiced on a consid-
(5) erable scale during two jerky little tours—one in Switzerland the first summer, and the other late in the winter, when they all ran down to Florence and then, at the end of ten days, lik-ing it much less than they had intended, strag-
(10) gled back in mysterious depression. They had returned to Nice "for ever," as they said; but this didn't prevent their squeezing, one rainy muggy May night, into a second-class railway-carriage—you could never tell by
(15) which class they would travel—where Pemberton helped them to stow away a won-derful collection of bundles and bags. The explanation of this manoeuvre was that they had determined to spend the summer "in some
(20) bracing place"; but in Paris they dropped into a small furnished apartment—a fourth floor in a third-rate avenue, where there was a smell on the staircase and the *portier*[1] was hateful—and passed the next four months in blank
(25) indigence.

The better part of this forced temporary stay belonged to the tutor and his pupil, who, visiting the Invalides[2] and Notre Dame, the Conciergerie and all the museums, took a hun-
(30) dred rewarding rambles. They learned to know their Paris, which was useful, for they came back another year for a longer stay, the general character of which in Pemberton's memory today mixes pitiably and confusedly with that
(35) of the first. He sees Morgan's shabby knicker-

bockers—the everlasting pair that didn't match his blouse and that as he grew longer could only grow faded. He remembers the particular holes in his three or four pairs of
(40) colored stockings.

Morgan was dear to his mother, but he never was better dressed than was absolutely necessary—partly, no doubt, by his own fault, for he was as indifferent to his appearance as a
(45) German philosopher. "My dear fellow, so are you! I don't want to cast you in the shade." Pemberton could have no rejoinder for this—the assertion so closely represented the fact. If however the deficiencies of his own wardrobe
(50) were a chapter by themselves he didn't like his little charge to look too poor. Later he used to say "Well, if we're poor, why, after all, shouldn't we look it?" and he consoled him-self with thinking there was something rather
(55) elderly and gentlemanly in Morgan's disre-pair—it differed from the untidiness of the urchin who plays and spoils his things. He could trace perfectly the degrees by which, in proportion as her little son confined himself to
(60) his tutor for society, Mrs. Moreen shrewdly forbore to renew his garments. She did noth-ing that didn't show, neglected him because he escaped notice, and then, as he illustrated this clever policy, discouraged at home his public
(65) appearances. Her position was logical enough—those members of her family who did show had to be showy.

During this period and several others Pemberton was quite aware of how he and his
(70) comrade might strike people; wandering lan-guidly through the Jardin des Plantes[3] as if they had nowhere to go, sitting on the winter days in the galleries of the Louvre, so splen-didly ironical to the homeless, as if for the
(75) advantage of the steam radiators. They joked about it sometimes: it was the sort of joke that

GO ON TO THE NEXT PAGE

1 1 1 1 1 1 1 1 1 1 1 1

was perfectly within the boy's compass. They figured themselves as part of the vast vague hand-to-mouth multitude of the enormous
(80) city and pretended they were proud of their position in it—it showed them "such a lot of life" and made them conscious of a democratic brotherhood. If Pemberton couldn't feel a sympathy in destitution with his small com-
(85) panion—for after all Morgan's fond parents would never have let him really suffer—the boy would at least feel it with him, so it came to the same thing. He used sometimes to wonder what people would think they were—to
(90) fancy they were looked askance at, as if it might be a suspected case of kidnapping. Morgan wouldn't be taken for a young patrician with a tutor—he wasn't smart enough— though he might pass for his companion's
(95) sickly little brother. Now and then he had a five-franc piece, and except once, when they bought a couple of lovely neckties, one of which he made Pemberton accept, they laid it out scientifically in old books. This was sure
(100) to be a great day, always spent at the used book stands on the quays, in a rummage of the dusty boxes that garnish the parapets. Such occasions helped them to live, for their books ran low very soon after the beginning of their
(105) acquaintance. Pemberton had a good many in England, but he was obliged to write to a friend and ask him kindly to get some fellow to give him something for them.

___

[1] Hall porter or custodian.
[2] Famous Paris monument; site of the tomb of Napoleon.
[3] Botanical garden.

13. The primary purpose of the passage is to

(A) denounce the ill treatment of an exceptional child
(B) describe a boy's reactions to his irresponsible parents
(C) portray a selfish and unfeeling mother and son
(D) recount an outsider's impressions of an odd family
(E) advocate an unusual educational experiment

14. It can be inferred from lines 10–25 that the reason for the Moreens' sudden departure from Nice had to do with

(A) ill health
(B) changes in climate
(C) educational opportunities
(D) financial problems
(E) shifts of mood

15. According to lines 17–25, Pemberton's visit to Paris can be described as all of the following EXCEPT

(A) gratifying
(B) sudden
(C) instructive
(D) elegant
(E) frugal

GO ON TO THE NEXT PAGE ⟶

1 1 1 1 1 1 1 1 1 1 1

16. Lines 30–35 suggest that the narrator is making these comments about Pemberton's travels with the Moreen family

(A) on Pemberton's return with the Moreens to Nice

(B) in response to visiting Paris for the first time

(C) some time after Pemberton's wanderings with the Moreens

(D) in answer to Morgan's questions about his childhood

(E) in an effort to write down his memoirs

17. The tone of Morgan's speech to his tutor (lines 45 and 46) can best be described as

(A) apathetic

(B) bitter

(C) teasing

(D) exasperated

(E) self-righteous

18. The statement that "the deficiencies of his own wardrobe were a chapter by themselves" (lines 49 and 50) serves to

(A) indicate the author's intention to cover this topic in a separate chapter

(B) separate Pemberton's problems from those of Morgan and the rest of the Moreens

(C) suggest that Pemberton was allotted insufficient closet space by the Moreens

(D) establish Pemberton's inability to learn to dress himself appropriately

(E) convey Pemberton's sensitivity about the disreputable state of his clothes

19. According to lines 61–67, Mrs. Moreen most likely ceases to spend money on new clothing for Morgan because

(A) she and her husband have grown increasingly miserly with the passage of time

(B) the child is so small for his age that he needs little in the way of clothing

(C) she is unwilling to offend Pemberton by dressing his pupil in finer garments than Pemberton can afford

(D) she resents the child and intentionally neglects him, spending money on herself that should be his

(E) she has only enough money to buy clothes for the family members who must appear in polite society

20. As described in lines 41–67, Mrs. Moreen's approach toward Morgan can best be described as

(A) stern but nurturing

(B) fond but pragmatic

(C) cruel and unfeeling

(D) tentative but loving

(E) doting and overprotective

GO ON TO THE NEXT PAGE ⇒

1 1 1 1 1 1 1 1 1 1 1 **1**

21. The author most likely describes the galleries of the Louvre as "so splendidly ironical to the homeless" (lines 73 and 74) because

    (A) homeless and other destitute people are not allowed within the museum
    (B) people in the galleries make sarcastic comments about poorly dressed museum goers
    (C) the Louvre originated as a shelter for the homeless of Paris
    (D) their opulence contrasts so markedly with the poverty of those who lack homes
    (E) the museum does an excellent job of teaching poor people about different styles of life

22. Morgan and Pemberton regard the "hand-to-mouth multitude" of Paris (lines 77–83) with a sense of

    (A) amusement
    (B) condescension
    (C) indifference
    (D) identification
    (E) resentment

23. In line 93, "smart" most nearly means

    (A) intelligent
    (B) painful
    (C) fashionable
    (D) impudent
    (E) resourceful

24. An aspect of Pemberton's character that is made particularly clear in the final paragraph is his

    (A) tendency to joke about serious matters
    (B) longing to have a younger brother
    (C) concern for how he appears to others
    (D) reluctance to accept gifts from Morgan
    (E) pride in his identification with the poor

STOP

If you finish before time is called, you may check your work on this section only. Do not work on any other section in the test.

Section 2

TIME—25 MINUTES
24 QUESTIONS

For each of the following questions, select the best answer from the choices provided and fill in the appropriate circle on the answer sheet.

Each of the following sentences contains one or two blanks; each blank indicates that a word or set of words has been left out. Below the sentence are five words or phrases, lettered A through E. Select the word or set of words that best completes the sentence.

Example:

Fame is ----; today's rising star is all too soon tomorrow's washed-up has-been.

(A) rewarding   (B) gradual
(C) essential   (D) spontaneous
(E) transitory

1. Because the salt used to deice highways in snowbelt states is highly _____ , it can turn the reinforcing bars in the concrete on highways, bridges, and parking garages into rusty mush.

   (A) adhesive
   (B) obvious
   (C) diluted
   (D) corrosive
   (E) profitable

2. Although the book might satisfy Bloom's hard-core fans, it is _____ by its monotonous citations and its _____ style.

   (A) marred...slipshod
   (B) warped...elegant
   (C) enhanced...impeccable
   (D) unified...laconic
   (E) annotated...exhaustive

3. Sociobiology, the study of the biological and evolutionary basis of social behavior, is a _____ discipline, part biology and part sociology, that requires an understanding of both fields.

   (A) summary
   (B) hybrid
   (C) prolific
   (D) hypothetical
   (E) pedantic

4. By nature he was a _____, demanding that his subordinates follow his orders _____.

   (A) pessimist...positively
   (B) dissident...noncommittally
   (C) martinet...meticulously
   (D) despot...magnanimously
   (E) virtuoso...obsequiously

5. Publishers have discovered that Black America is not a _____ of attitudes and opinions but a rich mixture lending itself to numerous expressions in print.

   (A) concoction
   (B) medley
   (C) monolith
   (D) paradox
   (E) controversy

GO ON TO THE NEXT PAGE

2 2 2 2 2 2 2 2 2 2 2

Read the passages below, and then answer the questions that follow. The correct response may be stated outright or merely suggested in the passages.

Questions 6–9 are based on the following passages.

Passage 1

Should a novelist be allowed to take liberties with the lives of historical figures? This question has engaged critics for centuries,
Line with some supporting the cause of historical
(5) accuracy and others weighing in on the side of artistic freedom. There is, to my mind, a difference between Daniel Defoe's use of the story of Alexander Selkirk, who endured four years as a castaway, to create his character
(10) Robinson Crusoe, and Doctorow's wholesale appropriation of historical personages such as Booker T. Washington and Emma Goldman, whose fame or notoriety he capitalizes on as he makes them "interact" with his fictional
(15) characters.

Passage 2

What do I love best about the novels of E. L. Doctorow? The answer to that is simple. I love the way he mixes up fact and fiction to create something new and magical. Take
(20) _Ragtime_, for example. In _Ragtime_ he throws together Emma Goldman, the anarchist; Harry Houdini, the "escapologist"; Sigmund Freud, the father of psychology; and Henry Ford, the father of the Model T, turning these historical
(25) figures into characters in a novel. Freud and Jung actually went to Coney Island on their visit to America. _That_ the historians can document. Did they take a ride through the Tunnel of Love, as in the novel? Who knows? But
(30) what a fantastic idea.

6. In line 3, "engaged" most nearly means
   (A) hired
   (B) absorbed
   (C) betrothed
   (D) pursued
   (E) misled

7. In Passage 1, the author's attitude toward Doctorow's "wholesale appropriation of historical personages" (lines 10 and 11) can best be characterized as one of

   (A) grudging admiration
   (B) anxious bewilderment
   (C) objective neutrality
   (D) fundamental disapproval
   (E) unconditional acceptance

8. The author of Passage 2 mentions Freud and Jung's ride through the Tunnel of Love in order to

   (A) take issue with the novelist's disregard for facts
   (B) document a historic encounter
   (C) correct a critical misapprehension
   (D) commend a happy invention
   (E) evoke a sense of nostalgia

9. Unlike the author of Passage 2, the author of Passage 1

   (A) discusses a phenomenon
   (B) draws a contrast
   (C) formulates a hypothesis
   (D) poses a question
   (E) quotes an authority

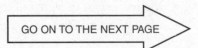
GO ON TO THE NEXT PAGE

2 2 2 2 2 2 2 2 2 2 2 2

Questions 10–15 are based on the following passage.

The style of the renowned modern artist Pablo Picasso changed radically in the course of his long career, as he reacted to new artistic stimuli and fresh ways of seeing the world. In this excerpt from a survey of Picasso's art, the critic Alfred Barr considers the impact of Black African art on Picasso's work, in particular on his painting Les Demoiselles d'Avignon (The Girls of Avignon).

Traditionally, *Les Demoiselles d'Avignon* was indeed supposed to have been influenced by African Negro sculpture but Picasso has since
Line denied this, affirming that although he was
(5) much interested in Iberian[1] sculpture he had no knowledge of Negro art while he was at work on *Les Demoiselles*. Only later in 1907, he states, did he discover Negro sculpture.

Quite recently however Picasso has
(10) assured us that the two right-hand figures of *Les Demoiselles* were completed some time after the rest of the composition. It seems possible therefore that Picasso's memory is incomplete and that he may well have painted
(15) or repainted the astonishing heads of these figures *after* his discovery of African sculpture, just as only a year before, stimulated by Iberian sculpture, he had repainted the head of Gertrude Stein's portrait months after he had
(20) completed the rest of the picture . . . .

The discovery and appreciation of African Negro sculpture among the artists of Paris in the early 1900's is still a somewhat confused story. It seems probable that as early as 1904
(25) Vlaminck began to take an interest in this hitherto neglected art. Shortly afterwards he introduced Derain to his new enthusiasm, and before long Derain and his fellow *fauve*[2] Matisse began to form collections. Vlaminck's
(30) admiration lay more in the romantic and

exotic values of the masks and fetishes but Derain and Matisse found in them unhackneyed aesthetic values involving the bold distortion and structural reorganization of natural
(35) forms.

It is strange that Picasso, who had met Matisse by 1906, should have been unaware of Negro art until the middle of 1907 when, as he says, he discovered it for himself almost
(40) accidentally while leaving the galleries of historic sculpture in the Trocadéro. However, the discovery, he affirms, was a "revelation" to him and he began immediately to make use of it. Whatever general stimulation the *fauves*
(45) had got from African art there is little specific trace of it in their painting. But several of Picasso's works of 1907–08 incorporate African forms and possibly colors to such an extent that the title "Negro Period" has hith-
(50) erto been applied to his art of this time, including *Les Demoiselles d'Avignon*. Actually, Iberian sculpture continued to interest him and often its forms were fused (and by critics confused) with those of the Congo and
(55) the Guinea Coast.

For instance the *Woman in Yellow* has long been considered one of the important paintings of Picasso's Negro period but it now seems clear that this hieratically impressive
(60) figure is related to Iberian bronzes even more closely than are the three earlier figures of *Les Demoiselles d'Avignon* which it resembles in style. As Sweeney has pointed out, the face and pose are remarkably similar to an archaic
(65) votive figure from Despeñaperros. The ocher color and striated patterns, however, may have been suggested by Negro art. More African in

GO ON TO THE NEXT PAGE

2 2 2 2 2 2 2 2 2 2 2

form is the *Head*, which may have been
inspired by the almond-shaped masks of the
(70) Ivory Coast or French Congo.

———————

[1]The term Iberian refers to the peninsula in southwest
Europe that is made up of Spain and Portugal.

[2]The *fauves* were a group of twentieth-century French
artists noted for vivid colors and striking contrasts.

10. The opening paragraph suggests that
     Picasso would have agreed with which of
     the following statements?

     (A) In painting *Les Demoiselles d'Avignon*,
         he was directly inspired by black art.
     (B) In painting *Les Demoiselles d'Avignon*,
         he may have been indirectly
         influenced by African sculpture.
     (C) In painting *Les Demoiselles d'Avignon*,
         he explicitly copied Iberian models.
     (D) In painting *Les Demoiselles d'Avignon*,
         he may have been influenced by
         ancient Spanish art.
     (E) In painting *Les Demoiselles d'Avignon*,
         he lost interest in Iberian sculpture.

11. As shown in lines 12–20, Picasso reacted
     to new artistic stimuli by

     (A) attempting to reproduce them
         faithfully
     (B) deciding to come back to his artistic
         roots
     (C) rethinking already completed works
         of art
     (D) beginning to collect inspiring
         examples
     (E) forgetting his earlier influences

12. In the second paragraph, the author

     (A) poses a question
     (B) refutes a misapprehension
     (C) makes a hypothesis
     (D) cites the testimony of authorities
     (E) contrasts two unlike situations

13. According to lines 36–41, Picasso first
     became acquainted with African art

     (A) through another artist
     (B) on a trip to Africa
     (C) through an art historian
     (D) in an art gallery
     (E) in a book of reproductions

14. In line 50, "applied to" most nearly means

     (A) spread on
     (B) credited to
     (C) placed in contact with
     (D) used to designate
     (E) requested as

15. We can infer from lines 63–65 that
     Despeñaperros is most likely

     (A) a town on the Ivory Coast of Africa
     (B) the name of a young French girl from
         Avignon
     (C) a contemporary artist known to
         Picasso
     (D) a location on the Iberian peninsula
     (E) the name of a village near Avignon

GO ON TO THE NEXT PAGE

2 2 2 2 2 2 2 2 2 2 2

Questions 16–24 are based on the following passage.

Taken from the writings of Benjamin Franklin, the following excerpt, published in 1784, demonstrates Franklin's attitude toward the so-called savages of North America and reveals something of what these Native Americans thought about the white men and women who had come to their land.

Savages we call them, because their manners differ from ours, which we think the perfection of civility; they think the same of
Line theirs.
(5)   Perhaps, if we could examine the manners of different nations with impartiality, we should find no people so rude as to be without rules of politeness, nor any so polite as not to have some remains of rudeness.
(10)   The Indian men, when young, are hunters and warriors; when old, counselors, for all their government is by counsel of the sages; there is no force, there are no prisons, no officers to compel obedience or inflict punish-
(15) ment. Hence they generally study oratory, the best speaker having the most influence. The Indian women till the ground, dress the food, nurse and bring up the children, and preserve and hand down to posterity the memory of
(20) public transactions. These employments of men and women are accounted natural and honorable. Having few artificial wants, they have abundance of leisure for improvement by conversation. Our laborious manner of life,
(25) compared with theirs, they esteem slavish and base; and the learning, on which we value ourselves, they regard as frivolous and useless.
   An instance of this occurred at the treaty of Lancaster, in Pennsylvania, in the year
(30) 1744, between the government of Virginia and the Six Nations. After the principal business was settled, the commissioners from Virginia acquainted the Indians by a speech that there

was at Williamsburg a college, with a fund for
(35) educating Indian youth; and that, if the Six Nations would send down half a dozen of their young lads to that college, the government would take care that they should be well provided for, and instructed in all the learning of
(40) the white people. It is one of the Indian rules of politeness not to answer a public proposition the same day that it is made; they think that it would be treating it as a light matter, and that they show it respect by taking time to
(45) consider it, as of a matter important. They therefore deferred their answer till the day following; when their speaker began by expressing their deep sense of the kindness of the Virginia government in making them that
(50) offer, saying:
   "We know that you highly esteem the kind of learning taught in those colleges, and that the maintenance of our young men, while with you, would be very expensive to you. We are
(55) convinced, therefore, that you mean to do us good by your proposal, and we thank you heartily. But you, who are wise, must know that different nations have different conceptions of things; and you will therefore not take
(60) it amiss, if our ideas of this kind of education happen not to be the same as yours. We have had some experience of it. Several of our young people were formerly brought up at the colleges of the northern provinces: they were
(65) instructed in all your sciences; but when they came back to us they were bad runners, ignorant of every means of living in the woods, unable to bear cold or hunger. They knew neither how to build a cabin, take a deer, nor kill
(70) an enemy, spoke our language imperfectly, were therefore neither fit for hunters, warriors, nor counselors; they were totally good for nothing.

GO ON TO THE NEXT PAGE →

We are, however, not the less obliged by (75) your kind offer, though we decline accepting it; and, to show our grateful sense of it, if the gentlemen of Virginia will send us a dozen of their sons, we will take care of their education, instruct them in all we know, and make *men* of (80) them."

16. According to Franklin, Indian leaders maintain their authority by means of their

   (A) warlike ability
   (B) skill as hunters
   (C) verbal prowess
   (D) personal wealth
   (E) punitive capacity

17. In line 17, "dress" most nearly means

   (A) clothe
   (B) adorn
   (C) medicate
   (D) straighten
   (E) prepare

18. To which of the following does Franklin attribute the amount of leisure time for conversing available to the Indians?

   I. Their greater efficiency and productivity
   II. Their simpler, more natural lifestyle
   III. Their distinctive set of values

   (A) I only
   (B) II only
   (C) I and II only
   (D) II and III only
   (E) I, II, and III

19. Franklin's purpose in quoting the speech that concludes the excerpt is primarily to

   (A) demonstrate the natural oratorical abilities of Indians
   (B) condemn the Virginians' failure to recruit Indian students for their schools
   (C) give an example of the Indian viewpoint on the benefits of white civilization
   (D) describe a breakdown in communications between Indians and whites
   (E) advocate the adoption of Indian educational techniques

20. The Indians' chief purpose in making the speech seems to be to

   (A) tactfully refuse a friendly gesture
   (B) express their opinions on equality
   (C) gratify their intended audience
   (D) describe native American customs
   (E) request funds to start their own school

21. According to this passage, the Indians' idea of education differs from that of the gentlemen of Virginia in that the Indians

   (A) also believe in the education of young women
   (B) have different educational goals
   (C) teach different branches of science
   (D) include different aspects of nature
   (E) speak a different language

22. In line 69, "take" most nearly means

   (A) endure
   (B) transport
   (C) confiscate
   (D) capture
   (E) accept

GO ON TO THE NEXT PAGE

2   2   2   2   2   2   2   2   2   2   2

23. The Indians responsible for the speech would probably agree that they

    (A) have no right to deny Indian boys the opportunity for schooling
    (B) are being insulted by the offer of the commissioners
    (C) know more about the various branches of science than the commissioners do
    (D) have a better way of educating young men than the commissioners do
    (E) should not offer to educate the sons of the gentlemen of Virginia

24. The tone of the speech as a whole is best described as

    (A) aloof but angry
    (B) insistently demanding
    (C) grudgingly admiring
    (D) eager and inquiring
    (E) courteous but ironic

STOP

3 3 3 3 3 3 3 3 3 3 3

Section 3

TIME—20 MINUTES
19 QUESTIONS

For each of the following questions, select the best answer from the choices provided and fill in the appropriate circle on the answer sheet.

Each of the following sentences contains one or two blanks; each blank indicates that a word or set of words has been left out. Below the sentence are five words or phrases, lettered A through E. Select the word or set of words that best completes the sentence.

Example:

Fame is ----; today's rising star is all too soon tomorrow's washed-up has-been.

(A) rewarding   (B) gradual
(C) essential   (D) spontaneous
(E) transitory

Ⓐ Ⓑ Ⓒ Ⓓ ●

1. Before the 1960s, African-American cartoonists labored mostly without mainstream recognition, their work _____ African-American magazines, journals, and newspapers.

    (A) confined to
    (B) unconscious of
    (C) irrelevant to
    (D) unacceptable to
    (E) derided by

2. Calculation and planning informed the actress's every word and gesture: there was not a _____ moment in her entire performance.

    (A) spontaneous
    (B) tasteful
    (C) histrionic
    (D) lethargic
    (E) poignant

3. None of her students minded when Professor Rivera's lectures wandered away from their official theme; her _____ were always more fascinating than the topic of the day.

    (A) summaries
    (B) digressions
    (C) intimations
    (D) metaphors
    (E) imprecations

4. Though Widow Douglas hoped to reform Huck, her sister Miss Watson _____ him _____ and said he would come to no good end.

    (A) called...amendable
    (B) declared...qualified
    (C) pronounced...incorrigible
    (D) proclaimed...optimistic
    (E) professed...cured

5. Critics point out that, far from moving _____ closer to its goals, the field of behavioral genetics is _____ the same problems that have always plagued it.

    (A) intermittently...composed of
    (B) dramatically...divorced from
    (C) inexorably...mired in
    (D) steadily...acclaimed for
    (E) uniformly...enhanced by

6. Rebuffed by his colleagues, the initially _____ young researcher became increasingly _____.

    (A) outgoing...withdrawn
    (B) boisterous...excitable
    (C) diligent...tolerant
    (D) theoretical...pragmatic
    (E) tedious...polished

GO ON TO THE NEXT PAGE

3 3 3 3 3 3 3 3 3 3 3 3

Read the passages below, and then answer the questions that follow. The correct response may be stated outright or merely suggested in the passages.

Questions 7–19 are based on the following passages.

The following passages concern the learning and behavior of infants during the first months of life. The first passage comes from a popular guide for new parents, the second from a textbook on child development.

Passage 1

The two-month-old baby has hardly roused himself from the long night of his first weeks in this world when he is confronted
Line with some of the profound problems of the
(5) race. We invite him to study the nature of reality, to differentiate self and non-self, and to establish useful criteria in each of these categories. A project of such magnitude in academic research would require extensive laboratory
(10) equipment and personnel; to be fair about it, it has taken just that to reconstruct the experiments of the infant. And there are few grown and fully accredited scientists who can equal the infant for zeal and energy in sorting out
(15) the raw data in this project. His equipment is limited to his sensory organs, his hands, his mouth, and a primitive memory apparatus.

At two months, as we have seen, he recognizes an object that we know to be a human
(20) face and we know to be an object outside himself. But to the baby this is just an image, an image incidentally that he can't differentiate from the mental image, the picture in memory. But this face is one piece in the jigsaw puz-
(25) zle—a key piece, we think. Then gradually in the weeks to come the association of breast or bottle, of hands, voice, a multitude of pleasurable sense experiences begin to cluster around this face and to form the crude image of a
(30) person.

Meantime the infant is conducting a series of complicated experiments in sensory discrimination. We must remember that in the early months he does not discriminate
(35) between his body and other bodies. When he clutches the finger of his mother or his father he doesn't see it as someone else's finger and his behavior indicates that he treats it exactly the same as he does his own finger. It takes
(40) him some time, in fact, to recognize his own hand at sight and to acquire even a rudimentary feeling that this is part of his own body. In the first group of experiments he discovers that the object that passes occasionally in front
(45) of his eyes (which *we* know to be his hand) is the same as the object with visual and taste qualities that he can identify. In another experimental series he discovers that the sensations that accompany the introduction of *this* object
(50) into his mouth are different from those experienced when he takes a nipple into his mouth, or a toy, or his mother's or father's finger.

Passage 2

Very soon after birth, environmental forces, or response contingencies, begin to
(55) operate in conjunction with the infant's built-in response repertoire to produce learned changes in behavior. It will not be long before the baby, instead of awaiting a touch near the mouth to open it, will do so when the bottle or
(60) nipple is seen approaching it. Or the head may be turned in the appropriate direction when the baby is placed in the accustomed feeding posture. Such anticipatory gestures symbolize the essence of learning. Such response systems
(65) are the classically conditioned or Pavlovian variety, because they involve elicited behavior.

GO ON TO THE NEXT PAGE

3   3   3   3   3   3   3   3   3   3   3

Operant conditioning is in a sense also anticipatory; the infant makes a response pre- sumably in anticipation of receiving a reward.
(70) Response consequences serve as reinforcers of the behavior, then, and tend to perpetuate the behavior. Thus an infant who spontaneously makes a sound, which is then followed by an attractive consequence such as sweet fluid or
(75) the smiling presence of the mother, will very likely repeat the act with increasing frequency as time (and reinforcement) goes on. Similarly, a response which is followed by an aversive consequence, such as a frightening
(80) noise, will tend not to be repeated in the future. The infant thus behaves in accordance with expectations about the availability of positive reinforcers or punishments, based upon past experience.
(85) It must be clear by now that thought begins at birth. There are psychologists who would not want to term the anticipatory ges- tures just spoken of as thought. Even they, however, would have difficulty pinpointing
(90) the stage of development or learning at which the onset of thought occurs. It is perhaps more meaningful to speak of increasing levels of symbolization.
A number of developmental theorists have
(95) postulated stages of thought development. While no two systems or theories of cognition or thought development are exactly the same, most are agreed that the baby begins with a primitive appreciation of what is there and
(100) what is not, and most agree that early in life what is not there is unimportant to the child. Only with increasing cortical development, cognitive complexity, and experience in sens- ing, perceiving, and storing information does
(105) the child begin to take into consideration the current absence of past stimulation and to consider how things are different or might be different than they are. Such "mental manipu- lations" occur later and set the stage for very
(110) symbolic higher thought processes of which mature persons are capable.

7. By stating that a two-month-old baby confronts "some of the profound problems of the race" (lines 1–5), the author means that the infant

(A) will start to figure out what is real and what is imaginary
(B) is far more intelligent than we may think
(C) begins to understand that dreams are not real
(D) begins to locate his physical boundaries
(E) soon learns to communicate with the world outside itself.

8. The author of Passage 1 compares a baby with a scientist (lines 12–15) in order to make the point that

(A) infants are tireless in their efforts to understand their environments
(B) infants use a form of the scientific method
(C) scientific experimentation is very time-consuming
(D) an infant is a human laboratory
(E) many scientific studies have been done on how infants learn

9. The author of Passage 1 apparently believes that during infancy learning begins with

(A) feeling loved
(B) the baby's senses
(C) images that the infant sees
(D) ideas stored in the infant's memory
(E) repetition of certain sights and sounds

GO ON TO THE NEXT PAGE

3 3 3 3 3 3 3 3 3 3 3

10. The account in Passage 1 of how an infant learns to discriminate between has own body and the body of others suggests that

(A) all babies follow one of several well-defined patterns
(B) the sequence is highly structured and precise
(C) some babies learn more quickly than others
(D) there are several different theories about how the process works
(E) male babies learn differently from female babies

11. According to Passage 1, an important milestone in infant development apparently occurs when a baby learns

(A) to grasp someone else's finger with his hand
(B) to remember objects like a mother's face even when the object is out of sight
(C) that his mother and father have different faces
(D) that his own hand has a distinctive smell and taste
(E) that his own hand is different from another person's hand

12. The behavior of infants discussed in the first paragraph of Passage 2 occurs because

(A) infants feel emotions just as adults do
(B) every baby responds to the environment in certain predictable ways
(C) every baby is born with certain instincts
(D) infants naturally learn to respond to certain stimuli in the environment
(E) healthy babies do not need to be taught to ingest food

13. The author uses the phrase "classically conditioned" response system (lines 64–66) to mean that infants

(A) use built-in response contingencies to satisfy their basic needs
(B) cry when they are hungry
(C) respond to their environments early in life
(D) can be trained to learn from their environments
(E) learn to elicit certain behaviors from their caregivers

14. With regard to an infant's capacity to think, the author of Passage 2 believes that

(A) newborns are capable of thought
(B) thought develops even without external stimulation
(C) real thought does not occur until an infant has had some experience
(D) the development of memory triggers thought
(E) all newborns have the same thoughts

15. The author suggests that the term "symbolization" (line 93) be used to refer to

(A) fright that infants feel after hearing a loud noise
(B) vivid images in an infant's mind
(C) the difference between positive and negative reinforcement
(D) a form of mental activity occurring in an infant
(E) an infant's memory

GO ON TO THE NEXT PAGE

3　3　3　3　3　3　3　3　3　3　3

16. Passage 2 implies that one can determine the maturity of people's thought processes by

    (A) observing their capacities to think abstractly
    (B) measuring the speeds at which their minds work
    (C) checking their rates of intellectual growth
    (D) assessing the sizes of their memory banks
    (E) evaluating their abilities to retain information

17. The authors of both passages agree that early in life newborns learn

    (A) to manipulate ideas in a primitive form
    (B) to differentiate between things that are not there and things that are
    (C) what to do when they feel discomfort
    (D) to distinguish between behaviors that provide pleasure and behaviors that don't
    (E) to influence the immediate environment

18. Compared to Passage 1, Passage 2 places more emphasis on the

    (A) research being done to understand newborn infants
    (B) parents' role in helping an infant develop
    (C) external indications of an infant's thought patterns
    (D) emotional growth of infants
    (E) psychology of thought development

19. In contrast to the author of Passage 2, the author of Passage 1 describes the development of an infant's thought with greater

    (A) attention to theory
    (B) authority
    (C) seriousness of purpose
    (D) scientific evidence
    (E) accuracy

STOP

Answer Key

Section 1

1. D	5. A	9. C	13. D	17. C	21. D
2. D	6. B	10. E	14. D	18. E	22. D
3. B	7. E	11. D	15. D	19. E	23. C
4. B	8. E	12. A	16. C	20. B	24. C

Section 2

1. D	5. C	9. B	13. D	17. E	21. B
2. A	6. B	10. D	14. D	18. D	22. D
3. B	7. D	11. C	15. D	19. C	23. D
4. C	8. D	12. C	16. C	20. A	24. E

Section 3

1. A	5. C	9. B	13. C	17. B
2. A	6. A	10. B	14. A	18. E
3. B	7. D	11. E	15. D	19. B
4. C	8. A	12. D	16. A	

Analysis of Test Results

I. Check your answers against the answer key.

II. Fill in the following chart.

Sentence Completion Number Correct	Section 1 (Questions 1–8) _____		Section 2 (Questions 1–5) _____	Section 3 (Questions 1–6) _____		Total _____
Passage-Based Reading Number Correct	Section 1 (Questions 9–24) _____		Section 2 (Questions 6–24) _____	Section 3 (Questions 7–19) _____		Total _____

III. Interpret your results.

Sentence Completion   Number Correct _____

Passage-Based Reading   Number Correct _____

Subtotal _____

Guessing Penalty: Subtract 1/4 point for each incorrect answer.   _____
(Do not take off points for questions you left blank.)

TOTAL SCORE _____

	Sentence Completion Score	Passage-Based Reading Score	Total
Excellent	18–19 Correct	43–48 Correct	60–67
Very Good	14–17 Correct	33–42 Correct	46–59
Good	11–13 Correct	25–32 Correct	35–45
Fair	9–10 Correct	20–24 Correct	28–34
Poor	6–8 Correct	12–19 Correct	17–27
Very Poor	0–5 Correct	0–11 Correct	0–16

Answer Explanations

Section 1

1. **(D)** One would expect restoration and cleaning to enhance or improve the murals' colors. Instead, the colors *deteriorated* or grew worse.

2. **(D)** In contrast to the loneliness of writing, Mr. Doyle appreciates the *sociability* of working with others on films.

3. **(B)** This *important* trade involving vast quantities of textiles was so vital to the economy that not even a war could stop it. Thus, it *continued* or kept on taking place through the Revolutionary War.

4. **(B)** The astronomers resemble the doctors in their use of X rays to examine things that are concealed or *hidden*.

5. **(A)** The phrase "anything but" signals an extreme degree of contrast. When trees go dormant, the process is decidedly not *sleepy* or sluggish, and the change is extreme or *radical*.

6. **(B)** Lavish carvings decorating a throne are a form of *embellishment* (decoration; ornamentation).

7. **(E)** "But" signals a contrast. Though one can dispute the way the author treats certain details, one cannot find fault with her main arguments or theses. They are *irreproachable* (flawless; blameless).

8. **(E)** Oates has invented or *coined* a new word to *describe* a particular genre.

9. **(C)** By adopting a masculine pseudonym, a woman writer *assumed* it or took it as her own.

10. **(E)** The fact that a highly respected fellow poet like Southey could maintain that women should not pursue writing as a career suggests the Brontes' decision to disguise their gender by using masculine pseudonyms was *justified*.

11. **(D)** The author's remark that the dead or dying giant squid showed little vitality or life on surfacing is *ironic*: it wryly points up the contrast between the vigor of Verne's fictional devilfish and the sluggishness of the squid trapped in nets or washed ashore.

12. **(A)** The squid's actions in "aggressively attacking" its prey clearly suggest that it *is a more active predator than previously supposed*.

13. **(D)** The tutor, who is not related to the Moreens and is therefore an outsider to the group, is telling the story of his relationship to this unusual family.

14. **(D)** The Moreens' sudden shifts are apparently motivated by financial problems, for the class they travel in and the apartment they stay in vary with their financial state.

15. **(D)** Living as he did in a small, uncomfortable apartment and dressing shabbily in threadbare clothes, Pemberton did not lead an *elegant* life during his visit to Paris. Use the process of elimination to answer this question.

    - Pemberton's visit to Paris was *gratifying*; he found his rambles with Morgan rewarding. You can eliminate (A).
    - Pemberton's visit to Paris was *sudden*; the Moreens suddenly gave up their villa in Nice and headed for Paris. You can eliminate (B).

- Pemberton's visit to Paris was *instructive*; he and Morgan "learned to know their Paris." You can eliminate (C).
- Pemberton's visit to Paris was *frugal*; he and Morgan seldom had any money, and when they did have some, they were very careful about what they spent it on. You can eliminate (E).

16. **(C)** Lines 30–35 state that the Moreens "came back another year for a longer stay, the general character of which in Pemberton's memory today mixes pitiably and confusedly with that of the first." The narrator's reference to "Pemberton's memory *today*" indicates that he is speaking *some time after* the events recounted in this tale. The narrator is telling the story of events his friend Pemberton remembers from years past.

17. **(C)** In telling his tutor that he does not wish to outshine him or cast him in the shade by dressing better than he does, Morgan is affectionately *teasing* Pemberton.

18. **(E)** To say that something is a chapter by itself is a way of saying that it would take an entire chapter of a book to deal with that subject fully. Thus, Pemberton is asserting that his wardrobe's shortcomings are major. Clearly, he is *sensitive about the disreputable state of his clothes.*

19. **(E)** Mrs. Moreen does not spend money for new clothes for Morgan because he does not make public appearances, that is, does not appear in "polite society." She does spend money on new clothes for the family members who move in polite circles. She loves Morgan and does not neglect him intentionally. This suggests that *she has only enough money to buy clothes for the family members who must appear in polite society.*

20. **(B)** Mrs. Moreen loves Morgan ("Morgan was dear to his mother"), but she shrewdly refrains from buying him new clothes when she realizes that nobody "important" will see how he is dressed. Her attitude is *fond* (loving) *but pragmatic* (practical).

21. **(D)** Morgan and Pemberton consider themselves "part of the vast vague hand-to-mouth multitude of" Paris and feel conscious of being part of a "democratic brotherhood." Thus, on some levels, even if partly in jest, they *identify* with the poor.

22. **(D)** Here the irony lies in the *contrast* between the splendors of the great museum and the shabbiness of the poor and homeless who flock to it for shelter and a bit of warmth.

23. **(C)** A young patrician is the child of an aristocratic family. Given Morgan's shabby clothing, he does not look smart or *fashionable* enough for people to consider him a member of the aristocracy.

24. **(C)** The opening sentence of the final paragraph states that Pemberton was "quite aware of how he and his comrade might strike people." The paragraph then proceeds to give examples of Pemberton's self-consciousness about appearances, as he wonders "what people would think they were" and fancies or imagines they are getting odd looks from people because they are such a mismatched pair. Clearly, the paragraph particularly brings home Pemberton's *concern for how he appears to others.*

Section 2

1. **(D)** Salt eats away iron bars, turning them into rusty mush, by the process known as corrosion; salt is a highly *corrosive* substance.

2. **(A)** The writer is criticizing Bloom's book, which is *marred* (damaged) by its *slipshod* or sloppy style. *Although* is a contrast signal. Its use signals that the writer is *not* satisfied by Bloom's book.

3. **(B)** Because sociobiology combines aspects of two fields it is a *hybrid* or combined discipline (just as a mule, the offspring of a horse and an ass, is a hybrid animal).

4. **(C)** By definition, a *martinet* (stickler for discipline) would want his subordinates to follow orders *meticulously*, treating every detail with extreme care.

5. **(C)** By definition, a *monolith* is something solidly uniform, an undifferentiated whole. Black America, however, is a mixture of different attitudes and opinions; it is not monolithic at all.

6. **(B)** The question has engaged or *absorbed* critics, occupying their attention.

7. **(D)** The author of Passage 1 maintains that Doctorow has capitalized on the fame or notoriety of real people. His attitude toward this "wholesale appropriation" is one of *fundamental disapproval*.

8. **(D)** The author of Passage 2 considers Freud and Jung's trip through the Tunnel of Love "a fantastic idea." To him it is *a happy invention*, one that he is delighted to *commend*.

9. **(B)** The author of Passage 1 states that "There is . . . a difference" between Defoe's use of Selkirk and Doctorow's appropriation of Washington, Goldman, and other historical figures. He *draws a contrast* between the practices of the two authors, pointing out how they differ.

10. **(D)** Picasso admitted that at the time he was working on *Les Demoiselles* "he was much interested in Iberian" or ancient Spanish sculpture. Thus, *he may have been influenced by ancient Spanish art*.

11. **(C)** Picasso had been moved in the past to *rethink completed works*. "Only a year before, stimulated by Iberian sculpture, he had repainted the head of Gertrude Stein's portrait months after he had completed the rest of the picture."

12. **(C)** In asserting that Picasso's memory might have been inaccurate and that he might have repainted the heads after his discovery of African sculpture, the author is *making a hypothesis* about what actually took place.

13. **(D)** Picasso was in the sculpture galleries of the Trocadero when he ran across African carvings.

14. **(D)** The title "Negro Period" has been given to this period or *used to designate* it, distinguishing it from Picasso's art of earlier times.

15. **(D)** The author asserts that experts today agree the *Woman in Yellow* is quite closely related to Iberian bronze statues. To back up this assertion, he cites Sweeney's observation that the *Woman in Yellow* looks remarkably similar to an ancient votive figure from Despeñaperros. Thus, it seems most likely that Despeñaperros is *a location on the Iberian peninsula* associated with ancient Iberian bronzes.

16. **(C)** If "the best speaker" has the most influence in the Indians' counsels, clearly the Indian leaders maintain their authority by means of their *verbal prowess* or skill.

17. (**E**) To dress food is to *prepare* it so that it can be cooked.

18. (**D**) You can answer this question by using the process of elimination.

   - Statement I is untrue. Franklin never states that the Indians are more productive than the whites. Therefore, you can eliminate (A), (C), and (E).
   - Statement II is true. According to Franklin, the Indians have abundance of leisure because they have "few artificial wants." They work only to satisfy their simple physical needs. When compared with the whites' laborious manner of life, theirs is a *simpler, more natural lifestyle*.
   - Statement III is also true. The Indians do not value the time-consuming learning valued by the whites because they have a different, *distinctive set of values*. Therefore, you can eliminate (B).
   - Only (D) is left. It is the correct answer.

19. (**C**) Just before he quotes the speech, Franklin states that the Indians look on the learning of the whites as useless. In recounting this instance of Indian diplomacy, he is *giving an example of the Indian viewpoint on the benefits of white civilization*.

20. (**A**) In assuring the commissioners that they recognize both the commissioners' good intentions and wisdom, the Indians are being most diplomatic. However, they are not agreeing to the commissioners' offer. Instead, they are declining or *tactfully refusing* it.

21. (**B**) While the education provided the Indians in the colleges of the northern provinces included all the white men's sciences, it did not prepare these young men for life in the woods. Thus, it did not meet the Indian elders' educational goals. It is clear that the Indians and the gentlemen of Virginia *have different educational goals*.

22. (**D**) To "take" a deer in this context is to kill or *capture* it; the speaker is describing how the white man's education fails to prepare young men to become hunters.

23. (**D**) The Indians state that a white college education made worthless good-for-nothings out of young Indians. They also assert that they can make men out of the Virginian commissioners' sons. Thus, it seems likely that the Indians would agree that they *have a better way of educating young men than the commissioners do*.

24. (**E**) In expressing their gratitude for the offer and thanking the Virginians for their intent, the Indians are being most *courteous*. In making the Virginians an offer they realize the Virginians are unlikely to accept, they are somewhat *ironic* as well.

Section 3

1. (**A**) Until the 1960s, the work of African-American cartoonists was largely limited or *confined* to African-American publications; their cartoons generally did not appear in the mainstream, general press.

2. (**A**) The actress thinks out every move she makes. Consequently, her performance is not *spontaneous* (unplanned, impulsive).

3. (**B**) To wander away from one's subject is to *digress*; the students enjoyed the professor's *digressions* or departures from the assigned topic.

4. **(C)** Miss Watson *pronounces* (asserts) that Huck cannot be reformed; she calls him *incorrigible* (uncorrectable). *Though* is a contrast signal. Its use signals that, unlike her widowed sister, Miss Watson has *no* hope of being able to reform Huck.

5. **(C)** Rather than moving *inexorably* (relentlessly, unstoppably) closer to its goals, the field is stuck or *mired in* its usual problems. The phrase "far from" is a contrast signal. Its use signals that the second missing word means the opposite of "moving *inexorably* closer."

6. **(A)** To be rebuffed is to be rejected or slighted. Being ignored by one's co-workers could make an *outgoing*, sociable person become unsociable and *withdrawn*.

7. **(D)** The phrase refers to the task of differentiating "self and nonself." In other words, the infant *begins to locate his physical boundaries*, learning where his own body ends and the rest of the world begins.

8. **(A)** The passage says that few scientists "can equal the infant for zeal and energy." An infant, therefore, is *tireless in his efforts* to figure things out.

9. **(B)** Throughout the passage, the author points out the vital role of the *baby's senses* in learning. See, for example, "sensory organs" (lines 15–17), "sense experiences" (lines 25–30), and "sensory discrimination" (lines 31–33).

10. **(B)** The infant conducts a step-by-step "series of complicated experiments," which can be described only as *highly structured and precise*.

11. **(E)** In lines 47–52 the passage describes the infant's discovery that *his own hand is different from another person's hand*.

12. **(D)** The fundamental principle of stimulus-response behavior, which is discussed in the passage, is that organisms, including infants, *naturally learn to respond to certain stimuli in the environment*.

13. **(C)** Stimulus-response conditioning is a "classical," universally acknowledged principle of behavioral psychology. We see evidence of it in newborns when they *respond to their environments early in life*. Pavlov, whose experiments with dogs is widely known, was one of the first scientists to describe the principle.

14. **(A)** The author states that *newborns are capable of thought* in lines 85 and 86.

15. **(D)** Because psychologists cannot agree on a precise definition of "thought," the author suggests "symbolization" as an alternative word to describe *the activity that takes place in an infant's mind*.

16. **(A)** Mature thought is that which allows the mind to consider "how things are different or might be different than they are." Such speculation demonstrates *a capacity to think abstractly*.

17. **(B)** Much of Passage 1 discusses how newborns begin *to differentiate between things that are not there and things that are*. In Passage 2 the author states that "the baby begins with a primitive appreciation of what is there and what is not."

18. **(E)** Passage 1 stresses the behavior that a parent might observe as a newborn infant learns to think. Passage 2, on the other hand, focuses on behavior in terms of the *psychology of thought development*.

19. **(B)** Passage 2 is written more tentatively; that is, the author recognizes that many assertions regarding infant thought are theoretical and that not all psychologists agree on every theory. In comparison, Passage 1 sounds like the voice of *authority*. This is probably as it should be, for nervous parents want to be told exactly what is going on with their newborns.

ANSWER SHEET
CRITICAL READING TEST 2

Section 1

1. Ⓐ Ⓑ Ⓒ Ⓓ Ⓔ
2. Ⓐ Ⓑ Ⓒ Ⓓ Ⓔ
3. Ⓐ Ⓑ Ⓒ Ⓓ Ⓔ
4. Ⓐ Ⓑ Ⓒ Ⓓ Ⓔ
5. Ⓐ Ⓑ Ⓒ Ⓓ Ⓔ
6. Ⓐ Ⓑ Ⓒ Ⓓ Ⓔ
7. Ⓐ Ⓑ Ⓒ Ⓓ Ⓔ

8. Ⓐ Ⓑ Ⓒ Ⓓ Ⓔ
9. Ⓐ Ⓑ Ⓒ Ⓓ Ⓔ
10. Ⓐ Ⓑ Ⓒ Ⓓ Ⓔ
11. Ⓐ Ⓑ Ⓒ Ⓓ Ⓔ
12. Ⓐ Ⓑ Ⓒ Ⓓ Ⓔ
13. Ⓐ Ⓑ Ⓒ Ⓓ Ⓔ

14. Ⓐ Ⓑ Ⓒ Ⓓ Ⓔ
15. Ⓐ Ⓑ Ⓒ Ⓓ Ⓔ
16. Ⓐ Ⓑ Ⓒ Ⓓ Ⓔ
17. Ⓐ Ⓑ Ⓒ Ⓓ Ⓔ
18. Ⓐ Ⓑ Ⓒ Ⓓ Ⓔ
19. Ⓐ Ⓑ Ⓒ Ⓓ Ⓔ

20. Ⓐ Ⓑ Ⓒ Ⓓ Ⓔ
21. Ⓐ Ⓑ Ⓒ Ⓓ Ⓔ
22. Ⓐ Ⓑ Ⓒ Ⓓ Ⓔ
23. Ⓐ Ⓑ Ⓒ Ⓓ Ⓔ
24. Ⓐ Ⓑ Ⓒ Ⓓ Ⓔ
25. Ⓐ Ⓑ Ⓒ Ⓓ Ⓔ

Section 2

1. Ⓐ Ⓑ Ⓒ Ⓓ Ⓔ
2. Ⓐ Ⓑ Ⓒ Ⓓ Ⓔ
3. Ⓐ Ⓑ Ⓒ Ⓓ Ⓔ
4. Ⓐ Ⓑ Ⓒ Ⓓ Ⓔ
5. Ⓐ Ⓑ Ⓒ Ⓓ Ⓔ
6. Ⓐ Ⓑ Ⓒ Ⓓ Ⓔ
7. Ⓐ Ⓑ Ⓒ Ⓓ Ⓔ

8. Ⓐ Ⓑ Ⓒ Ⓓ Ⓔ
9. Ⓐ Ⓑ Ⓒ Ⓓ Ⓔ
10. Ⓐ Ⓑ Ⓒ Ⓓ Ⓔ
11. Ⓐ Ⓑ Ⓒ Ⓓ Ⓔ
12. Ⓐ Ⓑ Ⓒ Ⓓ Ⓔ
13. Ⓐ Ⓑ Ⓒ Ⓓ Ⓔ

14. Ⓐ Ⓑ Ⓒ Ⓓ Ⓔ
15. Ⓐ Ⓑ Ⓒ Ⓓ Ⓔ
16. Ⓐ Ⓑ Ⓒ Ⓓ Ⓔ
17. Ⓐ Ⓑ Ⓒ Ⓓ Ⓔ
18. Ⓐ Ⓑ Ⓒ Ⓓ Ⓔ
19. Ⓐ Ⓑ Ⓒ Ⓓ Ⓔ

20. Ⓐ Ⓑ Ⓒ Ⓓ Ⓔ
21. Ⓐ Ⓑ Ⓒ Ⓓ Ⓔ
22. Ⓐ Ⓑ Ⓒ Ⓓ Ⓔ
23. Ⓐ Ⓑ Ⓒ Ⓓ Ⓔ
24. Ⓐ Ⓑ Ⓒ Ⓓ Ⓔ
25. Ⓐ Ⓑ Ⓒ Ⓓ Ⓔ

Section 3

1. Ⓐ Ⓑ Ⓒ Ⓓ Ⓔ
2. Ⓐ Ⓑ Ⓒ Ⓓ Ⓔ
3. Ⓐ Ⓑ Ⓒ Ⓓ Ⓔ
4. Ⓐ Ⓑ Ⓒ Ⓓ Ⓔ
5. Ⓐ Ⓑ Ⓒ Ⓓ Ⓔ
6. Ⓐ Ⓑ Ⓒ Ⓓ Ⓔ
7. Ⓐ Ⓑ Ⓒ Ⓓ Ⓔ

8. Ⓐ Ⓑ Ⓒ Ⓓ Ⓔ
9. Ⓐ Ⓑ Ⓒ Ⓓ Ⓔ
10. Ⓐ Ⓑ Ⓒ Ⓓ Ⓔ
11. Ⓐ Ⓑ Ⓒ Ⓓ Ⓔ
12. Ⓐ Ⓑ Ⓒ Ⓓ Ⓔ
13. Ⓐ Ⓑ Ⓒ Ⓓ Ⓔ

14. Ⓐ Ⓑ Ⓒ Ⓓ Ⓔ
15. Ⓐ Ⓑ Ⓒ Ⓓ Ⓔ
16. Ⓐ Ⓑ Ⓒ Ⓓ Ⓔ
17. Ⓐ Ⓑ Ⓒ Ⓓ Ⓔ
18. Ⓐ Ⓑ Ⓒ Ⓓ Ⓔ
19. Ⓐ Ⓑ Ⓒ Ⓓ Ⓔ

20. Ⓐ Ⓑ Ⓒ Ⓓ Ⓔ
21. Ⓐ Ⓑ Ⓒ Ⓓ Ⓔ
22. Ⓐ Ⓑ Ⓒ Ⓓ Ⓔ
23. Ⓐ Ⓑ Ⓒ Ⓓ Ⓔ
24. Ⓐ Ⓑ Ⓒ Ⓓ Ⓔ
25. Ⓐ Ⓑ Ⓒ Ⓓ Ⓔ

1 1 1 1 1 1 1 1 1 1 1 1 1

CRITICAL READING TEST 2

Section 1

Time—25 minutes
24 Questions

For each of the following questions, select the best answer from the choices provided and fill in the appropriate circle on the answer sheet.

Each of the following sentences contains one or two blanks; each blank indicates that a word or set of words has been left out. Below the sentence are five words or phrases, lettered A through E. Select the word or set of words that best completes the sentence.

Example:

Fame is ----; today's rising star is all too soon tomorrow's washed-up has-been.

(A) rewarding   (B) gradual
(C) essential   (D) spontaneous
(E) transitory

 Ⓐ Ⓑ Ⓒ Ⓓ ●

1. The museum administration appears to be singularly ____ the comforts of its employees, providing an employee health club, a lending library, and a part-time social worker to help staff members with financial or domestic problems.

    (A) ignorant of
    (B) indifferent to
    (C) attentive to
    (D) exploited by
    (E) uninvolved in

2. The assemblyman instructed his staff to be courteous in responding to requests from his ____, the voters belonging to the district he represented.

    (A) collaborators
    (B) interviewers
    (C) adversaries
    (D) constituents
    (E) predecessors

3. Trees native to warmer climates are genetically programmed for shorter, milder winters and are therefore ____ to both cold snaps and sudden thaws.

    (A) indifferent
    (B) restricted
    (C) vulnerable
    (D) accessible
    (E) attributed

4. Although, as wife of President John Adams, Abigail Adams sought a greater voice for women, she was not a feminist in the modern sense; she ____ the ____ view of women as "beings placed by providence" under male protection.

    (A) anticipated...current
    (B) regretted...heretical
    (C) distorted...outmoded
    (D) repudiated...radical
    (E) accepted...traditional

GO ON TO THE NEXT PAGE

Critical Reading Test 2

5. An unattractive feature of this memoir is the casually dismissive, often downright ____, comments the author makes about almost all of her former colleagues.

   (A) elegiac
   (B) euphemistic
   (C) objective
   (D) contemptuous
   (E) laudatory

6. There was some stagecraft behind the supposedly ____ moments photographed by Doisneau; in a legal dispute last year, Doisneau ____ that he had paid two models to pose for his famous *The Kiss at the Hotel de Ville*.

   (A) innocent…disproved
   (B) candid…acknowledged
   (C) theatrical…regretted
   (D) affected…intimated
   (E) spontaneous…urged

7. The protagonist of the poem "Richard Cory" appears ____ but has no real joy in his gifts and possessions; he ____ his feelings with a mask of lightheartedness.

   (A) talented…manifests
   (B) nonchalant…adapts
   (C) jovial…camouflages
   (D) affluent…suppresses
   (E) acquisitive…unburdens

8. Always less secure in herself than she liked to admit, she too often ____ disagreement as ____ and opposition as treachery.

   (A) rewarded…virtue
   (B) construed…betrayal
   (C) condemned…detachment
   (D) invited…provocation
   (E) interpreted…drollery

GO ON TO THE NEXT PAGE

Read each of the passages below, and then answer the questions that follow the passage. The correct response may be stated outright or merely suggested in the passage.

Questions 9 and 10 are based on the following passage.

Strangely enough, among the high points of the Jewish Museum's exhibition entitled *Wild Things: The Art of Maurice Sendak*, is a
Line small alcove off the main gallery. Decked out
(5) with soft pillows, a shaggy rug, and a generous assortment of Sendak books, this retreat from the museum's crowds was inspired by Max's imaginary bedroom in *Where the Wild Things Are,* perhaps Sendak's most famous
(10) children's tale. Walking through the exhibit's thematically arranged rooms, exploring the artist's Eastern European roots, his connections to Brooklyn's Jewish community, and his links to Germany, land of the Holocaust and of
(15) the brothers Grimm, I was increasingly drawn to this simple room where a weary mother could read to her sleepy child.

9.   In line 6, "retreat" most nearly means

   (A) departure
   (B) haven
   (C) evacuation
   (D) recession
   (E) recoil

10.   The author's tone in the final lines of the passage can best be characterized as

   (A) quizzical
   (B) weary
   (C) ironic
   (D) melancholy
   (E) appreciative

Questions 11 and 12 are based on the following passage.

In pre-Victorian times, despite the widespread belief that a woman's place was in the home, some strong-minded women found
Line opportunities to participate actively in scien-
(5) tific work. In *Before Victoria,* Elizabeth Denlinger points out that, at that time, the sciences were, to some extent, still in their infancy: they had not yet become official parts of the university curriculum, and therefore
(10) were open to women. Thus, Caroline Herschel, acting as assistant to her brother William, in the late eighteenth century performed basic astronomical research. The first woman to discover a comet, in later years
(15) Herschel catalogued every discovery she and her brother had made, creating research tools still in use today.

11.   In the passage, the author does all of the following EXCEPT

   (A) provide an example
   (B) cite an authority
   (C) mention a time frame
   (D) refer to a cliché
   (E) propose a solution

12.   An aspect of Herschel's work that the passage points out is the

   (A) way in which it ignores the conventional wisdom
   (B) extent to which it continues to be helpful nowadays
   (C) degree to which it depended on academic support
   (D) kinds of astronomical devices that she employed
   (E) limitations imposed on her by society

Critical Reading Test 2

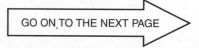
GO ON TO THE NEXT PAGE

1 1 1 1 1 1 1 1 1 1 1 1

Questions 13–24 are based on the following passage.

In this excerpt from The Joy of Music, *the composer and conductor Leonard Bernstein describes the characteristics of the ideal conductor.*

For the qualities that distinguish *great* conductors lie far beyond and above what we have spoken of. We now begin to deal with the
Line intangibles, the deep magical aspect of con-
(5) ducting. It is the mystery of relationships—conductor and orchestra bound together by the tiny but powerful split second. How can I describe to you the magic of the moment of beginning a piece of music? There is only one
(10) possible fraction of a second that feels exactly right for starting. There is a wait while the orchestra readies itself and collects its powers; while the conductor concentrates his whole will and force toward the work in hand; while
(15) the audience quiets down, and the last cough has died away. There is no slight rustle of a program book; the instruments are poised and—bang! That's it. One second later, it is too late, and the magic has vanished.
(20)   This psychological timing is constantly in play throughout the performance of music. It means that a great conductor is one who has great sensitivity to the flow of time; who makes one note move to the next in exactly the
(25) right way and at the right instant. For music, as we said, exists in the medium of time. It is time itself that must be carved up, molded and remolded until it becomes, like a statue, an existing shape and form. This is the hardest to
(30) do. For a symphony is not like a statue, which can be viewed all at once, or bit by bit at leisure, in one's own chosen time. With music, we are trapped in time. Each note is gone as soon as it has sounded, and it never can be
(35) recontemplated or heard again at the particular instant of rightness. It is always too late for a second look.

So the conductor is a kind of sculptor whose element is time instead of marble; and
(40) in sculpting it, he must have a superior sense of proportion and relationship. He must judge the largest rhythms, the whole phraseology of a work. He must conquer the form of a piece not only in the sense of form as a mold, but
(45) form in its deepest sense, knowing and controlling where the music relaxes, where it begins to accumulate tension, where the greatest tension is reached, where it must ease up to gather strength for the next lap, where it
(50) unloads that strength.
     These are the intangibles of conducting, the mysteries that no conductor can learn or acquire. If he has a natural faculty for deep perception, it will increase and deepen as he
(55) matures. If he hasn't, he will always be a pretty good conductor. But even the pretty good conductor must have one more attribute in his personality, without which all the mechanics and knowledge and perception are
(60) useless; and that is the power to *communicate* all this to his orchestra—through his arms, face, eyes, fingers, and whatever vibrations may flow from him. If he uses a baton, the baton itself must be a living thing, charged
(65) with a kind of electricity, which makes it an instrument of meaning in its tiniest movement. If he does not use a baton, his hands must do the job with equal clarity. But baton or no baton, his gestures must be first and always
(70) meaningful in terms of the music.
     The chief element in the conductor's technique of communication is the preparation. Everything must be shown to the orchestra *before* it happens. Once the player is playing
(75) the note, it is too late. So the conductor always has to be a beat or two ahead of the orchestra . . . . And he must hear two things at the same time: what the players are doing at any moment, and what they are about to do a

GO ON TO THE NEXT PAGE ⇨

1   1 1 1 1 1 1 1 1 1 1   1

(80) moment later. Therefore, the basic trick is in the preparatory upbeat. If our conductor is back again on page one of Brahms's *First Symphony*, he must show, in his silent upbeat, the character of the music which is about to
(85) sound. Whether he thinks of it as tense and agitated, or weighty and doom-ridden, his upbeat should show this, in order to enable the orchestra players to respond in kind. It is exactly like breathing: the preparation is like
(90) an inhalation, and the music sounds as an exhalation. We all have to inhale in order to speak, for example; all verbal expression is exhaled. So it is with music: we inhale on the upbeat and sing out a phrase of music, then
(95) inhale again and breathe out the next phrase. A conductor who breathes with the music has gone far in acquiring a technique.

But the conductor must not only make his orchestra play; he must make them want to
(100) play. He must exalt them, lift them, start their adrenaline pouring, either through cajoling or demanding or raging. But however he does it, he must make the orchestra love the music as he loves it. It is not so much imposing his will
(105) on them like a dictator; it is more like projecting his feelings around him so that they reach the last player in the second violin section. And when this happens—when one hundred players share his feelings, exactly, simultane-
(110) ously, responding as one to each rise and fall of the music, to each point of arrival and departure, to each little inner pulse—then there is a human identity of feeling that has no equal elsewhere. It is the closest thing I know
(115) to love itself. On this current of love the conductor can communicate at the deepest levels with his players, and ultimately with his audience. He may shout and rant and curse and insult his players at rehearsal—as some of our
(120) greatest conductors are famous for doing—but if there is this love, the conductor and his

orchestra will remain knit together through it all and function as one.

Well, there is our ideal conductor. And
(125) perhaps the chief requirement of all this is that he be humble before the composer; that he never interpose himself between the music and the audience; that all his efforts, however strenuous or glamorous, be made in the ser-
(130) vice of the composer's meaning—the music itself, which, after all, is the whole reason for the conductor's existence.

13. In the first paragraph, in creating an initial impression of the qualities of the ideal conductor for the reader, the author makes use of

   (A) reference to musical notation
   (B) contrast to the musicians
   (C) comparison with other leaders of ensembles
   (D) narration of a sequence of events
   (E) allusion to psychological studies

14. The passage is most likely to have been preceded by a discussion of

   (A) the deficiencies of conductors whom the author has known
   (B) how the conductor relates to the composer
   (C) ways in which the orchestra complements the conductor
   (D) the technical skills needed to be a reasonably competent conductor
   (E) the qualities that transform a conductor into a superior musician

GO ON TO THE NEXT PAGE →

15. The conductor's decision as to the moment when to begin a piece of music can best be described as

(A) tentative
(B) imperceptible
(C) intuitive
(D) trivial
(E) hypothetical

16. In stating that "with music, we are trapped in time" (lines 32 and 33), the author is being

(A) resigned
(B) wistful
(C) ironic
(D) figurative
(E) resentful

17. The author mentions sculpting chiefly in order to

(A) place conducting in perspective as one of the fine arts
(B) contrast it informally with conducting
(C) help the reader get an image of the conductor's work
(D) illustrate the difficulties of the sculptor's task
(E) show how the study of sculpture can benefit the conductor

18. In line 44, "mold" most nearly means

(A) decaying surface
(B) fixed pattern
(C) decorative strip
(D) organic growth
(E) cooking utensil

19. Lines 51–55 indicate that the author believes that the ideal conductor's most important attributes are

(A) innate
(B) transient
(C) technical
(D) symbolic
(E) unclear

20. The author regards the conductor's baton primarily as

(A) a necessary evil
(B) a symbol of strength
(C) an electrical implement
(D) an improvement over hand gestures
(E) a tool for transmitting meaning

21. In dealing with musicians, the author believes conductors

(A) must do whatever it takes to motivate them to perform
(B) should never resort to pleading with their subordinates
(C) must maintain their composure under trying circumstances
(D) work best if they love the musicians with whom they work
(E) must assert dominance over the musicians autocratically

22. In lines 105–107, the author mentions "the last player in the second violin section" primarily to emphasize

(A) the number of musicians necessary in an orchestra
(B) the particular importance of violins in ensemble work
(C) how sensitive secondary musicians can be
(D) how the role of the conductor differs from that of the musician
(E) the distance across which the conductor must communicate

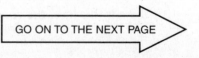

GO ON TO THE NEXT PAGE

23. The author regards temperamental behavior during rehearsals on the part of conductors with

    (A) disapprobation
    (B) tolerance
    (C) bemusement
    (D) regret
    (E) awe

24. To the author, the conductor's primary concern is to maintain

    (A) rapport with the audience
    (B) authority over the orchestra
    (C) the respect of the musicians
    (D) the tempo of the music
    (E) the integrity of the musical piece

STOP

Critical Reading Test 2

2 2 2 2 2 2 2 2 2 2 2 2

Section 2

TIME—25 MINUTES
24 QUESTIONS

For each of the following questions, select the best answer from the choices provided and fill in the appropriate circle on the answer sheet.

Each of the following sentences contains one or two blanks; each blank indicates that a word or set of words has been left out. Below the sentence are five words or phrases, lettered A through E. Select the word or set of words that best completes the sentence.

Example:

Fame is ----; today's rising star is all too soon tomorrow's washed-up has-been.

(A) rewarding   (B) gradual
(C) essential   (D) spontaneous
(E) transitory

Ⓐ Ⓑ Ⓒ Ⓓ ●

1. Just as all roads once led to Rome, all blood vessels in the human body ultimately _____ the heart.

   (A) detour around
   (B) shut off
   (C) empty into
   (D) look after
   (E) beat back

2. One of photography's most basic and powerful traits is its ability to give substance to _____, to present precise visual details of a time gone by.

   (A) romance
   (B) premonition
   (C) mysticism
   (D) invisibility
   (E) history

3. Michael purchased a season subscription to the symphony in order to gratify his _____ classical music.

   (A) predilection for
   (B) subservience to
   (C) impatience with
   (D) divergence from
   (E) reservations about

4. The president was _____ about farm subsidies, nor did he say much about the even more _____ topic of unemployment.

   (A) expansive...interesting
   (B) wordy...important
   (C) uncommunicative...academic
   (D) noncommittal...vital
   (E) enthusiastic...stimulating

5. As more people try to navigate the legal system by themselves, representing themselves in court and drawing up their own wills and contracts, the question arises whether they will be able to _____ judicial _____ without lawyers to guide them.

   (A) await...decisions
   (B) overturn...stipulations
   (C) avoid...quagmires
   (D) forfeit...penalties
   (E) arouse...enmity

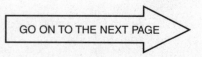
GO ON TO THE NEXT PAGE

Read the passages below, and then answer the questions that follow. The correct response may be stated outright or merely suggested in the passages.

Questions 6–9 are based on the following passages.

Passage 1

With cries of delight and occasional tears, ornithologists around the world celebrated the sighting in Arkansas of the ivory-billed wood-
Line pecker. Long thought to be extinct, the ivory-
(5) bill was first sighted in February of 2004 by a kayaker in Big Woods country. Later visual encounters seemed to corroborate the original sighting, but doubt remained until one sighting was captured on video. Despite the blurred,
(10) grainy quality of the footage, the team of Cornell researchers identified the woodpecker by its size, markings, and characteristic plumage. To bird-lovers, the rediscovery of the ivory-bill seems miraculous, "almost like
(15) finding Elvis," and they are grateful for a sec-ond chance to protect this unique bird and the Big Woods in which it lives.

Passage 2

Although the public appears to be taking the ivory-billed woodpecker's rediscovery as
(20) fact, much skepticism still exists among bird-watchers unconvinced by the Cornell Ornithology Laboratory's video and audio recordings that the ivory-bill lives. Even the Cornell scientists have begun to hedge.
(25) According to Cornell's Russell Charif, "Our interpretation of these data is that they provide suggestive and tantalizing, but not conclusive, new evidence of living ivory-bills in this region." Unfortunately, the ivory-billed wood-
(30) pecker controversy is not just a philosophical debate—it has real-world implications as well. The Department of the Interior has earmarked $10 million to preserve the ivory-bill's habitat; that means $10 million less available to pro-
(35) tect other species, such as the Kirtland's warbler.

6. Which best expresses the relationship between Passage 1 and Passage 2?

(A) Passage 2 urges the continuation of the policies endorsed in Passage 1.
(B) Passage 2 presents a hypothesis in support of the conclusions drawn in Passage 1.
(C) Passage 2 provides a scientific explanation for the advances described in Passage 1.
(D) Passage 2 questions the validity of the celebration mentioned in Passage 1.
(E) Passage 2 mocks those who support the viewpoint presented in Passage 1.

7. Passage 2 as a whole suggests that its author would most likely react to the final sentence of Passage 1 with

(A) resentment
(B) enthusiasm
(C) suspicion
(D) compassion
(E) trepidation

GO ON TO THE NEXT PAGE

2 2 2 2 2 2 2 2 2 2 2

8. According to lines 23 and 24 of Passage 2 ("Even…hedge"), the Cornell scientists

    (A) are now being intentionally noncommittal
    (B) believe strongly in the validity of their case
    (C) seek to engage their opponents in debate
    (D) are employing questionable methods
    (E) expect to profit from an uncertain situation

9. In both passages, the discussion of the ivory-billed woodpecker controversy focuses on the challenges of

    (A) preserving the habitats of endangered species
    (B) allocating funds for wildlife management
    (C) distinguishing among closely related species of birds
    (D) convincing the Department of the Interior to take a stand
    (E) proving a supposedly extinct species to be extant

Questions 10–15 are based on the following passage.

Largely unexplored, the canopy or treetop region of the tropical rain forest is one of the most diverse plant and animal communities on Earth. In this excerpt from a 1984 article on the rain forest canopy, the naturalist Donald R. Perry shares his research team's observations of epiphytes, unusual plants that flourish in this treetop environment.

The upper story of the rain forest, which we investigated, incorporates two-thirds of its volume. This region can be divided arbitrarily
Line into a lower canopy, extending from 10 to 25
(5) meters above the ground, an upper canopy, reaching a height of 35 meters, and an emergent zone that encompasses the tops of the tallest trees, which commonly grow to heights of more than 50 meters. The canopy is well
(10) lighted, in contrast to the forest understory, which because of thick vegetation above receives only about 1 percent of the sunlight that falls on the treetops. In the canopy all but the smallest of the rain forest trees put forth
(15) their leaves, flowers and fruit. It also contains many plants that exist entirely within its compass, forming vegetative communities that in number of species and complexity of interactions surpass any others on the earth.
(20) Among the most conspicuous features of vegetation in the canopy of the tropical rain forest are epiphytes. About 28,000 species in 65 families are known worldwide, 15,500 of them in Central and South America; they
(25) include species of orchids, bromeliads, and arboreal cacti as well as lower plants such as lichens, mosses, and ferns. Thousands more epiphyte varieties remain unidentified.

The Greek meaning of the word epiphyte
(30) is "plant that grows on a plant," and they carpet tree trunks and branches. Epiphytes sprout from seeds borne by the wind or deposited by animals, their roots holding tight to the interstices of the bark. Yet they are nonparasitic;
(35) their hosts provide them with nothing more than a favorable position in the brightly lighted canopy. For nourishment epiphytes depend on soil particles and dissolved minerals carried in rainwater, and on aerial deposits of humus. The
(40) deposits are the product of organic debris, such as dead leaves from epiphytes and other plants, that lodges among epiphyte roots.

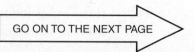

GO ON TO THE NEXT PAGE

Water is directly available to epiphytes only when it rains; other plants have continuous (45) access to moisture trapped in the soil. As a result many epiphytes have developed features that collect and retain rainwater. Some, including orchids and arboreal cacti, have succulent stems and leaves, with spongy tissues that store (50) water, as well as waxy leaf coatings that reduce the loss of moisture through transpiration.[1] Many orchids have bulbous stem bases; other families of epiphytes impound water in tanks formed by tight rosettes of leaves or in cups (55) shaped by the junctions of broadened petioles[2] and stems. Some species possess absorbent, spongelike root masses that soak up and hold water. Bromeliads, a Central and South American family, can hold reserves of several (60) gallons within their cisternlike bases, forming "arboreal swamps" that attract insects of many species, earthworms, spiders, sow bugs, scorpions, tree frogs, and insect-eating birds.

---

[1] Passage of water through a plant to the atmosphere.

[2] Slender stalks that attach a leaf to the stem.

10. In lines 9–13, the author characterizes the floor or understory of the rain forest as relatively

    (A) insignificant
    (B) windy
    (C) thick
    (D) obscure
    (E) voluminous

11. In lines 16 and 17, "compass" most nearly means

    (A) a curved arc
    (B) an instrument for determining direction
    (C) passageway
    (D) boundaries
    (E) specifications

12. It can be inferred that which of the following is true of epiphytes?

    (A) They lack an adequate root system.
    (B) They cannot draw moisture from tree trunks.
    (C) They are incapable of transpiration.
    (D) They are hard to perceive in the dense rain forest canopy.
    (E) They originated in the Southern Hemisphere.

13. According to lines 46–48, epiphytes are particularly adapted to

    (A) independent growth
    (B) a cloudless environment
    (C) the dissipation of rainwater
    (D) drawing sustenance from a host
    (E) the retention of liquid

14. Epiphytes have direct access to water only when it rains because

    (A) they lack the ability to collect moisture
    (B) the frequency of rain keeps them excessively wet
    (C) the thick canopy protects them from rainstorms
    (D) they lack connections to water in the ground
    (E) dead leaves and other organic debris cover their roots

15. Desert cacti are likely to resemble arboreal cacti most in their

    (A) tolerance of extremes of heat and cold
    (B) dependence on tree trunks for support rather than nourishment
    (C) development of features to cut down the loss of moisture
    (D) lack of roots connecting them to the ground
    (E) absence of variations in size

Critical Reading Test 2

GO ON TO THE NEXT PAGE

2 2 2 2 2 2 2 2 2 2 2 2

Critical Reading Test 2

Questions 16–24 are based on the following passage.

In this excerpt from the novel A Tale of Two Cities, *Charles Dickens describes the journey of a coach carrying mail and passengers to the seaport town of Dover.*

It was the Dover road that lay, on a Friday night late in November, before the first of the persons with whom this history has business.
Line The Dover road lay, as to him, beyond the
(5) Dover mail, as it lumbered up Shooter's Hill. He walked uphill in the mire by the side of the mail, as the rest of the passengers did; not because they had the least relish for walking exercise, under the circumstances, but because
(10) the hill, and the harness, and the mud, and the mail, were all so heavy, that the horses had three times already come to a stop, besides once drawing the coach across the road, with the mutinous intent of taking it back to
(15) Blackheath.

With drooping heads and tremulous tails, the horses mashed their way through the thick mud, floundering and stumbling between whiles as if they were falling to pieces at the
(20) larger joints. As often as the driver rested them and brought them to a stand, with a wary "Wo-ho! so-ho then!" the near leader violently shook his head and everything upon it—like an unusually emphatic horse, denying that the
(25) coach could be got up the hill. Whenever the leader made this rattle, the passenger started, as a nervous passenger might, and was disturbed in mind.

There was a steaming mist in all the hol-
(30) lows, and it had roamed in its forlornness up the hill, like an evil spirit, seeking rest and finding none. A clammy and intensely cold mist, it made its slow way through the air in ripples that visibly followed and overspread
(35) one another, as the waves of an unwholesome sea might do. It was dense enough to shut out

everything from the light of the coachlamps but these its own workings, and a few yards of road; and the reek of the laboring horses
(40) steamed into it, as if they had made it all.

Two other passengers, besides the one, were plodding up the hill by the side of the mail. All three were wrapped to the cheekbones and over the ears, and wore jack-boots.
(45) Not one of the three could have said, from anything he saw, what either of the other two was like; and each was hidden under almost as many wrappers from the eyes of the mind, as from the eyes of the body, of his two compan-
(50) ions. In those days, travelers were very shy of being confidential on a short notice, for anyone on the road might be a robber or in league with robbers. As to the latter, when every posting-house and ale-house could produce some-
(55) body in "the Captain's" pay, ranging from the landlord to the lowest stable nondescript, it was the likeliest thing upon the cards. So the guard of the Dover mail thought to himself, that Friday night in November, one thousand
(60) seven hundred and seventy-five, lumbering up Shooter's Hill, as he stood on his own particular perch behind the mail, beating his feet, and keeping an eye and a hand on the arm-chest before him, where a loaded blunderbuss lay at
(65) the top of six or eight loaded horse-pistols, deposited on a substratum of cutlass.

The Dover mail was in its usual genial position that the guard suspected the passengers, the passengers suspected one another and
(70) the guard, they all suspected everybody else, and the coachman was sure of nothing but the horses; as to which cattle he could with a clear conscience have taken his oath on the two Testaments that they were not fit for the journey.

GO ON TO THE NEXT PAGE

2 2 2 2 2 2 2 2 2 2 2

16. It can be inferred that the passengers are walking because

    (A) they need fresh air and exercise
    (B) they are afraid of being robbed
    (C) their trip is over
    (D) the guard is suspicious of them
    (E) the coach cannot carry them uphill

17. In creating an impression of the mail coach's uphill progress for the reader, the author uses all of the following devices EXCEPT

    (A) description of its surroundings
    (B) humorous turns of phrase
    (C) contrast with more attractive areas
    (D) exaggerated comparisons
    (E) references to geographic locations

18. The purpose cited as supporting the argument that some brute animals are endowed with reason most likely is

    (A) the driver's intent to use the whip to motivate the horses
    (B) the passengers' willingness to walk by the side of the coach
    (C) the horses' determination to turn back to Blackheath
    (D) the traveler's resolve to undertake such a rugged journey
    (E) the guard's aim to quell any manifestations of mutiny

19. The passage suggests that the rattle referred to in line 26 most likely was

    (A) the call of the driver to the horses to halt
    (B) the clatter of the wooden wheels upon the cobblestones
    (C) the jangle of the harness when the horse shook his head
    (D) the creaking of the wagon's joints under the strain
    (E) the sound of the coachman using his whip

20. In line 26, "started" most nearly means

    (A) began
    (B) jumped
    (C) set out
    (D) went first
    (E) activated

21. In lines 31–36, the author includes the description of the mist primarily to emphasize the

    (A) nearness of the sea
    (B) weariness of the travelers
    (C) gloominess of the surroundings
    (D) transience of the journey
    (E) lateness of the hour

22. In line 55, "the Captain" most likely refers to

    (A) the master of a sailing ship
    (B) a police officer
    (C) a highwayman
    (D) an innkeeper or hotel employee
    (E) a town official

23. The attitude of the passengers toward one another shown in lines 67–70 can best be described as

    (A) conspiratorial
    (B) guarded
    (C) benevolent
    (D) resentful
    (E) pugnacious

24. The use of the word "genial" in line 67 is an example of

    (A) understatement
    (B) archaism
    (C) simile
    (D) digression
    (E) irony

STOP

3 3 3 3 3 3 3 3 3 3 3

Section 3

For each of the following questions, select the best answer from the choices provided and fill in the appropriate circle on the answer sheet.

Each of the following sentences contains one or two blanks; each blank indicates that a word or set of words has been left out. Below the sentence are five words or phrases, lettered A through E. Select the word or set of words that best completes the sentence.

Example:

Fame is ----; today's rising star is all too soon tomorrow's washed-up has-been.

(A) rewarding   (B) gradual
(C) essential   (D) spontaneous
(E) transitory

---

1. Supporters of the proposed waterway argue that it will _____ rather than _____ railroad facilities, since the waterway will be icebound during the only months when the railroads can absorb much traffic.

    (A) limit…extend
    (B) build…destroy
    (C) weaken…help
    (D) surpass…equal
    (E) supplement…threaten

2. Although he was widely celebrated as a radio and motion picture star in the 1940s, George Burns enjoyed his greatest _____ after his return to the screen in the "Oh God" films of the 1980s.

    (A) respite
    (B) collaboration
    (C) renown
    (D) disappointment
    (E) inducement

3. Despite some personal habits that most people would find repulsive, naked mole rats are _____ housekeepers.

    (A) slovenly
    (B) indifferent
    (C) meticulous
    (D) perfunctory
    (E) repugnant

4. Biography is a literary genre whose primary _____ is an ability to _____ imaginatively the inner life of a subject on the basis of all the knowable external evidence.

    (A) requisite…reconstruct
    (B) consequence…disregard
    (C) peculiarity…envision
    (D) weapon…undermine
    (E) claim…counteract

5. Many scientific discoveries are a matter of _____ : Newton was not sitting on the ground thinking about gravity when the apple dropped on his head.

    (A) serendipity
    (B) experimentation
    (C) casuistry
    (D) technology
    (E) principle

6. In prison Malcolm X set himself the task of reading straight through the dictionary; to him, reading was purposeful, not _____.

    (A) deliberate
    (B) retentive
    (C) critical
    (D) desultory
    (E) exhaustive

GO ON TO THE NEXT PAGE

Critical Reading Test 2

3 **3** **3** **3** **3** **3** **3** **3** **3** **3** **3** **3**

Read the passages below, and then answer the questions that follow. The correct response may be stated outright or merely suggested in the passages.

Questions 7–19 are based on the following passages.

The following passages, written in the 1960s, explore the roots of anti-Japanese and anti-Jewish feelings in America during the first half of the twentieth century.

Passage 1

Prejudice, the sociologists tell us, is learned behavior. Twentieth-century Californians learned the lesson well. Although
Line racial prejudice, directed at various ethnic
(5) groups, flourished throughout the United States during the period under discussion, nowhere north of the Mason-Dixon line did any single group encounter the sustained nativist assault that was directed against
(10) California's Japanese. There seem to be four chief reasons for this. First, the Japanese were of a distinct racial group; no amount of acculturation could mask their foreignness. Second, unlike the Chinese, they rapidly began to chal-
(15) lenge whites in many businesses and professions—as a group, Japanese in the United States became very quickly imbued with what, in Europeans, would be called the Protestant ethic. Third, the growing unpopularity of their
(20) homeland . . . further served to make immigrants from Japan special objects of suspicion. These three conditions would have made any large group of Japanese a particularly despised minority anywhere in the United States.
(25) Finally, the fact that most of the Japanese were in California probably made things worse, for California probably had a lower boiling point than did the country at large.

California, by virtue of its anti-Chinese
(30) tradition and frontier psychology, was already conditioned to anti-Orientalism before the Japanese arrived. Other special California characteristics abetted the success of the agitation. In the prewar years, the extraordinary
(35) power of organized labor in northern California gave the anti-Japanese movement a much stronger base than it would have enjoyed elsewhere; in the postwar years, open-shop southern California proved almost
(40) equally hospitable to an agitation pitched to middle-class white Protestants. In the two periods anti-Japanese sentiment flourished among completely disparate populations: the first- and second-generation immigrants who
(45) were the backbone of California's labor movement, and the Midwestern émigrés who came to dominate the southern California scene. For most of these Californians, opposition to the Japanese was based upon fears which were
(50) largely nonrational.

Passage 2

To say that anti-Semitism in America sprang chiefly from the difficulties of integrating large numbers of first- and second-generation immigrants is, inferentially, to stress its
(55) similarity to other kinds of anti-immigrant sentiment—to put it in the same class with dislike of the Irish, Italians, Japanese, Mexicans and other transplanted minorities, while making allowances for the differential
(60) characteristics of each group. Likewise, this approach minimizes distinctions often made between different kinds of anti-Semitism, in that it relates all of them to a common root. Yet we must also consider the role of irrational
(65) anti-Semitic fantasies that had no direct connection with real problems of ethnic integration. The ideological hatreds spread by the agitator and the fanatic have had a place in American history, too.

GO ON TO THE NEXT PAGE

(70)   Unlike . . . more ordinary social prejudices
. . . , ideological anti-Semitism condemns the
Jews as incapable of assimilation and disloyal
to the basic institutions of the country. In its
more extreme forms, it portrays them as
(75) leagued together in a vast international con-
spiracy. The alleged plot usually centers on
gaining control of the money supply and
wrecking the financial system; sometimes it
extends to polluting the nation's morals
(80) through control of communications and entertainment. The supposed eventual aim is to
overthrow the government and establish a
superstate. In America, anti-Semitism of this
kind has not been so well organized or so pro-
(85) ductive of violence as other racial and religious phobias. But it has enjoyed an unusually
rich and complex imagery.
        Religious motifs, by and large, have not
figured prominently in American anti-Semitic
(90) thought. Except among certain preachers
spawned by the Fundamentalist movement of
the 1920s (notably Gerald Winrod and Gerald
L. K. Smith), one looks in vain for a clearly
religious animus. Though not entirely lacking
(95) in references to the treachery of Judas, ideological anti-Semitism has always dwelled
mainly on the power of Shylock. Whether the
Jew appears in his traditional role as exploiter
or in his later incarnation as Bolshevik, his
(100) subversive influence supposedly flows from
an unwillingness or inability to abide by the
existing economic morality.

7. The author of Passage 1 makes the point
    that prejudice against the Japanese in the
    twentieth century

    (A) began in California
    (B) was comparable to racial prejudice in
        the South
    (C) was taught in the schools of
        California
    (D) often bred violence
    (E) was a shameful chapter in the history
        of California

8. Passage 1 implies that the Japanese would
    not have faced such intense prejudice if

    (A) their physical appearance had been
        different
    (B) they had arrived in California via
        New York
    (C) they had emigrated to California a
        century earlier
    (D) they had settled in southern
        California
    (E) Californians had themselves been
        recent immigrants

9. Passage 1 suggests that, after Japanese
    immigrants arrived in California, they

    (A) joined unions
    (B) often went on welfare until they got
        jobs
    (C) created Japanese ghettos in several
        cities
    (D) worked hard to be successful
    (E) contributed technical skills to the
        state's work force.

10. According to information in Passage 1,
    World War II

    (A) provided California's Japanese
        population temporary relief from
        prejudice
    (B) caused prejudice against the Japanese
        to intensify
    (C) had little impact on prejudice against
        the Japanese
    (D) diverted the hatred from Japanese
        civilians to the Japanese military
    (E) shifted the center of anti-Japanese
        feeling in California

GO ON TO THE NEXT PAGE

11. One can infer from Passage 1 that hostility toward the Japanese flourished in California because

(A) California was closer to Pearl Harbor than any other state
(B) Californians are more intolerant than other Americans
(C) Japan-bashing was an official policy of the labor unions in the state
(D) Japanese were quickly buying up buildings, land, and other property throughout the state
(E) American workers felt threatened by Japanese workers

12. The author of Passage 2 believes that anti-Semitism in America differs from other forms of prejudice because

(A) it is based on a long tradition
(B) anti-Semites tend to be more hateful than other types of bigots
(C) most anti-Semites are fanatics
(D) it comes in many forms and guises
(E) each ethnic minority experiences prejudice in a different way

13. The term "ideological hatreds" (line 67–69) refers to prejudice

(A) only against Jews
(B) that is openly declared in public
(C) that existed in an earlier era
(D) that is inspired by the victims' beliefs and values
(E) that has gone out of control

14. The author of Passage 2 implies that violence against Jews in the United States has been

(A) fed by social anti-Semitism rather than ideological anti-Semitism
(B) has been directed mostly at first-generation Jewish immigrants
(C) has helped other minorities to cope with violence against them
(D) has been more verbal and psychological than physical
(E) has been less severe than violence against other minorities

15. Passage 2 indicates that avid anti-Semites fear Jews for all of the following reasons EXCEPT that

(A) it is hard to tell a Jew from a non-Jew
(B) Jews crave power
(C) Jews are immoral
(D) the media are controlled by Jews
(E) Jews do not value democracy

16. Gerald Winrod and Gerald L. K. Smith (lines 92 and 93) are cited as anti-Semites

(A) who advocated the violent treatment of Jews
(B) whose hatred of Jews was based largely on religion
(C) who sought to convert Jews to Christianity
(D) who alleged that Jews were a danger to the United States
(E) who founded the Christian Fundamentalist movement in the United States

GO ON TO THE NEXT PAGE

3   3   3   3   3   3   3   3   3   3   3

17. Based on the two passages, it is fair to say that prejudice against the Jews in the United States compared to prejudice against the Japanese

    (A) has been more violent
    (B) has been more strenuously opposed by fair-minded people
    (C) is more complex and diffuse
    (D) has a longer history
    (E) has increased at a greater rate since World War II

18. The authors of both passages appear to agree that

    (A) prejudice in the United States is gradually diminishing
    (B) prejudice in the United States is gradually increasing
    (C) prejudice is based on irrational thinking
    (D) physical appearance is a major cause of prejudice against both Jews and Japanese
    (E) stereotypes are hard to break

19. In their explanations of the causes of prejudice, both authors

    (A) stress economic reasons
    (B) focus on the historical roots of prejudice in America
    (C) are hopeful that justice will eventually prevail
    (D) agree that the Japanese and the Jews have been scapegoats
    (E) think that extreme nationalism may lie at the heart of bigotry

Critical Reading Test 2

STOP

If you finish before time is called, you may check your work on this section only. Do not work on any other section in the test.

Answer Key

Section 1

1. C	5. D	9. B	13. D	17. C	21. A
2. D	6. B	10. E	14. D	18. B	22. E
3. C	7. C	11. E	15. C	19. A	23. B
4. E	8. B	12. B	16. D	20. E	24. E

Section 2

1. C	5. C	9. E	13. E	17. C	21. C
2. E	6. D	10. D	14. D	18. C	22. C
3. A	7. C	11. D	15. C	19. C	23. B
4. D	8. A	12. B	16. E	20. B	24. E

Section 3

1. E	5. A	9. D	13. D	17. C
2. C	6. D	10. E	14. A	18. C
3. C	7. B	11. E	15. A	19. A
4. A	8. A	12. D	16. B	

Analysis of Test Results

I. Check your answers against the answer key.

II. Fill in the following chart.

Sentence Completion Number Correct	Section 1 (Questions 1–8) _____		Section 2 (Questions 1–5) _____	Section 3 (Questions 1–6) _____		Total _____
Passage-Based Reading Number Correct	Section 1 (Questions 9–24) _____		Section 2 (Questions 6–24) _____	Section 3 (Questions 7–19) _____		Total _____

III. Interpret your results.

Sentence Completion   Number Correct _____

Passage-Based Reading   Number Correct _____

Subtotal _____

Guessing Penalty: Subtract 1/4 point for each incorrect answer. _____
(Do not take off points for questions you left blank.)

TOTAL SCORE _____

	Sentence Completion Score	Passage-Based Reading Score	Total
Excellent	18–19 Correct	43–48 Correct	60–67
Very Good	14–17 Correct	33–42 Correct	46–59
Good	11–13 Correct	25–32 Correct	35–45
Fair	9–10 Correct	20–24 Correct	28–34
Poor	6–8 Correct	12–19 Correct	17–27
Very Poor	0–5 Correct	0–11 Correct	0–16

Critical Reading Test 2

Answer Explanations

Section 1

1. **(C)** Given the examples listed, the administration seems unusually considerate of or *attentive to* the well-being of its employees.

2. **(D)** By definition, an assemblyman's *constituents* are the voters who belong to the district he represents.

3. **(C)** If trees have adapted to survive short, mild winters, then they're not likely to do well in harsh winters with extreme temperature changes. In fact, they will prove *vulnerable to* (defenseless against) cold snaps and sudden thaws.

4. **(E)** Unlike a contemporary feminist, Abigail Adams *accepted* the then-*traditional* view of the roles of women and men.

   The second clause of the sentence serves to explain in what way Abigail Adams was unlike feminists today.

5. **(D)** The author is making highly negative comments, ones that go beyond being casually dismissive (indifferent or disapproving) to being bluntly *contemptuous* (scornful).

6. **(B)** Though people assumed Doisneau's pictures were unposed, he *acknowledged* (admitted) he had staged some shots that were supposed to have been *candid* (informal, unposed).

7. **(C)** The *jovial*-appearing Cory used a mask of lightheartedness to *camouflage* or disguise his underlying depression.

8. **(B)** Someone insecure would be likely to *construe* (interpret) disagreement as *betrayal* (disloyalty).

9. **(B)** The retreat to which the author finds herself drawn is a *haven* or refuge.

10. **(E)** The author values the quiet, comfortable retreat. Her tone is *appreciative*.

11. **(E)** Consider the choices in turn. The author provides the example of Herschel; eliminate (A). She cites Denlinger as an authority; eliminate (B). She mentions a time frame, pre-Victorian times, and the late eighteenth century; eliminate (C). She refers to that tired old cliché about a woman's place being in the home; eliminate (D). She does not, however, *propose a solution*. The correct choice is (E).

12. **(B)** In the final sentence of the passage, the author points out that Herschel's astronomical catalogues are still in use, an indication of the *extent to which* her work *continues to be helpful nowadays*.

13. **(D)** The author tells or *narrates* what happens during the period of time just before the conductor gives the upbeat to signal the orchestra to begin.

14. **(D)** The opening of the first paragraph states that "the qualities that distinguish *great* conductors," the qualities about which the author is going to speak, "lie far beyond and above what we have spoken of." Clearly, he has just been speaking of other qualities that conductors must possess. However, these are not the high, artistic skills that one needs to be a great conductor. They are merely *the technical skills needed to be a reasonably competent conductor*.

15. **(C)** The magic moment for beginning a piece of music is the moment that "feels exactly right" (lines 10 and 11). The conductor's decision is based on instinct, on feelings, not on logic; it is *intuitive*.

16. (**D**) The author does not mean we are literally trapped or captive; he is being *figurative* or metaphorical.

17. (**C**) Throughout the passage, the author uses different approaches to give the reader an idea of the nature of just what a conductor does. Here, he compares a conductor's working with time to a sculptor's working with physical blocks of stone. He does this to *help the reader get an image of the conductor's work.*

18. (**B**) "Mold" here is a *fixed pattern* or shape.

19. (**A**) The author states that "no conductor can learn or acquire" the mysteries or most important attributes of conducting. The "natural faculty for deep perception" is inborn or *innate.*

20. (**E**) The author looks on the baton as a tool he uses to help him communicate with the orchestra, in other words, as *a tool for transmitting meaning.*

    (A) is incorrect. The author does not consider the baton either necessary (he can gesture equally clearly with his hands) or evil.

    (B) is incorrect. The author is not talking about the baton as a symbol; he is talking about it as an instrument that gets used.

    (C) is incorrect. In talking of the baton's being "charged with a kind of electricity," the author is being figurative, not literal. He does not literally look on the baton as an electrical appliance or tool.

    (D) is incorrect. The author never states a preference for one means of communication over the other.

21. (**A**) The author suggests a variety of things the conductor can do to get a performance out of the musicians—cajoling (coaxing), demanding, raging. Clearly he believes conductors *must do whatever it takes to motivate* the musicians to want to perform.

22. (**E**) The author is talking about projecting his feelings, conveying his emotions so vividly and intensely that they reach each and every one of his hundred musicians, no matter where in the orchestra they are. Thus, in singling out the "last" player, the one farthest back, in the "second" violin section, the section behind the first violins, he is emphasizing *the distance across which the conductor must communicate.*

23. (**B**) The author's concern is for the orchestra to learn to function as a whole. He views the temperamental behavior of conductors—ranting, cursing, insulting musicians—with *tolerance,* accepting these actions as either unimportant personal quirks on the part of the conductor or tactical moves in the conductor's grand design to stimulate the musicians to play at their best.

24. (**E**) In dedicating himself to "the service of the composer's meaning" (lines 129–132), the conductor is laboring to maintain *the integrity of the musical piece* in accordance with the composer's design.

Section 2

1. (**C**) To complete the comparison, in the same way that the roads all led to the city of Rome, the heart of the Roman Empire, the blood vessels all lead to or *empty into* the heart.

2. (**E**) To give the visual details of past events is to make *history* real to people.

3. (**A**) A *predilection* or fondness *for* classical music could well lead someone to subscribe to the symphony for a season.

4. **(D)** The president did not say much about farm subsidies: he was *noncommittal*, taking no clear position on this important issue. He also did not say much about the more important or *vital* issue of unemployment.

   (C) is incorrect. While it would be possible in this context to describe the president as *uncommunicative* about farm subsidies, it would be inaccurate to describe the critical issue of unemployment as merely *academic* (theoretical; of no practical significance).

5. **(C)** In navigating tricky legal waters, one hopes to be able to *avoid* judicial *quagmires* (marshes; swamps) in which one might bog down.

6. **(D)** Passage 2 reports the skepticism felt by many bird-watchers about the ivory-bill's alleged rediscovery and points out the tentativeness of the researchers' claims. In doing so, it *questions the validity of the* ornithologists' initial *celebration*.

7. **(C)** The final sentence of Passage 1 speaks of the rediscovery of the ivory-bill as miraculous. The author of Passage 2 looks on such miracles with *suspicion*. Lacking strong evidence that would make him a believer, he remains unconvinced.

8. **(A)** To hedge is to avoid making a clear, direct response or statement. Thus, in beginning to hedge, the Cornell scientists *are now being intentionally noncommittal.*

9. **(E)** Passage 1 describes the many sightings and the corroborative video recording evidence that had to be completed before the research team was ready to present its case. Passage 2 discusses the challenge of finding conclusive evidence of living ivory-bills in the Big Woods region. Both passages emphasize that *proving a supposedly extinct species to be extant* has presented challenges to the researchers involved.

10. **(D)** The shadowy, gloomy understory is dimly lit or *obscure*.

11. **(D)** The plants that exist only within the compass of the canopy live within its *boundaries*.

12. **(B)** The tree trunks provide the epiphytes only with a good location up in the canopy. Being nonparasitic, epiphytes *cannot draw moisture* (or any nourishment whatsoever) *from tree trunks.*

13. **(E)** Having developed features that collect and retain rainwater, epiphytes clearly are particularly well suited to the *retention* (holding; storing up) *of liquid.*

14. **(D)** Because epiphytes do not sink their roots into the earth, *they lack connections* to the earth and thus do not have direct access *to water in the ground.* They have direct access to water only when it rains.

15. **(C)** Both desert cacti and arboreal cacti grow in environments in which access to moisture is difficult to achieve. The desert cacti lack access to moisture because the amount of rainfall in desert regions is minimal and little moisture exists in the soil. The arboreal cacti lack access to moisture because they grow high up in the canopy with no root connections to the soil. Thus, both kinds of cacti have had to develop *features to cut down* or reduce *the loss of moisture.*

16. **(E)** The passengers are walking because the coach cannot carry them uphill. Note that the horses have already come to a stop three times.

17. **(C)** The author describes the immediate, rather unwholesome area. However, he never *contrasts it with more attractive areas.*

18. **(C)** Given the inclement weather, the muddy footing, and the uphill struggle, the fact that *the horses* (brute animals) *strongly attempted to turn back to Blackheath* suggests that they were more reasonable creatures than the humans who forced them to struggle on.

19. **(C)** The lead horse *shook his head* and everything upon it, that is, his head and his harness, which made a rattling noise.

20. **(B)** It is not surprising that, at the sudden, emphatic noise the nervous passenger started or *jumped*.

21. **(C)** All the descriptive terms in the paragraph—mist "like an evil spirit," "waves of an unwholesome sea," fog "dense enough to shut out everything from the light"—emphasize the *gloominess* and dark melancholy of the scene.

22. **(C)** The sentence that immediately precedes the reference to the Captain maintains that anyone on the road might be in league with robbers, that is, might be a robber's accomplice or confederate. Thus, to be in the Captain's pay means to be a robber's paid accomplice, and the Captain is clearly a highway robber or *highwayman*.

23. **(B)** Viewing one another with suspicion, the passengers maintain a *guarded* or wary stance.

24. **(E)** By definition, *genial* means cordial or friendly. However, the situation shown here is grim and unfriendly rather than genial. Thus, the word is being used in an *ironic*, unexpected way.

Section 3

1. **(E)** Currently, the railroads can take on additional shipping only during the winter; at other times of the year, they can't absorb any more traffic. During the winter months the waterway could not take traffic away from the railroads (an icebound waterway is useless as a route for traffic). Thus, those in favor of the waterway argue that it will *supplement* or be a desirable addition to railroad facilities and will not *threaten* or endanger the railroads.

2. **(C)** George Burns had even greater celebrity or *renown* in the 1980s than he had known in the 1940s.

3. **(C)** "Despite" signals the contrast between the mole rat's repulsive, disgusting habits and its *meticulous*, painstakingly careful cleaning of its burrow.

4. **(A)** It is a major *requisite* (requirement or necessity) of the genre that the biographer be able to *reconstruct* or mentally build up again his or her subject's inner life.

5. **(A)** The dictionary defines *serendipity* as good luck, and aptitude for making valuable discoveries by accident. Newton's discovery of the law of gravity is a classic example of serendipity at work.

6. **(D)** The opposite of a purposeful, determined action is a *desultory*, aimless one.
   "Not" is a contrast signal. The missing word must be an antonym or near-antonym for "purposeful."

7. **(B)** In the first paragraph the author, by likening the prejudice against the Japanese to the prejudice below the Mason-Dixon line, argues that anti-Japanese feeling *was comparable to racial prejudice in the South*.

8. **(A)** The intensity of anti-Japanese feeling is explained in part by the fact that the Japanese "were of a distinct racial group; no amount of acculturation could

mask their foreignness" (lines 11–13). Logically, then, had *their physical appearance been different*, they might not have experienced such intense hatred.

9. **(D)** Among the causes of prejudice against the Japanese was the rapidity with which the Japanese immigrants adopted the so-called Protestant ethic, which includes the notion that you must *work hard to be successful.*

10. **(E)** Before the war, anti-Japanese feelings were most intense in northern California. Afterward, southern California became the locus of prejudice. World War II, then, *shifted the center of anti-Japanese feeling.*

11. **(E)** The passage explains that labor unions provided the base of the anti-Japanese movement. Presumably, labor unions voiced their opposition because members felt that their jobs were being *threatened by Japanese workers.*

12. **(D)** The author of Passage 2 cautions readers not to confuse anti-Semitism with other forms of anti-immigrant sentiment, but to be mindful of "different kinds of anti-Semitism." The passage then describes *many forms and guises* (appearances) of anti-Semitism.

13. **(D)** The author refers to ideological anti-Semitism as that which has "no direct connection with . . . ethnic integration." In other words, it is hatred of others' assumed *beliefs and values*, such as the anti-Semitic notion cited in the passage that Jews want to take control of the United States.

14. **(A)** According to the passage, ideological anti-Semitism has not been as "productive of violence as other racial and religious phobias." When violence has occurred, therefore, it has been inspired or *fed by social anti-Semitism.*

15. **(A)** The second paragraph of the passage lists several explanations for hatred of Jews, but not that *it is hard to tell a Jew from a non-Jew.*

16. **(B)** In the third paragraph Winrod and Smith are cited as examples of anti-Semites *whose hatred of Jews was based largely on religion.* As the passage says, except for Winrod and Smith, "one looks in vain for a clearly religious animus" to explain anti-Semitic feelings.

17. **(C)** The first passage pinpoints California as the center of anti-Japanese feeling and gives several precise explanations for its growth in that state. In contrast, Passage 2 portrays anti-Semitism as a *more complex and diffuse* (widespread) form of bigotry. It describes various reasons for anti-Semitism and fails to identify a place or region where it is concentrated.

18. **(C)** Both authors cite *irrational thinking* as the cause of prejudice. The first says the "opposition to the Japanese was based upon fears which were largely nonrational" (lines 47–50), while the second refers to the role played by "irrational anti-Semitic fantasies" (lines 64–67).

19. **(A)** *Economic reasons* dominate both authors' explanations of prejudice. The Japanese were hated for challenging whites in many businesses and professions, for working hard, and for competing with American workers for jobs. Jews were accused of plotting to take control of America's money supply, wrecking the financial system, and taking over the communications and entertainment industries.

ANSWER SHEET
CRITICAL READING TEST 3

Section 1

1. Ⓐ Ⓑ Ⓒ Ⓓ Ⓔ
2. Ⓐ Ⓑ Ⓒ Ⓓ Ⓔ
3. Ⓐ Ⓑ Ⓒ Ⓓ Ⓔ
4. Ⓐ Ⓑ Ⓒ Ⓓ Ⓔ
5. Ⓐ Ⓑ Ⓒ Ⓓ Ⓔ
6. Ⓐ Ⓑ Ⓒ Ⓓ Ⓔ
7. Ⓐ Ⓑ Ⓒ Ⓓ Ⓔ

8. Ⓐ Ⓑ Ⓒ Ⓓ Ⓔ
9. Ⓐ Ⓑ Ⓒ Ⓓ Ⓔ
10. Ⓐ Ⓑ Ⓒ Ⓓ Ⓔ
11. Ⓐ Ⓑ Ⓒ Ⓓ Ⓔ
12. Ⓐ Ⓑ Ⓒ Ⓓ Ⓔ
13. Ⓐ Ⓑ Ⓒ Ⓓ Ⓔ

14. Ⓐ Ⓑ Ⓒ Ⓓ Ⓔ
15. Ⓐ Ⓑ Ⓒ Ⓓ Ⓔ
16. Ⓐ Ⓑ Ⓒ Ⓓ Ⓔ
17. Ⓐ Ⓑ Ⓒ Ⓓ Ⓔ
18. Ⓐ Ⓑ Ⓒ Ⓓ Ⓔ
19. Ⓐ Ⓑ Ⓒ Ⓓ Ⓔ

20. Ⓐ Ⓑ Ⓒ Ⓓ Ⓔ
21. Ⓐ Ⓑ Ⓒ Ⓓ Ⓔ
22. Ⓐ Ⓑ Ⓒ Ⓓ Ⓔ
23. Ⓐ Ⓑ Ⓒ Ⓓ Ⓔ
24. Ⓐ Ⓑ Ⓒ Ⓓ Ⓔ
25. Ⓐ Ⓑ Ⓒ Ⓓ Ⓔ

Section 2

1. Ⓐ Ⓑ Ⓒ Ⓓ Ⓔ
2. Ⓐ Ⓑ Ⓒ Ⓓ Ⓔ
3. Ⓐ Ⓑ Ⓒ Ⓓ Ⓔ
4. Ⓐ Ⓑ Ⓒ Ⓓ Ⓔ
5. Ⓐ Ⓑ Ⓒ Ⓓ Ⓔ
6. Ⓐ Ⓑ Ⓒ Ⓓ Ⓔ
7. Ⓐ Ⓑ Ⓒ Ⓓ Ⓔ

8. Ⓐ Ⓑ Ⓒ Ⓓ Ⓔ
9. Ⓐ Ⓑ Ⓒ Ⓓ Ⓔ
10. Ⓐ Ⓑ Ⓒ Ⓓ Ⓔ
11. Ⓐ Ⓑ Ⓒ Ⓓ Ⓔ
12. Ⓐ Ⓑ Ⓒ Ⓓ Ⓔ
13. Ⓐ Ⓑ Ⓒ Ⓓ Ⓔ

14. Ⓐ Ⓑ Ⓒ Ⓓ Ⓔ
15. Ⓐ Ⓑ Ⓒ Ⓓ Ⓔ
16. Ⓐ Ⓑ Ⓒ Ⓓ Ⓔ
17. Ⓐ Ⓑ Ⓒ Ⓓ Ⓔ
18. Ⓐ Ⓑ Ⓒ Ⓓ Ⓔ
19. Ⓐ Ⓑ Ⓒ Ⓓ Ⓔ

20. Ⓐ Ⓑ Ⓒ Ⓓ Ⓔ
21. Ⓐ Ⓑ Ⓒ Ⓓ Ⓔ
22. Ⓐ Ⓑ Ⓒ Ⓓ Ⓔ
23. Ⓐ Ⓑ Ⓒ Ⓓ Ⓔ
24. Ⓐ Ⓑ Ⓒ Ⓓ Ⓔ
25. Ⓐ Ⓑ Ⓒ Ⓓ Ⓔ

Section 3

1. Ⓐ Ⓑ Ⓒ Ⓓ Ⓔ
2. Ⓐ Ⓑ Ⓒ Ⓓ Ⓔ
3. Ⓐ Ⓑ Ⓒ Ⓓ Ⓔ
4. Ⓐ Ⓑ Ⓒ Ⓓ Ⓔ
5. Ⓐ Ⓑ Ⓒ Ⓓ Ⓔ
6. Ⓐ Ⓑ Ⓒ Ⓓ Ⓔ
7. Ⓐ Ⓑ Ⓒ Ⓓ Ⓔ

8. Ⓐ Ⓑ Ⓒ Ⓓ Ⓔ
9. Ⓐ Ⓑ Ⓒ Ⓓ Ⓔ
10. Ⓐ Ⓑ Ⓒ Ⓓ Ⓔ
11. Ⓐ Ⓑ Ⓒ Ⓓ Ⓔ
12. Ⓐ Ⓑ Ⓒ Ⓓ Ⓔ
13. Ⓐ Ⓑ Ⓒ Ⓓ Ⓔ

14. Ⓐ Ⓑ Ⓒ Ⓓ Ⓔ
15. Ⓐ Ⓑ Ⓒ Ⓓ Ⓔ
16. Ⓐ Ⓑ Ⓒ Ⓓ Ⓔ
17. Ⓐ Ⓑ Ⓒ Ⓓ Ⓔ
18. Ⓐ Ⓑ Ⓒ Ⓓ Ⓔ
19. Ⓐ Ⓑ Ⓒ Ⓓ Ⓔ

20. Ⓐ Ⓑ Ⓒ Ⓓ Ⓔ
21. Ⓐ Ⓑ Ⓒ Ⓓ Ⓔ
22. Ⓐ Ⓑ Ⓒ Ⓓ Ⓔ
23. Ⓐ Ⓑ Ⓒ Ⓓ Ⓔ
24. Ⓐ Ⓑ Ⓒ Ⓓ Ⓔ
25. Ⓐ Ⓑ Ⓒ Ⓓ Ⓔ

Critical Reading Test 3

1 1 1 1 1 1 1 1 1 1 1 1 1

CRITICAL READING TEST 3

Section 1

TIME—25 MINUTES
24 QUESTIONS

For each of the following questions, select the best answer from the choices provided and fill in the appropriate circle on the answer sheet.

Each of the following sentences contains one or two blanks; each blank indicates that a word or set of words has been left out. Below the sentence are five words or phrases, lettered A through E. Select the word or set of words that best completes the sentence.

Example:

Fame is ----; today's rising star is all too soon tomorrow's washed-up has-been.

(A) rewarding   (B) gradual
(C) essential   (D) spontaneous
(E) transitory

Ⓐ Ⓑ Ⓒ Ⓓ ●

1. Though financially successful, the theater season, once again, is more noted for its _____ than for its original productions.

    (A) musicals
    (B) revivals
    (C) failures
    (D) rehearsals
    (E) commercials

2. During the Ice Ages, musk oxen ranged as far south as Iowa, in North America, and Spain, in Europe, but in recent centuries the species has been _____ arctic tundra habitats, such as Greenland and the arctic islands of Canada.

    (A) barred from
    (B) confined to
    (C) dissatisfied with
    (D) enervated by
    (E) unknown in

3. Just as an orchestra cannot consist only of violins, a society cannot consist only of managers, for society is an _____ in which different parts have different _____.

    (A) anarchy…powers
    (B) edifice…complaints
    (C) organism…functions
    (D) institution…results
    (E) urbanity…ambitions

4. A _____ person is one who will _____ something on the slightest of evidence.

    (A) restive…forget
    (B) garrulous…criticize
    (C) maudlin…censure
    (D) phlegmatic…condemn
    (E) credulous…believe

5. That the brain physically changes when stimulated, instead of remaining _____ from infancy to death, as previously thought, was Dr. Marian Diamond's first, and perhaps most far-reaching discovery.

    (A) mutable
    (B) static
    (C) sensory
    (D) vigorous
    (E) fluid

GO ON TO THE NEXT PAGE

Critical Reading Test 3

6. There were _____ in her nature that made her seem an _____ enigma: she was severe and gentle; she was modest and disdainful; she longed for affection and was cold.

    (A) aspirations…irreducible
    (B) contradictions…inexplicable
    (C) distortions…impetuous
    (D) disparities…interminable
    (E) incongruities…irrelevant

7. At a time when biographies that debunk their subjects are all the rage, it is refreshing to have one idol who not only lives up to her legend but also _____ it.

    (A) complicates
    (B) surpasses
    (C) compromises
    (D) rejects
    (E) subverts

8. *Morphing* is a term _____ for the metamorphosis of one shape into another, such as the smooth formation of a live actor from a silvery puddle as seen in *Terminator 2.*

    (A) coined
    (B) denigrated
    (C) simulated
    (D) mistaken
    (E) repudiated

GO ON TO THE NEXT PAGE

1 1 1 1 1 1 1 1 1 1 1

Read each of the passages below, and then answer the questions that follow the passage. The correct response may be stated outright or merely suggested in the passage.

Questions 9 and 10 are based on the following passage.

"Paint me as I am," said Oliver Cromwell[1] to the artist Lely. "If you leave out the scars and wrinkles, I will not pay you a shilling."
Line Even in such a trifle, Cromwell showed good
(5) sense. He did not wish all that was characteristic in his countenance to be lost, in a vain attempt to give him regular features and smooth cheeks. He was content that his face should show all the blemishes put on it by
(10) time, by war, by sleepless nights, by anxiety, perhaps by remorse; but with valor, policy, authority, and public care written on it as well. If great men knew what was in their best interests, it is thus that they would wish their
(15) minds to be portrayed.

——————
[1]Oliver Cromwell led the forces of Parliament during England's Civil Wars; he was Lord Protector of England, Scotland, and Ireland from 1653 to 1658 during the republican Commonwealth.

9. The author views Cromwell's choice about the way in which he wanted to be painted with

(A) detachment
(B) condescension
(C) cynicism
(D) approbation
(E) distaste

10. The passage suggests that painters who conceal their subjects' blemishes and imperfections

(A) are more skillful than those who portray their subjects with greater accuracy
(B) are better paid than those who paint more realistically
(C) reveal their subjects' inner beauty
(D) expose their own aesthetic preferences
(E) are doing their subjects no real favor

Questions 11 and 12 are based on the following passage.

On receiving the Congressional Medal for Distinguished Civilian Achievement, Dr. Jonas Salk declared, "I feel that the greatest
Line reward for doing is the opportunity to do
(5) more." People worldwide would agree that, in his forty-year medical career, Salk did a stunning amount for humanity. His work developing the first polio vaccine was the opening shot in a war that has led to the disease's vir-
(10) tual eradication. (In 2001, polio, which once paralyzed hundreds of thousands of children annually, claimed only 600 new victims worldwide.) Though Salk's vaccine has been superseded by Albert Sabin's cheaper oral
(15) vaccine, Salk's legacy and name live on.

11. In the course of the passage, the author does all of the following EXCEPT

(A) use a metaphor
(B) cite a statistic
(C) quote a historic figure
(D) describe a process
(E) make an assertion

12. In lines 6–7, "stunning" most nearly means

(A) gorgeous
(B) perplexing
(C) amazing
(D) critical
(E) unique

GO ON TO THE NEXT PAGE

1 1 1 1 1 1 1 1 1 1 1 1

Questions 13–24 are based on the following passage.

The following passage is taken from an article by a contemporary poet about Clement Clarke Moore, the nineteenth-century writer best known as the author of "A Visit From Saint Nicholas."

If he wasn't a myth maker himself, at least Clement Clarke Moore was a great myth refiner. He started with St. Nicholas, giver of
Line presents, whom the Dutch settlers had brought
(5) over to New York. Moore's portrait of the good saint is as fleshy and real as some Frans Hals painting of a burgher:

    The stump of a pipe he held tight in his teeth,
(10)   *And the smoke it encircled his head like a wreath.*

But with American efficiency, Moore combines the figure of St. Nicholas with that of Kris Kringle, who (in Norwegian lore)
(15) helped the saint by driving a reindeer-drawn sleigh. Moore fires Kris, leaving St. Nick to do his own driving. The result is our own American Santa Claus. Moore removes St. Nick's bishop's miter, decks him out in fur,
(20) gives him a ruddy face and a pot belly, hands him a sack of toys and calls him an elf—suggesting a pointed cap. Thomas Nast, our most authoritative Santa Claus delineator, stuck closely to Moore's description, and ever since,
(25) few artists have dared depart from it.

To see how good Moore's imagination is, you have only to compare his version of St. Nicholas with Washington Irving's of a few years earlier. In 1809, in "Knickerbocker's
(30) History of New York," Irving makes St. Nick a friendly Dutch-American deity "riding jollily among the tree-tops" in (of all things) a wagon, not only on Christmas but also on any old holiday afternoon. What pulled that silly
(35) wagon Irving doesn't say, or why it didn't snag itself on a branch and bust both axles.

But Moore in his genius provides St. Nick with reindeer power. And by laying marvelous names on those obedient steeds, he makes
(40) each one an individual. Though ruminants may be poorly designed for flight, Moore doesn't worry his head about aerodynamics; he just sidesteps the whole problem. Dasher, Dancer, Prancer, and the rest of the crew sim-
(45) ply whiz up to the rooftop by pure magic. It never occurs to us to question such a feat. We are one with Moore's protagonist, a man with "wondering eyes."

Delving into John Hollander's recent
(50) Library of America anthology "American Poetry: The Nineteenth Century," I was glad to find "A Visit From St. Nicholas" right there along with works by Whitman, Emily Dickinson and Jones Very. Professional decon-
(55) structionists may sneer, but popular demand has fixed the poem securely in our national heritage. If Mr. Hollander had left it out, it would have been missed. Statistics are scarce, but it seems likely that Moore's masterwork
(60) has been reprinted, recited and learned by heart more often than any other American poem—and that goes for "The Raven," "Casey at the Bat," and Sylvia Plath's "Daddy."

To be sure, mere popularity doesn't make
(65) a work of art great. If it did, then "September Morn," that delicate tribute to skinny-dipping once reproduced on calendars hung in barbershops and pool halls galore, would be a better painting than "Nude Descending a Staircase"
(70) any day. And yet a poem like Moore's that has stuck around for 171 years has to have something going for it.

GO ON TO THE NEXT PAGE →

1 1 1 1 1 1 1 1 1 1 1

Well then, what? I submit that the poem's immortality may be due not only to Moore's (75) perfecting a great myth, but also to his skill in music-making. It is a moribund reader who doesn't feel the spell of its bounding anapests, as hard to ignore as a herd of reindeer on your roof. Poets today tend to shy away from such (80) obvious rhythms. They shrink too from alliteration, which, applied badly, seems bric-a-brac. But Moore lays it on thick, and makes it work like a charm: the "fl" sounds in "Away to the window I flew like a flash," the hard "c" (85) sounds in "More rapid than eagles his coursers they came." As for his rhymes, most clunk along unsurprisingly (like "house" and "mouse"), but a few sound Muse-inspired. If any later versifier ever hits upon another pair (90) of rhyming words as fresh and precise as these, let him die smug:

He sprang to his sleigh, to his team gave a whistle,
And away they all flew like the down of
(95) *a thistle.*

History doesn't tell us whether Moore's daughters, who first received the poem as a Christmas present in 1822, were disappointed at not getting dolls instead. Anyhow, it is a (100) safe bet that, a hundred years from now, many a more serious and respectable poem will have departed from human memory like the down of a thistle, while Moore's vision of that wonderful eight-deer sleigh will go thundering on. (105) "A Visit From St. Nicholas" may be only a sweet confection, yet how well it lasts. On a cold winter night, it can warm you to the quick: a homemade verbal cookie dipped in Ovaltine.

13. The passage serves primarily to

   (A) inform the reader of a new anthology featuring "A Visit from St. Nicholas"
   (B) encourage contemporary poets to adopt the literary techniques used by Clement Clarke Moore
   (C) give an instance of a great work of art that has won universal renown
   (D) correct a misconception about the origins of Santa Claus
   (E) explain the enduring appeal of a classic example of light verse

14. By calling Clement Clarke Moore "a great myth refiner," the author intends to convey that Moore

   (A) was skillful at explaining myths
   (B) created brand new legends
   (C) studied the origins of myths
   (D) transformed old myths into something new
   (E) disdained the crudity of early mythology

15. Moore's sources for his Saint Nicholas can best be described as

   (A) eclectic
   (B) pagan
   (C) meager
   (D) illusory
   (E) authoritative

GO ON TO THE NEXT PAGE

Critical Reading Test 3

16. We can infer from lines 22–25 that Thomas Nast most likely was

    (A) an imitator of Moore's verse
    (B) a critic of Moore's changes to traditional figures
    (C) an illustrator of Moore's poem
    (D) an iconoclastic artist
    (E) a competitor of Moore's

17. Which statement best summarizes the point made in lines 26–48?

    (A) Moore's portrait of Saint Nicholas antedates Washington Irving's interpretation.
    (B) Irving's version of Saint Nicholas surpasses the one created by Moore.
    (C) Moore's interpretation of Saint Nicholas is less friendly than Irving's interpretation.
    (D) Moore preferred his version of Saint Nicholas to Irving's variant.
    (E) Moore showed greater creativity than Irving in constructing his picture of Saint Nicholas.

18. The statement in lines 46–48 ("We are one . . . eyes'") is best interpreted as conveying the idea that

    (A) we share the identity of the protagonist
    (B) we too view the proceedings with astonishment and awe
    (C) we do not understand the attraction of what takes place
    (D) we question the events as they occur
    (E) we also resemble Saint Nicholas in nature

19. The author's attitude toward "professional deconstructionists" (lines 54–57) can best be described as

    (A) respectful
    (B) dismissive
    (C) adulatory
    (D) timorous
    (E) perplexed

20. In line 62, "goes for" most nearly means

    (A) aims at
    (B) passes for
    (C) holds true for
    (D) gives approval to
    (E) attacks physically

21. In line 64, "mere" most nearly means

    (A) insignificant
    (B) involuntary
    (C) momentary
    (D) simple
    (E) problematic

22. In line 76, the author uses the word "moribund" to emphasize the reader's

    (A) immortality
    (B) fear of dying
    (C) ignorance of mythology
    (D) reservations about magic
    (E) insensitivity to verse

1 1 1 1 1 1 1 1 1 1 1

23. The author regards Moore's use of the rhyming words "whistle" and "thistle" with

    (A) self-satisfaction and complacency
    (B) amusement and condescension
    (C) delight and admiration
    (D) interest yet envy
    (E) derision and disdain

24. One aspect of the passage that might make it difficult to appreciate is the author's apparent assumption that readers will

    (A) prefer the realistic paintings of Hals to later artworks
    (B) have read Hollander's anthology of American poetry
    (C) be acquainted with statistics about the memorization of verse
    (D) understand the author's childhood associations with Saint Nicholas
    (E) already be familiar in great detail with Moore's poem

STOP

If you finish before time is called, you may check your work on this section only. Do not work on any other section in the test.

Critical Reading Test 3

2 2 2 2 2 2 2 2 2 2 2 2

Section 2

Time—25 minutes
24 Questions

For each of the following questions, select the best answer from the choices provided and fill in the appropriate circle on the answer sheet.

Each of the following sentences contains one or two blanks; each blank indicates that a word or set of words has been left out. Below the sentence are five words or phrases, lettered A through E. Select the word or set of words that best completes the sentence.

Example:

Fame is ----; today's rising star is all too soon tomorrow's washed-up has-been.

(A) rewarding   (B) gradual
(C) essential   (D) spontaneous
(E) transitory

Ⓐ Ⓑ Ⓒ Ⓓ ●

1. Despite the current expansion of fencing association membership in America, the governing body of world fencing fears that fencing could be in danger of _____ if it does not become more _____ to spectators.

   (A) monotony…intelligible
   (B) overcrowding…resistant
   (C) extinction…accessible
   (D) corruption…cordial
   (E) remoteness…handy

2. Precision of wording is necessary in good writing; by choosing words that exactly convey the desired meaning, one can avoid _____.

   (A) redundancy
   (B) complexity
   (C) duplicity
   (D) ambiguity
   (E) lucidity

3. Despite the _____ size of her undergraduate class, the professor made a point of getting to know as many as possible of the more than 700 students personally.

   (A) negligible
   (B) modest
   (C) infinitesimal
   (D) daunting
   (E) moderate

4. Biographer Janet Malcolm maintains that biography is a spurious art, for the orderly narrative it creates is _____; the "facts" aren't facts at all, but literary _____.

   (A) illusory…inventions
   (B) genuine…commonplaces
   (C) informative…allusions
   (D) brilliant…triumphs
   (E) sincere…criticisms

5. Something in Christopher responded to the older man's air of authority: he looked _____, accustomed to _____.

   (A) magisterial…command
   (B) monumental…intimidate
   (C) diffident…domineer
   (D) masterful…obey
   (E) decisive…fret

GO ON TO THE NEXT PAGE
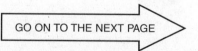

Read the passages below, and then answer the questions that follow. The correct response may be stated outright or merely suggested in the passages.

Questions 6–9 are based on the following passages.

Both passages relate to English author Jane Austen and her readers. Passage 1 is taken from E. M. Forster's 1924 review of Chapman's edition, The Works of Jane Austen. *Passage 2 is taken from an article written in 2005.*

Passage 1

I am a Jane Austenite, and, therefore, slightly imbecile about Jane Austen. My fatuous expression and airs of personal
Line immunity—how ill they set on the face, say,
(5) of a Stevensonian. But Jane Austen is so different. One's favorite author! One reads and re-reads, the mouth open and the mind closed. Shut up in measureless content, one greets her by the name of most kind hostess, while criti-
(10) cism slumbers. The Jane Austenite possesses none of the brightness he ascribes to his idol. Like all regular churchgoers, he scarcely notices what is being said.

Passage 2

Line   Jane Austen never suffered fools gladly,
(15) nor should we. Her letters and novels are filled with sharp, cutting comments—zingers, remarks that startle, even shock, the unwary reader. At the ball there "was a scarcity of Men in general, & a still greater scarcity of
(20) any that were good for much." Zing! Who, reading that caustic comment, can ever again think of Austen as Gentle Jane? As Natalie Tyler says, "She is the one person whose insights about yourself you would most fear
(25) because you realize that her perceptions are penetrating, perspicacious, and piercingly accurate."

6. Passage 1 supports which of the following generalizations about the Jane Austenites?

    (A) They also enjoy the novels of Robert Louis Stevenson.
    (B) They are irregular in their reading habits.
    (C) Their approach to Austen's works is analytical but constructive.
    (D) They grow increasingly immune to Austen's appeal.
    (E) Their reverence for Austen is uncritical.

7. The author of Passage 2 views Austen primarily as

    (A) an ironic observer
    (B) an ardent feminist
    (C) a petty quibbler
    (D) an objective witness
    (E) a reluctant critic

8. The author of Passage 2 does all of the following EXCEPT

    (A) pose a question
    (B) cite an authority
    (C) define a term
    (D) provide an example
    (E) propose a hypothesis

9. Both passages support the generalization that Austen

    (A) was restricted by the limitations of her society
    (B) was unusually sensitive to her environment
    (C) is less popular today than in years past
    (D) possessed an acute intellect
    (E) is more reverent than other authors

GO ON TO THE NEXT PAGE

Critical Reading Test 3

2 2 2 2 2 2 2 2 2 2 2 2

Questions 10–15 are based on the following passage.

In this excerpt from The Way to Rainy Mountain, *the writer N. Scott Momaday tells of his grandmother, a member of the Kiowa tribe, who was born at a key time in Kiowa history.*

I like to think of my grandmother as a child. When she was born, the Kiowas were living the last great moment of their history.
Line For more than a hundred years they had con-
(5) trolled the open range from the Smoky Hill River to the Red, from the headwaters of the Canadian to the fork of the Arkansas and Cimarron. In alliance with the Comanches, they had ruled the whole of the southern
(10) Plains. War was their sacred business, and they were among the finest horsemen the world has ever known. But warfare for the Kiowas was preeminently a matter of disposition rather than of survival, and they never
(15) understood the grim, unrelenting advance of the U.S. Cavalry. When at last, divided and ill-provisioned, they were driven onto the Staked Plains in the cold rains of autumn, they fell into panic. In Palo Duro Canyon they aban-
(20) doned their crucial stores to pillage and had nothing then but their lives. In order to save themselves, they surrendered to the soldiers at Fort Sill and were imprisoned in the old stone corral that now stands as a military museum.
(25) My grandmother was spared the humiliation of those high gray walls by eight or ten years, but she must have known from birth the affliction of defeat, the dark brooding of old warriors.
(30) Her name was Aho, and she belonged to the last culture to evolve in North America. Her forebears came down from the high country in western Montana nearly three centuries ago. They were a mountain people, a mysteri-

(35) ous tribe of hunters whose language has never been positively classified in any major group. In the late seventeenth century they began a long migration to the south and east. It was a journey toward the dawn, and it led to a
(40) golden age. Along the way the Kiowas were befriended by the Crows, who gave them the culture and religion of the Plains. They acquired horses, and their ancient nomadic spirit was suddenly free of the ground. They
(45) acquired Tai-Me, the sacred Sun Dance doll, from that moment the object and symbol of their worship, and so shared in the divinity of the sun. Not least, they acquired the sense of destiny, therefore courage and pride. When
(50) they entered upon the southern Plains they had been transformed. No longer were they slaves to the simple necessity of survival; they were a lordly and dangerous society of fighters and thieves, hunters and priests of the sun.
(55) According to their origin myth, they entered the world through a hollow log. From one point of view, their migration was the fruit of an old prophecy, for indeed they emerged from a sunless world.

10. The author of this passage indicates in lines 12–16 that the Kiowas waged war predominantly because they

(A) feared the Comanches
(B) wanted more land
(C) were warlike in nature
(D) had been humiliated by the cavalry
(E) believed they would perish otherwise

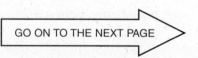
GO ON TO THE NEXT PAGE

2 2 2 2 2 2 2 2 2 2 2

11. Compared to the Kiowa warriors, the cavalrymen were

(A) more idealistic about warfare
(B) exceptionally fine horsemen
(C) vulnerable to divisiveness
(D) unswerving in determination
(E) less given to brooding

12. The author's grandmother directly experienced

(A) imprisonment at Fort Sill
(B) the bleak attitude of the older Kiowa men
(C) the defeat at Palo Duro Canyon
(D) the loss of the tribe's provisions
(E) surrender to the white soldiers

13. The author views the Kiowas of the late seventeenth and eighteenth centuries with a sense of

(A) urgency
(B) ambivalence
(C) remorse
(D) admiration
(E) irony

14. By "their ancient nomadic spirit was suddenly free of the ground" (lines 43 and 44), the author most nearly means

(A) the wanderers were now free to worship the sun
(B) the acquisition of horses liberated them to rove more freely
(C) they did not have to pay the Crows for the gift of horses
(D) the oldest of the migratory Kiowas lacked ties to the soil
(E) they no longer believed in the earth spirits of their ancestors

15. An "origin myth" (line 55) as used by the author is

(A) a theory of reproduction told to Native American children
(B) a religion the Kiowas learned from the Crows
(C) a type of tale known only to Kiowas
(D) an explanation of how the Kiowas came into being
(E) a natural tale about trees and the sun

Questions 16–24 are based on the following passage.

African elephants now are an endangered species. The following passage, taken from an article written in 1989, discusses the potential ecological disaster that might occur if the elephant were to become extinct.

The African elephant—mythic symbol of a continent, keystone of its ecology and the largest land animal remaining on earth—has
Line become the object of one of the biggest,
(5) broadest international efforts yet mounted to turn a threatened species off the road to extinction. But it is not only the elephant's survival that is at stake, conservationists say. Unlike the endangered tiger, unlike even the
(10) great whales, the African elephant is in great measure the architect of its environment. As a voracious eater of vegetation, it largely shapes the forest-and-savanna surroundings in which it lives, thereby setting the terms of existence
(15) for millions of other storied animals—from zebras to gazelles to giraffes and wilde-beests—that share its habitat. And as the ele-phant disappears, scientists and conservation-ists say, many other species will also disap-
(20) pear from vast stretches of forest and savanna, drastically altering and impoverishing whole ecosystems.

GO ON TO THE NEXT PAGE

Critical Reading Test 3

2 2 2 2 2 2 2 2 2 2 2

It is the elephant's metabolism and appetite that make it a disturber of the environment
(25) and therefore an important creator of habitat. In a constant search for the 300 pounds of vegetation it must have every day, it kills small trees and underbrush and pulls branches off big trees as high as its trunk will reach.
(30) This creates innumerable open spaces in both deep tropical forests and in the woodlands that cover part of the African savannas. The resulting patchwork, a mosaic of vegetation in various stages of regeneration, in turn creates a
(35) greater variety of forage that attracts a greater variety of other vegetation-eaters than would otherwise be the case.

In studies over the last twenty years in southern Kenya near Mount Kilimanjaro,
(40) Dr. David Western has found that when elephants are allowed to roam the savannas naturally and normally, they spread out at "intermediate densities." Their foraging creates a mixture of savanna woodlands (what the
(45) Africans call bush) and grassland. The result is a highly diverse array of other plant-eating species: those like the zebra, wildebeest and gazelle, that graze; those like the giraffe, bushbuck and lesser kudu, that browse on tender
(50) shoots, buds, twigs and leaves; and plant-eating primates like the baboon and vervet monkey. These herbivores attract carnivores like the lion and cheetah.

When the elephant population thins out,
(55) Dr. Western said, the woodlands become denser and the grazers are squeezed out. When pressure from poachers forces elephants to crowd more densely onto reservations, the woodlands there are knocked out
(60) and the browsers and primates disappear.

Something similar appears to happen in dense tropical rain forests. In their natural state, because the overhead forest canopy shuts out sunlight and prevents growth on the
(65) forest floor, rain forests provide slim pickings

for large, hoofed plant-eaters. By pulling down trees and eating new growth, elephants enlarge natural openings in the canopy, allowing plants to regenerate on the forest floor
(70) and bringing down vegetation from the canopy so that smaller species can get at it.

In such situations, the rain forest becomes hospitable to large plant-eating mammals such as bongos, bush pigs, duikers, forest
(75) hogs, swamp antelopes, forest buffaloes, okapis, sometimes gorillas and always a host of smaller animals that thrive on secondary growth. When elephants disappear and the forest reverts, the larger animals give way to
(80) smaller, nimbler animals like monkeys, squirrels and rodents.

16. The passage is primarily concerned with

(A) explaining why elephants are facing the threat of extinction
(B) explaining difficulties in providing sufficient forage for plant-eaters
(C) explaining how the elephant's impact on its surroundings affects other species
(D) distinguishing between savannas and rain forests as habitats for elephants
(E) contrasting elephants with members of other endangered species

17. In line 5, "mounted" most nearly means

(A) ascended
(B) increased
(C) launched
(D) attached
(E) exhibited

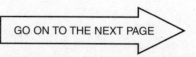
GO ON TO THE NEXT PAGE

2 2 2 2 2 2 2 2 2 2 2 2

18. In the opening paragraph, the author mentions tigers and whales in order to emphasize which point about the elephant?

   (A) Like them, it faces the threat of extinction.
   (B) It is herbivorous rather than carnivorous.
   (C) It moves more ponderously than either the tiger or the whale.
   (D) Unlike them, it physically alters its environment.
   (E) It is the largest extant land mammal.

19. A necessary component of the elephant's ability to transform the landscape is its

   (A) massive intelligence
   (B) threatened extinction
   (C) ravenous hunger
   (D) lack of grace
   (E) ability to regenerate

20. The author's style can best be described as

   (A) hyperbolic
   (B) naturalistic
   (C) reportorial
   (D) esoteric
   (E) sentimental

21. It can be inferred from the passage that

   (A) the lion and the cheetah commonly prey upon elephants
   (B) the elephant is dependent upon the existence of smaller plant-eating mammals for its survival
   (C) elephants have an indirect effect on the hunting patterns of certain carnivores
   (D) the floor of the tropical rain forest is too overgrown to accommodate larger plant-eating species
   (E) the natural tendency of elephants is to crowd together in packs

22. The passage contains information that would answer which of the following questions?

   I.   How does the elephant's foraging affect its surroundings?
   II. How do the feeding patterns of gazelles and giraffes differ?
   III. What occurs in the rain forest when the elephant population dwindles?

   (A) I only
   (B) II only
   (C) I and II only
   (D) II and III only
   (E) I, II, and III

GO ON TO THE NEXT PAGE

Critical Reading Test 3

23. In line 76, "host" most nearly means

    (A) food source for parasites
    (B) very large number
    (C) provider of hospitality
    (D) military force
    (E) angelic company

24. Which of the following statements best expresses the author's attitude toward the damage to vegetation caused by foraging elephants?

    (A) It is an unfortunate by-product of the feeding process.
    (B) It is a necessary but undesirable aspect of elephant population growth.
    (C) It fortuitously results in creating environments suited to diverse species.
    (D) It has the unexpected advantage that it allows scientists access to the rain forest.
    (E) It reinforces the impression that elephants are a disruptive force.

STOP

If you finish before time is called, you may check your work on this section only. Do not work on any other section in the test.

3 3 3 3 3 3 3 3 3 3 3 3

Section 3

For each of the following questions, select the best answer from the choices provided and fill in the appropriate circle on the answer sheet.

Each of the following sentences contains one or two blanks; each blank indicates that a word or set of words has been left out. Below the sentence are five words or phrases, lettered A through E. Select the word or set of words that best completes the sentence.

Example:

Fame is ----; today's rising star is all too soon tomorrow's washed-up has-been.

(A) rewarding   (B) gradual
(C) essential   (D) spontaneous
(E) transitory

Ⓐ Ⓑ Ⓒ Ⓓ ●

1. A subway modernization program intended to ____ a host of problems ranging from dangerous tracks to overcrowded stairwells has failed to meet its schedule for repairs.

    (A) augment
    (B) initiate
    (C) deplore
    (D) disclose
    (E) eliminate

2. To astronomers, the moon has long been an ____, its origin escaping simple solution.

    (A) interval
    (B) ultimatum
    (C) enigma
    (D) affront
    (E) opportunity

3. The amusements of modern urban people tend more and more to be ____ and to consist of the ____ of the skilled activities of others.

    (A) strenuous…contemplation
    (B) healthful…enjoyment
    (C) solitary…sharing
    (D) passive…observation
    (E) intellectual…repetition

4. As matter condenses out of the thin disk of hot gas and dust revolving around a new sun, it ____ into larger particles, just as snowflakes stick together as they fall.

    (A) crashes
    (B) protrudes
    (C) coalesces
    (D) evaporates
    (E) dissolves

5. The term *mole rat* is a ____, for these small, furless rodents are neither moles nor rats.

    (A) pseudonym
    (B) digression
    (C) misnomer
    (D) nonentity
    (E) preference

6. Einstein's humility was so ____ that it might have seemed a pose affected by a great man had it not been so obviously ____.

    (A) spurious…genuine
    (B) convincing…assumed
    (C) profound…sincere
    (D) heartfelt…hypocritical
    (E) modest…contrived

GO ON TO THE NEXT PAGE

Critical Reading Test 3

3 3 3 3 3 3 3 3 3 3 3

The questions that follow the next two passages relate to the content of both, and to their relationship. The correct response may be stated outright in the passage or merely suggested.

Questions 7–19 are based on the following passages.

These passages are portraits of two fathers. The first appeared in a contemporary novel, the second in a memoir written in the 1990s by a person looking back on experiences in the San Francisco Bay area.

Passage 1

In 1948 my father was serving his second term as sheriff of Mercer County, Montana. We lived in Bentrock, the county seat and the
Line only town of any size in the region. In 1948
(5) its population was less than two thousand people. . . .

Many of the men in Mercer County had spent the preceding years in combat. (But not my father; he was 4-F. When he was sixteen a
(10) horse kicked him, breaking his leg so severely that he walked with a permanent limp, and eventually a cane, his right leg V-ed in, his right knee perpetually pointing to the left.) When these men came back from war they
(15) wanted nothing more than to work their farms and ranches and to live quietly with their families. The county even had fewer hunters after the war than before.

All of which made my father's job a rela-
(20) tively easy one. Oh, he arrested the usual weekly drunks, mediated an occasional dispute about fence lines or stray cattle, calmed a few domestic disturbances, and warned the town's teenagers about getting rowdy in
(25) Wood's Cafe, but by and large being sheriff of Mercer County did not require great strength or courage. The ability to drive the county's rural roads, often drifted over in the winter or washed out in the summer, was a much more
(30) necessary skill than being good with your fists

or a gun. One of my father's regular duties was chaperoning Saturday night dances in the county, but the fact that he often took along my mother (and sometimes me) shows how
(35) quiet those affairs—and his job—usually were.

And that disappointed me at the time. As long as my father was going to be sheriff, a position with so much potential for excite-
(40) ment, danger, and bravery, why couldn't some of that promise be fulfilled? No matter how many wheat fields or cow pastures surrounded us, we were still Montanans, yet my father didn't even look like a western sheriff. He
(45) wore a shirt and tie, as many of the men in town did, but at least they wore boots and Stetsons; my father wore brogans and a fedora. He had a gun but he never carried it, on duty or off. I knew because I checked, time
(50) and time again. When he left the house I ran to his dresser and the top drawer on the right side. And there it was, there it always was. Just as well. As far as I was concerned it was the wrong kind of gun for a sheriff. He should
(55) have had a nickel-plated Western Colt .45, something with some history and heft. Instead, my father had a small .32 automatic, Italian-made and no bigger than your palm. My father didn't buy such a sorry gun; he con-
(60) fiscated it from a drunken transient in one of his first arrests. My father kept the gun but in fair exchange bought the man a bus ticket to Billings, where he had family.

GO ON TO THE NEXT PAGE ⟹

3 3 3 3 3 3 3 3 3 3 **3**

Passage 2

He was good-looking, in a Southern,
(65) romantic poet sort of way. He needed those
good looks, one of the aunts said; why else
would my otherwise sensible mother have
married a man like him, an actor-writer
hyphenate who lived on dreams and spent his
(70) free evenings carrying a spear at the Opera
House. But that was in later times, when he
had moved out of the rundown communal
house in the Berkeley Hills, leaving my
mother and the ever-changing cast of nominal
(75) uncles and aunts to patch the ancient water
heater and pump out the basement when the
overpressured valve finally blew. He needed
separateness to write, he said, solitude, something we'd never given him, and he was tired,
(80) tired of being dragged from his study to tend
to the latest household eruption that bubbled
up "like gas from a Calistoga mud bath," he
said, with relentless regularity.

He looked tired by then, as tired of us as
(85) we were of him, of forgotten birthdays and
surprises that failed to surprise. When he did
bring us a present, I even wondered why, for it
was always somehow off: last season's hot toy
no one played with any more, or a complicated
(90) model no boy could assemble without a
father's help. Which we never got. He was an
actor, after all, not tech crew, an artist, not
someone who could fix a toy.

If he was an actor, we were props at best.
(95) Reluctant ones—had there been a Plantagenet
Pleasure Faire, he would have strutted his
hour as Wicked Dick III, while Geoffrey and I,
thrust into burlap sacks, were hauled off, two
little princes in shabby tights, to be disposed
(100) of elsewhere. That was his glory, kinging it.
Living History,[1] he called it, and in the early
days he followed the fairs up and down the
state, living the Renaissance first in Agoura,
then in Marin, finally winding up the acting

(105) season with Victoria's England in San
Francisco or even Oakland for one or two
slow years.

Not that anyone ever hired him to act the
king. No, he was a minor figure even on that
(110) rude stage, a charming but lesser nobleman in
Elizabeth's court, an attentive councilor in
Victoria's entourage. But he shared the perks
of royalty, such as they were, stood center
stage in black velvet pantaloons while the
(115) September sun burned overhead, or posed
handsomely (in a Prince Albert coat, no less)
as the royal party made its way through the
Christmas crowds at Dickens Fair. Why he
stuck to it, I never understood. Certainly not
(120) for the pay.

Between fairs he wrote, or thought of
writing, shut up in his study, into which we
children were not allowed, or did research for
his one-man-shows (in which he played a
(125) series of writers, one per show, so that one
year we saw his Edgar Allan Poe, another
year, his Ambrose Bierce). He was a writer, or
at least a writer once removed, writing down
other men's words and speaking them as if
(130) they were his own. At times it seemed he
thought they were his own, he paraphrased
them so freely, vamping upon the themes of
The Devil's Dictionary.[2] And he probably
thought we were his own as well, as little
(135) acquainted with us as he was. And so we were,
if only by example and heredity.

---

[1] Since the 1960s, California's Living History Centre has
produced fairs and festivals in northern and southern
California. The Renaissance Pleasure Faire is set in the
time of Queen Elizabeth I; the Dickens Christmas Fair
and Pickwick Comic Annual, in the time of Queen
Victoria.
[2] A book of diabolical epigrams by Ambrose Bierce.

GO ON TO THE NEXT PAGE

Critical Reading Test 3

7. In Passage 1 the narrator uses the parenthetical material (lines 8–13) to

    (A) suggest that his father became sheriff to compensate for his disability
    (B) highlight the difference between his father and other men in Mercer County
    (C) justify his father's peaceful nature
    (D) belittle his father
    (E) indicate that the voters felt sorry for his father when they elected him sheriff

8. Mentioning that Mercer County "had fewer hunters after the war than before" (lines 17 and 18) is the author's way of saying that

    (A) the men had had their fill of shooting and death
    (B) the men worked long hours and had no time for hunting
    (C) the narrator's father prevented the men from hunting
    (D) the men thought hunting was too dangerous
    (E) many of the hunters were killed in the war

9. By describing his father's work clothes (lines 44–48), the narrator is suggesting that his father

    (A) wanted to dress like other men
    (B) didn't take the sheriff's job seriously
    (C) was pretty dull
    (D) was a nonconformist
    (E) was concerned about his image

10. By wishing that his father had a gun with "some history and some heft" (lines 54–56), the narrator means

    (A) an antique gun
    (B) a more expensive gun
    (C) a gun used in the war
    (D) a gun that could be worn in a holster
    (E) a more impressive gun

11. In Passage 1 which of the following best describes the narrator's feelings about his father?

    (A) Regret
    (B) Hostility
    (C) Resentment
    (D) Affection
    (E) Indifference

12. The narrator of Passage 2 compares himself and his brother to "props" (line 94) because they

    (A) reinforced their father's image as a parent
    (B) were assets to theatrical productions
    (C) were physical objects handled onstage
    (D) supported their father's dramatic efforts
    (E) possessed essential attributes their father lacked

13. In line 110, "rude" most nearly means

    (A) roughly made
    (B) deliberately impolite
    (C) highly vigorous
    (D) inconsiderate
    (E) tempestuous

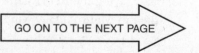

3 3 3 3 3 3 3 3 3 3 3

14. The narrator mentions his father's sharing the perks of royalty (lines 112–118) in order to emphasize that his father

    (A) had gone far in his chosen field
    (B) wanted to share these privileges with his children
    (C) had a particularly regal demeanor
    (D) demanded only the best for himself
    (E) received very little for his efforts

15. In Passage 2, which of the following is NOT an accurate description of the narrator's father?

    (A) He was not dependable to his children.
    (B) He enjoyed being the center of attention.
    (C) He had an appealing appearance.
    (D) He was well liked by those who shared his home.
    (E) He was uncomfortable with his responsibilities.

16. The narrator's purpose in writing this portrait of his father was

    (A) to show readers the effects of a bohemian lifestyle on one man
    (B) to help himself understand his complex feelings toward his father
    (C) to illustrate the importance of open communication among members of a family
    (D) to tell about the difficulties of his boyhood
    (E) to praise his father, a man he both loved and feared

17. In which respect is the portrait of the father in Passage 1 similar to the portrait in Passage 2?

    (A) In both passages we see the father through the eyes of a young boy.
    (B) Both passages portray the father as deficient in some important way.
    (C) In both passages we get to know intimate details of the father's life.
    (D) Both passages tell us as much about the narrator as about the father.
    (E) Both passages imply that the narrators would like to emulate their fathers.

18. As presented in the two passages, the relationship between each narrator and his father is

    (A) loving
    (B) competitive
    (C) cautious
    (D) distant
    (E) tense

19. The authors of both passages come across as

    (A) loyal sons
    (B) intolerant of their fathers
    (C) respectful of their fathers
    (D) rebellious sons
    (E) puzzled by their fathers

 STOP

If you finish before time is called, you may check your work on this section only. Do not work on any other section in the test.

Critical Reading Test 3

Answer Key

Section 1

1. **B**	5. **B**	9. **D**	13. **E**	17. **E**	21. **D**
2. **B**	6. **B**	10. **E**	14. **D**	18. **B**	22. **E**
3. **C**	7. **B**	11. **D**	15. **A**	19. **B**	23. **C**
4. **E**	8. **A**	12. **C**	16. **C**	20. **C**	24. **E**

Section 2

1. **C**	5. **A**	9. **D**	13. **D**	17. **C**	21. **C**
2. **D**	6. **E**	10. **C**	14. **B**	18. **D**	22. **E**
3. **D**	7. **A**	11. **D**	15. **D**	19. **C**	23. **B**
4. **A**	8. **E**	12. **B**	16. **C**	20. **C**	24. **C**

Section 3

1. **E**	5. **C**	9. **C**	13. **A**	17. **B**
2. **C**	6. **C**	10. **E**	14. **E**	18. **D**
3. **D**	7. **C**	11. **A**	15. **D**	19. **E**
4. **C**	8. **A**	12. **C**	16. **B**	

Analysis of Test Results

I. **Check your answers against the answer key.**
II. **Fill in the following chart.**

Sentence Completion Number Correct	Section 1 (Questions 1–8)		Section 2 (Questions 1–5)	Section 3 (Questions 1–6)		Total
	_____		_____	_____		_____
Passage-Based Reading Number Correct	Section 1 (Questions 9–24)		Section 2 (Questions 6–24)	Section 3 (Questions 7–19)		Total
	_____		_____	_____		_____

III. **Interpret your results.**

Sentence Completion   Number Correct _____

Passage-Based Reading   Number Correct _____

Subtotal _____

Guessing Penalty: Subtract 1/4 point for each incorrect answer.   _____
(Do not take off points for questions you left blank.)

TOTAL SCORE _____

	Sentence Completion Score	Passage-Based Reading Score	Total
Excellent	18–19 Correct	43–48 Correct	60–67
Very Good	14–17 Correct	33–42 Correct	46–59
Good	11–13 Correct	25–32 Correct	35–45
Fair	9–10 Correct	20–24 Correct	28–34
Poor	6–8 Correct	12–19 Correct	17–27
Very Poor	0–5 Correct	0–11 Correct	0–16

Critical Reading Test 3

Answer Explanations

Section 1

1. **(B)** The contrast here is between *revivals* (new productions of old plays) and original productions.

2. **(B)** "But" signals a contrast. In the Ice Ages, musk oxen ranged or roamed over much of the Northern Hemisphere. In recent times, however, they have been *confined* or limited *to* the far northernmost regions.

3. **(C)** The comparison suggests society is an *organism* made up of many parts serving different roles or *functions*.

4. **(E)** By definition, someone *credulous* or gullible readily *believes* things without having much reason to do so.

5. **(B)** "Instead" signals a contrast. The missing word must be an antonym or near-antonym for "physically changes." Something *static* or unchanging by definition does not physically change.

6. **(B)** To be sometimes harsh and sometimes gentle is to act in *contradictory* ways. Such inconsistencies in behavior might well make someone seem an *inexplicable* enigma, a mystery that could not be explained.

7. **(B)** To debunk the subject of a biography is to expose the false claims about that person's virtues, to poke holes in the legend, so to speak. The subject of this biography, however, deserves the praise she has been awarded. She is even better than tales paint her, *surpassing* her legend.

8. **(A)** To come up with or invent a name for something new is to *coin* a term.

9. **(D)** Stating that Cromwell showed good sense in his insistence on an honest portrait, the author views this choice with *approbation* (approval).

10. **(E)** If to be portrayed accurately, warts and all, is in the best interests of great men, then painters who misrepresent their subjects by concealing their blemishes and imperfections *are doing their subjects no real favor.*

11. **(D)** Use the process of elimination to answer this question. The author uses a metaphor: Salk's release of the vaccine was "the opening shot in a war." Therefore, you can eliminate (A). The author cites a statistic: polio claimed 600 new victims in 2001. Therefore, you can eliminate (B). The author quotes Salk, a historic figure whose legacy lives on. Therefore, you can eliminate (C). The author makes several assertions. Therefore, you can eliminate (E). Only (D) is left. It is the correct answer. The author never *describes a process.*

12. **(C)** In helping wipe out a disease that had crippled children for centuries, Salk did an *amazing*, stunning amount for humanity.

13. **(E)** Throughout the passage, the author praises Moore's "sweet confection," demonstrating its strengths and showing reasons for its popularity over the years. Thus, the passage chiefly serves to *explain the enduring appeal of this classic example of light verse.*

14. **(D)** Moore did not invent any new myths. However, he *transformed the old myths* of Kris Kringle the sled driver and Saint Nicholas the bishop into our archetypal Santa Claus.

15. **(A)** Moore uses sources from a variety of traditions—Norwegian, Dutch, possibly even American. To compose something out of elements drawn from such a variety of sources is by definition to be *eclectic*.

16. **(C)** To delineate Santa Claus is to depict or portray him. The *illustrator* Thomas Nast closely based his illustrations of Santa Claus on Moore's own words.

17. **(E)** One contrasts Moore's St. Nick with Irving's in order to see just how very good and imaginative a job Moore did compared to Irving. Moore goes beyond Irving in furnishing Santa with steeds, naming these steeds, and differentiating them from one another. In doing so, he shows considerable *creativity*.

18. **(B)** We never think of questioning what the poem says because, like the poem's protagonist, we are too awestruck by what we see to ask any questions. We view what occurs *with astonishment and awe*.

19. **(B)** The author disregards or *dismisses* the sneers of the professional deconstructionists (literary critics, members of a literary school with little respect for light verse). He believes the lasting popularity of the piece should outweigh the deconstructionists' petty criticisms.

20. **(C)** The phrase "that goes for 'The Raven'" means "that also *holds true for* 'The Raven.'" The author is asserting that he has not ignored the claims of popular favorites like "Casey at the Bat" and "The Raven" in saying Moore's poem is probably our most popular American poem.

21. **(D)** "Mere" popularity here means *simple* popularity, considered apart from any other quality a work of art might possess.

22. **(E)** A moribund reader is someone figuratively dead or *insensitive to the verse* he or she reads. (*Moribund* literally means approaching death; dormant.)

23. **(C)** The author presents this pair of rhyming words as one of Moore's "Muse-inspired" better pairings. Clearly, he regards Moore's use of these words with both *delight* in the rhyme and *admiration* for the rhymester.

24. **(E)** The author does not bother to summarize the story of "A Visit From Saint Nicholas" for the reader. He refers blithely to its anapests and alliteration, mentions its protagonist (whom someone unfamiliar with the poem, not knowing any better, might have confused with Saint Nick), and generally assumes that anyone reading his article will *already be familiar in great detail with Moore's poem*.

Section 2

1. **(C)** "Despite" signals a contrast. Right now, fencing in America is in a stage of growth; the fencing association's membership is expanding. However, the association fears that fencing will not grow but die out (face *extinction*) if spectators cannot understand what's going on. Thus, fencing needs to become more *accessible* (comprehensible).

2. **(D)** Precise wording reduces the chances of *ambiguity* (confusion about meaning).

3. **(D)** It would be a *daunting* (discouraging) task to get to know over 700 people in the course of one semester. Such a large group is in itself *daunting*.

4. **(A)** "Spurious" means false or fake. Malcolm argues that biographers make up or *invent* the facts they narrate, so the orderly narrative you read and take as historically true is actually *illusory* (deceptive; unreal).

5. **(A)** By definition, *magisterial* means authoritative or *commanding*.

6. **(E)** The author of Passage 1 compares the Jane Austenites to "regular church-goers" who "scarcely notice what is being said," and asserts that "criticism slumbers." Thus, Passage 1 supports the generalization that the Austenites' *reverence for Austen is uncritical*.

7. **(A)** Stressing Austen's caustic comments and penetrating perceptions, the author of Passage 2 depicts her primarily as *an ironic observer*.

8. **(E)** Use the process of elimination to answer this question. Does the author of Passage 2 pose a question? Yes, she asks, "Who, reading that caustic comment, can ever again think of Austen as Gentle Jane?" Eliminate (A).

   Does the author of Passage 2 cite an authority? Yes, she quotes the critic Natalie Tyler. Eliminate (B).

   Does the author of Passage 2 define a term? Yes, she defines *zingers* as "remarks that startle, even shock, the unwary reader." Eliminate (C).

   Does the author of Passage 2 provide an example? Yes, she provides an example of a zinger: Austen's comment on the scarcity of men, particularly "any that were good for much." Eliminate (D).

   Does the author of Passage 2 propose a hypothesis? No, she does not. The correct choice is (E).

9. **(D)** Passage 1 refers to the "brightness" which the Jane Austenite ascribes to his idol. Passage 2 quotes Tyler on Austen's "penetrating, perspicacious, and piercingly accurate" perceptions. Clearly, the two passages agree that Austen *possessed an acute intellect*.

10. **(C)** The author states that warfare for the Kiowas "was preeminently a matter of disposition rather than of survival." In other words, they *were warlike in nature*.

11. **(D)** The author comments that the Kiowas "never understood the grim, unrelenting advance of the U.S. Cavalry." They lacked the *unswerving determination* that kept the cavalrymen pursuing their foes long after a band of Kiowas would have changed its course.

12. **(B)** Born too late to experience the actual fighting and famine, the author's grandmother did experience *the bleak,* cheerless *attitude* of the defeated warriors, "the dark brooding" *of the older Kiowa men*.

13. **(D)** Describing the Kiowas as "a lordly and dangerous society of fighters and thieves, hunters and priests of the sun" (lines 53 and 54), members of a courageous and proud tribe, the author clearly regards them with *admiration*.

14. **(B)** Before they acquired horses, the Kiowas were tied to the ground, forced to move slowly in the course of their journey toward the dawn. Once they had horses, however, they were *liberated to rove more freely*; their wandering spirit was no longer tied down.

15. **(D)** The Kiowas' origin myth describes how "they entered the world through a hollow log." Thus, it is *an explanation of how they came to be* on Earth.

16. **(C)** The author's emphasis is on the elephant's importance as a "creator of habitat" for other creatures.

17. **(C)** To mount an effort to rescue an endangered species is to *launch* or initiate a campaign.

18. **(D)** The elephant is "the architect of its environment" in that it *physically alters its environment,* transforming the landscape around it.

19. **(C)** The author states that it is the elephant's metabolism and appetite—in other words, its voracity or *ravenous hunger*—that leads to its creating open spaces in the woodland and transforming the landscape.

20. **(C)** In this excerpt from a newspaper article, the author objectively reports the effect of the decline in the elephant population on other species that inhabit the savanna. His style can best be described as *reportorial.*

21. **(C)** Since the foraging of elephants creates a varied landscape that attracts a diverse group of plant-eating animals and since the presence of these plant-eaters in turn attracts carnivores, it follows that *elephants have an indirect effect on the hunting patterns of certain carnivores.*

22. **(E)** You can arrive at the correct answer choice through the process of elimination.

    Question I is answerable on the basis of the passage. The elephant's foraging opens up the surroundings by knocking down trees and stripping off branches. Therefore, you can eliminate (B) and (D).

    Question II is answerable on the basis of the passage. Gazelles are grazers; giraffes are browsers. Therefore, you can eliminate (A).

    Question III is answerable on the basis of the passage. The concluding sentence states that when elephants disappear the rain forest reverts. Therefore, you can eliminate (C).

    Only (E) is left. It is the correct answer.

23. **(B)** The author is listing the many species that depend on the elephant as a creator of habitat. Thus, the host of smaller animals is the *very large number* of these creatures that thrive in the elephant's wake.

24. **(C)** The author is in favor of the effect of elephants on the environment; he feels an accidental or *fortuitous result* of their foraging is that it allows a greater variety of creatures to exist in mixed-growth environments.

Section 3

1. **(E)** A modernization program logically would attempt to *eliminate* or get rid of problems.

2. **(C)** Something that cannot be solved with ease remains a mystery or *enigma.*

3. **(D)** If you simply watch or *observe* the skilled activities of others, you are *passive,* that is, inactive.

4. **(C)** The key phrase here is "stick together." Small particles of matter join together to form larger ones. In other words, they coalesce.

5. **(C)** A *misnomer* (incorrect designation) by definition misnames something. The writer here is arguing that mole rats have been given the wrong name.

6. **(C)** Einstein's humility was not a pose that he put on for an audience. His *profound,* deep humility was clearly *sincere* (genuine; unfeigned).

7. **(C)** Throughout the passage, the narrator, a small boy, wishes that his father had been a tougher, more heroic sheriff. *To justify his father's peaceful nature* to

himself as well as to his reader, he explains why his father had not gone to war like other men.

8. **(A)** We are told that, when the men returned from war, they "wanted nothing more than to work their farms and ranches and to live quietly with their families." In essence, the war veterans *had had their fill of shooting and death*.

9. **(C)** The narrator disapproves of his father's clothes. At least the other men "wore boots and Stetsons." All told, the boy thinks that his father is *pretty dull*, especially for a sheriff in Montana.

10. **(E)** The boy wishes that his father carried a "nickel-plated Western Colt .45," perhaps one that had been carried by a gunslinging sheriff in the old West. In short, his gun should have been a *more impressive* firearm.

11. **(A)** The passage is tinged with the boy's *regret* that his father was not a tougher, more glamorous sheriff. In fact, he says that aspects of his father's job "disappointed" him.

12. **(C)** Theatrical properties or props are usually movable items (not costumes or furniture) that actors use onstage during a performance. Note how the author describes the boys' likely fate, to be hauled offstage as if they were inanimate *physical objects* (lines 94–100).

13. **(A)** The stage is rude in the same sense that "the rude bridge that arched the flood" is rude: it is a *roughly made*, somewhat primitive structure.

14. **(E)** The narrator uses the phrase "such as they were" to dismiss the supposed perks or privileges of stage royalty. Considering that his father's reward was to stand under a hot sun wearing a heavy costume, it is clear that his father *received very little for his efforts*.

15. **(D)** Given that he forgot their birthdays and never helped them fix their toys, the narrator's father clearly was "not dependable to his children." He "enjoyed being the center of attention": he gloried in acting like a king and starring in one-man shows. He "had an appealing appearance," evinced by the good looks that attracted his wife. He "was uncomfortable with his responsibilities," tired of dealing with household problems. All he lacked was the liking of *those who shared his home*, who grew to be as tired of him as he asserted he was of them.

16. **(B)** The narrator has told the story of his father to better *understand his complex feelings toward his father*, who abandoned his family responsibilities in pursuit of ambitions the narrator neither shares nor fully understands.

17. **(B)** The authors of the two passages portray their fathers as *deficient in some important way*. The father in Passage 1 is not tough and courageous enough to suit his son, and the father in Passage 2 is flawed in many ways—from his inability to succeed in his career to his destructive self-centeredness.

18. **(D)** Neither son seems to have a close relationship with his father. In essence, they are *distant*.

19. **(E)** The author of Passage 1 seems to be asking how a man can be both a sheriff in Montana and a wimp at the same time. It's *puzzling* to the boy. The author of Passage 2 analyzes his father closely, but not with a sense of confidence in his findings. In many ways the father remains *puzzling*. As the passage says, the author never understood why the father endured his low-paid, uncelebrated career as an actor working for fairs.